Torkel Aschehoug and Norwegian Historical Economic Thought

Anthem Other Canon Economics

Anthem Press and The Other Canon Foundation are pleased
to present the **Anthem Other Canon Economics** series. The Other Canon – also
described as 'reality economics' – studies the economy as a real object rather than as
the behaviour of a model economy based on core axioms, assumptions and techniques.
The series includes both classical and contemporary works in this tradition, spanning
evolutionary, institutional and Post-Keynesian economics, the history of economic
thought and economic policy, economic sociology and technology governance,
and works on the theory of uneven development and in the tradition of
the German historical school.

Other Titles in the Series

A 'Short Treatise' on the Wealth and Poverty of Nations (1613)
Antonio Serra, edited by Sophus A. Reinert

Competitiveness and Development: Myth and Realities
Mehdi Shafaeddin, with a foreword by Erik S. Reinert

*Development and Semi-periphery: Post-neoliberal Trajectories
in South America and Central Eastern Europe*
Edited by Renato Boschi and Carlos Henrique Santana

*Economists and the Powerful:
Convenient Theories, Distorted Facts, Ample Rewards*
Norbert Häring and Niall Douglas

Knowledge Governance: Reasserting the Public Interest
Edited by Leonardo Burlamaqui, Ana Célia Castro
and Rainer Kattel, with a foreword by Richard Nelson

*The Politics of Enlightenment:
Constitutionalism, Republicanism, and the Rights of Man in Gaetano Filangieri*
Vincenzo Ferrone, translated by Sophus A. Reinert

Thorstein Veblen: Economics for an Age of Crisis
Edited by Erik S. Reinert and Francesca Linda Viano

Torkel Aschehoug and Norwegian Historical Economic Thought

Reconsidering a Forgotten Norwegian Pioneer Economist

Mathilde C. Fasting

ANTHEM PRESS
LONDON · NEW YORK · DELHI

Anthem Press
An imprint of Wimbledon Publishing Company
www.anthempress.com

This edition first published in UK and USA 2013
by ANTHEM PRESS
75–76 Blackfriars Road, London SE1 8HA, UK
or PO Box 9779, London SW19 7ZG, UK
and
244 Madison Ave #116, New York, NY 10016, USA

British Library Cataloguing-in-Publication Data
A catalogue record for this book is available from the British Library.

Library of Congress Cataloging-in-Publication Data
A catalog record for this book has been requested.

ISBN-13: 978 0 85728 075 6 (Hbk)
ISBN-10: 0 85728 075 9 (Hbk)

This title is also available as an ebook.

CONTENTS

ACKNOWLEDGEMENTS

After finishing my first education as an economist, I spent a decade working both in large private companies and on starting my own business. Gradually, a wish to learn more about the origins of my discipline and intellectual history in general led me to share my time between my private business and a fulltime study of intellectual history (*idéhistorie*), first finishing a bachelor's and then a master's degree. The topic of my master's thesis was the history of economic thought in the late seventeenth and early eighteenth centuries, addressing the economic motivation of self-interest. This path led me to an inspiring lecture by Professor Erik Reinert, whom I had not met before. In a moment of inspiration, I left him my contact details, and just a few months later he suddenly called me and asked if I would be interested in looking at the Norwegian economist Torkel Aschehoug. I was in my car at the time, but the name Aschehoug rang a bell. When I came home, I quickly found out that Aschehoug was the brother of my great-great-grandfather. And what's more, I had in my office a first edition of his complete *Socialøkonomik*.* My reply to Reinert was, of course, yes. With his invaluable help, I became acquainted with my supervisor Professor Jürgen Backhaus, and my project turned into a doctoral thesis and now a book about Torkel Aschehoug. I wish to thank them both: Reinert for making it possible, and Backhaus for critical and encouraging comments during the process.

An insightful seminar about Aschehoug in 2009 also gave me valuable inspiration for my work, and I wish to thank Professor Arild Sæther especially for including me in other seminars, for constructive and interesting talks, and for providing me with analyses of Norwegian economic thought concerning entrepreneurs and the influence of Alfred Marshall on Norwegian economic thought. I will also extend my thanks to Professor Sylvi Endresen, who participated at the Aschehoug seminar and worked with me on a seminar paper and presentation at the Heilbronn Symposium about Aschehoug and his views on labour.

I also need to mention Professor Øystein Sørensen, who has been most helpful and encouraging for my work on Anton Martin Schweigaard and his Norwegian economic reforms. This also includes Professor Lars Fr. H. Svendsen, who has given me constructive advice for the structure of my dissertation and insightful comments on philosophical issues. I have also had valuable and inspiring talks during various stages of the process with Professor Anne-Lise Seip, Professor Francis Sejersted, Professor Rune Slagstad and the conservative politician and former minister of culture Lars Roar Langslet, who included Aschehoug in his recent book presenting portraits of Norwegian conservative thinkers (*Konservatisme på norsk*, 2011). I also wish to thank Professor Sverre Christensen

---

* I have used these four volumes as my research copies for this book.

at Senter for næringslivshistorie, BI (Centre for Business History), who invited me to a stimulating meeting with his colleagues to present and discuss my project. A last thanks goes to Agnar Sandmo, professor of economics at my former school, the Norwegian School of Economics and Business Administration, for a critical review of my doctoral thesis before the submission of the work to the editors of the book manuscript.

The editors at Anthem must also be thanked warmly, for critical reviews of the manuscript, valuable comments and corrections, and for professional assistance with editing of the final book.

Since Torkel Aschehoug had just a small family and was close to his brother (my great-great-grandfather), it has been most interesting to search for private information about his life and the life of his family. I extend my thanks to my aunt, Inger Kloster Jensen, for providing me with old family information and a genealogical table, and for the contact she made with Torkel Aschehoug's great grandchild, Kirsti Berulfsen, who died last winter. In her apartment hung the original painting of Torkel Aschehoug that is used on the cover of this book.

Finally, my heartfelt thanks go to my family, who have encouraged me and tolerated my many hours of reading and writing, not only during the week, but also on weekends and holidays.

Oslo, April 2013

Chapter 1

INTRODUCTION

Following World War II, historical schools of economics have generally been neglected within the arena of economic theory, because of the strong positions held by the classical and neoclassical schools of economic thought. In recent years, and especially after the financial crisis of 2008, a revaluation of this way of seeing the economy is emerging. Historical thought was not limited to Germany, but flourished in neighbouring countries like Norway. To complete the picture of the development of political economy, namely the development of historical and institutional approaches to economics, this book will contribute to the Norwegian part of the broader European picture of late nineteenth-century economic thought.

The story is told through the life and works of Norway's most influential economist and an important intellectual and jurist during the last decades of the nineteenth century, Torkel Halvorsen Aschehoug (1822–1909). This book will analyse his economic thought and how he developed it in a Norwegian context with an extensive international orientation. However, economics was not an international science in his day, nor did he write in any well-known international languages. It is a paradox that his genuinely international thought has remained a secret to the international history of economic ideas. The re-evaluation of his thought in this book will be most valuable for all readers interested in the history of economic thought and of Norwegian political economy and intellectual history in general, and it will make his work accessible to a non-Scandinavian-speaking audience. The intention here is to make an account of Aschehoug's personal academic history and explain how this highly educated Norwegian intellectual managed the adoption of the new economic theories developed in several European countries during the 1890s and the first decade of twentieth century, and combined them with insights from the German historical school and the English classical economics he had studied in his youth.

Aschehoug was well into his sixties when he left active politics and embarked on his economic project, which he continued until his death. Interestingly, this coincided with a profound change and a rapid development of economic thought internationally. How was this to influence Aschehoug? What did the marginal revolution mean to his way of thinking? And how were the *Methodenstreit* and discussions between different schools of economic thought influencing him?

The analysis will place Aschehoug in the context of nineteenth-century Norwegian society and, moreover, his economic thought will be discussed both in relation to his Norwegian colleagues and in relation to international economists, namely German, French and British. His extensive use of sources shows a strong German affiliation; Wilhelm Roscher (1817–1894), Adolph Wagner (1835–1917) and especially Gustav von Schmoller

(1838–1917) are quoted throughout his major economic work, *Socialøkonomik*. Written from 1903 to 1908, *Socialøkonomik* comprises more than twenty-two hundred pages, and lists almost nine hundred different sources in the first edition and more than a thousand in the second (note that all references will be to the first edition).

Another important influence comes from British economist Alfred Marshall (1842–1924), the single most quoted author in *Socialøkonomik*, in terms of both his marginal theory and his general outlook on economics. A third connection is also evident between Aschehoug and the French economist Jean-Baptiste Say (1767–1832), particularly when it comes to the concept of the entrepreneur in economic theory. This is a topic that is highly relevant to discuss in relation to contemporary economics, as are two others: his theory of labour and his theory and discussion of economic crises. Aschehoug's theory of crises also contains many detailed observations that can be found in more recent theories. Aschehoug was especially cognizant of the reasons for economic crises, and this confirms the overall impression of Aschehoug's *Socialøkonomik* as a most learned and theoretically solid work. Finally, the development in understanding international trade and trade policies is discussed, focusing on how a relatively liberal economist had to renounce his liberal principles when facing the political realities of the turn of the century.

There has never been a thorough analysis of the economic thought of Aschehoug, and his main work, *Socialøkonomik*, has not been translated into any other European language. The ambition of this book is to unearth a body of literature which – due to its language of publication – is not available to the international community of scholars, and to offer a critical reconstruction and make it available in English. It must be added that all quotes from Aschehoug are my translations from Norwegian to English, unless otherwise stated, to fill an important gap in the Norwegian historical tradition of economic thinking. As English today is the lingua franca of academics, knowledge that is not communicated in English is often lost. If the scholar writes and publishes in English, the chances are greater for the work to be analysed and made useful, whereas scholars from Norway would not be analysed unless someone who reads and understands the original language is able to transmit and translate the original texts. Due to a much greater knowledge of other languages, many late nineteenth-century scholars were able to read and communicate in most major European languages, such as French, German, English and Italian. Norwegian intellectuals were usually trained in at least two or three of these languages in addition to their native tongue. The intention is to present the thoughts of a Norwegian scholar in English, with extensive quotations and explanations of the original Norwegian texts.

In addition, it is worth mentioning that what is understood by economics nowadays is different from how the economists of the nineteenth century saw themselves and their field of research. The lines were blurred between what today would be considered as clearly different disciplines, and university professors were the products of holistic knowledge and multieducational backgrounds. This interdisciplinary approach to economics is most valuable and rewarding when reading and analysing the works of Aschehoug; it is a perspective lacking for most mainstream economists today, though there are exceptions. Aschehoug was living and writing in a period where the gradual disintegration of science was taking place – the process towards separate disciplines. As the historian Franklin

Baumer puts it: science itself was breaking up into the sciences. Political and historical thought also ceased, to a large extent, to speak a universal or general language, and became steadily more partisan. History, which was a special case, gained greatly in importance and prestige. That is, history now concerned itself more with the individual, the particular and the unrepeatable than with general laws. It was one of the principal and most significant developments in nineteenth-century thought.[1] Aschehoug was at the centre of this *scisma*: he held on to the desire of the German historical school to explain 'the whole' (*die Ganzheit*) and to be scientific without oversimplifying.

Further, the difficulty of the term 'economics' needs to be mentioned. The title of Aschehoug's work, *Socialøkonomik*, is understood as 'the science of economics' or 'political economy'. When Aschehoug uses the term *socialøkonomi* or *økonomi*, these have been translated into 'economic activity' or simply 'economy'. Another element is the prefix of the title, *social-* (which means the same in English, now written as *sosial* in modern Norwegian). Twenty years before the publishing of his work, Aschehoug started the Statsøkonomisk forening. Here the prefix is 'state-', and so this is commonly understood as 'political economy'. In Germany, the term that was chosen for the British political economy was *Nationalökonomi*, and later the political part of political economy was called *Staatswissenschaft*. Aschehoug's choice of the prefix 'social-' indicates that he wanted to place his theories into a social and political context, not keeping it to the national or state level, which today would be more similar to macroeconomics, a term that is avoided in this work. I have tried to respect the differences of the terms in all my translations and presentations, and eventual disagreements or errors are my responsibility.

Wherever appropriate and possible, the current relevance of Aschehoug will be mentioned, while recognizing that drawing lessons over such a large timespan might be risky. I will attempt to uncover and reconstruct the forgotten economic, empirical and historical tradition to which he belonged. Aschehoug was a jurist as well as an economist. He obtains objectiveness by discussing different aspects of a topic, not by applying *a priori* conditions and describing ideal situations. His goals as a scholar are closely tied to the practical relevance of his analyses. By pointing out how Aschehoug goes about presenting and using the empirical-historical method in economic analysis, I will show how it is possible to discern a pattern that is clearly different from mainstream economics. His method has a much broader scope and an innumerable multitude of nuances and clear observations.

As all histories are chronological, the two main methods of organizing a history will naturally be by 'school' or by 'topic'.[2] These are overlapping. The problem with defining schools is that it means grouping individuals that are not necessarily alike. Furthermore, it also means choosing a set of characteristics that may be disputable. Such an approach will also require a careful and pinpointed definition of the 'school'.

Can Torkel Aschehoug be assigned to a special school of economic thought? The answer is both yes and no. He first and foremost belonged to a Norwegian tradition. It becomes clear that Aschehoug recognized and synthesized all international economic theories of his time. He analysed their history, their strengths and weaknesses, and adapted them to the Norwegian context. By using this empirical-historical approach, he is much closer to the historical school than to the classical school in the tradition of David Ricardo (1772–1823). Aschehoug was an economist, but he was also a humanist, being just as interested in economic and juridical theory as in the practical application, thus bringing forth deeply human and insightful analyses of society and economic activity. To Aschehoug, economic thinking was profoundly embedded in all social and political thinking, as well as in typically humanist thought. To place Aschehoug's thought in mainstream theoretical economics would be too easy and would not capture the many nuances of his thought. Economics is not isolated, nor is the analysis of Aschehoug. He greatly elaborated, and was the main protagonist of, a Norwegian historical-empirical tradition in economics during the nineteenth and early twentieth centuries in Norway. His approach continued in 'mainstream economics' for two decades after his death in 1909. Subsequently, this tradition went out of favour in Norway with Ragnar Frisch (1885–1973) and the foundation of the Oslo school of economic thought in the 1930s. Since then no attempt has been made to re-establish and analyse the thinking of Aschehoug. The neglect of Aschehoug, the economist, is reinforced by the fact that Norwegian economics students are offered no courses, not even elective, in the history of their chosen area of interest.

The editors of *Norsk idéhistorie* (Norwegian history of ideas) might be quoted in order to explain what often happens in smaller, peripheral countries. When Norwegian thinking is analysed, the question often arises of whether the ideas are original or if they are plagiarizing other European ideas. During decisive periods in Norwegian history, the Norwegians have had close ties and connections with other European cultures and the literary exchange of ideas among intellectuals has been substantial. It must also be remembered that Norwegian intellectuals throughout history have read Latin as well as the main European vernaculars. The nineteenth century may be classified as a decisive period in Norwegian history, a period when European influence was particularly strong.[3] The main point of the editors of *Norsk idéhistorie* is that: 'No matter where ideas and impulses come from, they have their special Norwegian manifestation. Sometimes ideas come without too much adaption, and sometimes they must be said to be profoundly changed.'[4] Another important observation made relates to what criteria must be used in order to consider an idea original, important or interesting. Even if an idea lacks originality, it might be influential and it might capture the essence or spirit of the period in question. Ideas that are important in the development of a certain science, like economics, are usually not mainstream, and they can usually be traced back to original thinkers. In the case of Aschehoug, it is more relevant and fruitful to look at how he absorbed these ideas, how he perceived them, and how he then adapted them to the Norwegian context in order to educate his students and the general intellectual Norwegian public. Economic theories are not 'neutral' when it comes to economic development. If there are discrepancies between theories and the order of society, an adoption of theory will lead to a change in the existing conditions of society. The ideas and principles underlying practical policies will also change according to general changes in society. When different concepts are applied, they carry meaning and ideas. And finally, it is relevant and important to present the theoretical discussions between Aschehoug and his colleagues about the Norwegian scientific economic development.

Applied Sources

Between 1847 and 1908, Aschehoug wrote more than three thousand pages on economics, as well as letters, articles, commission reports and pamphlets. His main work, *Socialøkonomik*, will be the core text in the analysis, together with relevant articles published in *Statsøkonomisk Tidsskrift* (Journal of political economy) between 1887 and 1908.[5] These documents and texts can be found in the Norwegian National Library. A list of these letters and documents and a list of his published works are appended. Since this book does not include Aschehoug's political career, or his legal career, the works that belong to this context are not quoted. This also means that most of the relevant sources are from the period between the 1870s and the early 1900s, and are concentrated on texts that are relevant for his economic thought. As stated, these texts have had to be translated; all quotes in the original language are included in notes, and in the text they are either translated quotes, or explained and commented passages of texts. Although this may seem inconvenient, it is hopefully valuable for other scholars to use in later research.

Since *Socialøkonomik* and the articles in *Statsøkonomisk Tidsskrift* were written for academic and scientific purposes, and the analysis has been concentrated on his career as a professor of economics, the interpretation of his political and public statements have been less important. The analysis of Norwegian political life in the nineteenth century has been done in great detail, which is not the case for the history of economic thought. Two of the main secondary sources are the doctoral thesis about Aschehoug written by Anne-Lise Seip in 1974, *Vitenskap og virkelighet: Sosiale, økonomiske og politiske teorier hos T. H. Aschehoug 1845 til 1882* (Science and reality: Social, economic and political theories of T. H. Aschehoug 1845–1882), and Trond Bergh and Tore Jørgen Hanisch's *Vitenskap og politikk: Linjer i norsk sosialøkonomi gjennom 150 år* (Science and politics: Norwegian (social) economics of the last 150 years) from 1984. They have two somewhat different purposes in this book. The first has been most valuable because of its thorough use of sources, especially political documents; the second has been useful for gaining a comprehensive overview and analysis of Norwegian economic thought. Seip focuses on Aschehoug as a politician. Bergh and Hanisch place Aschehoug in the Norwegian economic tradition, but state that their aim is not to look at international impulses. Importantly, they look at the relationship between scientific development and practical economic policies, which can be said of Seip's analysis as well. Bergh and Hanisch further underline the strong desire among the early Norwegian economists to be useful, meaning they emphasize the relevance and applicability of their works and analyses. A third source for the thought of Schweigaard, in addition to his own published works, has been the doctoral thesis of Øystein Sørensen, *Anton Martin Schweigaards politiske tenkning* (The political thought of Anton Martin Schweigaard) from 1988. His perspectives on liberalism and the position of Schweigaard have been most valuable in the analysis of Aschehoug.

Structure and Contents

In order to introduce Aschehoug, a presentation of his background, education and career followed by an overview of the nineteenth-century Norwegian economic and political context will make up the first part of this book. To Norwegian readers this second part may be well known, and the ambition is not to be original, rather it is to unearth the context in which Aschehoug belonged. Aschehoug's biography is by no means a full picture of his life, it is more precisely directed at introducing elements in his life that are relevant for understanding his economic works.

The second part of the Norwegian context is dedicated Aschehoug's teacher, Anton Martin Schweigaard (1808–1870), generally considered to be the first Norwegian economist. Many Norwegian historians have discussed and analysed Schweigaard, the most recent contribution being *Anton Martin Schweigaard: Professorpolitikeren* (2010), edited by Ola Mestad. After giving a brief general presentation of Schweigaard, the aim here is to concentrate on topics that are relevant to the later analysis of Aschehoug, namely Schweigaard's position on method and scientific approach – first by looking at his article 'Om den tyske filosofi' (On the German philosophy) and secondly by looking at his lectures on political economy. The relevance of the article on philosophy is that it explains Schweigaard's view on method, whereas his lectures provide his general position on economics and politics. Finally, a much-discussed topic among Norwegian historians has been to what extent Schweigaard was a liberalist and a follower of laissez-faire. Without elaborating in detail to what extent this might be true, it is attempted to show that it is important to make a distinction between laissez-faire and free trade. Sørensen's analysis is followed, and henceforth Schweigaard is placed as a free trade adherent, but not as a laissez-faire follower. This is also Aschehoug's position.

In the next two chapters Norwegian economic thought during the last decades of the nineteenth century and the first decade of the twentieth century is analysed, starting with a small presentation of Aschehoug's colleagues and continuing with Aschehoug's theoretical position. A complete section in his *Socialøkonomik* is dedicated to theory and method, and it will be the basis of the analysis. There was no *Methodenstreit* in Norway during Aschehoug's lifetime, only a small discussion that took place in the mid-1890s.[6] This discussion concludes the chapter about Norwegian economic thought. The empirical tradition dominated, and henceforth also the methods that were applied. Statistics became important, as well as analyses of historical events with the intention of understanding and uncovering casual connections, and chains of causes and effects. The English classical economists focused on the incentives of the marketplace as an external driving force for man and the cosmopolitical and general aspects of economics. Aschehoug and his contemporaries, although acutely aware of the role of markets, emphasize the national context and history in order to develop their economic thought. This is much closer to a historical, empirical approach, which can be connected both to British empiricism and to the German historical school.

To Aschehoug, history is not only 'a comprehension of the past' or even a way of finding the origins of the present in the past, but it is also a study of the incessant movement in human life, of continual change and development. Society is understood more as an open-ended evolution, or as conditioned by a changing environment, ushered by the dynamics of the French and Industrial Revolutions.

Chapter 5 will describe the development of Aschehoug's thought through his works and texts from 1848, with a clear focus on 1870 onwards, when Aschehoug concentrated on scientific economic thought, wrote his magnum opus in economics, and founded and conducted the Statsøkonomisk forening (Association of Political Economy). It will be shown that there is continuity in Aschehoug's work, as well as an ability to acquire new knowledge and adapt and process it in an attempt to create a sound foundation for the economic discipline. The foundation of the Statsøkonomisk forening is of major importance to the development of a professional milieu of economics in Norway. It was an arena for discussions of current economic and social issues, and also a vehicle for professionalizing economics and presenting new theoretical works, followed by minutes from the scientific discussions that took place after the lectures. Finally this chapter presents his main work, *Socialøkonomik*. The early drafts and a complete list of contents in English are included in appendixes. This is primarily done in order for non-Norwegians to understand the huge range and depth of his work. Unfortunately, the scope of this project is too limited to conduct a thorough analysis of later editions of *Socialøkonomik* and of what happened in detail after the death of Aschehoug in 1909. However, it is clear that after two decades the work of Aschehoug disappeared, and with it a tradition of thought, due to the emergence in the 1930s of what was later called the Oslo school in economics.

The last part of this book is twofold: one part concentrates on the international influence on Aschehoug, and the other looks at selected topics in Aschehoug's *Socialøkonomik* that may be relevant to contemporary economics. The international influence is divided into three parts: the German historical school, the adaption of Marshall's marginal theory and the general French influence. After a small presentation of the German historical school and how Aschehoug describes this tradition in *Socialøkonomik*, I compare Aschehoug with Gustav von Schmoller. The purpose of this comparison is to show the many similarities between the two economists, and thereby establish the obvious connection between the German and Norwegian economic thought of this period. Discrepancies are also commented on, the most important being the harsher conflicts and debates in Germany compared to the more homogenous Norwegian milieu. Another is to what extent the empirical-historical method and historical thought were met with opposition. This came from more classical liberal economists, and from Austrian economists in the so-called *Methodenstreit*, and later in the value debates referred to as the *Werturteilsstreit*. Even though the Norwegian economists and Aschehoug did not meet the same opposition and subsequently did not have to defend themselves, the empirical-historical tradition was gradually lost during the 1930s and onwards, as was also the case in Germany. The analysis of the German historical school and Schmoller in this chapter leans heavily on different secondary sources in English, as I am not fluent in German.

Secondly, the British influence is described by the pivotal introduction of marginal theory in Norway, led by the protagonist Alfred Marshall. This chapter also presents a new turn in Norwegian economic thought. Marginal theory was an important theoretical development during the last decades of the nineteenth century, and Aschehoug quickly set himself the task of acquiring a deep understanding of this new theory. Understanding and developing marginal theory represents the single most difficult task for Aschehoug in *Socialøkonomik*. What is equally interesting, and probably also explains why Aschehoug did not elaborate to the same extent on the Austrian perspective on marginal theory, is that Marshall and Aschehoug had the same principle view on economics.

Thirdly, the French influence is addressed in order to demonstrate the unique material that makes up the analysis of Aschehoug. The most influential French thinker was Jean-Baptiste Say. A general presentation of Say is provided in the section entitled 'The French Liberal School', and in addition, Say is of paramount importance to the chapter about the entrepreneur. Aschehoug's position towards positivism, ethical thought and socialism in the French tradition is also commented on in this chapter. Generally, Aschehoug disapproves of socialism, but he approaches socialist thought in a neutral way. For example, Aschehoug was the first 'conservative' economist in Norway to accept Karl Marx (1818–1883) as a scientist, and he mentions socialist principles in neutral terms in his *Socialøkonomik*. Economists like Nassau W. Senior (1790–1864), John McCulloch (1789–1864), Frédéric Bastiat (1801–1850) and John Stuart Mill (1806–1873) renewed and developed classical theory without altering its core, which made it difficult on a theoretical level to refute the socialist theories of Marx and Friedrich Engels (1820–1895).[7] A socialist revolution was never a serious issue in Norway, henceforth the Norwegian 'conservative' economists did not have to defend themselves like many of their European colleagues.

The final part consists of different selected topics that might be relevant for contemporary economics. In this process it has been necessary to make choices, because the scope and depth of Aschehoug's work is too extensive to be analysed in detail within the limits of this book. Topics are partly chosen out of perceived relevance and partly out of theoretical interest. The first topic is Aschehoug's views of labour, which is also part of a forthcoming book. As this is a joint article between Sylvi Endresen and me, I have chosen to leave out most of her contribution and later add a couple of perspectives, without abandoning the main idea that Aschehoug saw the worker and labour as more than just a production factor. This fact is also related to the social questions that were an important part of the debates and papers presented at the Statsøkonomisk forening. The second topic is an analysis of the more interesting and relevant perspectives on the entrepreneur, where Say plays an important part in the Norwegian views and theoretical tradition. The entrepreneur is seen as a fourth production factor, the centre of economic activity.

A further chapter covers discussions about trade and trade policies, presented in the Norwegian nineteenth-century context and in the works of Schweigaard. This shows that Aschehoug and his colleagues did not change radically from the earlier free trade position of Schweigaard, but they faced a more difficult international climate, with more widespread protectionist policies and the termination of the Swedish–Norwegian free trade agreement. Nevertheless, they were pragmatic in their approach, which will be shown by presenting the different commissions and debates at the Statsøkonomisk forening, emphasizing the final one, which took place in 1903.

The difficult international climate is also the backdrop for the extensive analysis that Aschehoug makes on economic crises, in which he aims to understand the different underlying conditions that cause them. During the lifetime of Schweigaard economic crises were present, but not to the same extent, and the phenomenon was not discussed in detail in his lectures. It is to the credit of Aschehoug that more than one hundred years ago, Norwegian economics had a comprehensive, and in many aspects modern, analysis of economic crises. It would be relevant and interesting to look even closer into the different theories that Aschehoug presents and make a comparison with later theories – a topic for a later project, perhaps.

The legacy of Aschehoug is summed up in the last chapter, as well as the main conclusions of this book. Other topics that merit further analysis are the large part of *Socialøkonomik* that covers money and credit theories, and the financial sector, including the central bank. These issues mainly constitute the third volume of *Socialøkonomik*. Since *Socialøkonomik* itself is an encyclopaedic work, there are certainly other perspectives to analyse. I hope that this book will lay the ground for a renewed interest in the work of Torkel Aschehoug and his contemporaries.

Chapter 2

BIOGRAPHY

General Background and Childhood

Torkel Halvorsen Aschehoug was born on 27 June 1822 in Rakkestad in south-east Norway and died on 20 January 1909 in Oslo.[1] His father was Halvor Aschehoug and his mother was Anne Christine Darre. Torkel was the oldest of five children. He had two sisters, Anne Cathrine and Nicoline. Only Anne Cathrine married, while Nicoline remained a spinster and lived with her mother for many years. They died within a year of each other. Torkel also had two brothers, both named Nils Stockfleth Darre. The first died at only one year old, while the youngest became a judge in the small town of Horten and had a close relationship with Torkel throughout his life, Torkel being only six years older than him.[2]

Shortly after Aschehoug's death, Professor Joh. K. Bergwitz made a presentation at the Statsøkonomisk forening on 28 November 1910 entitled 'A Presentation of Professor Aschehoug, His Family and Ancestry'. Bergwitz points out that 'the personality of an outstanding man is best understood by looking at the conditions within the society in which he lived. [...] But closer, and first and foremost, the man must be understood from his forefathers, his ancestry and his relatives on all sides.'[3] In the following, a brief outline of his family background is provided followed by a resume of his professional career, focusing on the elements that can provide a background for his career as an economist.

The Aschehoug family was active, both locally and nationally. Thorkil Aschehoug (1756–1838) was the grandfather of Professor Aschehoug. He was the local parson as well as parish pastor in Rakkestad, and for a while also worked as a government official (*konsistorialraad*).[4] Thorkil was an imperious master of his congregation. The young people confirmed by Thorkil did not dare marry later in life without asking his permission.[5] He worked as a pastor in Rakkestad for 53 years, and received the honorary title 'jubilation teacher'. He certainly made a deep impression on the history of the county.[6] Thorkil was a pioneer in many areas; among other things a library was set up at the rectory based on his own valuable collection of books. Thorkil also worked as a mediator and only a few cases ended in court during his 27 years of practice. He saw to it that a midwife was trained. He opened a post office in the rectory and himself worked as its postmaster for 40 years. He established a granary to take care of the food supply for the local needy. Christie writes that the pastor himself organized the distribution of food, and that he provided the needy with free care and board at the rectory. During the battle of the union dissolution in 1814, the rectory found itself in the middle of the fight between Swedish and Norwegian troops, when it functioned as a hospital.

In 1814, Thorkil was elected to represent his county, Smålenene, in the Norwegian parliament. He was re-elected as his county's elected parliamentary representative in 1822 and also joined the Court of Impeachment. The same assignments and interests were continued by his three sons, all of whom were pastors. One of them, Halvor, was the father of Professor Aschehoug. Christie notes, 'We can observe a common thread through the assignments of the Aschehougs, the love and care of their local county and the people living there. Three of the Aschehoug pastors were mediators, in addition we find them as chairmen of the commission of health, the school board, the commission of the poor, as mayors and as representatives to the Norwegian parliament.'[7] Thorkil was fittingly called the 'elderly father' of the county. At the age of 79, after 53 years as a pastor, Thorkil wrote the following resignation to the king on 13 April 1835:

For almost 18 years I have been completely blind in my right eye, and the left is exhausted, my speech is strenuous, because I have lost all my teeth, my senses are dull because of a recent paralysation and my right hand is so weak that I can barely write. [...] I humbly ask to resign from my office [...] hoping that my request is heard by the Majesty. [...] Possibly I am the only pastor who has worked uninterruptedly in the same congregation in Your Majesty's two kingdoms for more than 50 years.[8]

This clearly proves the valuable contribution this tenacious pastor had made to his family and his native Rakkestad. Aschehoug himself was clearly of the same stock, being active to the bitter end, dying a few years older than his grandfather. It is also worth mentioning that Torkel early in life saw the consequences of poverty and learned how important it was to take care of one's community and of one's fellow man, and help as much as one could.

Aschehoug's uncle Johan succeeded his father in Rakkestad. Aschehoug was 16 years old at the time, having lost his own father, Halvor, to tuberculosis at the age of 43, when he was only 7 and a half years old. He grew up with his mother, two younger sisters and brother, living on the small farm of Hov close to Fredrikshald. Nevertheless, the small family stayed in close contact with the large family at the rectory in Rakkestad. Grandparents, and later uncles, supported the fatherless flock in many ways.[9] The family ties were strong among the large Aschehoug family. Aschehoug's mother's pension was small, so the money they inherited from grandfather Thorkil was spent on the education of the two brothers, Torkel and Nils. The brothers also contracted tuberculosis in their youth, but unlike their father they both survived and lived to be more than eighty years old.

As mentioned, the family of Torkel Aschehoug was well represented in both local and national administration. Torkel's father, Halvor, represented Smålenene in parliament in 1824 and in 1827–28. Halvor became a pastor in Idd, close to the Swedish border, in 1820 after passing his exam in theology in Copenhagen with distinction. Halvor received the following recommendation from Bishop Bech: 'I congratulate the parish that shall have H. A. as their pastor and spiritual advisor.' Svendsen writes in his history of Norwegian pastors that Halvor 'had a kind and amiable presence, as well as a bright mind, and he won the love, trust and admiration of his parish with his comprehensive knowledge, diligence and industriousness'.[10] However, he must also have possessed quite a temper, because it is said that after his law studies he worked for a short time in the department of law, where at some point he had a disagreement with his superior (who of course was wrong), whereupon Halvor slapped him and left the office.[11]

Torkel Aschehoug married twice. Firstly he was married to his cousin Anne Cathrine, who unfortunately died early. He then married her younger sister Johanne Bolette. Both were daughters of the pastor in Rakkestad, his uncle Johan. This second marriage was happy, and their home was open and welcoming. They received many guests, both official and professional, as well as family, friends and relatives.

The profoundly deaf son of Torkel and his first wife Anne Cathrine, Halvor, founded the Aschehoug bookstore together with his second cousin, Hieronymus, son of another Aschehoug pastor in Rakkestad, Jens Bjerch Aschehoug. The bookstore later became the well-known Norwegian publishing house Aschehoug. A small family anecdote illustrates how much the family cared for each other: Torkel's mother and sister Nicoline shared a dress coat all their lives, which they used alternately when they went out, allowing only one of them at a time to appear decently in public. Their savings were supposed to support Torkel's two deaf children, Halvor and Johan (one with each wife). But since Torkel and his younger sister Anna both lived well financially, they renounced their maternal inheritance to the benefit of their brother, Nils Stockfleth Darre, who needed the money more than they did.[12]

Torkel's mother, Anne Christine Darre, was the daughter of Lieutenant (*Premierløitnant*) Nils Stockfleth Darre and Anne Christine Darre provided her sons 'with the education Ellen Aschim.[13] Ulla Meyer writes of her:

> Those who at any point in time have heard our great jurist, economist, historian and politician Torkel Halvorsen Aschehoug talk about his mother must get the strongest impression of the respect and love he always felt for her. He was also well aware of the close connection they had all through her life, and he never forgot what his mother had meant and done for him and his sisters and brother from their earliest childhood.[14]

Anne Christine Darre provided her sons 'with the education their talents deserved', which shows a strength, selflessness and a 'spirit that calls for respect'.[15] She was her son's natural advisor and supporter all her life, and died at the age of 84 in 1883. The unmarried sister, Nicoline, died one and a half years before her mother, while the other sister married in Denmark. The brother, Nils, married Helene Larsen, and moved to the small town of Horten where he worked as a district recorder. The two brothers and their families remained close throughout their lives. A letter from Aschehoug's niece Lela (Helene) to her sister Clara in Oslo described Aschehoug's health problems and occasional bad temper later in life. She wrote that she came to Oslo hoping to avoid having dinner at the house of 'uncle professor' (Torkel), since he always talked about his stomach problems.[16] In 1886, *Departements-tidende* reported that Aschehoug had been excused of his tiresome examination responsibilities at the university.[17] Aschehoug's health was described as poor and the faculty wanted him to prioritize scientific work and not 'exhausting and demanding student tutoring', because they believed that it would be an 'irresponsible misuse of one the best scientists at the university'.[18]

Bergwitz concludes his presentation of the Aschehoug family by saying that Torkel came from a typical Norwegian family. His closest relations were all government officials (*embetsmenn*), either pastors or officers, but his family tree also included farmers and smallholders who came from reduced circumstances.[19] Bergwitz's conclusion says as much about the author as it says about Aschehoug:

We can better understand that Professor Aschehoug had an insatiable thirst for knowledge, and that he continuously worked his whole life through, by widening his horizon of his never-ending studies of people and society, ending with a rare and finely tuned analytical capability. From his humble family at Aas [Rakkestad] he inherited his meticulous diligence, a trait that is not a part of the national character, at least not in the elevated classes and well down in the middle classes of our society. An unusual harmony, eagerness and work enthusiasm was united, bringing about wonderful and great results. My hope is that many humbly will follow the example of our deceased, highly esteemed and irreplaceable dear professor![20]

Studies and Travels: European Influences

Torkel Aschehoug became a student at the University of Oslo at the age of 17 in 1839.[21] His fellow students remarked more on his 'unhealthy looks and sickly complexion', ignoring his 'intellectual capabilities'.[22] It turned out that he was far from fragile, living until he was 86, and that his spirits were unusually well developed. The Danish economist Harald Westergaard (1853–1936) writes in his obituary, 'Aschehoug was undoubtedly one of Norway's best sons, highly esteemed in all Scandinavian countries for his profound studies no less than for his sincere character and his great amiability.'[23]

In 1844, at the age of 22, Aschehoug graduated with a law degree from the University of Oslo. In September two years later, he received a scholarship from the Norwegian state and travelled to London. In order to present him as an economist, his own report from this scholarship will be used. He remained abroad for almost one and a half years, first in England and thereafter travelling on the continent, finally spending a couple of months in Sweden. It was clearly not law and jurisprudence that were the main purpose of his travels, but studies of statistics and political economy. Earlier in 1846, he had become a research fellow in political economy (*statsøkonomi*) at the university. England was considered the best place to go because of its developed institutions and theories in economics, according to Aschehoug an 'ideal example of the workings of political economy'.[24] England already had, at the time, a well-developed economy and economic theories were being put into practice.[25] In his official report from his travel Aschehoug writes,

Anyone who wants to form an individual opinion about the multiple and complicated phenomena of English society development, should observe English institutions and businesses, because it was on English soil that political economy first flourished, and it is from English statistics that political economists have obtained the most complete and trustworthy facts, wherefrom their theories have been constructed.[26]

But he continues by saying,

> This circumstance is said to have given the doctrine itself an English mark, which
> has to be removed before it can be given a general validity. Whatever is assumed, it is
> sure that this question about the character of discipline cannot be overlooked, but to
> solve it one has to acquire a lively understanding of the English social circumstances
> that only a sojourn in the country could provide.[27]

He continues by saying that only a stay in England would lead to a satisfactory
comprehension of English economic activity. England was widely recognized as the most
important country in the world in terms of its level of economic development. It seems
that he believed at this point that the political economy of England was fully developed,
and that all the theoretical analyses of the English scientists were more or less complete.
He adds that some of their theories were adapted to English circumstances, institutions
and society. Under these circumstances, he states that it 'would be appropriate to learn
about the statistical method that was developed in England, and to understand as
thoroughly as possible the development of English society'.[28] In order to understand
English society, Aschehoug believed that the best way would be to study the sectors of
society which could not be understood without staying in the country itself.

The scholarship was of great importance for his further career. He became enthusiastic
about the promising development in statistics and economics and especially how it was
applied in politics. Aschehoug had two points of interest that came up during his stay in
England, both of which followed him for the rest of his life. These were the problem of
'distribution' of wealth and the conflict between private and public interests. The problem
of distribution came up when he was a member of the Poverty Commission and later in
all discussions about social policies, and the other was closely related to the workings of
free trade. Aschehoug worked all his life with questions of how economic activity should
be organized in society when public and private interests do not necessarily coincide.
England was to become his model country when it came to pragmatic policies combined
with scientific expertise in order to reform and develop society.

Aschehoug was in England during two important events in 1847: the railway crisis
and the trade crisis, both of which would influence his later practical work. Aschehoug
chose to study the workings of the railway institutions as well as the credit sector, both
examples of great importance for English society. The task he set for himself was to
look at how free trade, as a principle of economics, functioned in those areas of society
where private and public interests might be incompatible. He came to the conclusion that
'private construction without state control would in the long run lead to a loss to society'.
Even though some enterprises in the beginning could be rentable, private construction
would eventually lead to the creation of monopolies, in such a way that 'liberty, although
it elsewhere creates competition, in this case excludes it'.[29] Further comments about
trade policies are made in the chapters about professor Anton Martin Schweigaard
(1808–1870) and the chapter about trade policies in the work of Aschehoug. The
other point of interest that could hardly be overlooked upon arrival in London was the
1846–47 English credit crisis. Interestingly enough, he observed that it was the credit

problems that led to the trade crisis, and that some people had already, in the autumn of 1846, 'anticipated the storm that had to come', but that they were not taken seriously.[30] Economic crises are treated separately in a later chapter, but the time frame for this project is not large enough to include a more thorough analysis of money, credit and financial issues.

During his stay in England, Aschehoug met many prominent people with whom he remained in contact for the rest of his life, people of interest whom he came to admire and could ask for advice. One of them was, in Aschehoug's own words, 'the man whose guidance was of utmost importance to me': bank director George Warde Norman. Norman was an economist, a director in the Bank of England, a lay judge, a 'Poor Law guardian' and a landowner. In addition he was a liberal and a utilitarian.[31] Norman was of great value to Aschehoug during his stay and also later in life. He taught Aschehoug many things about English society and politics which could not have been obtained by reading books. Norman knew people like David Ricardo, James Mill, Lord Overstone (bank director Samuel Jones-Loyd) and Charles Darwin personally. Furthermore, Norman was well acquainted with Norwegian circumstances, because of his close business relationships with Norwegian traders, which made him well qualified to provide suitable advice and suggestions.[32] Aschehoug revisited Norman after his first travels in 1850, and Norman introduced him to Charles Darwin. There are no clear signs of typical Darwinist thought in the works of Aschehoug, nor social-Darwinist thought, but the belief in progress and development was implicit in his scientific thought. Aschehoug wrote of this meeting in 1899, almost fifty years later, that it was with a 'keen interest' that he came to 'visit and talk to this famous man'.[33] The most important element of his thinking was the belief that scientific work would lead to results that could be used in practical and political decision making. The meeting was probably mentioned as a curiosity, but meeting Darwin as early as 1850 would also have given Aschehoug a special position to evaluate personally and follow the debates about the works of Darwin all through the last part of the nineteenth century. Langslet also mentions that Aschehoug in fact defended two university colleagues, the botanist Axel Blytt and the philosopher Waldemar Dons, both being accused of Darwinist sympathies and as a consequence denied positions.[34]

Aschehoug did not study English theoretical texts, but did study documents of practical value and purpose. He was interested in current English political and economic debate, and by studying pamphlets, official documents, and commission reports and propositions, he gained a clear understanding of how economic theory was tried out and used in practical politics. This was valuable experience for his later political career. Through debates, theories were discussed in relation to practical problems, and to Aschehoug this was a demonstration of how the usefulness of theories was tested out and how practical solutions had their theoretical foundation. Aschehoug commented in his travel report that 'the practical sense of the English had brought about, not a [...] blind belief in theory, nor in customs, but a solid foundation of practical facts, already systematized and collected for many years'.[35] Aschehoug pointed out the advanced use of statistics as a tool to analyse 'actual information'. Moreover, the debates were tools themselves through which different opinions and interests were discussed, as well as the use of different theories and analyses of facts. He complimented the well-developed

English organization of commissions and parliament committees on the way they collected statistical data and used the information as a foundation for law propositions and other reports. He believed that critical debate and discussions about economic and social circumstances in the press and other literature were unsurpassed in England.[36]

Some of the most important knowledge that Aschehoug brought back with him to Norway was how commission work was conducted in England, something that he made use of almost immediately after his return. He could observe how statistical data were collected, adapted and used in economic debates. In England, historical statistics had already been used for a while, so the basis was the most advanced in Europe. Aschehoug also looked at legislation in the study of real estate and compared how the legislation of a country influenced the structure of real estate in different European countries, especially in the case of England and Ireland.[37] He wrote that 'the study of the legislation of real estate and its influence on the national wealth took much of my time during my stay in England'.[38]

After a short private trip to the continent during the summer of 1847, Aschehoug stayed for four months in Sweden with Professor Per E. Bergfalk (1798–1890) from Uppsala, who was a professor of economic jurisprudence and political economy (state economics). He was at the time also a member of the Law Preparation Committee in Stockholm. The difference in the historical development of Norway and Sweden and how it had influenced the development of economic activity was the most important study he conducted during his sojourn. He clearly acknowledged that the natural conditions in the two countries differed, but he concluded that the differences in historical as well as juridical development were equally important. He further pointed out that Sweden had always had a stricter customs system, and economic liberty had been partly *de jure*, partly *de facto* greater in Norway than in Sweden. He admired the technical education that was established in Sweden; in his view this was at a much higher level than any comparable education in Norway. Technical education was important to 'the creation and development of productive forces in the country'.[39] Later comments about his teacher Schweigaard showed that Aschehoug perceived technical progress as more important than Schweigaard, who was more interested in trade as a means to generate welfare.

As already mentioned, Aschehoug had to write a formal report about his travels. It is dated 15 May 1848, but there are no comments or traces that can be seen in relation to the February revolution in 1848.[40] In the final part, Aschehoug mentions poverty problems and comments on questions about distribution of wealth, but it has a more scientific purpose and is not related to the actual events of 1848. Formally, his stay ended in December 1847, and this might be the answer to why it is not mentioned. Aschehoug was not easily knocked off his perch. From the beginning of his career he held on to the belief that economics, statistics, law and social sciences had to be used actively to support political decisions. He claimed all his life that political economy was a science that used impulses and empirical facts from a broad spectre of knowledge from many areas of society, and thereby developed as an interaction between theory and practical life. Political economy was an experience-based discipline, therefore historical knowledge was important.

After his return from Sweden, Aschehoug worked for a short period at the University of Oslo before he became a clerk at the Ministry of Finance, working for Minister Jørgen

H. Vogt. His responsibilities were of the scientific kind, among others the history of taxation. A few years later he was temporarily appointed principal officer. However, soon after an opportunity at the University of Oslo came up, and in the autumn of 1852 he was offered a teaching position in law.[41] Aschehoug was to be affiliated to the university for the rest of his life, and he was often referred to as a 'professor-politician', working with law, economics and history.

A Brief Outline of His Academic Career

First and foremost, it is important to bear in mind that this book does not include the huge efforts and the prominent position Aschehoug had as a professor of law, some of his works still prevailing at the Faculty of Law at the University of Oslo. This outline will present his academic and economic career. Norwegian historians like Slagstad, Seip, Sejersted and Langslet have all commented mostly on his legal works and his participation in debates concerning juridical and constitutional questions.

During his education, Aschehoug became acquainted with Anton Martin Schweigaard, who was both his teacher and later his colleague. Schweigaard influenced the thought of Aschehoug in many ways. Later in life Aschehoug further developed economics professionally, and also took part in the division of law and economics at the university by introducing a written exam in economics (*statsøkonomi*) in 1905.[42] Schweigaard wanted to integrate the two disciplines, something that Aschehoug had supported until the debate at the university at the beginning of the twentieth century. It was the professionalization of the discipline and different theoretical developments that brought about a need to establish a dedicated chair in economics and a pure economic written exam system. There were no political economy exams at the university before 1870. This was the year that Schweigaard died and Aschehoug took over the teaching responsibilities of economics (then called *statsøkonomi*). According to Bergh and Hanisch, Aschehoug was persuaded to accept the chair after Schweigaard, and he became a professor of the combined law, statistics and economics in 1870.[43] He had already been a professor of law since 1862 and a university teacher since 1852.[44] In 1886, Aschehoug took over the chair in pure economics (meaning without law and statistics) after Ebbe Hertzberg (1847–1912), who had held this position since the creation of a pure chair in economics had been established in 1877, still at the time called *statsøkonomi*, the British equivalent of political economy.[45]

After 1877, Aschehoug was the protagonist of Norwegian economics until his death in 1909. As a consequence of Aschehoug's diligent work, 'political economy' was established at the University of Oslo in 1905. The program was divided into three parts: theoretical, empirical and practical economics. Hanisch and Sæther underline the strong belief Aschehoug had about the importance of economic theory in order to solve present-day economic and political problems.[46]

A fellow professor, Bredo Morgenstierne (1851–1930), contemplates Aschehoug's academic career in his 80th birthday speech:

When Professor Aschehoug, in 1886, received the chair in pure economics, he was 64 years old and had had a long working career. He had to a large extent been working with economic issues, both theoretically and practically, although his main study had been within history and jurisprudence, as well as other topics of law. One would have thought that a man, even with the capacity of Aschehoug, in his 60s, 70s and even the beginning of his 80s, working with the publication of his two main treatises, *The Constitution of Norway and Denmark until 1814* and *The Current Constitution in Norway*, would not have been capable of closely following world literature in economics, and certainly not have been able to consume and analyse it all in order to satisfy his scientific demands to master the discipline fully and independently. It was a huge body of knowledge that met the already older man when he agreed to accept the offer of a chair in economics, meaning that he was to become the protagonist of his country, being the first spokesman of this most important discipline and making the extensive body of international economic literature meaningful and accessible, as well as adapted to Norwegian intellectuals.[47]

One of Aschehoug's students, Thorvald Aarum (1867–1926), who also revised *Socialøkonomik*, wanted an integration of law, history, mathematics and economics as a basis for the political economy or state economy. Aarum was a lawyer himself, but later became a professor of economics, and he wanted to introduce a separate exam in political science following the Danish model. But in the end, the professional and theoretical aspects of economics carried the greatest weight. Economics was consequently gradually removed from practical and political life and more directed towards the disciplinary and professional development of theory and method.[48]

When Schweigaard died in 1870, this coincided with a period during which classical economic thought was challenged from different angles. The German historical school, the marginalists and Marxist economists all criticized classical economics in different ways. The difference between the classical school and the historical school was mainly that the latter found the basis of economics in historical, empirical analyses and not in abstract assumptions. At first, the differences in economic thought were smaller and not incompatible, but the contrasts became more visible later on. In Norway, the critique of the classical school was initially rejected, but later on Aschehoug was clearly influenced by ideas from the historical school. Furthermore, Aschehoug had been interested in history and empirical and statistical analyses all his life, thus he could adhere to many of the principles of the historical way of thought.

Aschehoug also spent time going through the different schools of thought in his *Socialøkonomik*, from their early beginnings until contemporary developments. Aschehoug himself, however, is harder to categorize, even though he has been described as a classical, conservative economist, often being seen together with Schweigaard. This is probably too superficial. He was clearly influenced by a historical way of thought. It is possible to draw a line from Ludvig Holberg (1664–1754) and the eighteenth century to Aschehoug. Holberg represents the beginning of a distinctive Norwegian tradition in economics, characterized by a pragmatic, practical and ethical approach to economic theory.[49] Even though Aschehoug chose to go to England at the age of 24, it was not to study the classical economists at the British universities, but to study statistics and the workings of different commissions, and to understand preparatory analysis for practical economic decision making. To Aschehoug it became vital to support economic activities that were of major use and interest to society, such as the development and construction of railways and the creation of savings banks. *Socialøkonomik* has extensive chapters that describe such activities. The idea was that these activities needed support in the beginning to become well established, and that they could not be economically rentable, or even created, without the state intervening in a transitional phase. The crucial distinction is between the appeal to free trade and a free economy and the wish to have a passive state, where a laissez-faire politics is connected to the latter. The Norwegian intent was to have as much free trade as possible, and at the same time create solid and durable industries. The most important division, both for Aschehoug and Schweigaard, is between the wish to give everybody an opportunity to follow their interests and to intervene when individual interest and common interest do not coincide sufficiently. These issues are discussed later.

The analyses of society that he conducted during his workings for the Smallholder Commission (Husmannskommisjonen) and the Poverty Commission (Fattigkommisjonen), give an insight into an early Norwegian attempt to apply scientific methods to investigate and solve the problems of society.[50] Statistics were being used as an auxiliary discipline to provide empirical facts. Economics was supposed to explain the facts that statistical investigation revealed, but at the same time economics should be based on statistical laws. Aschehoug thought that statistics were the future sources of empirical facts. It was a plight to bring forward this information. Many of the chapters concerning practical matters in *Socialøkonomik* use statistics extensively. Statistical information was substantially increased from a modest level in Aschehoug's youth to the publication of *Socialøkonomik* after 1900.

In 1877, the independent Norwegian statistical office, the Central Bureau of Statistics (Statistisk sentralbyrå or SSB), was established. This was previously part of the ministry of internal affairs under the name of the Statistical Office. Anders Nicolai Kiær (1838–1919), also a student of Schweigaard, was appointed the bureau's first director. Empirical thought already hugely influenced Norwegian economics, as was the case in Germany at the same time. Nevertheless, Bergh and Hanisch point out that the historical learnings and workings of Schweigaard and Aschehoug started much earlier. It is therefore correct to say that Norway followed its own way in the development of an empirical-historical tradition. Bergh and Hanisch claim to see a close affiliation between Aschehoug and other Norwegian economists and English classical theory and liberal politics, as well as an influence from the French liberal economist Jean-Baptiste Say.[51] As will be shown, the influence of Say is substantial, as well as of the Briton Alfred Marshall. Statistics and historical analyses were also influenced by similar approaches from Germany. In his youth, Aschehoug participated in two large international statistical congresses, in Vienna in 1857 and in Berlin in 1863.

Anne-Lise Seip comments that the 'harmony-liberal' views of Aschehoug came under pressure during the 1870s.[52] Her view of Aschehoug's harmony liberal position is one example of a common opinion held about Aschehoug. She refers to a debate about customs in parliament in 1879, where he had to defend the free trade system. He claimed that liberalism had become more polished and refined, at the same time as a protectionist wave had become more widespread. How this comment might suggest that the free trade views were more nuanced than Seip perceived is commented on in the chapter about Schweigaard and later in the chapter about Aschehoug and trade policies. In the 1870s, Seip argues, Aschehoug stuck to free trade as the best alternative, and believed that it was the contemporary economic crises that caused a temporary rise in protectionist politics.[53] This is nevertheless an example of how Aschehoug treated theory and praxis:

> Generally the majority [in the Customs Commission] claimed that an augmentation in the prices of goods was a necessary consequence of all customs; and the protective tariff was a subsidy of certain classes [in the society] at the cost of others. [...] The keyword was 'concentration', 'sharing of production' between countries, and 'mutual gain', all indicating a classical distribution thought building on the idea that only industries that leaned on natural conditions, sound natural resources and 'interest and inherited knowledge' were rentable.[54]

Aschehoug did not believe that the state should encourage investments in uncertain industries through customs politics, but rather that they should promote sound industrial development. Comments on Aschehoug and his trade policies can be found in a later chapter, where the focus will be on what is written in *Socialøkonomik*, although a few remarks from earlier statements will be included where appropriate. He was pragmatic, something that became more visible as he grew older. Seip claims, 'Harmony and integration, the two main ideas of social thought of the 1850s, wound up in the background both in thought and argumentation during the 1870s.'[55] I will argue that Aschehoug was more consistent in his approach and that when she ends her analysis in 1882, she misses an important part of his scientific work that clearly displays continuity and an elaborated perspective on theory and practical policies in economics. As his knowledge expands, so do his analyses and theories.

Political Context: Aschehoug the Politician

Aschehoug as a politician is one of the main topics in Seip's *Vitenskap og Virkelighet: Sosiale, økonomiske og politiske teorier hos T. H. Aschehoug 1845 til 1882*, published in 1975, after a seven-year-long doctoral thesis project from 1966 to 1973. She explicitly states that her purpose is to investigate how his political and social theories were applied in his role as an active politician and how they influenced his opinions and ideas about society.[56] Seip mostly uses public documents, such as governmental propositions (*Stortingsmeldinger*), commission reports (*kommisjonsinnstillinger*), governmental negotiations (*Stortingsforhandlinger*) and newspaper articles, mostly from *Morgenbladet* (the morning journal) and *Christiania-posten*. She also includes Aschehoug's personal letters as well as his published works, with a clear time span from 1845 to 1882. This means that *Socialøkonomik* and most articles in *Statsøkonomisk Tidsskrift* are not part of her main analysis and are only mentioned occasionally.

Aschehoug was a regular columnist in *Morgenbladet* for two decades, where he freely expressed his meanings with a 'masterly pen'.[57] This lasted until at least 1868. Seip says that his views, and those of the government, often coincided and that his influence was substantial.

Her description of Aschehoug as a politician is thorough, although with a somewhat negative bent. She describes Aschehoug as a 'harmony-liberal' and, in many cases, conservative when it came to questions about voting rights. Seemingly the term 'harmony-liberal' has a negative slant to her. She also underlines his will to compromise, citing his contemporaries, who accused him of lacking 'independence and self-esteem', 'opinions and steadiness' and 'strength and courage to move on'.[58] She describes a person that did not live up to the expectations of a new leadership after Schweigaard, someone who held on to outworn ideals about the political system, and who was a loser in the debate about parliamentarism. She also sees his personal appearance as a hindrance, although this is not consistent, as she gives examples to suggest either way. Maybe the expectations after the highly influential and dominating Schweigaard were too high; perhaps 'the boots were too big to fill'. Sometimes the term 'professor-politician' is used to refer to these nineteenth-century men, and I suggest that this describes Aschehoug, being a professor first and a politician second, whereas the opposite describes Schweigaard: he was a 'politician-professor'.

Aschehoug was 'number two' after the charismatic Schweigaard. He may have been more productive theoretically, with much higher standards, deeper analyses and with updated perspectives, but as the change in political reality coincided with his succession of Schweigaard, he was bound to fail. He lacked the political ability, the authority and impact of his predecessor. Langslet points out that this opinion about Aschehoug has been somewhat influenced by the context, time and coincidences in the 1870s. In a harsher political climate, knowledge and solid arguments were less appreciated than before.[59] The analyses of Anne-Lise and Jens Arup Seip from the 1970s clearly highlights the negative sides of Aschehoug; the context has been pushed deeply into the background. Aschehoug was aware of the situation himself, saying that he was used to losing, and that no one, until his 80th birthday had called him amiable.

Aschehoug's personality is best found in his many letters, as Anne-Lise Seip highlights. She says that a 'more friendly, respected and well-liked' picture manifests itself.[60] She admits that historians have often drawn a negative picture of him, based on his failures as a politician, which might be superficial and not properly understood within the actual context. Aschehoug commented himself, in a governmental negotiation (*stortingsforhandling*) from 1874, that 'while the victory always covers all faults, the defeat often displays and exposes them in too sharp a light'.[61]

Aschehoug had many different assignments during his life and career, some of them more important to his work as an economist than others. As already mentioned, Aschehoug studied the workings of commissions during his stay in England, and on his return to Norway in 1850, at only 28 years old, he was appointed as member of the Smallholder Commission. Three years later he became a member of the Poverty Commission, whose aim was to outline a proposition for a new law about the workings of the Poor Law authorities. Both commissions were to influence Aschehoug substantially in his later work with social problems and questions, and through these workings he was able to try out the interaction between economic theories and practical problem solving. Other commissions were the Malt Tax Commission (1857) and the Tax Commission (1861). Later, he was the chairman of the Customs Commission, which will be commented on in the analysis of Aschehoug and trade policies.

Seip draws attention to something Aschehoug himself wrote in the proposition from the Smallholder Commission. In this he wrote that enlightenment and education were the answers to a concrete political challenge, namely to preserve the peace of society and maintain harmony.[62] Education was defined as a task for society, an obligation and an offer to the labour classes. The Norwegian social scientist Eilert Sundt (1817–1875) was a member of the Poverty Commission together with Aschehoug and they belonged to the same generation.[63] Aschehoug believed that Sundt had both a theoretical insight as well as a practical perspective and that he had the ability to see variations and explain them.[64] Concrete insight into the causes and consequences of the workings of the Poor Law administration should result in guidance for further development and contribute to a deeper understanding of the practical workings of social laws and social institutions, and thereby create a platform for the necessary reforms.[65]

The interaction between practical economic life and economic theory, and the connection between law and economics, were to characterize Aschehoug throughout his life. Legislation was to become an instrument to reformers like Aschehoug and Schweigaard, both professors in law and in economics. The aim was to put theory into practice. In his obituary to Aschehoug, professor Francis Hagerup (1853–1921) writes, 'Finally, last but not least, must be mentioned the substantial efforts Aschehoug made to his country as an active politician.'[66]

Aschehoug became a member of the Norwegian parliament (Stortinget) in 1868, a position he held until 1883, and became a chairman of the conservative party after the death and resignation of Schweigaard. He had a close relationship with several contemporary politicians, including Frederik Stang (1808–1884), the first prime minister of Norway, his grandchild Fredrik Stang d.y. (1861–1941), a chairman of the conservative party (now Høyre), and Johan Sverdrup (1816–1892), the prime minister following the introduction of the parliamentary system in 1884 and chairman of the left liberal party (Venstre). Aschehoug took part in the debate about the introduction of the parliamentary system, opposing it, something that certainly contributed to his limited success as chairman of the conservative party and later on to his resignation.[67] During the beginning of the 1880s, Aschehoug complained about his health and looked upon the demanding committee work as 'drudgery', as described in his personal letters.[68] He was 60 years old and wanted to concentrate his efforts on scientific work, which we now know was specifically economics.[69]

Public Assignments and Different Academic and Personal Interests

Aschehoug had many assignments; among others he was a member of the supervisory commission of the College of Agricultural Engineering at Aas from 1861 to 1871.[70] In the 1850s, he was a member of the Society for the Promotion of General Education (Selskabet for folkeopplysningens fremme) and the Scandinavian Society (Skandinavisk selskab). Of importance to his discussions about credit and saving banks was his assignment as a member of the board of directors at the Norwegian central bank from 1874 to 1885, the administration of the Widow Funds from 1872 to 1874 and the board of directors of Den norske Creditbank (the Norwegian credit bank) from its foundation in 1856 until his death in 1909. His interest in the importance and development of the railway system had already been born in his youth, and he was a member of the board of directors of the main railway from 1865 to 1871.[71] Aschehoug also greatly contributed to the foundation of SSB in 1876, as mentioned above in connection to Anders Kiær.

Aschehoug's daughter, Anna Sewell, was married in London to Thomas Sewell, a descendant of a business partner of George W. Norman. She published a statement in the French press after the death of her father. The statement presents all his honorary titles: most importantly were the 'docteur en droit' and his different chairs at the University of Oslo. In addition, Aschehoug had received the highest honorary title in Norway: commander of the cross (*kommandørkorset*) of the St Olavs orden. He was a commander of the first class of the Danish order Dannebrogordenen and of the Swedish Nordstjärneordenen, as well as being a commander of the French Legion of Honour (Æreslegionen). In terms of international scientific affiliations and membership, these included: the Kongelige danske forening for historie og nasjonale språk (Royal Danish Association of History and National Language), the Statistiske forening (Statistical Association) in London, the Institut de France, and the Internasjonale institutt for internasjonal rett (International Institute of International Law). He was also honorary doctor at the academy in Lund (Sweden), a member of the Kongelige svenske vitenskapsforening (Royal Swedish Scientific Society) in Uppsala and doctor in law at the Kongelige akademiet Albertine (Royal Academy Albertine) in Königsberg.[72]

Scientific, Legal and Historical-Statistical Works

During his career, Aschehoug published an impressive amount of scientific papers, books, treatises, articles and commission reports, as well as his main work about public law *Norges offentlige rett* (Norwegian public law), which was published in three volumes between 1875 and 1885. Furthermore, he wrote several historical works, the most important being *Statsforfatningen i Norge og Danmark intil 1814* (The constitution of Norway and Denmark until 1814), which was published in 1866. Together with K. J. Berg and the Danish lawyer and politician A. F. Krieger (1817–1893) he was the editor of the five volumes of *Nordisk retsencyklopædi*, where he was responsible for the article about Nordic constitutional rights.[73] As already stated, these works will not be analysed in this project due to the time and scope available. Seip provides a small analysis of these works, and she comments that the *Statsforfatningen* must be read as an important historical work, giving a thorough historical background for the constitution in Norway, and argues that the 'science of history should uncover causes and developments, something that brought history methodically closer to the natural sciences [...] the possibility that historical research had to find causes and demonstrate chains of causes'.[74] The *Statsforfatningen* did not have a chapter about method, something that *Socialøkonomik* has. This chapter will be analysed as a core part later.

In 1889, Bredo Morgenstierne followed Aschehoug's position as a professor of law (*stats- og forvaltningsrett*), and in 1900 he published *Lærebog i den norske statsforfatningsret*, a work that was explicitly meant to be a textbook version of the copious volumes of Norwegian public law by Aschehoug, revised in the beginning of the 1890s. Morgenstierne followed to a large extent the central ideology of constitution in Aschehoug's own work; division of power and the individual rights of citizens (especially in the economic sphere) were vital premises to the interpretation of the constitution. But Morgenstierne thought that the premises of the constitution were absolute and could not be tampered with, a thought that deviated from Aschehoug's own interpretation. In addition, Morgenstierne's general political theory was more conservative than that of his predecessor Aschehoug.[75] In his obituary of Aschehoug, Morgenstierne comments that in his main work of jurisprudence, 'he meticulously quotes thousands of references of every parliamentary debate, foreign constitutional laws, literature and so forth, saving his predecessors an enormous amount of work. Along with his excellent qualities, his magnum opus of Constitutional Law will remain the main source of jurisprudential knowledge, both for scientists and for politicians in our country.'[76]

His historical interest and extensive knowledge of history is also clearly visible all through *Socialøkonomik*. A couple of independent smaller articles form the basis of several chapters in *Socialøkonomik*, many of which were published in *Statsøkonomisk Tidsskrift* (see Appendix C). Two articles were especially important for the ongoing work with *Socialøkonomik*, the articles about crises and marginal theory.

In 1898, Aschehoug published an article entitled 'De økonomiske kriser og depressioner i det 19. aarhundre' (The economic crises and depressions during the nineteenth century), as well as a shorter article about revenue and income, 'Afkastning og indtækt'. Aschehoug had lived long enough to observe many of them. When he later wrote the about the crises in the last volume of *Socialøkonomik*, he built on this article, as well as commenting and broadening his perspective, including the crisis in US in 1907. His presentation was, as always, nuanced and solid. Economic crises are treated in Chapter 12 of this book.

In 1900, Aschehoug started the publishing of *Værdi- og prislærens historie* (History of the theory of value and prices), a three year project from 1900–1902. *Værdi- og prislærens historie* was reviewed by Thorstein Veblen (1857–1929), who regretted that Aschehoug did not develop the theme further, something Aschehoug later did in *Socialøkonomik*.

> This slight volume on the history of value and price theories comes nearer being a sketch than a monograph. The reason for so characterizing it is not its insignificance of bulk, but rather its compact form and concise presentation together with an easy and graceful touch and the absence of any attempt to follow the inquiry out exhaustively at any one point. It covers the history of doctrine since Adam Smith, with some slight reference to earlier writers, and shows such wide and intimate familiarity with the literature of the subject, and such sympathetic, and at the same time critical, appreciation of the many writers and points of view, as to leave the reader with a hearty regret that Professor Aschehoug has not chosen to deal more exhaustively with his subject.[77]

In 1903, he published a short review of the history of the value of money in Norway compared to Western Europe, 'Kort oversigt over den norske mynt- og pengeværdis historie, sammenlignet med Vesteuropas'. The last article he published was in 1908, when he reviewed the publication of K. A. Wieth-Knudsen's *Formerelse og fremskridt*.

Some of these articles will be used in my analysis of topics in *Socialøkonomik*, especially the one about crises and the large one about price and value theory. An obituary in *Norsk retsvidenskap* written by Francis Hagerup in 1909 sums up his activity in this manner: 'His scientific project covered a large field of interests. His interest in economics was born in his early youth, and lead to his employment at the Ministry of Finance. Economics was also his main occupation during the last decades of his life. The fruits of this magnum opus, that will surely maintain his name, is: "*Socialøkonomik*, a scientific presentation of the economic activity of human society"'.[78]

This presentation has emphasized Aschehoug as an economist and commented on his political career. Aschehoug was also a highly esteemed professor of law, which this presentation does not highlight other than to mention his most important works. The portrait that Langslet presents concentrates on Aschehoug as a conservative politician and professor of law, which might be illuminating for a Norwegian audience. Anyone who might wish to look at Aschehoug's juridical works should aim at presenting this part of his career.

Chapter 3

NORWEGIAN ECONOMIC AND POLITICAL CONTEXT IN THE NINETEENTH CENTURY

This chapter will give an outline of the Norwegian economic and political context in the nineteenth century. The main emphasis will be on Anton Martin Schweigaard in order to trace the origins of Aschehoug's thought. Other earlier economists are only mentioned briefly when appropriate. In order to understand the small and backward country Norway was at the beginning of the century, and how much it had changed by the time of Aschehoug's death in 1909, this outline will show different aspects and theories of this development. The role of active politics in order to create a well-functioning economy is also mentioned. To a Norwegian reader, this outline may be well-known history. The aim is nevertheless to present the early framework in which Aschehoug grew up and worked.

The Norwegian Political and Social Context in the Nineteenth Century

To understand what kind of economic approach was adapted in Norway during the nineteenth century, a summary of the general Norwegian context and political system is necessary.[1] The development of Norway from a small, rural country to a modern industrial power started and progressed during the nineteenth century. Society was created in the tension between the *embetsstand* (intellectuals/bureaucrats) and the popular movements – firstly the free Norwegian landholders, later the labour movements. The authors of *Norske idéhistorie*, as well as the philosopher Gunnar Skirbekk in his new analysis of Norwegian modernity, *Norsk og moderne*, underline that the development was distinctly Norwegian (or Scandinavian) – not, as is often claimed, just an adaptation of European experiences.[2] The interaction between government officials and popular movements was relatively peaceful and focused on cooperation when compared to other European countries. According to the Norwegian historian Kåre Amundsen, the period between 1814 and 1890 can be described as the transition from an agrarian society to a private-capitalistic industrial society, especially prominent after 1840. From 1890 to 1940 economic growth and industrialization continued, albeit suffering setbacks from various crises such as the World Wars and the stock market crash in 1929.[3]

Amundsen notes that gradual change from a mercantilist to a liberal economic society from 1814 to 1890 happened without any major disturbances, and the transition was relatively straightforward.[4] He further sums up three main principles of public tasks: firstly, secure domestic and foreign peace, take responsibility for poor relief, and promote general education; secondly, participate in economic activities where public operation is preferred to private; thirdly, to a certain extent accept protection customs in order to secure the national existence of certain industries.[5]

Protestant ethics and religious value orientation also permeated popular movements, resulting in claims for individual freedom and equality, ending with Norwegian independence in 1905. Almost one hundred years earlier in 1814, Norway established its own constitution, but remained in union with Sweden. Ever since the end of the four-hundred-year union with Denmark, Norway had been politically independent in all national matters. The union with Sweden was a union of two countries, internally independent, but having the same international political regime. The constitution of 1814 was founded on the ideas from the French Revolution and the US Declaration of Independence. The idea of freedom that was embedded in the constitution was more cosmopolitical than national. The human reason was coupled with freedom, and enlightened reason lead to freedom and vice versa. The constitution was a progressive one, but in reality only a few were entitled to vote during most of the nineteenth century. The need for a political elite that could bring the country forward was prevailing, at least until the people were educated and enlightened enough to govern themselves.

The enlightenment ideas of freedom, equality and rationality had their unique reception in Norway. 'It is more a question of a pragmatic, nonutopian adaption, with the farmer as the hegemonic figure', says the historian Øystein Sørensen in *Norsk idéhistorie*.[6] Ideas were introduced and accepted through a pragmatic and peaceful process, finding the necessary compromises when needed. Sørensen writes in *Norsk idéhistorie* that this was probably the reason why the forceful reactions between German romanticism and French Enlightenment thought were not as present as in other European countries.

Norway was a country without a nobility, without a capitalist elite or bourgeoisie, with the exception of a few. Of about 900,000 inhabitants in 1814 only 1,700 to 1,800 were *embetsmenn*, and a handful were entrepreneurs and capitalists.[7] Around 90 per cent were farmers (or smallholders) who, to some extent, were literate and who were well represented at the constituent assembly at Eidsvoll in 1814. The government officials were educated in Copenhagen, and they were generally well acquainted with international ideas and circumstances. These numbers were slightly altered by the end of the century, but Norway still had just a handful of people with any political or economic power. Only 0.2 per cent of the inhabitants were *embetsmenn* – mainly university-educated jurists, Lutheran priests and a couple of military officers. They had a dual role, acting as both government officials and as active politicians. When the parliamentary system was introduced, other classes of society gradually gained more political power. The power was passed from government officials to a new oppositional elite which comprised many farmers. The government officials were people that were educated, but who did not necessarily have economic resources. In many cases they were also farmers, as were the priests. Christiania was just a small town, and many of these people were scattered around the country to administer local needs.

The term 'farmer' needs an explanation. The farmer was a free and independent, but rather small, landholder. The *odal* rights, which the reformist absolutist Danish regime had been about to abolish before 1814, were included in the 1814 Constitution of the

Kingdom of Norway. The many small independent farmers, peasant proprietors and free tenants were enfranchised.[8] The farmer was, on the other hand, also related to ideas of romanticism, but these ideas eventually became part of the Enlightenment ideas. The Norwegian farmer was then an enlightened figure tainted by ideas of romanticism. The farmer was not only the symbol of equality and freedom, but also an educated and virtuous figure. The cliché was that farmers, but not any kind of farmers, inhabited Norway.[9] They were relatively well educated, and most importantly they were free, independent and equal. At least, this has been the prevalent idea about the Norwegian soul for almost two hundred years. In reality this is of course a simplification, but it is important to bear it in mind in order to see how the political and economic regime developed in Norway during the nineteenth century. The cliché was not as far fetched as it could have been. The Norwegian population was mostly employed in primary industries – farming and fisheries – whereas nobilities and economic elites were almost nonexistent, something that of course influenced the ideas of economic development.[10]

Furthermore, the Swedish historian, Bo Stråth, offers a comprehensive analysis of the *volk* (folk) dimension in Norway by the end of the nineteenth century: 'Social protest and claims for more democracy originated in a broader popular coalition in which the labour movement was, or rather, became, the driving force, though not to the exclusion of others. Farmers also formed an integral part of this coalition.'[11] Some important implications can be drawn from this concerning the historical development in Norway. The Norwegian farmer is difficult to include within the concept of a peasant, which has the connotation of subordination in it, connected to a feudal hierarchy. According to Stråth, the Norwegian farmer is a figure between the yeoman and the freeholder in an English context, being more like a farmer at the turn of the century. Farmers have played an important role in the formation of Norwegian society by solving the conflict between freedom and equality. Stråth claims that the tension between freedom and equality was more easily contained in Norway because of the pragmatic dimension connected to it. He says, 'There emerged in the pragmatic bargaining cultures a paradoxical positivist quest for perfection in search of public welfare, […] religious revivalism and political pragmatism in a contradictory but consistent way.'[12] Norwegian farmers were active figures both economically and politically; Nina Witoszek says that they were 'too conservative to be radical but too radical to be conservative'.[13] And it is easy to see the political dimensions in Aschehoug's background; although his close family were parish priests, they were indeed farmers as well. Their daily political and social tasks were, among other things, the practical administration of poor relief. The farmers were often local administrators and therefore independent at the same time as being part of political life, many being the local representative to the Storting (parliament).

Individualization and dehierarchization through the development of the church, making the Lutheran church a *volk* church, was still another step towards equality and democracy. Cultural and educational development also followed a nonelitarian path. To sum up, the Norwegian society was empirically and pragmatically oriented.[14] In order to see the difference between the continental and German emerging welfare state and the Norwegian or Scandinavian development, Bo Stråth offers a comprehensive analysis. He argues that the emerging welfare states in Scandinavia at the end of the nineteenth century had a universalistic dimension. This was due to a close communicative connection between the social democrats, social liberals and reforming conservatives, Aschehoug belonging to the latter. The Scandinavian countries followed rapidly the changes and proposals made by Bismarck in Germany, the difference being that farmers and all 'classes' in society were part of the discussion from the beginning. Stråth emphasizes that welfare projects were a 'mixture of self-defined needs among the lower classes and the fear of social and political revolt among the ruling classes. In Scandinavia the gravitation point [...] was closer to the former.'[15] Skirbekk repeats this view in his analysis and calls these deep learning processes among people for the distinctive *volk* dimension. All Scandinavian languages have words like *folkelighed*, *folkhem* and *folkedanning*, which are almost completely impossible to translate, but meaning something common, for everybody and also transmitting a meaning of equality. The French call it *le charme discret des pays nordiques*.[16]

Stepping back to the middle of the century, another historian, Jens Arup Seip described the 70 years between 1814 and 1884 as the *embetsmannsstaten* – the state of the government officials. They constituted the political elite gained through their education and superior knowledge. And they had little competition, either from the farmers or from other (nonexistent) elites. They knew each other from friendship, marriages and professional activities, forming a small, but nationwide, network. A group of young intellectuals formed during the 1830s a small, informal circle called *intelligenskretsen*, publishing their views through the magazine *Vidar* and later also the journal *Den constitutionelle*.[17]

The protagonist of this circle was Schweigaard. Many of his ideas about the development of Norwegian society started out in this circle, which included many jurists. Aschehoug was, in his youth, a great admirer of the somewhat older affiliates in *intelligenskretsen*. As will be discussed, the circle saw communications in the widest sense as paramount to the modernization of society, as well as a general liberalization of trade. Also, a universal education was part of their vision. An educated population would enhance economic development. The main ideas from the Enlightenment coupled with a belief in progress were embedded in their ideas about the development of society. The Norwegian national building project was founded on reforming and ameliorating institutions to create a modern *Rechtsstaat* and improve economic development. The historian Anton Fredrik Andersen states in his thesis that the eagerness of the Norwegian professors to engage in the practical institution building, both private and public, was greater than in many other European countries. Given the scarce possibilities of raising an economic elite, the state was a natural vehicle to implement reforms. Fronted by Schweigaard, the ideas of this circle of intellectuals for reforming the state and modernizing Norway would appear. They shaped Aschehoug's youth and the early beginnings of economic thought in Norway.[18]

Parliamentarism was introduced in 1884, but democratic and political development started 70 years earlier in 1814. In this period a profound reciprocal trust was built into the political system, based on a deep respect for the opinions and positions of others. As Skirbekk puts it, 'It can be described as a fundamental trust in political opponents as reasonable persons and to legal institutions as fair, just and useful.'[19] This does not imply that there were no debates or even harsh disagreements, but rather that solutions, in the end, were sought through compromise and respect for the minority. This pragmatic approach and mentality is deeply rooted in what Skirbekk calls a 'pastoral Enlightenment', enhancing a will to seek compromises, sharing and taking responsibility and seeking agreements through 'enlightened' discussions. Cooperation is a better term than conflict to describe Norwegian politics, although the 1884 parliamentary discussions and the 1905 union discussions were heated. Bearing these general observations in mind, it will be easier to understand how the thoughts of Aschehoug were shaped and formed during his adolescence and professional career.

Nineteenth-Century Economic Development in Norway: A Backward Country Becoming Industrialized

The economic development of Norway is, in many ways, mirrored in the approach of Aschehoug's economic theory. This is not surprising, since he emphasizes history, both through his analysis and through the presentation of statistics. Some historians present the Norwegian economic development as technology driven; others underline the demand dimensions and the market. There are also discrepancies when it comes to the role of the state versus the private initiative. Presentations of Schweigaard usually point out his role as a modernizer, and Rune Slagstad calls the Norwegian way 'governmental-tainted capitalism'. In order to understand Norwegian economic development, and to relate it to Aschehoug, this small analysis will focus on the entrepreneurial factor, the credit and capital conditions, and trade and customs development. The other important aspect that is being discussed among historians is institutional preparations and readiness and how it affects economic development.

Before the Napoleonic Wars Norway was a peripheral country in Europe. Apart from fisheries, mining and the lumber industry, which had an international market, the primary agrarian activities were local. There was, however, one important difference compared to other peripheral countries, the Norwegian farmer was a small but free individual, living by the produce of his farm. During the nineteenth century, Norway became an industrialized country, integrated into the industrialized part of the world.

In 1814, following the wars, Norway was in a miserable economic state. Independent Norwegian institutions (not based in Copenhagen) were to a great extent lacking, but it is worth mentioning that continuity was present as well. Of the 150 Danish-born government officials that lived in Norway in 1814, only 26 returned to Denmark.[20] The first Norwegian university had been established only three years earlier in Christiania. It was a matter of building institutions and establishing an administration, and at the same time securing and developing the economy.[21] It was, at the same time, a governmental modernization process from above and an active participation from below, which makes the Norwegian modernization different from the French and the German, and the scientific development of economics differed as well, finding a Norwegian solution.[22] From above, the jurists were the protagonists, as lawmakers and institutional modernizers. From below, the farmers, and the often combined role of farmer and priests (the 'potato priests'), built up the local administration. Nina Witoszek claims that the North, conjured up by Scandinavian nation-building elites, was the North of a unique, 'pastoral Enlightenment' – it indicates an enduring rustic ingredient, a rural fantasy which is part and parcel of the Scandinavian self-image, but it also alludes to Scandinavian pastors and preachers, important agents and codifiers of the founding tradition.[23]

Economic growth was exceptionally high between 1835 and 1875, both quantitatively and qualitatively. From 1841 to 1866, the export of fish and lumber together doubled, and in 1866, shipping had grown to 12 per cent of the national income, the same as the fishery and lumber industries.[24] In the same span of 25 years the merchant fleet had grown by 250 per cent. The question among economic historians has been whether this growth was due to a (market) pull, a (production) push, or a combination of both, and how much a planned governmental interference meant to the development. The main purpose of the Norwegian historian, Francis Sejersted, in his theory about the historical and technological Norwegian development in the nineteenth century, is to show how Norway became a capitalistic, industrial country by a shift in the dynamics from a market-demand or pull perspective to a supply-technological or push perspective. He gives a coherent analysis of the economic, as well as political, development, and his conclusions are in line with what I perceive as a reliable overall picture of the Norwegian process from an agrarian to an industrialized country, the period coinciding with the lifespan of Aschehoug.[25]

The market-demand perspective can be described as export-driven growth, meaning that economic growth comes as a result of a demand for goods that can be exported. In the Norwegian case, this was lumber, fisheries and the transportation itself – shipping. Fritz Hodne, a Norwegian economic historian, is the protagonist of this view.[26] His main point is that entrepreneurs are using market possibilities. If there is a growth in a market, the suppliers will be there to satisfy it, given that they respond to the demand, something that Norway did, but other peripheral countries did not. The difference lies in the institutional and structural conditions. The question, then, is whether the institutions are needed before, or come as a result of, the growth.

The institutional, political and cultural readiness of Scandinavia brought the countries from poverty to plenty within a short period of time, even though the actual industrialization initially lagged behind. The catch-up was quick when it first started.[27] The estimated GNP per capita shows that the Scandinavian countries started out with US$219 in 1830 climbing to US$682 in 1913, closing the gap between themselves and the industrial core of continental Europe, including France and Germany. The modernization strategy of Schweigaard can be seen as a successful attempt to build up this cultural and institutional readiness in Norway. According to David Landes, Norway built on free enterprise and quick response, beginning with timber and raw fish, and soon developing processed products, clearly helped by improvements in transportation and banking (money and credit) institutions.[28] As we know, both transportation and banking development were staged by the Schweigaard and Stang government.[29]

The hypothesis that the Norwegian economy entered a phase of economic growth in the 1840s, partly by using new production technologies and partly benefiting from a freer international trade (e.g., the Navigation Act, 1849) is claimed by two Norwegian economic historians Fritz Hodne and Ola Honningdal Grytten at the Norwegian School of Economics and Business Administration (NHH), often referred to as the Bergen School. They belong to the school of thought that also emphasizes the market pull and the opportunities of growth that came from free(r) trade. They claim that technological progress was self-reinforcing. They attribute growth mainly to shipping and to fisheries and lumber industries becoming more advanced and delivering 'boiled products' instead of 'raw'. Of utmost strategic importance was, therefore, the opening of export markets for Norwegian products in the 1840s. Hodne stresses the 'individual factor', namely the entrepreneurs as being crucial. The initiative came from entrepreneurs, who seized the market opportunities.

Another Norwegian economic historian, Trond Bergh at the University of Oslo, adheres to the push/technological, production theory of growth. Generally, Norway seems to have used the opportunity of being a latecomer in a successful manner, something that Landes also underlines. Norway was the 'lucky, small imitator'. The opportunity of skipping mistakes, using newly developed technology and benefitting from the experience of others are probably paramount for the technological and industrial development in Norway. But initially, Norway did not possess the normal necessary resources to industrialize successfully, meaning there were no coal or ore mines, a small home market and no ambitions to industrialize. On the other hand, Norway did not, as mentioned earlier, have to struggle with land nobility, the Catholic Church or military elites, normal obstacles to institutional developments such as political democracy and industrial capitalism.[30] The Norwegians did not even possess an active bourgeoisie. But more importantly, the small, local bourgeoisie based in the smaller towns, together with egalitarian-oriented and free farmers in the countryside, made smaller businesses more successful. Also important was the widespread use of partnership in shipping (*partsredere*). Shipping, when combined with trade, was often a side business in order to conduct the business of trade.

Norwegian industrialization and the strategies used to industrialize have been discussed in relation to Schweigaard; many historians claim to see less enthusiasm for industry than for trade, communications and institutional building in his views. Schweigaard had said in the 1840s, 'All that can be expected from the future is that the country, using its own factories, will be capable of supplying itself with simple woven fabrics of mediocre quality, but will have to import higher quality fabrics.'[31] He thereby underlines the general impression from the Ministry of Finance that in 1842 stated, 'The difficulties with competition from foreign factories means that Norway will never be industrialized on a large scale.'[32] The last statement was obviously proven to be wrong by the turn of the century, but the statements show reluctance towards industrialization on a large scale. It is probably in this aspect that Schweigaard and Aschehoug differ the most. Aschehoug had the benefit of living through a couple of economic crises as well as seeing the development and change in shipping and the emerging industrialization, being especially strong in the last quarter of the nineteenth century.[33]

Even though Schweigaard did not see the opportunities in industrialization in the 1840s, he nevertheless worked hard to establish a sound monetary system with a convertible currency, as well as a credit system. Schweigaard wrote *Om Norges bank- og pengevæsen* in the 1840s, inspired by the works of another entrepreneur and economist Jacob Aall (1773–1844), and the development of a banking and monetary system continued. The third element, in addition to a growing population and a sound monetary system, was the amelioration of transportation. This did not only include shipping, but railways, roads, bridges, canals and harbours. Schweigaard worked on both these two framework conditions for industrialization. The growing population, together with a better transportation system, created a home market for many consumer goods. Aided by the growing export income, the home market grew as well.

Schweigaard also worked for a better education system, but there were no clear efforts towards technical and economic education until much later in the century. Bergh claims that the education level was low. The spread of technology did not happen because of a well-educated population. In 1850 only between 20 and 30 per cent of the population was literate. On the other hand, Bergh insists that a high general education was, not necessarily, a prerequisite for the adaptation of advanced technology. It sufficed that key clusters had the knowledge that was needed, or the opportunity to get it.[34] It appears that education was well adapted where it was needed, and therefore also efficiently applied. Since the adaptation of new methods came in smaller steps, Bergh asserts that industry slowly got the self confidence to risk larger projects and investments later (e.g., after 1900), calling it the 'Berlitz model', namely the lumber industry development process from lumber to pulp, to cellulose, and finally to paper.[35] Norway was successful in one aspect, which is the ability to adapt and diffuse new production methods in order to develop key cluster industries where the possibilities were already present. It is important to note that the adaptation was more than just copying, just as economic theory came to Norway from the Continent and from England to be discussed and reshaped to fit the Norwegian political and economic circumstances. One might say that the Norwegians were quick learners when they got the opportunity.

When the setbacks came for shipping and lumber, Norway was ready to industrialize quickly and sell more 'boiled products'. The growth in employment rose from 12,500 factory employed workers in 1850 to 101,000 in 1910. Pulp and paper employed only a few per cent in 1850 but was the second largest industry in 1910, with almost 15 per cent employed in this area.[36] Bergh does not see this transformation as a market pull, but rather as a technology push, transforming lumber to pulp and paper and gradually benefiting from waterfalls and electricity at the turn of the century.

Machinery was important, and much of it was imported from England. It was not only Aschehoug who travelled to England in the late 1840s; this was also common for technicians, mechanics and business managers. Germany was also important in many aspects when it came to know-how, especially in the wood-processing industry, but the Norwegians were, again, quick adapters and soon learned to make the machinery themselves. Later it was electrical equipment that came from Germany. Again, in industrialization, as well as in economic theory, Norway turned both to the Continent and Germany, and to England.

The broadest outline of the economic, political and technological development in Norway is, in my view as already stated, given by the historian Francis Sejersted. The kingdom of Denmark and Norway had a mercantilist economic system during the eighteenth century. This meant that political measures were taken to enforce the comparative advantages of the Norwegian mining and lumber production and trade, building on a small, but sustainable milieu of an entrepreneurial bourgeoisie. They were given privileges of trade and production. After the Napoleonic Wars Norway established its constitution, and just afterwards entered a union with Sweden (as mentioned, a union of two independent countries with a common king). This was a political and democratic boost, but economically Norway entered a phase of low growth and deep economic crises for many of the former businesses. Politically, Norway was close to starting anew, combining liberal ideas, modern political institutions and new general conditions for economic activities, based on equality of treatment (no privileges), protection of property and a stable monetary system. This indicates a willed or staged strategy, quite quickly resulting in a growing middle class of traders and producers – entrepreneurs, in the terms of Aschehoug. It must be underlined that this bourgeoisie comprised smaller businesses and industries, henceforth closely tied to their operations and employees, and it included many small freeholders. Jacob Aall noted during the 1840s that 'everything in our country is in some sense middle class'.[37]

A few words about demographic development might shed light on an increase in both the demand and supply of labour. Signs of a labour class were present, some got work in growing businesses. The post–Napoleonic War crisis also brought about changes in agriculture, resulting in an exceptional demographic growth, and in an increase of young people seeking work in the 1830s, and later a large migration from Norway to the US. Sejersted talks about a Schumpeterian 'creative destruction', opening for a new political regime, a larger middle class, and importantly a strong local governance, creating institutional requirements for new, local economic initiatives.[38] Sejersted also notes a change in mentality from an inward traditional thinking, to a new readiness for foreign impulses and ideas of progression.[39]

For a long time the main Norwegian exporting industries, including shipping, were astonishingly conservative, technologically speaking. The market pull hypothesis might be correct to explain the growth these industries had in the mid-century. As long as the growth was more than sustainable, the old technology worked. Around 1870, coinciding with the death of Schweigaard, the waves of international crises started, gradually creating a need for technological innovation and change. The political and institutional conditions were already present, as well as a functioning credit and monetary system.

Sejersted asserts that the Gerschenkronian scheme of a passive state and an active private banking system does not hold for Norway.[40] Norway never developed strong investment banks. The Norwegian banks were mostly small, local, saving banks and it continued to be so long after the turn of the century. The management of these banks was often identical to that of the local municipality politicians, thus playing a crucial role in local industrialization and development. Together with the central bank, the Norwegian banking system can be described as mostly public.

In the following an analysis of Schweigaard will be conducted, keeping these general remarks about the Norwegian economic and political development in mind. The early formation of the views of Aschehoug was closely linked to Schweigaard and his views on economics and politics in general.

Anton Martin Schweigaard: The First Norwegian Economist

Schweigaard has already been mentioned on numerous occasions. The last part of this chapter will look more closely at Schweigaard and his thoughts, as he represents the natural starting point for a presentation of Norwegian economic thought in the nineteenth century.[41] Two Norwegian economic historians, Bergh and Hanisch, wrote *Vitenskap og politikk* (Science and politics) in 1984. They see Schweigaard as the first important Norwegian economist in their historical presentation of Norwegian economics, and in particular the history of the Statsøkonomisk forening during the past 150 years. Even though they mention early on that his standards and methods do not satisfy the demands of today's economics, they see in Schweigaard the first serious attempts to gain a deeper understanding of the workings of economics and economic activity.[42] They especially praise his article about the Norwegian central bank and monetary system ('Om Norges bank og pengevæsen', 1836).[43] There are also forerunners to Schweigaard, among others Gregers Fougner Lundh (1786–1836), duly presented in a doctoral thesis by Anton Fredrik Andresen, about the foundation of the University of Oslo and economics in the early nineteenth century.[44] This thesis offers a comprehensive background for the development that preceded, and to some extent overlaps, my following presentation. Andresen asks: should economics be useful, civilizing or scientific? A century later, Aschehoug's economics was scientific and still useful, but not civilizing (a further discussion of the development of economics after the death of Fougner Lundh is included in Chapter 4).

Schweigaard did not leave any books or papers that explained his thoughts, except for a famous lecture held in 1847, gathered together around fifty years later by two Norwegians – the economist Oscar Jaeger (1863–1933) and Fredrik Stang d.y., a lawyer and the grandson of the former prime minister and close companion of Schweigaard, Frederik Stang. They published these collected papers under the name of *Ungdomsarbeider*, meaning his early works. This work contains lectures and small papers, and they have been the basis for an extensive discussion among Norwegian historians as to how to understand Schweigaard's position and economic thought. A small presentation of the different views will be conducted, as they are relevant for the comprehension of the development in Aschehoug's thinking. Aschehoug was a young student at the time Schweigaard held his lecture, and Schweigaard was Aschehoug's mentor and teacher. In order to understand Schweigaard as one of the Norwegian political protagonists of the nineteenth century, and at the same time explain the context of the Norwegian society that formed Aschehoug's views, a brief presentation of his work will follow, focusing on his methodical position, his general views on political economy, and his position as the protagonist of what is called the 'great modernization project of the nineteenth century'. Schweigaard was the first national strategic mind in a two-hundred-year tradition broadly presented in Rune Slagstad's *De nasjonale strateger* (The national reformers). Furthermore, comments on his article about the German philosophy and the question of free trade and laissez-faire will be made.

Before 1814, Norway was in a political union with Denmark, a close union that had lasted since the fifteenth century. Norway and Denmark were tightly connected both politically and economically, and as in other European countries, mercantilism and absolutism were mainstream until the last decades of the eighteenth century. A growing interest in liberal ideas could be seen in both countries, as the writings of Adam Smith were translated into Danish as early as 1779, just three years after the initial publication in 1776. The interest came from the bourgeois traders. The interest in economics was also picked up by the University of Oslo, and plans were made to establish a chair in economics together with other chairs that could give 'a suitable education and general knowledge, aimed at giving the candidates a practical and useful learning for their bourgeois activities'.[45] The plans were not realized, and economics was given only a small post together with philosophy, apparently because of a lack of economic resources.

The first decades of the nineteenth century did not bring forth any important economists, and it was not until economics was connected with the professoriate in law that the name of Anton Martin Schweigaard came up as the natural alternative in 1836. A combined post of law, statistics and economics was to become the academic platform for Schweigaard from 1840. The intellectual development manifested itself in the joint professoriate of law, state economics (*statsøkonomi*) and statistics at the University of Oslo, given to Schweigaard in 1840. It became a key discipline, law distancing itself from philosophy, and moving closer to economics and statistics. As Slagstad puts it, the philosophy of the principles of justice was replaced by statistical-economical utility calculations.[46] Professor in economics Olav Bjerkholt refers to the argument for moving and developing statistics at the university from the historical-philosophical faculty to the faculty of law in 1836: 'Statistics after the more recent adaptations, has stopped being a collection of curiosity and historical antiquities and has become important in juridical-economic affairs, because it partly contains the foundation of the organic and administrative legislation of the state and partly presents the facts of the applied national economics.'[47] Bjerkholt's conclusion gives Schweigaard his due in the development of Norwegian statistics, and he acknowledges the willed practical and political uses of statistics and the close connection between statistics and economics.[48]

Schweigaard then became a professor of economics in 1840, a combined professoriate of law, statistics and economics. He had been teaching statistics and economics (*statsøkonomi*) since 1837. In order to establish a chair at the University of Christiania, he saw the need to develop and conduct economic scientific and theoretical work adapted to Norwegian circumstances and experiences. He writes,

> If it were only a matter of translating the main international literature in political economy, it would have been easy. But in this case an independent, Norwegian discipline, that may justly serve Norwegian needs, is necessary. Guidance on improvements, to an understanding of our own economic and financial affairs and institutions, can only be obtained through a thorough scientific analysis and development of our economic institutions, their aims and their workings.[49]

A national expertise was needed, and the first step was a chair in economics. The second step was to develop appropriate Norwegian theoretical literature, but Schweigaard quickly became absorbed in politics and did not have sufficient time for this extensive scientific work.[50]

Bergh and Hanisch describe this as a distinctively Norwegian tradition that was to gain a great and long-lasting importance for economic thought in Norway. The joint juridical and economical professoriate lasted for more than fifty years, and its influence for almost a hundred (see further discussion in Chapter 4).[51] Bergh and Hanisch think that this institutional connection between law and economics was to put a distinctive Norwegian mark on the political questions of the nineteenth century, and they add that the liberal thought of Adam Smith was to influence Norwegian economic thought through Schweigaard, although it is clear that he was no imitator of Smith and his followers.[52] How this liberal thought was influencing Schweigaard has been thoroughly discussed by several Norwegian historians.

Schweigaard was, according to Bergh and Hanisch, the founder of what they chose to name 'the historical-statistical tradition in Norwegian (social) economics'.[53] Schweigaard wrote a couple of articles between 1835 and 1840 that can be found in *Ungdomsarbeider*, mentioned above. One of them was about the Norwegian bank and monetary system, and another outlined the history and principles of customs. In 1840, he also published *Norges statistik* (Norwegian statistics), which was the beginning of a systemization of statistics that was to become the basis of the later national accounts.[54] With this publication, statistics became more similar to current statistics, although it can be claimed that it was still rudimentary and that Aschehoug was the theoretical innovator in statistics. His statistical work is, according to Olav Bjerkholt, an example of an eminent 'applied economist', as opposed to a theoretical economist.[55]

The old ways of qualitative descriptions were replaced by a quantitative economic analysis in order to understand economic conditions, but still keeping its historical perspective. In fact, Aschehoug, who by the last part of the 1840s had become Schweigaard's student, started his career by continuing the statistical-historical works of Schweigaard. His 'On the Norwegian population from 1664–1666' came in 1848, and the preparatory work for the Poverty Commission came a few years later (also commented on in Chapter 6).[56] Statistics was to become an important auxiliary discipline in the development of economic thought in Norway. Another student of Schweigaard, Anders Nicolai Kiær (1838–1919) was appointed as the first manager of the Statistical Office, later to become the Central Statistical Bureau (Statistisk sentralbyrå).[57]

First and foremost Schweigaard was a politician, even though a recent book about him is called *Anton Martin Schweigaard: professor-politician* (I would have preferred the other way around: *politician-professor*). He held a position as a professor of law at the University of Oslo, but it is as a statesman that Schweigaard put his distinctive mark on Norwegian society during the mid-nineteenth century, this era being named *embetsmannsstaten* (*Beamtenherrschaft* in German) or the 'government officials state'.[58] Again, this is a statement that can be discussed, but as Ole Mestad writes, 'From 1842 until his death he was a delegate at the Storting, and he declined an offer to be Minister of Internal Affairs, leaving the job to his companion Stang, but regarding the Storting as his political arena [...] later almost leaving his scientific legal work, concentrating on economics and practical economic policy.'[59] Schweigaard was born just before the Norwegian Constitution was written in 1814, one of the earliest in Europe. Norwegian society was poor after the Napoleonic Wars, so it is fair to say that Norway had a liberal constitution before general economic growth and industrialization.[60]

Schweigaard was a promoter of the belief in practical and useful science in order to create a good society, as well as a believer in the possibility of deriving general laws from empirical data. This was, according to Jens Arup Seip, a general trait of Norwegian intellectual development during the first decades of the nineteenth century.[61] The first was inspired by a need for useful knowledge of society in general, whether it was sociological, economical or political. The inspiration was of course from the natural sciences, not only in method, but also in the attempts to conquer nature in order to ameliorate society. In Seip's words, the classical ideal of utility and of the technological-instrumental was believed to be useful also for the social sciences in general. The second bore the marks of positivism and sometimes 'realism' or 'materialism'.[62]

Schweigaard was in some ways influenced by the French socialist thinker Simonde de Sismondi (1773–1842). He had borrowed both *Etudes sur les sciences sociales* (Studies of the social sciences) and *Nouveaux principes d'économie politique* (New principles of political economy).[63] It is the combination of historical knowledge together with economic analysis that probably caught the attention and interest of Schweigaard. Sismondi was an inspiration for his theory of crises, which was not extensive, but nevertheless an early comprehension of economic business cycles. Sismondi writes about crises in his *Nouveaux principes*, and Schweigaard mentions in his lecture that 'a change in the economic business cycles is not just a consequence of natural or political causes [but also due to entrepreneurs and their changing economic activity]'.[64] As will be shown in Chapter 12, Aschehoug further developed the theory of crises.

Schweigaard's opinion of the state and the objectives of the state is another element in his views which makes it difficult to see him as a direct follower of the perceived liberalism (in nineteenth-century Norway) of Adam Smith and his followers. The idea of the state in the view of Schweigaard was 'to enhance the practical use of the national economy. [...] Ultimately Schweigaard was not a scientist in the narrow sense, he was a politician and an intellectual [with his specific ideas about the development of society] and law and economics were to help out in his political reform.'[65]

What did Schweigaard himself say about 'state economics'? In his comments from the period around the appointment in 1840, he claims that 'state economics [*statsøkonomi*] presupposes a thorough and deep understanding of state institutions, which are concerned with both the economic development and the management of both private and public economics'.[66] Firstly, the state is important, hence the naming of the discipline as 'state' economics. Secondly, state institutions can create the legal and economic framework both for the private and the public economic sectors. Thirdly, it also contains the idea of a practical and useful economics that could serve both the state and the economic sectors in society. The connection with statistics underlines this idea. Furthermore, Bergh and Hanisch bring forth another argument that Schweigaard used: the claim that Norway needed a tailor-made economics for Norwegian circumstances, because the general economic thought found internationally was too abstract and general to be put into practical use in Norway.

The aim of the Norwegian economics should then be to create an 'economic teaching that was distinctly Norwegian, and that could help to create valid guidance of what to correct and ameliorate, and to guide and strengthen general opinions about Norwegian financial and economic affairs and arrangements'.[67] This argument clearly underlines that Schweigaard perceived the close connection between economics and institutional and legal organization and the political aims he had for the development of Norwegian society.[68]

Bergh and Hanisch state that 'law and economics were seen as auxiliary disciplines for political reform work'.[69] To sum up his main modernizing strategy: he wanted a strong liberalization of the shipping industry, a public investment in communications and infrastructure, and a gradual liberalization of domestic trade and industry. Further comments are found later in this chapter and in Chapter 11.

The German Philosophy: About Method, Not Ontology

Included in his *Ungdomsarbeider* is an article called 'Om den tyske filosofi' (On the German philosophy), first published in Paris in 1835 in the French magazine *La France litteraire*, but not published in Norway before 1904. Some of the collected articles in *Ungdomsarbeider* were, in content, more philosophical and methodical than his later writings, which were mostly commentaries on the political debates. Schweigaard turned down German philosophy, because in his view, the German idealist philosophy claimed that humans constitute reality through cognition and thought. In his view, the mind could only be fully developed in encounters with reality and experience. He claimed that the world was organized in a rational way:

> When the German philosophers claim to know everything through an immediate revelation, when they acknowledge that speculation alone has the ability to bring forth true knowledge and thereby collect all in personalized abstraction – reason – what do they then do about experience? Yes, that is the question about which one easily could write monumental philosophical books, and yet, the question will remain unsolvable.[70]

The clear rejection of speculation is mostly due to the rejection of any influence on experience, not necessarily a rejection of reason itself. The article on German philosophy has been an issue for debate ever since, mainly about how it should be understood. Schweigaard was not attacking the German philosophy because he wanted to replace metaphysics with an empirical approach; it was rather to replace pure science with a consideration of utility, by widening the limits of economics to include moral considerations (which Andresen in his thesis remarks is closer to philosophy than to pure empirical thought).[71] Andresen further underlines that this debate about economics was similar to corresponding debates in Germany and England.[72]

A famous Schweigaard expression is *sagens natur* (in the nature of things).[73] The historian Nils Rune Langeland has analysed this expression in relation to Schweigaard's writings about philosophy, which has generally been understood as an acceptance of utilitarianism. His main point is that Schweigaard's critique of the German philosophy is about method, not about philosophy itself or ontology.[74] The Norwegian economist Hertzberg simply states, 'He was a jurist, an economist and an official person; these three tasks occupied both his complete time and his resources. He had his reasons for rejecting the German philosophy and leaning on an empirical world view.'[75]

Schweigaard clears the ground for widespread pragmatic solutions to specific juridical problems, and it could be added, for his approach in general. Towards the 'empty method of idealism', Schweigaard proposed the 'method of experience'.[76] Schweigaard himself writes, 'The German philosophers supplied the soul with an active and creative ability, without a connection with the real world, without basing it in the real world, neither in concrete facts or experiences, the soul creating its own ideas based on a supposed inner harmony that shall correspond to the outside world. [...] The German philosophy has done a lot of harm and lead astray many good souls; it is time to finish it up.' The words were harsh and direct, written by Schweigaard in his youth.[77] To 'base in reality' was to become the mantra of Schweigaard.[78]

He continues,

But could they proceed with this speculation until the ridicule: it will forever be impossible to hide that the postulates, which they claim are deductions given *a priori*, are alone sneaking results of previous abstractions, when they have taken a few steps outside these empty generalizations that could gain all kinds of meanings that one would want them to. [...] The authority that the results of experience enjoy is nil.[79]

He then sets up the British empiricist philosophical tradition as his ideal. He wants results, consequences and usefulness to be guiding the philosophy:

How could the German philosophers apply these empty principles? What could they present as positive results from this intuition, of this pure reason par excellence? [...] Is it not the best to solve the controversies between the parties [...] that judge them after the consequences [of the philosophy], the results and the usefulness of their teachings? Yes, this is the remedy that long gone has refuted this philosophy in France, and even more so in England, where the philosophical arbitrariness has always been fought by just and strong spirits.[80]

It might seem strange that Schweigaard should be as harsh as he is in his criticism, but he claims to have other Germans on his side: 'The social sciences have distanced themselves from the German philosophy, it is not only the small group of German historical jurists I refer to, but all that now have refuted the [German] philosophical pretentions.'[81] It was important to underline the need for empiricism and the reliance on experience. Hertzberg wrote a memoire of Schweigaard in 1883, *Professor Schweigaard i hans offentlige virksomhed*, and he generally sides with Schweigaard and is a great admirer.[82] Hertzberg's commentaries shed some light on these early writings of Schweigaard. He comments that it was 'the transcendental philosophers that at the same time claimed they were independent of reality but wanted to govern it that he rejected; an empirical synthesis of the different phenomena of life through the help of a modest abstraction within his own boundaries had not been criticized, rather he argued for such a connection between science and reality'.[83] Schweigaard didn't like conformist thought, neither in philosophy nor in historical approaches. According to Hertzberg, Schweigaard's position was more modern than that of his contemporaries: 'Just as his fear of false abstractions makes him an empiricist, he also sees how the dangers of too great a love of historical virtues and ways can hinder the unavoidable development.'[84] The development is important, and more important than the consideration of tradition. Sørensen describes Schweigaard as having an empiricist cognition; experience was not only a way of obtaining knowledge, but it was the highest possible form of cognition.[85] And finally, the newly published article 'Sagens natur' by Nils Rune Langeland underlines the methodical reasons for his writings and presents further details, which in this context is of less importance.[86]

These observations are made with examples illustrating the juridical views of Schweigaard, but they also apply to his general thoughts. The principles of development are, in Hertzberg's words, a combination of empirical facts, historically given axioms and general axioms, making him a progressive liberal thinker.[87] Bergh and Hanisch claim that his economic thought developed from his general thought and had its pattern from his juridical thought.[88] They further state that he took a middle position between natural law and the historical school, in clear opposition to German (but not British) thought on natural law. The laws he found in society as well as in nature were the most important goals of human cognition, but the laws could not be acknowledged by reason alone – empirical research was indisputably necessary.[89]

To Schweigaard, law was a result of history and was influenced both by national and local circumstances. As a consequence, law had to be understood through historical studies.[90] Could it then be said that Schweigaard, because of his rejection of the German philosophy, would turn to the opposite and join the historical school? According to Hertzberg the answer was no. Hertzberg argues that his view (on philosophy) was analytical-descriptive. He not only rejected the German philosophy, but also the German historical-juridical school. Hertzberg remarks on this 'peculiarity' in his theoretical thought: one should think that he would join the historical school, but in his article 'Views on the situation of jurisprudence in Germany', he sided with the opponent of the jurist Carl von Savigny (1779–1861), Anton Fredrich Justus Thibaut (1772–1840).[91] Thibaut didn't belong to any historical or philosophical school. According to Hertzberg, Schweigaard thought that Thibaut was the one that 'in liberal treatment, had a fresh and lively perception of reality as opposed to the bindings of law that generally rule all German jurists'. But later Schweigaard admits several times that his youthful attack on Savigny was slightly exaggerated. There had 'long ago ceased to be any distinct [incompatibility]. […] Strictly speaking the differences in view were more due to the scope of the legislative scope and obligations than to the development of the existing jurisprudence.'[92]

Schweigaard said about himself, 'It is not the best and most original thoughts that reveal themselves in writing. A person having within himself a system of thought doesn't necessarily want to manifest it in writing, because it is a real system while it's kept within the person itself, but it dies when it is confined to dogmas.'[93] Bergh and Hanisch quote Hertzberg and underline that Schweigaard assumed an empirical position: 'He was an empiricist, but just as much an idealist, because he saw the rational idea break through in both the actual and the spiritual world.'[94]

To conclude, in this context it is important to note the methodical comments Schweigaard makes, and which are supported by Hertzberg. Schweigaard never wrote explicitly about method, but as has been argued here, this small article about the German philosophy can be read as an argument for his methodical position. Further, seen together with his political career, it is plausible to assert that this way of seeing his article can illustrate Schweigaard's views on method, later elaborated by Aschehoug.

Schweigaard and His Lectures on Political Economy

The most famous and most debated documentation of the economical thought of Schweigaard is found in his lectures about political economy from 1847. It was not published until 1904, in his *Ungdomsarbeider*. The original manuscripts were lost, but the editors, Oskar Jaeger and Fredrik Stang d.y., managed to compare three different sets of lecture notes and thereby recreate the original manuscript.[95] The editors point out that Schweigaard had managed to give a coherent analysis of the political economy, including his basic scientific view, method and systemization, which was in their view still modern nearly sixty years later, even though new theories had been published and were still being debated.[96]

Schweigaard's introduction to his lectures is included in *Statsøkonomisk utsnitt* from 1940 by the two later Norwegian economists Wilhelm Keilhau (1888–1954) and Ragnar Frisch.[97] They state that

Two things may seem strange in this lecture. Firstly, that Schweigaard explicitly rejects building economics purely on certain limited economic terms, by claiming the economic interrelation with religious, moral and political conditions. This indicates a sociological view on economics, not a term that can be found in 1847. Secondly, that the leader of the nineteenth-century economic liberalism in Norway condemns in harsh terms the 'teachings of nonintervention' that under the misuse of the slogan 'laissez-faire' was promoted by the radical adherents to the Manchester School and harmony economics.[98]

These two professors judge Schweigaard in retrospect, pointing out a change in his political activity and a change in economics, and are clearly of the opinion that neither of these two aspects was to become reality. As will be shown, this view is consistent with the modernizing strategy that Schweigaard had and his perception of laissez-faire.

Differing opinions of these lectures have been published. Bergh and Hanisch, two Norwegian economists who wrote a complete overview of the Norwegian social economy in 1984, claim that Adam Smith and the classical school were of vital importance to Schweigaard.[99] It must be remembered that Schweigaard lived and worked earlier than Aschehoug, and that the texts of the classical school were probably the first texts he read. John Stuart Mill, for instance, published his work, *The Principles of Political Economy*, in 1848, and the lectures of Schweigaard were held in 1847. The works of Thomas Malthus (1766–1834), David Ricardo and Nassau Senior were known to Schweigaard as well as the works of Jean-Baptiste Say.[100] Bergh and Hanisch recognize his adaptation of economic terms and theory elements such as value and ground rent, the population theory of Malthus, and the law of Say. But on the other hand they perceive a critical approach when it comes to Ricardo, Senior and Mill. The British tradition was in some ways too liberal, and there is a closer affinity to continental economic thinkers such as

Say in France and F. B. W. von Hermann (1795–1868) and Karl Heinrich (1792–1870) in Germany. And finally, Schweigaard distanced himself from the theoretical political economy that had developed in England, especially Ricardo.

Schweigaard thought that Ricardo was oversimplifying his general theories. In his view, general ideas and models could be useful to grab an idea, but not to explain the workings of social economics in depth.[101] Ricardo had proclaimed that reasoning based on simplified principles was a way to get to the core of a problem, something Schweigaard could at times adhere to, but not when it came to doing it for the whole political economy.[102] That was *reductio ad absurdum*. Senior had claimed that the political economy 'depended more upon reasoning than upon facts', and Mill described it as 'essentially an *abstract* science and its methods as the method *a priori*'.[103] A parallel can be drawn with the arguments used by Schweigaard against the classical postulates of the natural law system, and the arguments used by the German historical school against the classical economics, perceived by them as a precisely natural law system.[104]

After the introduction of his lecture, the rest is in Mehlum's words: '[...] almost devoid of any discussions about the complex relations between state, governing, religion, politics and juridical circumstances. The six chapters generally refer to standard classical theory.'[105] Jaeger and Stang comment, 'What Schweigaard here presents is an elementary and pedagogical account of well-known economic theory, which should be part of a general education, but which unfortunately is not yet the case.'[106] Jaeger and Stang see his lectures as a short, but complete, overview of economics, that in its essence is unchanged (from 1847 to 1904), but which does not include the latest debates and developments in economics. The introduction of Schweigaard's lecture actually points out what Aschehoug is later doing, namely including economics in a comprehensive picture of society and politics. The critique that Schweigaard has towards the simplifications of classical economics (as it was in 1847) is then followed up later by Aschehoug. Interestingly, another historian Kåre Amundsen, writes in 1963 that Schweigaard emphasizes Say and the entrepreneur, something that breaks with the British classical economists.[107] To conclude, it is clear that Aschehoug continues and develops the foundation that Schweigaard lays in his lecture, but it is unfair to compare the two works, as Schweigaard's lectures are just a small pamphlet, whereas Aschehoug wrote many articles and more than two thousand pages in his *Socialøkonomik*. The scientific scope differs in their respective works, but many of Schweigaard's ideas can be found in Aschehoug.

What does Schweigaard state is the subject of political economy? In the opening paragraphs of his lecture he says, 'The task of political economy is to investigate the general causes that influence positively or negatively the welfare and wealth of civil society. The derived goal is to participate in the amelioration of general life conditions that secures so importantly the conditions for the moral development of nations.'[108] In the next paragraph he distances himself from the 'English school', which taught that political economy is the augmentation of the national wealth. Schweigaard underlines that it is the diffusion of general welfare of all that is the subject.[109] The British economist Nassau Senior had, for instance, defined political economy as 'the Science of Wealth', in order to base the discipline more scientifically.[110] Senior comments on other classical economists, and it is evident that he believes that political economy should be scientific, meaning a deductive science limited to the investigations of how to increase wealth, based on general principles of the functioning of economics.[111] Since Senior also gives his opinions on other classical economists in his introduction, it is even clearer how he tries to build a scientific basis for economics, meaning disregarding any attempt to make it a deductive or empirical discipline. He writes,

> The confining of the Science of Political Economy with the Sciences and Arts to which it is subservient, has seduced Economists sometimes to undertake enquiries too vague to lead to any practical results, and sometimes to pursue the legitimate objects of the Science by means unfit for their attainment. To their extended view of the objects of Political Economy is to be attributed the undue importance which many Economists have ascribed to the collection of facts, and their neglect of the far more important process of reasoning accurately from the facts before them. We are constantly told that it is a Science of facts and experiment, a Science *avide de faits*. The practical applications of it, like the practical applications of every other Science, without doubt, require the collection and examination of facts to an almost indefinite extent. The facts collected as materials for the amendment of the poor-laws, and the opening of the trade to China, fill more than twice as many volumes as could be occupied by all the Treatises that have ever been written on Political Economy; but the facts on which the general principles of the Science rest may be stated in a very few sentences, and indeed in a very few words. But that the reasoning from these facts, the drawing from them correct conclusions, is a matter of great difficulty, may be inferred from the imperfect state in which the Science is now found after it has been so long and so intensely studied.[112]

This is by no means the road that Schweigaard seems to follow, even though he sees the implications of widening the scope of political economy.[113] A political economy without reference to social society, to moral, political and juridical institutions, has 'no convincing force, because the purpose of the limitation of sciences is purely done to facilitate the comprehension of truth, and it should not be limited to "hide the view" of truth. Political economy is also not the centre of the social sciences, the purpose is to give it a direction without dismissing observations of importance and thereby reach the wrong conclusions.'[114]

Fifty years later Aschehoug starts his *Socialøkonomik* by defining the scope of the discipline first outlined by the term 'economics'. He says,

> Economics is the term used to describe the activity by which humans acquire and use resources to satisfy their needs. […] It is called private economy when the individual interest is concerned, and social or state economy when the society is concerned, but basically it is the same, it is only the angle that is different. In olden times economics [*socialøkonomi*] was called political economy or state economy. The Germans who started getting a sense of belonging to a nation called it national economy, a term that has been adopted by the Swedes and the Danes without the German historical experience.[115]

Aschehoug continues by defining the difference between *socialøkonomik* and *socialøkonomi*. The first is the term being used to define the science of economics; the second refers to the economic activity. Compared to Schweigaard, the definition of the purpose of economics is twofold: firstly, it is important to understand human economic activities in a meaningful way, and secondly, guidance should be given in order to organize these activities in the best manner for all. This is a strong defence for the practical use of economic theories as well as a clear reminder of the practical origins of the theories themselves. Aschehoug has the advantage of fifty years of debate over the definitions of political economy, and as always, he presents an overview of the different positions before giving his own considerations. Aschehoug seems to position himself in line with Schweigaard, although he does not mention him explicitly. The span of fifty years has brought new ideas and definitions, but the core concepts of Schweigaard still remain in the outlines of Aschehoug. Economics is a science that has to follow a certain method and system, but this should not solely be the deductive and general principles. In order to be useful, it must keep in touch with real life, real problems and empirical findings. As Schweigaard puts it, 'The products are made for the humans, and not vice versa.'[116]

Sørensen points out another important aspect of the difference between the dual goals of increased national wealth (*øke nationalrigdommen*) and increased general welfare (*almenvelstanden*). Schweigaard remarks that the increase in national wealth is of no use if it does not contribute to an increase in welfare not only for the well off, but also for the ones that have less to begin with. This indicates redistribution, even though he does not explicitly say how this should be implemented. He seems to think that an increase in national wealth will lead to a just distribution of it. Individual self-interest is the driving force for an increase in national wealth, but it cannot be counted on as a guarantee for either redistribution or investments in nonprofitable activities. He states that, 'If the nonintervention principle is abandoned as the ultimate postulate in the political economy, then there is a place for economic intervention from the general will [*samfundsviljen*].'[117] In other words, the state must intervene when it comes to the second goal, the redistribution of wealth. Even though he does not elaborate on this point in detail, he says in his lectures from the late 1850s that 'the important aim for the state in taxation is to see to it that the distribution of them is such that each will be taxed according to their capability'.[118] The intervention of the state for redistribution purposes was not through expropriation or other direct interventions. His position was that a general modernization would benefit all citizens, education would support the general morality, and juridical institutions would protect rights.

Schweigaard on Trade and Laissez-Faire: Important Distinctions

Another important topic in the lectures is the distinction drawn between free trade and laissez-faire.[119] Schweigaard himself writes,

If one instead of putting the greatest production outcome puts the greatest sum of general welfare as the ultimate purpose of political economy, then the advantage of the latter will be to disregard the postulate of the first [English school], that the greatest production is obtained by an unrestricted human activity within only the limits of the law. Self-interest is not only the ultimate force, but also the unrivalled leading star for the direction of human activity, meaning that all state intervention would represent a deviation and deterioration of the ultimate purpose of greatest production outcome. [...] The basic postulate of political economy would then have only one guideline, being to keep off all interference with economic activity, the so-called laissez-faire [seen by Schweigaard as a reaction to the earlier economic system mercantilism]. *This teaching of nonintervention, that has never been applied in any civilized public economy, will without doubt also disappear as a basic principle in the theory of political economy when the time of reaction has passed and the necessity of fighting one extreme by the other is overcome* [my emphasis].[120]

This is clear proof of Schweigaard's theoretical rejection of laissez-faire. Sørensen underlines the same point by giving other examples of how, both practically and theoretically, this was stated during his career as an active politician and a university professor.[121] Whereas three earlier (and partly contemporary) economists and historians, Ernst Sars (1913), Ebbe Hertzberg (1883) and later Wilhelm Keilhau (1930), describe Schweigaard as a liberal economist, Carl Lund and Jens Arup Seip both underline the fact that Schweigaard was a laissez-faire economist. The first claimed in 1958, 'Schweigaard remained all his life an adherent of the Manchester liberalism and may rightly be called its great prophet in our country.' It can be added that Fougner Lundh, Schweigaard's predecessor, had embraced the liberal fundaments of economics, but clearly refuted all forms of laissez-faire policies, especially emphasizing the importance of the role of the state and of the necessity to play an important part in helping new industries in their emerging phase, generally arguing that the state should intervene whenever public interests (*samfunnsinteressen*) needed something that private interests were incapable of providing.[122] These were the exact claims of Schweigaard, and they were both firmly placed on liberal grounds, never arguing for a nightwatchman state or a minimal state, both also emphasizing moral considerations, and having, as mentioned, the diffusion of general welfare (*almenvelstandens utbredelse*) in mind, emphasizing cultural and institutional conditions in this respect. Free trade was enhancing the augmentation of general welfare, but free trade arrangements should respect national needs for developing industries and opportunities.

Seip underlined his views on Schweigaard, first in an article about the Norwegian system in the time of the classical economic liberalism (1850–70) from 1959, and later in his magnum opus, *Utsikt over Norges historie* (View of Norwegian history) from 1974. Seip's arguments do not hold, because he faces a dilemma when he tries to explain the ideas of state interference. This is something he tries to solve by noting a shift in Schweigaard's position towards more laissez-faire after his lectures in 1847. Later, in 1988, Seip published another article, 'A. M. Schweigaard og liberalismens dilemma' (A. M. Schweigaard and the dilemma of liberalism), where his main hypothesis is that Schweigaard not only rejected laissez-faire, but that he also opposed important principles in the classical economic liberalism after his 1847 lectures.[123]

The question is whether Schweigaard was a defender of free trade and why he at the same time proposed protectionist customs in order to 'develop industrial strength and competence'. The discussion will not be continued here, instead a presentation of the lecture of Schweigaard will be included, and the conclusion of Schweigaard's position is mainly close to the views of Sørensen.[124] Chapter 11 further develops the views on this apparent dilemma between free trade and protectionist policies, focusing on the debates that followed after the lectures of Schweigaard throughout the last half of the nineteenth century. Generally, Schweigaard adhered to free trade between nations, but he was in many cases willing to adapt his politics to national needs. His modernizing strategy for Norway included many deviations from a free trade theory, because other measures were more adapted to increase national wealth and general welfare.[125] When Aschehoug later wrote about free trade and customs, his continuation of the Schweigaard position is clearly visible.

The main point of Sørensen is underlined when he analyses the confusion that is sometimes made between the English classical school and the Manchester liberalist school. He refers to William Grampp, who has studied the Manchester liberalist school, and who refutes both this confusion and the misconception that the all of those who were labelled Manchester liberalists defended a laissez-faire doctrine. According to Grampp, the Manchester liberalists were not a conformist group of thinkers, although they were united in the rejection of the 'corn laws' and by a general belief in free trade among nations. He states,

> In view of the heterogeneity of the Manchester School, there is nothing surprising in its not having had a consistent and comprehensive doctrine. Each of the groups in the school had their own reasons for wanting free trade. The belief that it was the quintessence of laissez-faire may come from supposing that anyone who wants free trade must hold such a doctrine.[126]

The methodical point Grampp makes is that of differentiating between the laissez-faire doctrine as an overall idea of non–state interference and free trade as only describing the idea of free exchange between nations. The conclusion is that it is perfectly possible to believe in free trade without adhering to the laissez-faire doctrine.[127] Another historian, H. Scott Gordon, has systematically taken this distinction further and explained why this confusion between the two has been so widespread. He says,

> A widespread development of free trade ideology developed in mid-nineteenth century England, but a similar laissez-faire ideology did not. A large part of the error which the historiography contains in its categorization of the period as one of laissez-faire is due to a false identification of laissez-faire and free trade. It is striking how often one finds the two phrases used synonymously by later writers.[128]

These views support Schweigaard's position as a follower of free (international) trade and as a nonbeliever in laissez-faire. After reviewing a couple of statements about Schweigaard and seeing the remarks he makes in practical political debates, it seems clear to me that Sørensen gives a trustworthy and correct picture of Schweigaard concerning his perception of laissez-faire. Schweigaard did on many occasions defend a free trade position, but he was pragmatic when it came to practical solutions. Free trade could be an ideal, but in many situations, other considerations were more pressing and were consequently chosen. A quote from Schweigaard's *Ungdomsarbeider*, namely his article on customs and the history of customs, 'Indførselstolden og dens historie', defends free trade against protectionism theoretically; his practical politics were a commonsensical adaptation of his theoretical position.[129] In his argument for free trade, Schweigaard also defended the predictability of state politics on customs.[130]

International trade was important to Schweigaard, and the abolition of the British Navigation Act in 1849 was of paramount importance to the flourishing of the Norwegian shipping industry and general international trade.[131] Nine years earlier, in 1840, Schweigaard had proclaimed, 'Make the Norwegian shipping as free as possible! This argument cannot be repeated too often and not strongly enough to anybody that sees Norway as a shipping nation. *The widest horizons are revealing themselves!*'[132] Increased international business meant increases in national income and prosperity. Schweigaard did not leave his free trade position; he was sticking to his ideals, but adapting them to his general modernization strategy for Norway. The shipping industry was the key to success in the industrial development of Norway, and it had to be administered and regulated in such a way that it would flourish as much as possible. Sørensen claims that shipping was probably more important to Schweigaard than an acceptance of a general theoretical doctrine about free trade.[133] The shipping industry meant more income, and the income could be used for general modernization and welfare. The shipping industry relied on free trade, and therefore free trade had to be supported. But not only were international communications important; just as important for the general modernization project were the construction of roads and railways, both being driven through as state projects or projects in joint ventures with private entrepreneurs. Shipping was, however, mostly privately owned. It might seem strange that Schweigaard didn't have a clear view of industrialization. His modernization was more focused on transport and communications. Schweigaard knew machinery and the mechanical industry, but he died in 1870 when the shipping fleet of Norway was still sailing.[134]

Schweigaard was a 'modernizer' of nineteenth-century Norwegian society, and the state played a major role in the modernization, more so than technical industrialization. In many ways, Schweigaard was conservative, as both his contemporaries and later historians have pointed out. He may well be seen as a conservative when it came to a democratization of the political system, but in the development of legal institutions, and of economic policies, he was a 'reformer'.[135] As mentioned, he reformed the banking and monetary system and generally the trade system. An extraordinary economic growth during his time as an active politician helped to bring about his goal of 'general welfare for everybody'. Change through the development of laws and regulations was to help people change when they could not do it by themselves, and to ensure a long-term perspective when that was needed. Changes were rooted in the utility of society as a whole, which did not make Schweigaard a utilitarian in the strict sense of Bentham, but which made him a practical national reformer.

The questions of free trade and of state intervention are intertwined in the views of Schweigaard. There are three main reasons why the state is needed in economic activity: the short-sightedness of the individual decision maker, the caring for resources that are considered free to everybody (like fresh water or forests) and the nonprofitable general infrastructure of the society like roads, railways and other communications. The ability to plan with a long-term perspective and the importance of communications that can be established and run by the state through tax income are both parts of Schweigaard's arguments for state intervention. Another principle of intervention can be found in his argument for customs to protect the establishment of national industries that otherwise would have had trouble in competing with cheaper imported goods. This kind of protection must be outlined in such a way that it could be removed when the industries had become sustainable without it, even though this, in many cases, could be difficult to decide. A quote from 1848 shows that he helped Modum Blaafarveværk in order to prevent the loss of jobs: 'It would be sad not to help this renowned factory and thereby condemn it to ruin.'[136]

The arguments for state intervention can also be found in Aschehoug's work, although with fifty years of political change and economic development in between. The emphasis on shipping was not as evident in Aschehoug as in Schweigaard, but other communications like roads and railways, post, and telegraphs were even more significant in the works of Aschehoug. The problem of capital was still prevalent around 1900, as it had been in 1850. The state was needed in the raising of capital for larger industrial projects; the alternative was to find international investors, which was also done. Banking and monetary politics also had Aschehoug's attention.[137]

Both Schweigaard and Aschehoug were engaged in the debates about education, and they both believed in the necessity of using knowledge in the modernization project. Moral issues, like alcohol, were also discussed, though in more detail in the works of Aschehoug. The only issue that came to the surface in the works of Aschehoug was industrialization and technological progress. Aschehoug had lived through both political (personal) crises and economic recessions, and he was able to integrate and analyse the role of industrialization, of labour and of economic theory to a much greater extent than his former teacher Schweigaard.

Sørensen mentions the term 'soft modernizing pressure from above', something that can be compared to Slagstad's 'state-tainted liberalism'. It was possible, then, for Schweigaard to reform the economic and many of the juridical institutions of Norwegian society. The changes were brought about without revolutions or strong objections from landowners or capital owners (both of which, historically, were scarce in Norway). Schweigaard was able to modernize by putting forth a plan that was adapted to Norwegian society, Norwegian history and economic conditions in Norway.

Chapter 4

NORWEGIAN ECONOMIC THOUGHT AND METHOD

Introduction

After Schweigaard the Norwegian milieu of economists grew. Aschehoug was the natural follower of Schweigaard, but he was not alone. Some of his most prominent contemporary economists (and jurists) were Hertzberg, Aarum, Morgenstierne and Jaeger.[1]

A presentation of Aschehoug's views on economic thought and specifically what he says about method and theory will be included. This chapter will end with a small section about the debate on methods which took place during the 1890s at the Statsøkonomisk forening. It was Oscar Jaeger who lectured about method, and the other economists participated in the debate which followed. They mostly accepted the presentation of Jaeger, at least after the turn of the century. The question was whether theoretical economics (and accordingly a more deductive method) should be divided from practical economics (accordingly a more inductive method). Aschehoug did not believe in such a sharp division between what he called the 'pure' and the 'applied' (social) economics (*socialøkonomik*), which is why he does not explicitly make this division through his *Socialøkonomik*, and why he accepts the dual use of methods, even though he distinguishes between *socialøkonomik*/economics and *socialøkonomi*/economy in the first chapter (see further comments later in this chapter).

First and foremost, is it possible to talk about a Norwegian historical school in economics? The answer is twofold. There are specific traits of a historical approach in method, namely the emphasis on studying statistics and history. As Grimmer-Solem puts it when he defines the German historical school: 'A heterodox variant of economics was the so-called "Historical School". Historical economics and closely related approaches such as institutionalism thrived in most European countries. [...] Such movements survived in parallel with neoclassical economics until well into the 1940s.'[2] Historical schools focus on statistics and have an empirical-factual emphasis, as well as strong attention to institutions and to social reform. Bergh and Hanisch comment on the German influence on method, observing that it was 'less theory and more facts' than the Norwegian school of thought during the 1870s and '80s.[3] 'The similarities between German and Norwegian economic thought is especially visible when it comes to method.'[4] They further claim that it is not apparent that this was only due to German influence, since Norwegian thought had a strong historical-empirical tradition that could be traced to the eighteenth century and that had British leanings as well. The development of German economic thought gave the Norwegian statistical work greater impact, and a substantial statistical development can be found in both countries during these years (after 1850). Amundsen underlines the general opinion of method and adapted theories to practical economic problems. See, for instance, chapter 3.2 in *Norsk sosialøkonomisk historie, 1814–1890*. Statistics had originally been the responsibility of professors of history at the university, based on the old German interpretation of statistics and the tradition from the University of Copenhagen. Fougner Lundh had to take on responsibility for statistics in the 1830s, and the ambition was the same throughout the nineteenth century: to describe as completely as possible the economic and social activity of the country (state).[5] And from the 1830s a clear ambition to develop statistics can be seen in discussions of what to measure, and many valid and useful comparisons were made of statistical theories over time in order to trace their development.[6] Statistics was to become the most important auxiliary discipline to economics: 'to be especially designed to provide information that could be useful for economics [*statsøkonomien*]', as Fougner Lundh argued in his lectures from 1835.[7] Andresen underlines in his doctoral thesis that this development was in line with similar considerations at universities in Germany, France and England. Aschehoug was to be the modernizer, not Schweigaard; Aschehoug investigated social and economic conditions and sought to reveal basic statistical relations, whereas Schweigaard was too superficial to be the innovator.[8]

Norwegian economic thought has never been labelled 'historical' like the German historical school. Nevertheless, Norwegian economic thought up to the 1920s had many similarities with the German historical school, and Norwegian economists followed German economic thought closely.[9] As an example of the more pragmatic attitude towards economic thought, a colleague of Aschehoug, Morgenstierne, wrote the following in an 1889 article 'Fattigondet og Socialismen' (The evil of poverty and socialism) in *Statsøkonomisk Tidsskrift*:

It is acknowledged that the state is not only a state of law, but also a cultural state; that it shall not only protect its citizens, but also promote the interests and support the material and intellectual development of its citizens. There are numerous ways in which the state already interferes in economic activity, partly by limiting individual freedom and partly by taking over the responsibility of certain enterprises. The limits for the activity of the state in this area [the economic] are just decided with an eye to individual freedom. Where these limits shall be drawn in each case will normally not be given. One state might be more socialistic; others will be more liberal. The first is currently the case with Germany, the second is the case with England, while our country may be described as being somewhere in between.[10]

Morgenstierne here exposes a dual influence, both German and British, placing Norway somewhere in between and thereby underlining the general hypothesis underlying this book, namely that Norwegian economic thought was a result of different ideas, adopted and processed to fit the Norwegian reality. This is later confirmed by Aarum, who clearly points out the international orientation and the belief in the need to adapt ideas and theories, and also adding that there is no Scandinavian economic science as such – similarities among them are rather due to a close relationship to international scientific milieus.[11]

Another observation concerning German influence is that early Norwegian economic thought read Adam Smith through the lenses of the German interpretation of him and his followers, one reason being that Norwegians read German, and as Andresen states, '"German economic thought" was corresponding well to [Fougner Lundh's] perception of economics.'[12] Norwegian economic thought was fundamentally liberal, accepting that economic policy had to respect the workings of economic activity and at the same time being clear about the role and importance of the state as well as the importance of proper institutions as premises for a properly functioning economy.

When Gregers Fougner Lundh died in 1836, Schweigaard's idea of economics was chosen over the ideas of another intellectual and historian, Ludvig Kristensen Daa (1809–1877). Schweigaard emphasized the importance of usefulness in statistics, arguing for a professoriate combining economics (*statsøkonomi*), statistics and law, seeing that statistics also dealt with historical information, but not wanting to let statistics be a part of the faculty of history.[13] Schweigaard also claimed that statistics should be relevant, concrete and realistic. In order for economics to be interesting and relevant, 'economics, in a Norwegian context, should provide correct guidelines about what to rectify and what to develop [...], something that included a thorough insight to the national institutions which were a condition for the development of the productive forces.'[14]

Generally, the historicist way of thinking had a strong position in Norway, and the need to contextualize economic behaviour and the value of historical research were accepted by the Norwegian, practically oriented economists. They acknowledged and encouraged historical and statistical research and favoured economic reforms based on the conclusions they could draw. There is, however, an apparent difference, if one should use the definition of the German historical school presented in the analysis of Shionoya:

> The real challenge of the German Historical School to mainstream economics was not the dichotomy between theory and history, between nomothesis and idiography, between generality and specificity, between universality and individuality, between deductivism and inductivism, and so on. Rather, it was the need to analyse the overall picture of society, based on the concept of the whole man, from evolutionary and comparative perspectives. From these perspectives, other crucial concepts such as history, ethics, and institutions will follow.[15]

The synthesis of history and theory, or the theoretical formulation of history is different from a mere collection and classification of historical data. The German historical school, seen like this, is a system of thought with similarities to the Norwegian school of thought. However, the difference is that Norwegians did not state this overall systematic theoretical formulation of history. Norwegian thought was closely connected to practical politics, and subsequently understanding and analysing historic events and empirical findings was essential. Aarum describes Aschehoug's own position towards the German historical school thus: 'Aschehoug was not negatively inclined to the historical school, but he could not join it because of its neglect of theory.'[16] Aarum further says that Aschehoug was inspired by the theoretical developments of the Austrians, as well as Alfred Marshall, and that he clearly saw the need of continuing this development.[17] Marshall's influence on Aschehoug is discussed in Chapter 7.

Pål Magnus Lykkja has written a comparative analysis of the economic theories of Schweigaard and Aschehoug between 1832 and 1882 as his master's thesis at the University of Oslo.[18] He traces Norwegian economic thought as far back as Ludvig Holberg (1684–1754) and the Danish-Norwegian mercantilist tradition, and mentions the German theoretical economic tradition. In order not to repeat the analysis, only a short account of his conclusions is given here.[19] Lykkja underlines the need for practical theories and the pragmatic attitude towards economics, quoting Aschehoug from 1876: 'People, when they apply the theories, are more sensible than when they are just making them.'[20]

Furthermore, the Norwegian philosopher and theologian, Anathon Aall (1867–1943), comments that, 'There was a general Norwegian opinion that the sciences of society should stay as close as possible to practical life; this is a tradition, namely the analytical-descriptive method that can be traced back to Holberg.'[21] The analytical-descriptive method may then be the product of both a German influence and an older Norwegian tradition. Lykkja shows that the German influence came to the Danish economists after Holberg during the second part of the eighteenth century. The most comprehensive analysis of the early nineteenth century development can be found in the doctoral thesis of Andresen, who explains in detail the different impulses and development in economic thought, underlining both the proper Norwegian ideas of economics as well as the different ideas coming from German, French and British thought. The empirical tradition is underlined both by the two Norwegian economic historians Bergh and Hanisch, and Lykkja. The question is how much was there before Schweigaard, what came from English empiricism, and how much the German historical school continued throughout the nineteenth century to influence Aschehoug. It is clear that the British influence later also came from Marshall.

The main question posed in this section, including the debate about method, is: was the general view of economics held by Aschehoug the leading one or were his views contested by any of his contemporaries, and what were their main fields of interest? The individual summary of each economist will be brief and is found in Appendix A of this book. It will focus on their general positions, a short list of economic works during the lifetime of Aschehoug, and eventual discrepancies will be highlighted concerning the general topics that are analysed in this book. Wilhelm Keilhau (1888–1954) is mentioned as the last economist belonging to the tradition of Schweigaard and Aschehoug.[22] He wrote a historical review of economic thought in Norway in which he presents the 'core' economists of the Aschehoug era. Bergh and Hanisch also make the distinction in the development of Norwegian economic thought: 'Norwegian economic thought was led by Schweigaard for almost thirty-five years, and in 1870 Aschehoug was the one that most clearly stood out to be his successor. [...] Norwegian economic thought was to expand strongly during the next decades [...], no longer being a "one-man-show".'[23] The politician Johan Sverdrup (1816–92), who was to become the first prime minister in Norway in 1884, underlined during a debate in 1869 (referred to in *Stortingstidende*), that 'it was not right to have such a tight connection between law and economics. [...] [The weakness of Norwegian economics] was the lack of disciplinary development, especially adapted to Norwegian conditions that might lead to a better comprehension of our Norwegian context.'[24] This was to change during the last decades of the nineteenth century, and the beginning of the twentieth century, as books and articles were written, education strengthened and a milieu grew around the Statsøkonomisk forening (see Chapter 5).

Aschehoug and His Presentation of Method in *Socialøkonomik*

Before analysing Aschehoug's own presentation of method in *Socialøkonomik*, there will be an analysis of the method and the general views on economics presented by a quote from Ebbe Hertzberg about early philosophers, which illustrates how Schweigaard was opposed to any speculative system, as shown in Chapter 3, and how he proposes an alternative possibility – empirical philosophy, based on what he calls the method of experience.[25] The philosophy should 'serve as a classification and universal method'.[26] The method is the key point in the philosophical thought of Schweigaard, the main reason why he does not like speculative thoughts and generalizations. Objective knowledge should be obtained through *induction*:

> That the basis of the secure objective knowledge is subjected to conditions, and lastly also the result of the most common induction, that nature is constant, that under the same conditions, on the same level of objective development, the same results are produced, the same phenomena appear; that nature in this way is reasonable, and that it is necessary to get advice from nature to obtain knowledge, what it says; that we cannot rule it without obeying it.[27]

He rejects general rules, his ideal is to use hypotheses as preliminary leading threads, and then analytically test them out by using empirical facts and ultimately try to falsify them. In addition, he emphasizes the historical dimension of knowledge.

Hertzberg, who sees a system in Schweigaard's philosophical thought, says that 'his method was the "analytical-descriptive", but even though he was an empiricist, he was also an idealist, in that he sees the idea of rationalism in both the physical and the mental world'.[28] It seems that Schweigaard would adhere to the British empiricism, but that he also had general ideas. However, in this analysis the main point is to show how this empirical leaning influenced his methodical approach to economics and how this later influenced the ideas of Aschehoug.

Even though John Stuart Mill is classified among the economists of the British classical school, he wrote in 1843, 'Between the primitive method of Deduction and that which I have attempted to characterize [a rational deductive method] there is all the difference which exists between Aristotelian physics and the Newtonian theory of the heavens.'[29] Lykkja comments that the classical school can be divided according to how much they supported the method of deduction, placing Mill in the direction of deduction.[30] He continues by asserting that Aschehoug was the first Norwegian to fully use the comparative method, which then later made his inductive and historical-comparative method similar to that of the German historical school.

Aschehoug seems to draw a line between economy as economic activity and economics as the scientific discipline.[31] Economy is the term for the human activity by which means are acquired to satisfy different needs.[32] These means are economic goods (*goder*). The economic activity of individuals is called private economic activity (*privatøkonomi*, *Privatwirtschaft*), whereas the aggregated level is called (macro)economic activity (*samfunnsøkonomi* or *socialøkonomi*, *Volkswirtschaft*). In this division, Aschehoug uses both Wagner and Schmoller's definitions found in Wagner's *Grundlegung* and in Schmoller's article 'Volkswirtschaftslehre und -methode' in Conrad's *Handwörterbuch der Staatswissenshaften (HBW)*. Aschehoug also calls attention to the fact that economics was derived from the British term 'political economy' or the German *Staatswirtschaft*, but that the Germans gradually started to use the term *Nationalökonomie*. This was, according to Aschehoug, because the Germans were not united as a German nation, and that by calling the economic activity 'national economics', they underlined this aspect.[33] Denmark and Sweden applied the German term, whereas the Norwegians kept the equivalent of the German *Staatswirtschaft* (*statsøkonomi*), but the frequent term was *socialøkonomik*, hence the title of Aschehoug's main economic work. This term is closer to the German *Sozialökonomie*, but the direct translation would be *Sozialwirtschaft*. In 1838, professor of history Henrik Steenbuch (1774–1839) explained in detail the different terms in circulation. He claimed that the original political economy (*statsøkonomi*) was in essence political and an adaption of the British term, whereas national economics (*nationaløkonomi*) was the scientific and theoretical discipline that was concerned with the natural laws of human economic action.[34] Today, these nuances are mostly gone, and the general term is economics (in Norwegian *samfunnsøkonomi* is usually used to label the discipline of economics).

Aschehoug claims to follow international economists when he divides the theoretical economic discipline and practical economic activity.[35] The main purpose is to define the tasks of the theoretical economic discipline – economics – which could never be only theoretical. Aschehoug is well aware of the different ways of defining economics, and he points out that these definitions vary a great deal. In the narrowest sense it is only a set of dogmas or systematic theories. To broaden this definition, economics should be giving guidelines for economic activity, and thereby not only describing and explaining current observations, but also pointing out how economic activity should be. Critics will claim that this definition will undermine the theoretical dimensions. Aschehoug seems to understand this point of view, showing how, among others, Senior, Cairnes and J. N. Keynes define economics. According to Aschehoug the most theoretical definition is given by Léon Walras in his *Eléments d'économie politique pure*.[36]

The overall problem is the neutrality of the economic discipline. In theory the theoretical discipline should be value free and not subdued by different interests or ideologies. But on the other hand, being scientists and at the same time trying to solve practical economic issues, economists may well often come up with solutions that are too superficial. Aschehoug is well aware of the difficulties concerning impartiality and how to define the scope of the theoretical discipline. He explains the German solution by saying that a line is drawn between the theoretical *Sozialökonomie* (*socialøkonomi*) and economic politics.[37] In general, the Germans agree that the first should clarify economic phenomena and causes, and the second should explain the different economic purposes of the state and society. Thereby the second follows the first. The first describes, the second prescribes. Some French economists make the same distinction, among others Jean-Gustave Courcelle-Seneuil (1813–92), A. E. Cherbuliez (1797–1869) and Maurice Block (1816–1901). Although, the dominant view among the French and also many of their British and American colleagues (which pleases Aschehoug) tends to be to see the discipline from both sides, theoretically and practically – the exception being Jevons, who in his *Theory of Political Economy* makes a systematic presentation of the abstract and elementary economic theorems.

Finally, Aschehoug draws his own conclusions, saying that a sharp division between pure and applied economics is not possible. The *socialøkonomik* discipline bases its theories on the internal or external facts of experience. Even the purest theoretical accounts will always have to use experience, because it was from the practical economic life and challenges that the economic discipline was born.[38] The search for general theorems drawn from practical life and experience started the scientific economic discipline. Aschehoug concludes by saying, 'Economic theorems, that have never had and could never have any practical use, are just empty fantasies. The main purpose of the economics will always be practical.'[39] This is a strong defence for the practical use of economic theories, as well as a clear reminder of the practical origins of the theories themselves.

The goal is twofold: firstly, it is important to understand human economic activities in a meaningful way; and secondly, guidance should be given in order to organize these activities in the best manner for all. Aschehoug here proposes a description and a prescription. The guidance should be tailor-made for the specific circumstances, both in time and scope. Hereby lies the difficulty, because getting a general and detailed overview of all human conditions is almost impossible, so Aschehoug claims that the true economic science will always be modest. Therefore it is of outmost importance to be aware of this when economic theories are being used for practical political purposes.[40] It is necessary to point out uncertainties, assumptions and reservations that are being made, when theories are being used in practical decision making.[41]

Civilization brings about changes in economic conditions, and these changes are not random, but caused by casual connections. Aschehoug mentions time as important; causes and effects drive development. He compares this to law and says, 'The economic conditions can be juxtaposed to the juridical institutions, both being formed and developed by the laws of causes.'[42] He further points out that changes in economic conditions or in juridical institutions will usually cause an interaction between the two. A change in economic affairs will normally cause changes in juridical institutions and vice versa. The task of the economic discipline is to clarify the nature and consequences of the forces that drive economic development. The study of economics is, then, the study of dynamic development.

This is an important claim; economics is dynamic in its nature, and not evolving around a specific balance point, or equilibrium. Aschehoug is clearly aware of the authors that write about equilibrium theories, and he says that although it is true that economic forces can have opposite effects, the old equilibrium, if it ever existed, will never be retained. Economic theories based on equilibrium are compared to mechanical sciences. Aschehoug finds great similarities between abstract economic theories and mechanical sciences, economics being driven by self-interest or the mechanics of utility. To Aschehoug, a more reliable and true understanding is that this comparison is only an analogy. Economic forces are both natural (in the sense of geographical and physical) and psychological, quoting Schmoller's remarks in Conrad's *HBW*.

The second chapter of *Socialøkonomik* outlines the method and system of the discipline of economics. As already mentioned, Aschehoug differentiates between the theoretical discipline, namely economics (*socialøkonomik*), and practical economic affairs, namely economy (*socialøkonomi*). This distinction is followed all through his *Socialøkonomik*, and the title of his main economic work is referring to the theoretical discipline, meaning that this is how he presents the scope and method of the science of economics.

He starts by giving an account of method. Firstly, it is important to investigate which facts should be included in the economic activity or that result from this activity. The starting point is a concrete investigation of the economy in order to get an overview. These facts are being described, mapped, classified and accounted for. Similarities and discrepancies, frequencies, correspondences and influences are important to clarify. If this is not done properly, the resulting analysis will be a thoughtless polyhistorical description, not useful for anything. The goal is to understand the complexity and the diversity, and thereby discover chains of causes and their interrelatedness.[43] Complexity has to be solved by continuous experience and investigation, and Aschehoug clearly believes that this is not a task for everyone. He states, 'A sound intellectual capability is necessary, one that at the same time is creative and has vision, but also has sufficient judgement to see if the vision is just imagination or if it is a rightful image of reality.'[44]

So what kind of method of economic discipline does Aschehoug claim is the best and why does he believe it to be so? He has already described what he calls the inductive or the empirical-realistic method.[45] But the process continues, because the established facts and the relation between them must be seen in a larger theoretical context and then used to test out other economic connections. Based on known facts and interrelations, one draws conclusions about the nonobserved facts and their relationship. This is the deductive or exact scientific method.[46] To Aschehoug, this is a continuous loop, because these postulates must again be subject to investigation and empirical research. They have to be verified and tested to see if they answer the questions and hypotheses they were constructed to give a response to.

Aschehoug provides a good overview of the different positions concerning scientific methods used in the economic discipline. An interesting remark is made about his Norwegian colleague Oskar Jaeger, who apparently gives his consent to the Austrian school in an article in *Statsøkonomisk Tidsskrift* from 1895, discussed in detail in the next section of this chapter.[47]

Important authoritative sources seem to be the article Gustav von Schmoller wrote in *HWB*, 'Volkswirtschaftslehre und -methode', which gives a broad account of German literature on the subject. He also mentions Carl Menger and the *Methodenstreit*, showing where to find Schmoller's and Menger's positions and answers, J. E. Cairnes's *Logical Method* (1875), J. N. Keynes's *The Scope and Method of Political Economy* (1891/1897), Palgrave's *Dictionary of Economics* and the articles by Sidgwick ('Deductive Method',

'Inductive Method' and 'Method of Political Economy'), Léon Say's *Nouveau dictionnaire d'économie politique*, and finally Maurice Block's *Progrès* (1897). These all treat the questions of method from different positions and also from different national viewpoints. It might be interesting to know how Aschehoug sees the use of method by earlier well-known economists. Aschehoug asserts that Adam Smith and also Malthus used both the inductive and deductive methods, while Ricardo mostly used the deductive, although Aschehoug claims that he also invoked the use of practical experience and that some of his smaller articles were clearly using the inductive method. In Aschehoug's view, Senior's main work is the obvious example of the deductive method being used to its extreme. John Stuart Mill also discusses the use of method extensively in his *System of Logic*. Many claim that he pushes the deductive method too far, this critique coming from the younger German historical school, but also from a few British economists, notably Cliffe Leslie (1826–82), Bonamy Price (1807–1888) and J. K. Ingram (1823–1907). It is well known that the Austrian school, represented by Menger and Böhm-Bawerk, opposed the inductive method. This is the view that Aschehoug himself adheres to, and it is important to keep in mind his position when it comes to the discussion of the German historical school (see Chapter 6).

According to Aschehoug, a further literary debate about these issues is superfluous. He claims that all parties more or less agree that both methods are necessary, the discrepancy is the balance between the two: 'Empirical facts are the input of science, but they have to be processed to be flesh and blood.'[48] An interesting observation is that earlier, the empirical basis was underdeveloped, and induction was often made with a weak foundation, thereby resulting in doctrines that were not always correct, and sometimes even wrong. A negligent deduction may also have resulted in wrong answers. Economics will always have to cope with uncertainties, and will never be able to achieve a complete overview or have the ability to verify hypotheses, like many natural sciences can by experimentation. The increasing complexity of economic life makes the task even more complicated.

There are, first and foremost, three different auxiliary disciplines that are of utmost importance to economics (*socialøkonomik*). The first is statistics. Statistics is in itself a discipline, but it is also a most helpful tool and an auxiliary discipline for many other disciplines, such as economics. Not surprisingly, England is mentioned as the most advanced country for statistical research and statistical history. Although the use of statistics is most valuable, Aschehoug also points out that there can be misuse, and wrong conclusions can be drawn if the researcher is not careful. This is just as much a problem for economics as the misuse of abstract reasoning.[49]

The next important auxiliary discipline is historical research. Historical conditions, the observed changes and the causes of these changes, can give valuable information and insight. Examples of this kind of research are Aschehoug's own 'History of money', 'History of banking' and 'History of economic crises'. Aschehoug is the first to admit that the discovery of true causes and explanations in historical research is difficult, but it should still be done.[50] The more valuable the statistical and historical information is, the more useful the deductive method will be.

Aschehoug then turns to the introduction of mathematics as the principal tool for the deductive method in economics. The so-called marginalist revolution came during the 1870s, and Aschehoug has clearly been able to follow the publications and the discussions during the following decades. He sees W. Stanley Jevons and Léon Walras as the protagonists of this mathematical thought in economics, but he also gives an account of others. These include the British economists Alfred Marshall, Philip Wicksteed (1844–1927) and Francis Y. Edgeworth (1845–1926), the American Irwin Fisher (1867–1947), the Germans C. W. F. Launhardt (1832–1918), J. Lehr (1845–94), J. L. Auspitz (1837–1906) and R. Lieben (1842–1919), the Italian V. Pareto (1848–1923), and to a certain extent his fellow citizen M. Pantaleoni (1857–1924), as well as the Scandinavians Harald Westergaard (1853–1936) and Knut Wicksell (1851–1926). Finally, Aschehoug mentions his own work 'The history of the theory of value and prices' from 1900–1902. Aschehoug correctly observes that the introduction of mathematics requires a deeper knowledge and training, and that mathematics eventually narrows the group of people that will be able to understand and read economic theories. Aschehoug draws the conclusion that mathematics will not become important to economics, because it will make economics inaccessible, a conclusion that today must be said is wrong.

There are also a few economists that do not value mathematics as an important tool for economics; Aschehoug mentions J. S. Mill, J. E. Cairnes (1823–75), C. Leslie, J. K. Ingram, W. Lexis (1837–1914) and P. P. Leroy-Beaulieu (1843–1916). Their main objection is that economic circumstances cannot be measured exactly and expressed in numbers. Aschehoug seems to take a position between the two extremes, accepting mathematics to a certain extent, but being careful about the belief that numbers give the only exact truth. In order to underline his point, he quotes the older Keynes (the father of John Maynard), in his *Scope and Method*, chapter VIII, where he goes through the method of economics and shows that mathematics, in a number of cases, can be useful. He also explains quantitative relations and developments.[51] Aschehoug does not apply or try to incorporate mathematic analyses in his economic theories, except when he explains marginal theory in his article published in *Statsøkonomisk Tidsskrift*. The mathematical explanations were left out later in the manuscript of *Socialøkonomik*.

Mathematics has brought a deeper understanding and more demands of stringency and logic to economic research. Aschehoug sees this as a positive development and claims that this logic and stringency has influenced other research methods of economics. As usual, Aschehoug also mentions the pitfalls. Mathematics can be misused to explain circumstances that might be explained just as well without it, but the more serious claim is that mathematics is becoming irrelevant if the number of uncertainties is too great. If the complexity of the matter is great, mathematic equations cannot be expected to give trustworthy answers, something Marshall also underlines in his *Principles* (see Chapter 7).[52]

What is, then, the right method of economics, and what can be the validity of economic theories? The debate about the law of nature and the claim that economic theorems are natural laws is to Aschehoug peculiar.[53] Although Adam Smith called his magnum opus *An Inquiry Into the Nature and Causes of the Wealth of Nations*, Aschehoug claims that Smith only attached a relative validity to his statements; and while Ricardo used the word 'laws', he intended this to mean principles, not universal laws.[54] According to Aschehoug, Smith did not see wealth as a result of permanent natural laws, because he understood that wealth is the result of free human actions that were not part of the causes. It seems as though Aschehoug interprets the term 'natural' to mean 'common' or 'average'. Aschehoug puts Mill and Malthus in the same category as Ricardo, both being attacked by continental economists. Aschehoug himself differentiates between natural laws and social and psychological laws, the last two being changeable. Although claims are made that there are certain physical or natural laws in economics, economics will mostly be based on what Aschehoug refers to as the nature of the human spirit and human culture. It is impossible to derive natural laws from human individuality or the cultural and historical aspect of society. It is misleading and inaccurate to refer to economic theories as natural laws.[55]

Aschehoug then moderates himself a little, saying that the term 'law' is used on many occasions, but that it does not necessarily mean a natural law. Many economic causes and effects are described as laws in the sense of describing and explaining economic relations that have certain validity in practical life.[56] The economy of society and the problems connected to it will not normally have complete and certain solutions. The complexity and uncertainty of economic circumstances are too great. Nevertheless, the task of economics is valuable, because economics can perform useful analyses of problems, clarify circumstances and contribute to future solutions, and sort out the important issues and questions. The validity of economic theories depends upon how many reservations and assumptions are being made. Their usefulness lies in the ability to isolate problems and analyse less complex relations, although one runs the danger of generalizing theories that oversimplify. The most important discussion is not about the theories themselves, but the assumptions and circumstances around them.[57]

The strength of economics lies in its comprehensiveness, and its ability to sort out the important matters. Its weakness is, on the other hand, the difficulty in deciding the importance of matters, but this can be solved by 'technical ability and a sound practical eye.'[58] The general issue for Aschehoug seems to be a warning of not believing in simplifications and generalizations. Time and time again he explains the complexity and uncertainty of economic affairs and the necessity to accept uncertainties. If a problem is unsolvable, it must be accepted. Being a professor of law, Aschehoug draws a quick outline between the different methods of law and economics. Laws have to be interpreted and decisions in courts have to be made, although the premises might be uncertain and obscured. Jurisprudence and legal usage are built on a sometimes uncertain basis, whereas economics is not tied by the demand of guidance in the same way and can therefore dismiss questions that are too complicated, meaning that there are no absolute claims for solutions.[59]

The last paragraph of Aschehoug's methodical outline concerns the use of terms and concepts – they are often badly or weakly defined. Many economists have the same claims.[60] Not only are the foundations often weak, but also the concepts are often used inconsistently in the same texts by the same authors. A more stringent use of concepts should be applied. As a jurist he points out that jurisprudence also has some of these problems, but to a lesser extent. Terms and concepts are continuously changing, and as long as the definitions and the foundations are being thoroughly explained, this is how it ought to be. Otherwise economics will become useless for its purpose of giving guidelines to practical decision making.[61]

Professor of law Francis Hagerup comments on the methodical views of Aschehoug in his obituary, claiming that his historical work is marked by a thorough and meticulous, as well as critical and detailed, selection of sources in order to describe institutions and their interrelations. Hagerup further says that he was far from grounding his analysis on uncertain hypothesis in order to show developments and driving forces. His method was the 'analytical-descriptive', giving a positive analysis of the given facts – following the British, more than the German, model in his jurisprudence work.[62]

To emphasize this approach of economics a quote from Joseph Schumpeter (1883–1950) – who in 1908 published his first book, *Das Wesen und der Hauptinhalt der theoretischen Nationalökonomie*, where he famously wrote about the *Methodenstreit* between Menger and Schmoller – might illustrate something that underlines the position that Aschehoug takes:

> With regard to their general argument, both sides [Schmoller and Menger] are mostly right. But one fails to appreciate the limits of the argument and overlooks that one party often thinks of problems differently from the other party. *Each method has its concrete areas of application, and it is useless to struggle for its universal validity.* [...] Our standpoint can be briefly characterised by the remark that historical and abstract methods are not inconsistent with each other, that the sole differences lies in their interests in different problems.[63]

There is also an important influence from Marshall concerning method. These comments can be found in the chapter about Aschehoug and Marshall. To sum up, Marshall had a significant influence on how Aschehoug adopted the deductive method when it came to marginal theory, and at the same time saw the inductive method as equally important. He emphasized, like Marshall, that it was the continuous interrelation between the two that was the most fruitful way of developing economics.

In the following, the Norwegian discussions about method in the 1890s will show that the younger economist Oscar Jaeger emphasized a more deductive approach based on his aim to separate theory and praxis.

The Norwegian Debate about Method

The Norwegians did not have any *Methodenstreit* during Aschehoug's lifetime. However, they followed the German-Austrian debates and had their own small discussion at the Statsøkonomisk forening. This discussion about method took place in the mid 1890s, but it was never harsh and the disagreements were not substantial. This underlines the somewhat 'in between' position that was adapted in Norway – neither a 'pure' deductive position, nor a 'pure' inductive. The influence came both from the continent and from British thought. There were nevertheless some disagreements, which will be presented here. These can be seen as a slow movement towards the division between science and politics that accelerated during the decades after Aschehoug.

The debate about method started when Oskar Jaeger published his doctoral dissertation *Den moderne statsøkonomis grundlæggelse ved Adam Smith* (The foundation of modern economics by Adam Smith) in 1895, printed in *Statsøkonomisk Tidsskrift*.[64] Jaeger thought that the economics of Smith had for too long been interpreted through the lenses of Ricardo.[65] The same year he held a trial lecture for his degree called *Den theoretiske statsøkonomis opgave og videnskabelige methode* (The task of theoretical economics and its method), which suggests, as mentioned earlier, that Oskar Jaeger sided with the Austrians concerning method. This is later confirmed by Aarum, stating that Jaeger followed the views of Menger, which were at the sharp divide between statistics and economic history on one side and theoretical and practical economics on the other, actually saying that economics was regarded as a theoretical science, closely connected to the reality of economic life.[66] The lecture and article were discussed at the Statsøkonomisk forening, and both Morgenstierne and Aschehoug were opponents. The same year, another economist, Einar Einarsen (1868–1913), published a theoretical article about the term 'capital' called 'Berebet kapital i økonomien' (The term capital in the economy). Bergh and Hanisch mention this article, saying that Einarsen went even further than Jaeger, but that he did not get any support for his 'pure' deductive views on economics.[67] Morgenstierne had also included a chapter about method in his *Socialøkonomiens grundræk* (A general analysis of social economics) in 1909, but he had begun developing ideas and writing drafts as early as 1890. His views were more in line with Aschehoug, but later he also argued for a greater division between theoretical and practical economics. Bergh and Hanisch point out that Aschehoug also agreed to this division to some extent, but that his *Socialøkonomik* was an example of the difficulties such a division would present in practice.[68] This is the main issue – should science and politics be separated? A more theoretical economics would establish and strengthen the scientific position of economics. On the other hand, it would distance itself from politicians that could not be expected to have the necessary schooling to understand complex economic theories.

In order to see the development in the debate about method in Norway, the lecture of Oskar Jaeger in which he draws a line between theoretical and practical economics will be used. This is something that Aschehoug does ten years later as well, and although he is aware of the many efforts to establish the scientific basis of economics, he does not follow the distinction in his *Socialøkonomik*. It might be added that this lecture probably is the first serious attempt to draw a distinct line between theory and practice in Norwegian economics; in other words, dividing theoretical economics and practical politics. Jaeger starts out by stating:

> What is in this country called state economics is in other countries called political economy, national economics or social economics, and is not a historical science. It contains a synthesis of all theoretical and practical knowledge, which can be divided in theoretical economics in which the task is to analyse general economic phenomena and their regularity, and in practical economics were one strives to find the postulates or maxims after which humans under different conditions may realise their economic intentions the best way possible.[69]

However, the difference between Jaeger and Aschehoug is probably that Jaeger emphasizes, to a much larger extent, the division between the practical and the theoretical element, underlining that they had fundamentally different approaches concerning method and that they should be kept apart.[70] In theoretical economics it is necessary to analyse the general aspects of economic phenomena, excluding all other elements except for those that are purely economic.[71] The individual phenomena are the responsibility of economic history and economic statistics.[72] But how then does Jaeger see the theoretical science? He underlines that empirical investigation is necessary in order to establish general laws or postulates, using history and statistics as indispensable disciplines. These sciences use the inductive method as opposed to the deductive method, also called the empirical-realistic method or the exact method. Jaeger sees these two as a kind of a hermeneutical process, starting and ending with concrete observation, but continuously in reciprocal interaction.[73] There were, for instance, some 'psychological laws' that could be discerned in economics: Jaeger identifies the 'will to satisfy needs with the least effort possible – to act economically' as such a law that could be used to deduce other postulates.[74]

Empirical facts were important, but they could change over time, and therefore they lacked what Jaeger calls a 'stamp of necessity'. They did not meet the ultimate theoretical need for a complete understanding of phenomena.[75] Economics is not like basic sciences such as psychology, or the natural sciences such as biology or physics. It is necessary to take into account, and investigate by induction, both psychological factors as well as the organization of society and the level of development.[76] Again, this is an example of how Jaeger tries to find out exactly how a theoretical discipline should be conducted. He must use empirical facts; but at the same time, he is clear about the necessity to be deductive in the approach. The general laws of theoretical economics can be tested out on empirical findings.[77] It is a difficult process, and Jaeger underlines the need to be strictly logical as a scientist when working with these issues.[78]

The difference between the approach of Aschehoug and Jaeger becomes visible when Jaeger underlines the necessity of abstraction and says that in theoretical economics it is 'not possible to isolate the individual causes, but one has to think about them as isolated and rationally deduct their distinct effects'.[79] Aschehoug would have called this a 'thought experiment', and in his presentation of method (above) many examples are found of his emphasis on why economics must be founded in reality and in the historical context.

Jaeger distances himself from a historical way of conducting economic analysis. He praises the attempts of Adam Smith and his successors when it comes to exact science, although he agrees that some of their postulates need revision and change, due to a prevalent deeper understanding of economics. And he credits the German historical school (Roscher, Knies, Hildebrand) for their great efforts in order to criticize the incomplete theories of the classical economists. But Jaeger also claims that they had a completely different methodical approach and thereby 'completely eradicate theoretical economics'. He gives an extensive account of their views, clearly to show how much he disagrees. He sees them as successful historians and statisticians, but not as economic scientists conducting theoretical economics. He accuses them of neglecting the importance of exact laws and theories. The quote from Jaeger is included in its original form and length.[80] His general view is that this approach will not give the necessary basic theoretical understanding of economics; it is necessary to establish a pure theoretical economic science in order to obtain certain knowledge about the workings of economics.[81]

So, where does Jaeger find his inspiration? He himself mentions Jevons, Walras, Menger and 'the greatest of them all', Böhm-Bawerk. They were the ones who were to reform the classical economic postulates and even completely alter the theoretical foundation of economics. They had reviewed the theories of the 'great masters' and emphasized to a great extent the necessity of using exact methods and a 'pure scientific approach'.[82] As already mentioned, Jaeger understands that classical economics needed a substantial revision, and that the reason why this had taken some time was partly the impact of the historical school, and partly the unwillingness of economists in the classical tradition to revise the old postulates and perceive some of the obvious errors. Due to the efforts of the historical school and the new willingness of classical economists to review older economic theories, a new theoretical foundation was now possible to work out.[83] He does not completely dismiss the historical economists, but when it comes to how theoretical economics should be conducted, he has nothing left for their methodical approach, although theoretical economists may use their empirical findings. As a last example in his article, he praises the new theories of capital that Böhm-Bawerk presents in his 'epoch-making' work, *Positive Theorie des Kapitales*.[84]

In order to recapitulate, the picture that is now presented of Jaeger's methodical views and his division of theoretical and practical economics is not in harmony with the emphasis that Aschehoug has on the deep intertwined relationship between practical and theoretical economics. They both see that both methods must be used, but Aschehoug 'stands on both legs', whereas Jaeger seems to prefer the exactness and the development of laws, and the further development of theoretical economics, later confirmed by Aarum.[85] It is symptomatic that the clearer the division between theoretical and practical economics became, the more deductive theoretical economics became. 'Science and politics' were no longer part of the same discipline, and the division started with this lecture held by Oskar Jaeger in 1895.

What may then be said about Aschehoug? He struggled with the development in value theory. Aschehoug belonged to the last generation of economist that aspired to write a book on economics that was at the same time a textbook and an original treatise. This is not possible if the division between theory and praxis is categorical. Even though the two of them both underline the interaction, and thereby probably did not disagree in many cases, the overall pictures they leave behind are different. For instance, Marshall did the same thing, but he lived long enough to make substantial revisions, making the theories more prominent.

There were never any large disagreements concerning method in Norway, rather it was an evolution in the perception of where to draw the line between science and politics. Morgenstierne, Aarum and Hertzberg did mostly accept the presentation of Jaeger, at least after the turn of the century. Even Aschehoug acknowledged the usefulness of isolating problems and analysing less complex relations, although one runs the danger of oversimplifying. It may then be concluded that the main views on economic theory and method were continued in the same manner as Schweigaard had proposed in his early lectures. But it may also be added that the general scientific development of economics gradually influenced the economists in a more theoretical direction, without losing the strong ties to empirical observation. Aarum later described the position of Jaeger in detail.[86]

Schweigaard had declared German philosophy of nature remote from reality and therefore un-Norwegian in the extreme. In particular, he scoffed at the *a priori* school, which proceeded 'without entering into any relation to the outer world, without deriving from it, without enriching itself with facts and experience'.[87] A quote from Nina Witoszek might be appropriate to end this discussion: 'The message was clear: the Norwegians embraced nature, God and reality [...]. The Norwegians cultivated healthy common sense [...]. [Norwegians had an] intellectual tradition of realism, common sense and dislike of abstractions [...]. A confidence in the unsullied authority of Reason as an agent of benevolent forces within nature remained dominant in the Norwegian intellectual tradition for the great part of the nineteenth century.'[88]

This was to be altered during the second decade of the twentieth century when it came to the scientific development of economics. Jaeger's views became prominent with the publication of his two economic works in the 1920s, and Aschehoug had died ten years earlier. The theoretical turn became clearer, and the basis in historical analyses was left behind. Many economists have later written textbooks in economics, and developed economic theories in separate articles or books. Aschehoug's attempt to include it all was simply too ambitious. As Marshall's *Principles of Economics* went through eight revisions, making marginal theory more and more prominent, Aschehoug's reviser, Aarum, did not contribute much in the way of editing the work, as there are only small differences between the first and the second edition, and no further revisions were made.

Chapter 5

DEVELOPMENT OF THE ECONOMIC THOUGHT OF ASCHEHOUG: STATSØKONOMISK FORENING AND THE *SOCIALØKONOMIK* PROJECT

Development of Aschehoug's Economic Thought

Although Aschehoug started his academic career in the 1840s, it was not until the 1870s that he concentrated on the formation and development of economic thought in Norway. The picture that is presented in the analysis of Anne-Lise Seip concentrates on his early years up until 1882. The full title of her book and doctoral thesis is *Vitenskap og virkelighet: Sosiale, økonomiske og politiske teorier hos T. H. Aschehoug 1845 til 1882* (Science and reality: Social, economic and political theories of T. H. Aschehoug 1845 to 1882). Admittedly, she does not analyse the development in his thought until the publication of *Socialøkonomik*, and one of the opponents of her doctoral thesis, Francis Sejersted, says that this development is lacking in her analysis. He believes that she does not fully appreciate how Aschehoug's superior knowledge of economics and general experience allowed him to develop a more nuanced and detailed system of thought over time.[1] Sejersted further underlines the importance of SSB and the close connection between its two successive managers, Anders Nicolai Kiær and Nicolai Rygg (1872–1957), and Aschehoug. The *Tabellkontoret for statens sentral for innsamling og bearbeiding av statistikk* (Office for the Central Collection and Processing of Statistics) was founded in 1861, and both Kiær and Aschehoug actively participated in its foundation. Kiær was also a committed member of the Statsøkonomisk forening. Furthermore, the younger Rygg started his career early and published his first article in *Statsøkonomisk tidskrift* in 1899.

Statistics were a part of Aschehoug's life from the very beginning of his academic career, and for many years he was a member of the 'Statistical Society' (Statistisk forening). In her work Seip focuses on the commissions in which Aschehoug participated, often as an expert on statistics and as a decision maker. Her main agenda is to analyse his political career in connection to his scientific work. She presents him as an active politician, although he was never a member of any government. He had an important political position, but he was not always diplomatic – as confirmed by Sejersted. The main concern in this analysis is Aschehoug's role as an economist, and the picture presented by Seip shows him to be a clear follower of Schweigaard – in her words a 'harmony-liberal'. This is true to some extent, but does not take into account what happened during the last decades of the nineteenth century, the foundation of the Statsøkonomisk forening and, of course, the huge efforts he made when preparing and publishing his *Socialøkonomik*. Aschehoug was a conservative, and in this context that is understood to be someone who would not push liberal ideas to an extreme; rather, he believed in capitalism and in the importance of entrepreneurs, as well as in a modern state that could facilitate economic activity. Seip's term 'harmony-liberal' is not appropriate. Although no one used the term during his lifetime, 'liberal conservative' would be a more valid description and can be traced in his thought throughout his life. As Slagstad puts it when he describes the jurist Aschehoug, 'The extraordinary feature of the theoretical position of Aschehoug is the combination of an antidemocratic conservatism and a constitutional liberalism.'[2]

Aschehoug did not write any specific economic articles before the foundation of the Statsøkonomisk forening, so a direct line can be drawn from his early trip to England (1847) to the foundation of the Statsøkonomisk forening (1883) and his appointment as a professor of economics. By doing this, the early picture of Aschehoug presented by Seip is accepted, but with modifications – highlighted in the earlier chapter about the Norwegian context and Schweigaard. Specifically, these include a reference to the different opinions presented about the liberal laissez-faire and the simplistic view of the method and scope of economics as a science, which can be found in an early comment from Aschehoug made when he was 24 years old, quoted in Seip. He says that he was 'sufficiently acquainted with the theory of the [economic] science'.[3] The full quote clarifies his point more, because he is choosing not to go to Scotland, nor to the universities in England, nor to the different factories in western England – he does not have the time. His full statement is:

> A person who wishes to study statistics and state economics [political economy] in Great Britain, may – assuming he is *sufficiently acquainted with the theory of the* [economic] *science* – have two goals. He may wish partly to gain a vivid and clear overview of the conditions and workings of British society and partly to become well acquainted with the method with which the British collect and process the facts which serve as the foundation of social science.[4]

The distinction is important, because it does not necessarily mean that Aschehoug feels that he has learned all there is to know, rather it displays a keen interest in the workings of economics, and an acknowledgement of the importance of collecting and processing historical and statistical facts in order to serve the purposes of society. It is worth noting that he uses the term 'social science' and not 'economics'. The clear division between social science and economics is not drawn in 1850. Fifty years later, Aschehoug still uses the term 'social economics' (*socialøkonomik*) – not 'political economy' or 'economics' – as the title of his work, choosing to keep the term social and joining it to economics.

Aschehoug maintained the scientific connection between economics, statistics and history throughout his life, but method and theoretical discussions became more important as the century came to an end. In a way, Aschehoug was growing together with the development of economic thought. His formative years were rooted in classical economics, taught by Schweigaard, but with a clear leaning towards an empirical approach. He started his economic work seriously during the *Methodenstreit*, the marginalist revolution and the reappraisal of classical economics, something that allowed his project to develop as he gradually adopted these new and important impulses, making them his own and finally presenting it all in *Socialøkonomik*. It is the purpose of this book to present his conclusions, and to point out what he has adapted and how he uses these important changes in international economic thought, to show how the formation of a whole science came about and what Norwegian ideas there were at the turn of the century.

Before the foundation of the Statsøkonomisk forening, Aschehoug expressed his views in newspapers, and during the different debates which took place in commission works and in parliament. For several years he was an active columnist in *Morgenbladet*, starting in 1847 and continuing all through the 1850s, and in *Christiania-posten* in the 1850s and 1860s. The previously mentioned debate about economics between Rolf Olsen and Aschehoug took place in *Morgenbladet* in the late 1840s. Seip analyses Aschehoug's economic thought mostly by using what he says and writes about in the commission reports and the governmental discussions and proposals (*Stortingsforhandlinger/Stortingsproposisjoner*). In this way, she creates a picture of his opinions on different topics, in the context of the real debate about political issues, which of course is important. On the other hand, a presentation of economics can also be seen by looking at what Aschehoug writes when he finally focuses his mind on economics and becomes a professor of the subject, which is being done here. A thorough analysis of selected topics in *Socialøkonomik* will follow in the next chapters, whereas the foundation of the Statsøkonomisk forening and the general structure, creation and comments on *Socialøkonomik* will be treated here.

Statsøkonomisk Forening

Aschehoug was one of the founding fathers and protagonists of the creation of the Statsøkonomisk forening (Verein für Statsökonomie/Association of Political Economy) on 4 December 1883. The informal meeting was initiated by Professor Aschehoug, Consul Heftye, Professor Hertzberg, Director Kiær (SSB), Mayor Rygh and Secretary of State Schweigaard (son of Anton Martin Schweigaard). 74 people registered as members, and Aschehoug, Heftye, Hertzberg, Kiær and Rygh were elected as members to the steering committee. The first formal meeting was subsequently held on 25 January 1884.[5]

Aschehoug was the chairman for more than twenty years from its foundation in 1883 until 1903. In 1887 the association started to publish a journal called *Statsøkonomisk Tidsskrift*. In this, economists, bureaucrats and others could publish their lectures from the meetings of the association, together with an account of the accompanying comments and debates. *Statsøkonomisk Tidsskrift* was one of the first genuine economic journals in the Nordic countries since the short life of *Danmarks og Norges oeconomiske Magazin* (1757–64) and the Danish *Nationaløkonomisk tidsskrift*, which was founded in 1873 and is still being published.

The association quickly gained influence within the economic-political arena. As Sejersted says, 'They opted for laying the premises for economic policies at the end of the nineteenth century.'[6] As the politician-professor monopoly of Schweigaard was more or less broken in 1870, the economic discipline gradually split from politics. This new direction was more visible when it came to textbooks and papers, in which new theories were discussed more as theories and not mixed with normative politics as much as before. The first steps towards a theoretical economic discipline can be traced back to the foundation of Statsøkonomisk forening, not only due to the death of Schweigaard, but also in parallel with an international development of economic thought.[7]

Admittedly, different topics of theoretical or practical importance were chosen, covering most of contemporary economic and political life. According to Bergh and Hanisch, the association was not a defence for the *embetsmannsstaten*, but a conservative adaptation to the parliamentary system that was introduced in 1884.[8] Neither was it an association with a specific political purpose, although many of its members were conservatives. Sejersted adds that the *embetsmenn* made up the core of the conservative Høyre (Right) party. Høyre was the party of government officials, and they never opposed state initiatives within what they perceived as normal and reasonable interference.[9]

The initial 74 members in 1883 grew to about 200 after ten years and again to more than 300 in the first decade of the twentieth century. It consisted of members with a conservative leaning, described as 'centre right' or 'reform conservative', something that could also easily apply to Aschehoug himself. The economists Hertzberg, Morgenstierne and Jaeger were prominent members. People from both the official bureaucracy and from private commerce and industry were members. The association soon became a forum for the enlightened elite of bureaucrats, government ministers, parliamentarians and economists, and Aschehoug was the driving force.[10]

The purpose of the association was, 'by means of lectures, discussions and the publishing of papers and scientific works, to contribute to the highlighting of issues of importance relating to political economy and social questions'.[11] Meetings were held monthly between October and April, and as mentioned, a steering committee prepared and conducted the meetings as well as being responsible for the journal. Later, dissertations and other scientific works were published as well, something that gave *Statsøkonomisk Tidsskrift* a good balance between practical economic and social debates, and a more thorough theoretical and methodical approach. Many of the lectures and debates were about public economics and public problems, usually connected to the role of the state in the development of the national infrastructure, such as railways, the telephone system and so forth. But there was also a growing concern about national economics (macroeconomics), questions of taxation, finance policies and the customs and trade policy.[12] The growing focus on social questions was clearly visible, with titles such as Morgenstierne's 'The evil of poverty and socialism', 'On insurance of unemployment' by Rygg, and 'Disability insurance' by Kiær. They also provided annual statistics concerning social conditions and comments in relation to the findings. Aschehoug himself was responsible for six articles during the first years of the journal, which made him the main contributor.

Although Aschehoug had believed most of his life that economic enlightenment and knowledge were important to a sound development in economic policy decisions, he became more pessimistic in his old age. During 1902 and 1903 the association had a long debate about ways to tackle the growth of the national debt, caused by economic crises. Hertzberg claimed that it was necessary to increase general knowledge of economics, something that Aschehoug supported, but about which he was more pessimistic. The mistakes of both public and private economic affairs were more a result of 'irresponsibility than lack of knowledge'.[13] Aschehoug philosophically formulated the current problem as follows: 'People were under the common and fatal inclination of overestimating the present demands and underestimating future demands, and believing more in what they hope for, than what they should fear.'[14]

Morgenstierne wrote about Aschehoug in 1902 for his 80th birthday:

The chairman of Statsøkonomisk forening, Professor Aschehoug, turned 80 years old on 27 June. This is an occasion that in itself is important enough to pay him this tribute. Not only was Professor Aschehoug among the promoters of the founding of this association, but he was also the one from which this initiative came. During the last 18 years he has been a constantly interested and energetic chairman, if illness has not occasionally prevented him. He has continually hosted the debates of the association, partly through his own presentations and partly by participating in the debates. These contributions have substantially increased the interest and appeal of the meetings. In the same vein, he has supported the journal [*Statsøkonomisk Tidsskrift*]. It is not possible to go through the 14 editions without coming across his name. He has treated many theoretical and practical issues of the greatest interest [...] not least the several monographs which give striking proof of this author's multifaceted insight, and ability to master an extensive range of literature, as well as his eloquent presentation ability. I will not be modest when I, on behalf of all the members, use this journal to extend my warm regards to Professor Aschehoug for his management of this association and his extensive written contribution.[15]

As has been shown, both Aschehoug and his colleagues published extensively in *Statsøkonomisk Tidsskrift*, participated in debates, reviewed all new international literature, and invited both business men, politicians and other enlightened members of the public to the meetings of the association. The impact of the association was visible in different policy decisions, and many of the members actively participated in different commissions as well as being members of parliament.

Aschehoug was the chief creator of a science of economics in Norway, especially after 1880. Statsøkonomisk forening was crucial in the foundation of a scientific economic milieu in Norway. Most intellectual questions and problems, both theoretical and practical, were brought up for discussion in the association. *Statsøkonomisk Tidsskrift* enhanced this development, especially when it came to publications of theoretical works and doctoral theses. Within a period of 16 years four theses were published, whereas before 1890 none were scientifically published in journals or in books.

During the same period official associations were established in many countries: the American Economic Association in 1885 and the British Economic Association (renamed the Royal Economic Society in 1902) in 1890, both after Statsøkonomisk forening. Journals were published: the *Quarterly Journal of Economics* (Harvard, 1887), the *Economic Journal* (Cambridge, 1891), the *Journal of Political Economy* (Chicago, 1892), and throughout Aschehoug's *Socialøkonomik*, Palgrave's famous *Dictionary of*

Political Economy was used extensively. The German equivalents are discussed in Chapter 6.

The *Socialøkonomik* Project: The Final Paramount Effort

Aschehoug started his economic scientific work late in life, when he turned 50 in 1872. Jurisprudence had dominated his scientific career until around 1870. He set out to adapt international economic theory to the Norwegian development of economic thought. He said, in 1869, that he could himself only 'present economics [...] with six hours of lectures a week during one semester; it has no scope larger than this'.[16] The difference between this quote and what he accomplished almost forty years later is enormous, and it also represents the developments which led to the foundation of the modern economic discipline in Norway.

The outline of his work will be presented here, focusing on the structure, working process and comments from colleagues, as well as the revision that was made after his death. There are also handwritten copies of his lectures in economics in the 1870s. He collected his lectures in ten small handwritten booklets from 1870 and 1871, including only a tiny fraction of what was later to become *Socialøkonomik*.

The works that became *Socialøkonomik* started in the 1880s, when Aschehoug had become a professor of the newly founded chair of economics and when a programme of economics was established at the university. The first edition of what should later become his magnum opus came in 1891. Aschehoug's own wish was that economic theory should become available in Norwegian, both for students and for a general educated public. His first edition had references to Böhm-Bawerk, Jevons, Menger, Schmoller and Walras.[17] Hanisch and Sæther write that 'Aschehoug decided, as early as 1886, to give an account of the science of economics in the Norwegian language. The first version of *Socialøkonomik* was completed in 1891. To a large extent, it was an edited version of his lectures in political economy from the 1870s, although he had taken into account developments in the intervening years.'[18] The difficulty in finishing the project was, as mentioned, developments within the theory of value, particularly Jevons's *Theory of Political Economy* (1871), Menger's *Grundsätze der Volkswirtschaftslehre* (1871) and Walras's *Éléments d'économie politique pure* (1874–77).

During the 1890s Aschehoug completed yet another version. Since these early versions only exist in handwritten manuscript, a brief presentation of the topics that he busied himself with during the 1890s is included in Appendix B. Some of these topics can be found in complete versions as articles in *Statsøkonomisk Tidsskrift*, others served as a basis for the final version of *Socialøkonomik*. Some economists are mentioned quite frequently in some of the small booklets, and they are indicated in brackets. Aschehoug has obviously read and quoted references throughout the process; handwritten notebooks with references and important quotes can be found in the Aschehoug archive.[19]

Many of the topics that were to become part of *Socialøkonomik* can be found in these drafts. Some of the topics have more than one draft (for instance, value and price theory), perhaps indicating that new information arrived as the work proceeded, something that is underlined both by himself and his colleagues. One of them, Morgenstierne, writes in *Statsøkonomisk Tidsskrift* in 1902,

> That Professor Aschehoug has completed this duty [being a professor of economics and reading all relevant literature] in an impeccable fashion is well known to all interested parties. The previously mentioned articles [in *Statsøkonomisk Tidsskrift*] are proof of this accomplishment. It is astonishing with what energy he has turned to this second, main, topic of his life, and with what energy he has attacked the tremendous amount of information that the modern literature of economics represents, and with what scientific superiority he has mastered this information, that up until now has only been partly available to evaluate for those who have been to lectures or meetings. His *Socialøkonomikens historie* [the first volume of *Socialøkonomik* about the history of economics] that is not as yet finished is close to becoming a picture of the whole development of society. The presentation is thoroughly clear and readable; the short sentences mirror the thought with an epigrammatic shortness that sticks in the memory.[20]

Morgenstierne continues:

> In a universal science like social economics or national economics, the first important task the scholars of a small country must complete is to create a window to world literature. No one can do it better or more completely than Aschehoug in his ongoing work. This is of course also, first and foremost, written for his own countrymen and for a Scandinavian-speaking audience. But luckily, the small people [Norwegians] are not only receiving, but also contributing to the body of world literature. The *Socialøkonomik* of Professor Aschehoug belongs to this body. If this work keeps what it promises, which I am certain it will, its comprehensiveness, universal overview and at the same time its scientific thoroughness and clear presentation will not find its equal in any country's literature. I then presume that translations in other languages will not be long in coming. Thanks and admiration will first and foremost be attached to Aschehoug's important body of work on theoretical and practical economics, and especially his *Socialøkonomik*, his long and meticulous studies and his rich and mature fruits of his experience.[21]

Socialøkonomik was a landmark in the economic development of Norway, and in the country's development of economics as a theoretical and applied science.

Aschehoug wrote and published *Socialøkonomik* in four volumes between 1903 and 1908. The postscript of the last volume is dated 15 November 1908, and Aschehoug died at the age of 86 on 20 January 1909. He started to publish his main work in economics when he was 80 years old. His aim was to present all relevant aspects of economics. It quickly became apparent that this would take time. William Scharling, the Danish professor of political economy pointed out that 'chapters after chapters were written, and time went by, because Aschehoug wanted to include all new knowledge and up-to-date theory, which meant that he had to read all the published literature in all relevant areas, to make his presentation as updated as possible'.[22] This aspect is as striking to readers of *Socialøkonomik* now as it was then, over a hundred years ago. Important textbooks and works that are published after 1900 are included, valuated and analysed. It is also worth noting that the intellectual level of Professor Aschehoug in no way shows his old age. The Danish economist Harald Westergaard notes in his obituary of Aschehoug that there are no signs of a man almost in his 90s with a fading mind. On the contrary, all current and actual questions and problems are discussed with references to literature being completely up to date.[23] Reading *Socialøkonomik* is like reading an encyclopaedia, and all major economists (and many more) from the economic canon up until 1908 are included. The author index shows more than nine hundred different authors. Aschehoug has meticulously been through all the literature he could lay his hands on. Even though some have accused him of not being creative and innovative, the four volumes show an experience and in-depth knowledge that is equally important in economics.

The first edition came in four volumes; the last was finished and published in November 1908. According to the former prime minister's grandson Fredrik Stang (1867–1941), who became minister of justice in 1912 and was one of many contemporary professors and politicians that praised the work of Aschehoug,

> When Aschehoug resigned from public life, he put all his efforts into his scientific work. Eventually, he concentrated completely on economics. Even though he had been interested in economics in his youth, he was, in reality, facing a new science when he returned to economics, and it was international literature that he dug into. Aschehoug threw himself passionately into this work, and he preferred the more modern literature and new economic developments in which to search for his information. But with a perception and an ability to elaborate which would surprise even a much younger man, and a power for empathy to this new world of thought, he completely absorbed it into his own thought. A few days before he turned 80, he started the publishing of an extensive presentation of economics. When he was 86, this magnum opus was finished. He immediately started his revisions with a new edition in sight. A month after, death interrupted his relentless work.[24]

Socialøkonomik presents a coherent analysis of contemporary economics.[25] Among others, Aschehoug has, for example, read the *Principles* by Alfred Marshall (fifth edition, 1907) and, out of curiosity, Wieth-Knudsens *Formerelse og fremskridt* (1908). Arild Sæther draws attention to the fact that Aschehoug is strongly influenced by Marshall, especially his theory of value.[26] Bergh and Hanisch write, 'The publishing of *Socialøkonomik* in four volumes was a milestone both in Norwegian and Nordic economics. It was the first thorough Norwegian textbook in economics and *it was so extensive and encyclopaedic that it was hardly paralleled by any international equivalent* [my emphasis].'[27] Selected parts of the first volume were translated into Finnish in 1904, otherwise it had just been available to a Scandinavian reading public.

Unlike later economic textbooks, *Socialøkonomik* is marked by a 'clear touch of life and reality'.[28] The ambition of *Socialøkonomik* was to be a synthesis after the German model, a complete presentation of economics or a *Handbuch*. In Aschehoug's opinion this didn't exist in the Nordic countries. *Socialøkonomik* is divided into ten parts (a detailed overview of the structure and contents is given in Appendix C) and follows a structure that can be seen in comparable works.[29] Each part has a solid foundation of information and analysis, as well as examples and statistics. Many parts are more extensive than in a normal standard textbook. The *Socialøkonomik* therefore deserves the German expression *Handbuch* – an overall, complete textbook.

How should an overall, complete textbook be presented? Aschehoug follows a tradition that divides economic activity into production, circulation (trade), distribution and consumption, although other economists have chosen to present it otherwise.[30] However, although the different parts of economic activity are interrelated, Aschehoug finds his division useful. A most important issue is the question of economic development and how this should be treated and represented. In this respect, Aschehoug clearly owes much to the German economists in terms of his layout and general presentation of economics: 'I shall follow their example'.[31] They begin their systematic presentations of economics with an analysis of the historical development of concepts. These presentations are called *Grundlegung* (introductions).[32] In the following two thousand pages of *Socialøkonomik*, Aschehoug continues to follow the German *Handbuch*, starting with a historical overview, followed by the theory of population, the scope of economic activity, and finally separate studies of the activities of production, circulation, distribution and consumption. This comparison is to be continued and substantiated by comparing Aschehoug's work to the work of Roscher and Schmoller.

There are two things that are worth mentioning: the first is Aschehoug's great admiration of his sources and the thoroughness of his presentation of other authors' views and theories; the other is one of the few weak points of the work, namely that it is sometimes difficult to dissect the opinions of Aschehoug himself, and thereby the importance he puts on the different theories and themes that he analyses. To find out what Aschehoug really means and what he sees as essential, one sometimes has to read between the lines, not because he does not have opinions, but because he formulates himself elegantly without being bombastic or direct. Nevertheless, after reading through this great work and being inside his thoughts, it is easier to see his position and to understand his priorities and his opinions. He becomes clear and is, as always, well formulated.

In his postscript he especially thanks Hertzberg and Jaeger as well as Kiær and Rygg:

I will extend my warmest thanks to [...] Rigsarkivar Hertzberg and Professor Jaeger, who with a great amiability have read through all my work, made comments and corrections, suggested ameliorations, some of great value. Director Kiær and Secretary Rygg have shown a similar helpfulness and controlled all my statistical information. [...] I have explicitly asked all of them to give me their opinions and comments, and I have in them found an invaluable support for which I am truly grateful.[33]

Noneconomists can find many great benefits in reading *Socialøkonomik*. It is pedagogical in its structure, and the presentations are clear, lucid and easily attainable. Readers with an economic education and interest will be able to use the extensive register of notes, as well as getting an overview of most historical-economic literature that was available in Europe at the beginning of the twentieth century. *Socialøkonomik* also has many references to works in disciplines like sociology, statistics, philosophy and general history. Another advantage is the capability of relating practical economic information found in local Norwegian or Scandinavian examples to economic theory. For instance, if Aschehoug writes about customs and tolls (chapter 80), he presents examples from his earlier career in the Customs and Tariffs Commission.

The analyses in *Socialøkonomik* are detailed, practical, sober-minded, never dogmatic, but critical and realistic, and as objective as possible. Aschehoug's main strength is his clear presentation of theories, the accuracy of his presentations and the impartial consideration of ideas, rather than an original and focused analysis of selected theoretical issues.[34] 'The fusion of reality and theory is the most characteristic trait of his intellectual personality. The two were deeply intertwined and during his life they were in the liveliest interrelation.'[35] These words belong to Francis Hagerup, and they confirm an important point that Anne-Lise Seip and many others would underline. Aschehoug always sought to combine theoretical studies with practical experience. To turn it around, Aschehoug thought that theoretical investigation was much more valuable and fruitful if it could find practical use. His main contribution remains in the fact that he was able to gather, analyse, incorporate and present the results of the quickly developing science of economics. He may be accused of being eclectic, because of his efforts in showing different opinions on various topics and problems.[36] This is not altogether a rightful accusation, as Aarum later adds: 'This characterization should not be put on his general scientific position. In important matters, he has exposed clear and independent opinions.'[37]

Aschehoug was a typical realist and had a sharp eye for the practical and the empirical. Still, his works show a clear understanding of ideological and philosophical thought, even though his conclusions and comments have a realistic basis. His theories always had to be rooted in reality in some way or other, and it is with this in mind that *Socialøkonomik* should be read.

Later Revisions by Aarum, the Reception and Use of *Socialøkonomik*

After the publication of the last volume of *Socialøkonomik* in 1908, the complete work was revised by one of the successors to Aschehoug, Peder Thorvald Aarum. Aarum states in his introduction that he has not changed the style and content of the work, only revised statistics and overviews. The elegant, precise and reader-friendly style was due to Aschehoug's habit of lecturing to himself before writing down the phrases and paragraphs.[38] Aarum's revised edition of *Socialøkonomik* became a standard textbook for all students in economics for two decades after Aschehoug's death.[39] Aarum himself wrote in 1927 that *Socialøkonomik* is of great educative importance for students of economics, and that it would keep its position as a *Handbuch* for a long time.[40] It is worth noting that after his death *Socialøkonomik* was perceived as a textbook, not an original theoretical work, even though William Scharling expressed the following at the death of Aschehoug: 'When I write, in full consciousness about the incompleteness of this hasty and small remark about such an important work, it is with the hope that it will be supplemented with a more thorough evaluation from one of the younger Norwegian economists, one of the disciples of Aschehoug.[41]

Socialøkonomik did not become required reading for students in economics in its original form, probably due to the encyclopaedic scope. Aarum and Jaeger struggled with the structure of the work, both wanting to draw a sharper line between theory and practical economics, as well as theory and history.[42] This is also symptomatic of the general struggle regarding the position of economics as a separate discipline, as well as about what to emphasize and where to draw lines. Aarum and Jaeger's textbooks took over during the 1920s. Marshall's influence continued (see discussions about Marshall), and his *Principles* was widely read by economic students, due to Aarum's recommendation and preference. One may then say that Aschehoug's praise of Marshall continued in the work of subsequent economists. Statistics was important as well, as part of the study of economics. It was the theoretical part that emerged as the most important and was to become the core of economics.

Aschehoug's *Socialøkonomik* contained analyses of different specific questions of the financial and historical-economic kind, although what was called social economics (*socialøkonomik*) constituted the main contents, which was also his main contribution.[43] Aarum remarks that a modern textbook adapted in scope and size was lacking. He considered *Socialøkonomik* too copious, and twenty years after Aschehoug's death, it needed theoretical revision in order to present new theories and developments.[44] But all the same, he credits Aschehoug for his huge efforts in attempting to present and explain economics in a coherent way in Norwegian, though many international textbooks could be found.[45]

The legacy of Aschehoug is summarized in the conclusion of this book. The struggle between practical and theoretical economics continued, and both Jaeger and Aarum participated in the public debate, although the earlier closeness to theory was gone. The reason was of course the theoretical turn, which implied more use of mathematics, and therefore was harder both to explain and to understand for people outside the economists' circle. The hopes of the 1870s economists that what was once called political economy would free itself from philosophy and law, and become a new science to match the logic and precision of mathematics and the physical sciences, were about to come true by the end of the 1920s. Aarum's final remark in 1927 was: 'I am of the opinion that the state of theoretical scientific approach in economics now contains the different theoretical directions of earlier epochs and that differences have been levelled into a more coherent and homogenous system. What is needed for the future is not an internal battle about different approaches and terms, but rather an application of theories that answers the main current questions of economics.'[46] The development in Norwegian economics was by the end of the 1920s still in its early phase, mainly concentrating on fundamental theoretical issues, not on the application of theories. According to Aarum, the main challenge for the near future was exactly the application and relevance of theories for economic decisions.[47]

A final remark can be made on the scope of Aschehoug's encyclopaedic effort. Although his enormous *Handbuch* was in many parts successful, it might be questioned if too much information was included. The editing that was not done by Aschehoug could have been done either by the publisher or by Aarum, who had the opportunity after Aschehoug died and was responsible for the revisions and publishing of the second edition. A solution that could have been more viable would have been to divide the project into what Jaeger called theoretical and practical economics. But as this analysis has shown, this was exactly the division that Aschehoug was not willing to do. Had Aschehoug been able to revise his work, it may be guessed that he would have concentrated more on marginal theory and maybe developed his original article in *Statsøkonomisk Tidsskrift* from the turn of the century. It was probably here that his contribution was most original.

Chapter 6

THE GERMAN HISTORICAL SCHOOL: SIMILARITIES, INFLUENCES AND DISCREPANCIES

A short presentation of the German historical school will be given, emphasizing the issues that are relevant for the parallel development in Norway. Thus, it is not a complete analysis of the German historical school or the views of Schmoller, but rather a summary of the relevant topics for Aschehoug and the foundation and development of the Statsøkonomisk forening as a vehicle for the progression and discussion of economic thought.

The Norwegian economists followed the development of German economic theory closely. A small analysis of *Statsøkonomisk Tidsskrift* shows that the annual presentation of new literature, debates, journals and books contained almost everything that was published in Germany.[1] Aschehoug quotes extensively from German authors, he comments on them and was clearly updated on German economic thought.[2] But as the late Norwegian economist Amundsen says, 'The political situation in Norway was closer to that in Britain than in the German states, and there was no substantial acceptance of the historical school among the Norwegian economists in the nineteenth century.'[3] This may be true when it came to the political situation, but it will be argued here that Amundsen errs in his comments about the influence of the German historical school theoretically. Why the Germans ended up emphasizing historical thought can be seen scientifically as a reaction towards what were perceived as the errors of the early classical school. In this respect the work of the school must be valued. To what extent the school mirrored German political circumstances is to the Norwegians less important, as the political situations in the two countries were different.

The previous chapter presented Norwegian economic thought and the debates about method. It could be said that the debate about scientific method is sometimes simplified as a fight between the atomistic and eternal versus the institutionalized and evolutionary, or as the deductive versus the inductive. The picture of Norwegian thought gives more elements to this debate, as will be the case in this presentation of the German historical school and the German debates about method. With the Norwegian tradition in mind, the purpose of this section is to see to what extent the German historical school influenced Norwegian thought and in what ways. In this chapter a short overview of the German historical school is presented, followed by Aschehoug's own presentation of the school, before an analysis of Schmoller and of the Schmoller/Aschehoug comparison is conducted. The purpose is not, of course, to give a complete picture of the German historical school, nor of all the details in the different debates, or different 'members'. The main idea is to understand to what extent this school, and especially Schmoller, was important to Aschehoug, how these two respectively influenced their own age, and what Aschehoug used from them and how he applied it. A preliminary observation is that the German historical school faced deeper and more troublesome debates – their 'arguments' were serious and more ideologically driven. In contrast, the Norwegian counterparts had a calmer, more pragmatic development, and their discussions were not divisive. However, the result for both schools was that they were neglected a few decades into the twentieth century.

A Small Presentation of the German Historical School

This is primarily a short presentation of the German historical school, but it is worthwhile remembering the close intellectual relationship between German and anglophone social economists before World War I.[4] An interesting observation that has been made recently in historical research reveals that 'the relationship between Austrian and German economics was much closer than was previously thought, and works on English and European historical economics, American Institutionalism and Progressivism, and Japanese social sciences have shown that historical economics was a phenomenon that hardly remained isolated to Germany.'[5] This underlines a connection that is highlighted in this book, namely the influence of German economic thought in Norway.

　　When it comes to a definition of what a historical school is, there are many suggestions. An early one can be found in Gide and Rist: 'The historical school is a broad reforming movement that brought realism and empiricism to economics,' and they quote Schmoller in order to explain that this was a reform which was needed: 'After the days of Adam Smith political economy seems to have suffered from an attack of anaemia.'[6] The broad appeal of this unorthodox approach was its strong statistical and empirical-factual emphasis, its focus on organizational processes and institutional structures, and its close connection to social reform and progressive movements.[7] In fact, it can be said that the German historical school emphasized the national and political concepts, rather than the universal and cosmopolitan.[8]

　　Another early comment is found in an article from 1885 by Alfred Marshall, which describes his views on the historical school and its achievements:

> It would be difficult to overrate the importance of the work that has been done by the great leaders of this [modern 'real' or historical] school [of economics] in tracing the history of economic habits and institutions. It is one of the achievements of our age, and is an addition of the highest value to the wealth of the world. It has done more than almost anything else to broaden our ideas, to increase our knowledge of ourselves, and to help us to understand the central plan, as it were, of the divine government of the world.[9]

The quote demonstrates his admiration and it highlights the important lessons from historical thought.[10] The main claim of the German historical school is not the denial of theory in general, but the need for more empirical studies before the theoretical formulation of wide and complicated phenomena in the historical perspective can be undertaken productively.[11]

Balabkins describes in a lively way what might be viewed as the soul of the German historical school: 'Slowly that outcry against the English classical school of economics, known in Germany as "Manchestertum", which signified the advocacy of unrestricted individual freedom from government intervention in industry and trade, became known as the German Historical School of Economics.'[12] This describes the German historical school as a protest movement, or an alternative economic thought. Balabkins points out what he calls the iron grip of the classical theory, especially in England, but also to some extent in Germany among the academic economists. He sums up the classical 'laws' thus: 1) the law of self-interest and the division of labour; 2) the law of diminishing returns; 3) the Malthusian law of population growth; 4) the iron law of wages; 5) the law of rent; 6) the law of capital accumulation; 7) the law of comparative advantage; 8) the law of value; 9) the quantity theory of money; and 10) Say's law of markets. His point is that these so-called laws were seen as irrevocable and universally applicable, regardless of time, place or existing institutions.[13] The idealistic concept of the state embedded in the thought of the German historical school brought about an idea of a policy-oriented economics, unlike the English classical thought, which had a universal perspective.[14] Shionoya outlines the main ideals of the German historical school: 'institution, evolution, and national policy', and the historical and ethical methods of the school were required to 'explore these key concepts'.[15]

A contemporary economist, Gustav Schönberg, juxtaposed the 'Manchester school' to the 'historical-ethical direction winning victory in German universities'.[16] Others have emphasized the middle perspective, that the German historical school is between socialism and liberalism.[17] This is a political argument, stating that the economists of the German historical school were politically driven. It is true that there were close connections between the political milieu and some of the central economists, but I believe this has to be read as a comment on the internal German context, within which the historical school developed. The political parts of the school were of less importance to the Norwegians. However, this protest to the Manchester school is clearly a protest towards the liberalism that this so-called school presented to the Germans.

Grimmer-Solem's hypothesis is that the German historical school represented a subtle, timely and effective empirical alternative to classical economics.[18] He further points out, in his introduction, that a broader social investigation became necessary in order to understand economic development. The empirical and historical approach was, according to Grimmer-Solem, a fruitful and enduring tension between theory and factual evidence. Finally, Joseph Schumpeter notes in his *History of Economic Analysis* (1954), 'though historical work done by economists was not itself a novelty, it was then [in the 1870s] undertaken on an unprecedented scale and in a new spirit. [...] In principle, if not quite in practice, the Schmollerian economist was in fact a historically minded sociologist in the latter term's widest meaning.'[19]

The use of the term 'German historical school' was highly unsystematic. Often the name 'historical school' was used interchangeably with 'socialists of the chair' or

Kathedersozialisten and the Verein für Sozialpolitik.[20] Grimmer-Solem gives an extensive overview of the different terms in use, something that also applies to Scandinavian struggles over names, with the terms 'social', 'national', 'state' or 'political' mentioned as a few examples. Anyway, it is important to understand that the term 'historical' is easily interpreted differently, both in the contemporary debate of the nineteenth century and up until today. To pinpoint the term, it is possible to use historical economics and emphasize the historical-empirical method and the close connection between economics and practical political decision making.

Literature normally makes a distinction between the older and the younger historical school, but no further comments are made here about the correctness of this division, nor about whether it is possible to group many different thinkers under this label. A brief summary of the most important economists identifies similarities, but also quite substantial differences. Just to recap, there seems to be a larger homogeneity in the Norwegian late nineteenth-century economic thought than can be seen in Germany at the same time. Wilhelm Roscher (1817–184) is considered to be the founder of the older German historical school.[21] He did not break with classical thought, but wanted to supplement it. Bruno Hildebrand (1812–1886) published his *Die Nationalökonomie der Gegenwart und der Zukunft* in 1848, in which he pleads for the 'reconciliation between capital and labour and suggested the necessary incorporation of the German labour class as responsible members of the reformed capitalistic economic and social order'.[22] Balabkins states that Hildebrand had a profound influence on Schmoller. Gide and Rist saw Hildebrand as young, active and ambitious.[23] Karl Knies (1821–1898) published *Die politische Ökonomie vom Standpunkte der geschichtlichen Methode* in 1853. In this he states that the classical laissez-faire did not lead to social welfare for all, and he opposed the strict deductive method of economic theory. According to Knies, economics was a historical science. Knies wanted to study economic phenomena in relation to social and political factors.[24] Knies was neither a socialist, nor a laissez-faire economist. His historical, statistical and institutional approach was the basis of his economics, and he used the inductive method. According to Gide and Rist he questioned the existence of natural laws and even laws of development. He thought that political economy was 'simply a history of ideas concerning the economic development of a nation at different periods of its growth'.[25]

Generally, Balabkins thinks that the objectives of the early or older German historical school represented by Roscher, Hildebrand and Knies were 'to fight and destroy the spreading socialist support for the overthrow of the existing social order and to overcome the legacy of the classical school of economics with its advocacy of "natural harmony", "hands-off" government, and the Manchester free trade policy'.[26]

The younger historical school can be dated to around 1870 and many scholars are associated with this school; among others, Lujo Brentano (1844–1931), Johannes Conrad (1839–1915), Ernst Engel (1821–1896), George Friedrich Knapp (1842–1926), Wilhelm Lexis (1837–1914), Albert Schäffle (1831–1903), Adolf Wagner (1835–1917) and, of course, Gustav von Schmoller (1838–1917). According to Carlson, they had three issues in common: firstly, economic laws are not general or universal like laws of nature; secondly, humans are not solely driven by self-interest in economic affairs; and, thirdly, they agreed that earlier economists had misused abstraction and deduction. Shionoya states that it is beyond question that Schmoller was the leader of the younger German historical school and was the towering figure of this school at its zenith.[27] Furthermore, Schmoller's idea of economic processes as interactions between the natural-technical and the psychological-ethical factors of society were inherited from the older historical school.

In the following, Schmoller will be used in my comparison between the Norwegian thought and Aschehoug and the German thought. Aschehoug was familiar with the work of the economists mentioned above and he applied their ideas to his own, but in this analysis the focus will be on Schmoller.

The German historical school aimed to be a broader social science, paying special attention to national needs and circumstances. The study of economics should also be normative in the sense that both ethical and teleological issues matter and are relevant to economics. Shionoya makes an important point about the ethical method as a scientific method, saying that it is assumed that human behaviour is motivated by various considerations other than self-interest, including morality, law, and customs.[28] A short version of their program might be summarized as follows: the national economy should not be isolated from other social or cultural sciences; the economy cannot be explained by starting with the individual since society is an organic unit; the economy is continuous and may only be understood by applying a historical perspective; theories are formed from an inductive process based on historical observations; and studies of institutions should be an integral part of economic studies.

Economic actions are complex and multifaceted. Economics should not content itself with just being descriptive and analytical, but should also have an ethical dimension, as mentioned, because the values and morals are embedded in the institutions.[29] Shionoya observes that the German historical school developed a characteristic methodology that explored the unique field of economic sociology or *Sozialökonomik* (the exact German translation of the title of Aschehoug's work *Socialøkonomik*) that was methodologically designed for the synthesis of history and theory. By this Shionoya means the theoretical formulation of 'reasoned history', which is different from a mere collection, classification, summarization and ad hoc explanation of historical data.[30] The purpose of the school was to analyse the overall picture of society from an evolutionary and comparative perspective.

It is important to understand the context of the German historical school and why history, politics and ethics became core issues. A detailed analysis of German history is not made, although these issues were important in the overall German development, the nation-building process, the challenges of social reform and the general political development that demanded justification. Grimmer-Solem gives a comprehensive statement about the German *Staatswirtschaft* that, to some extent, is comparable to the early Norwegian political development under Schweigaard:

> Reflecting the close relationship between absolute rulers and their universities [in Norway the connection between professors and politicians, *embetsmannsstaten*], economics in Germany grew out of *Staatskunst* (statecraft) and *Staatswirschaft*

(state economy), which had evolved as a training in crown administration and was therefore often also called '*Cameralien*' or '*Cammer-Sachen*' (cameralism). This *Staatswirtschaft* sought to balance the fiscal needs of the sovereign with the economic needs of his subjects, on the assumption that the strength and the security of the state was based on an economically flourishing, growing population. *Staatswirtschaft* and *Cameralien* were initially taught as a preparatory subject in practical philosophy, ethics and, politics in the philosophical faculty for higher studies in the faculties of theology, medicine, and especially law.[31]

The close connection between economics and law is also prominent in Norway. The special political situation in Norway – being in political union with Sweden but having an internal self-government – created the previously mentioned government structure where the same challenges of administration, modernization of institutions and of the economy were present. In Norway the term social economics was chosen, whereas in Germany political economy became *Nationalökonomi* and also *Volkswirtschaft*. *Staatswirtschaft* became the political part of political economy, called *Staatswissenschaft*. Furthermore, Harald Hagemann points out that the term *Staatswissenschaft* expresses the typical German symbiosis of state and economy, as opposed to the more theoretical and abstract economics of classical British political economics.[32]

An equivalent cannot be found in Norway during the late nineteenth century; the foundation of a *samfunnsvitenskapelig* faculty at the University in Oslo did not come until 1947.[33] This did not imply that these thoughts were new, they were clearly embedded in the thought of Schweigaard and of his followers, and were also part of the name of the economic association and journal – Statsøkonomisk forening and *Statsøkonomisk Tidsskrift* – combining state and economics, not dividing them. There is, however, one important distinction: the Norwegian economic thought and the creation of the Statsøkonomisk forening cannot be categorized as a protest movement – it was a continual process and a natural consequence of societal development. In Germany it might be said that the tensions were larger, and the conflicts more pressing.

There was, as shown, no equivalent to the *Methodenstreit* in Norway. But some important lessons can be drawn, which also came at a later time in Norway, not as a discussion about method, but as a discussion of what economics as a science should be, what the theoretical basis of economics is, and if and how the interaction between economics and politics should be conducted. To get the right perspective on this historical conflict, it is necessary to acknowledge that it was not about method itself, it was about how economic conclusions and policies could be drawn from using them. In hindsight, the real issue was the problems to be pursued – utility and price or institution and evolution. Neoclassical economists focused on the former, the historical economists on the latter.[34] On what grounds should conclusions be drawn and policies be made?

Another schism that became clearer was the gradual division between theoretical and practical economics, between 'science' and 'politics'. The *Methodenstreit* was also about how economics should be conducted, and therefore how far deduction should go and where to draw the line between the importance of empirical investigation and the possibility of deriving general conclusions. Grimmer-Solem gives an analysis of the *Methodenstreit* that explains and also clarifies differences; but most importantly, he also presents a comprehensive explanation as to why it might have been seen as more uncompromising when it took place than it does now. For example, Carl Menger (1840–1921) had admitted that for the study of 'organic phenomena' the 'exact-theoretical' methodology was not sufficient and required the 'empirical-realistic method' for a 'direct view of social phenomena'. He also later admitted that as society developed, purposive intervention by public authorities into formerly organically developed social institutions increased.[35]

Schmoller on the other hand had acknowledged the justification for a distinction between the historical-statistical (descriptive-individual) and the general-theoretical method, underlining the importance of interaction between the two.[36] And he agreed that 'one-sidedness' in these matters was not fruitful, although sometimes necessary in order to make a point. In 1894, ten years after his publication of *Die Irrthümer des Historismus in der deutschen Nationalökonomie*, Carl Menger wrote the following, indicating that the *Methodenstreit* had not been about method, but about the specific ends and purposes of scientific research:

> The difference that emerged between the Austrian school and a part of the historical economists of Germany was in no way one of method in the actual sense of the word. If the historical economists of Germany are frequently described – even in scientific works – as representatives of the inductive, and the Austrian economists, as such, as those of the deductive method, this does not reflect the actual situation. Neither the empirical direction of research in contrast to the rationalistic one, nor also induction in contrast to deduction remotely described the inner relationship of these learned schools. Both recognise in experience the necessary foundation for the investigation of real phenomena and its laws, both – as I presume – recognise in induction and deduction epistemological means which belong closely together and mutually support and supplement each other. *The basis of the real difference between the two schools which remains unbridged to the present day is a much more important one; it concerns the different views about the goals of research, about the system of tasks which science must solve in the field of economics* [my emphasis].[37]

The lesson of the *Methodenstreit* is the recognition that new theories would be formulated through the feedback between theoretical and historical approaches. However, Shionoya raises one important issue, which he perceives as a 'fundamental defect of the historical method': the methodological view that theory or law must be a summary or generalization of empirical facts.[38] The possibility of gaining enough information in order to present a complete picture of economic life is unattainable. The difficulties lie in where the line is drawn, when the historical, empirical investigation must be completed and conclusions reached.

Franz Boese, who in 1939 wrote an indispensible account of the activities of the Verein, has an interesting remark about Schmoller and method, quoting Schmoller from a letter to Lujo Brentano on 29 October 1905:

> Through my performance I only avoided that all members who stand further right feel embarrassed and hurt. As much as the left wing of the Verein is necessary as the

driving force, the right wing is equally necessary since it corrects overstatements and gives the Verein influence on the broad bourgeois classes whose social education is our main task. For social democrats we do not convert and influence anyway, least of all by our general assembly, more likely by our studies.[39]

This statement shows a keen interest in the academic influence on economic and social policies, and Hagemann remarks that Schmoller is a great realist.[40]

The *Methodenstreit* was well known to the Norwegian economic milieu. In many ways, their German colleagues expressed some of the same opinions, not necessarily opposing economic theory or even economic laws, but underlining the necessity not to deduce and theorize prematurely and disconnect from empirical facts and investigations. In Schmoller's view the most important issue was the need to differentiate between the scientific investigation of causes and subsequent explanations, and the creation of teleological systems, based on ideas and general postulates, as foundations for practical judgement and political action. He opposed the latter, but did not dismiss it. He did write an article on method in Conrad's *HWB* in 1893, but not any other later articles about method.

The *Methodenstreit* was, strictly speaking, about the empirical basis for doctrines and theory, and about the legitimacy of policies, of political ends and of the historical origins of the current society and its institutions.[41] These important issues were not solved after the *Methodenstreit* and they are still part of an ongoing debate in economics. An example of this can be found in Bruce Caldwell's analysis of Hayek, *Hayek's Challenge*:

> The Austrians and the German Historical School economists actually shared many views [...]. Both groups employed a variant of 'acting man' as their representative agent [...], both officially abhorred positivism [...], both also opposed Marxism [...], both saw the origins of social institutions as a principal question for economics [...]. Where the Austrians differed from the Germans was in a preference for investigating the topic theoretically rather than historically [...]. Both felt that institutions grow organically and reflect the characteristics of either a specific nation or people (Germans) or a specific set of cultural of social norms and values (Austrians).[42]

Caldwell is somewhat sceptical of the German historical school and also has critical comments on the 'revival' of the school in connection with the 150-year anniversary of the birth of Schmoller.[43] This is another example of how the controversies about schools and methods still exist.

The other large debate was about normative judgements and is usually referred to as the *Werturteilsstreit*. It took place later than the *Methodenstreit*, and escalated at the second meeting of the Verein in Vienna in 1909, the year Aschehoug died. It was primarily a dispute about whether economists or other social scientists should make normative judgements. This discussion can be seen as a critique of Schmoller, mainly from Max Weber, but also as a schism between social science and economics, and a clearer separation of social policy and social science proper.[44] Notably more than half of the members of the newly founded sociological association in 1910 were institutionally recognized as economists. The division of economics and economic policies can also be seen as a struggle about objectivity and value statements. Since Aschehoug died before this became an important part of the Norwegian discussion and a clearer division was formed, the German counterpart is not commented on further.

Before the Schmoller and Aschehoug comparison, an overview of what Aschehoug says about the historical school in *Socialøkonomik* will follow. This summary is limited to his chapter about the historical school, although references and quotes can be found throughout his work. As Aschehoug starts with a historical presentation, the founder of the historical school, Roscher, gets a somewhat more dominant position in this chapter than is the case in the rest of *Socialøkonomik*.

How Aschehoug Describes the German Historical School

Aschehoug dedicates a complete chapter to the historical school, and refers to German economists throughout his work.[45] In order to understand his views and his methodological position, it is useful to present his main thoughts and conclusions about the historical school, which are found in chapter 8 of the first edition. As shown, Aschehoug regards Wilhelm G. F. Roscher (1817–1894) as the founder of the so-called early historical school in economics in Germany. Roscher had in his *Geschichte der National-Oekonomik in Deutschland* divided the dogmatic history of economics in two: before and after Adam Smith, pointing out that the later history largely consists of comments from followers or from opponents.[46] The most durable opponents were found in the historical school, because of their emphasis on the continuity of social life. Being a professor of law, Aschehoug recognizes that the first steps to a historical approach were taken in German jurisprudence. Savigny was the protagonist, and the main idea was that every nation's law, as well as its *Geist*, had a national and historical basis, and was formed by the language, customs and practice of the people. The jurisprudence is not abstract, but a living belief or opinion. According to the school, there are no natural or general, unchangeable laws, and the goal is to get a complete knowledge of the development of institutions and laws. Aschehoug views this postulate with scepticism, as Schweigaard also did (see Chapter 3). He underlines that historical knowledge is certainly interesting and valuable, but that it is hard to get a complete historical overview, which complicates the analysis.[47]

Historical thought also came to influence economic thought. Aschehoug credits Adam Smith for using history to explain economic institutions and development, but he adds that it was not continued by his successors. It was, as mentioned, the Germans who came to see the importance of historical knowledge and came to acknowledge the fact that economic institutions were the products of a people's history, and could not be understood and developed without a historical perspective. Roscher's research and his ambition led to the establishment of the older, or early, German historical school, building on the principles and methods of the 'Savigny-Eichorn model' for jurisprudence.[48] Aschehoug clearly admires Roscher and comments on his work by saying that 'Roscher fulfilled his plan through the publishing of *System der Volkswirtschaft* and *Grundlagen der Nationalökonomik*'. Aschehoug describes these works as being 'the pride of nineteenth-century literature, demonstrating a vast knowledge and a mature judgement, impartiality and a noble philosophy of life.'[49]

Roscher claimed that the science of economics should include the historical development of people and their institutions. All aspects of life, including the economic aspects, are interrelated. In order to understand economic life, one had to know the language, the religion, the art, the sciences, the jurisprudence, the state and the economy of a nation or a people, the last three being the core. Aschehoug further says that Roscher did not want economics to describe how the economic sector should be organized. Rather it should investigate the workings and nature of economic activity and how needs could be satisfied in the most efficient way. Roscher presented a description of a four-stage theory of economic development, criticized by some for not being original and too-closely following the classical school. Aschehoug defends Roscher by saying that a closer reading brings forth new and valuable knowledge. He states that Roscher quickly gained an important position in Germany and was followed by Hildebrand and Knies.

It appears that Aschehoug does not adhere to what he perceives as the extreme need for historical knowledge in order to fulfil the ideal of what he sees at the ultimate goal of the historical school.[50] It might then be said that Aschehoug interprets the claim that one must have complete historical knowledge before being able to draw certain conclusions too literally. Others also asserted this critique, and the later development of the historical school was moderated.[51] But Aschehoug concludes his argument and says that science has to strive for knowledge and to seek out historical facts and connections for analysis. The ideal of a full historical overview is not attainable, but it doesn't mean one shouldn't try to make as much use as possible of what one has.[52]

As others also do, Aschehoug divides the German historical school in two: the older and the younger, placing Schmoller as the protagonist of the younger. The profession of economics at the end of the 1880s can be divided into two main camps: the 'old school' of conservative classical economists and the 'new school' of economists who supported both historical methods and marginal analysis, and who, in addition, favoured a more active role of the state in the economy.[53]

According to Aschehoug, Schmoller wanted even more accurate and meticulous historical information than his predecessors before trying to set up economic models and systems. In his concluding remarks about the historical school, he points out that the weakest point is the difficulty in gathering exhaustive historical information in order to ensure conclusions about economic activity. Nevertheless, he praises the valuable insights, efforts and contributions of the historical school, probably seeing that he used many of these insights in his own research.

Interestingly, Aschehoug also includes British and continental (French) historical thought when showing that the historical approach was not only a German initiative. The 'historical turn' is, according to Aschehoug, also useful when it comes to a re-evaluation and a critical reassessment of older economic thought. Historical insights should be used to rectify theories that are, by new historical knowledge, proven to be wrong.

Gustav von Schmoller: A Presentation of *Grundriss*

A thorough presentation of Schmoller's *Grundriss der allgemeinen Volkswirtschaftslehre* (Layout of general economics, 1901) is made, among others, by Nicholas Balabkins. Here only a brief outline will be given. The German equivalent of *socialøkonomik* – *Sozialökonomik* – is different from economic theory; it is a mixture of economic theory, economic sociology and economic history.

According to Backhaus, Schmoller's audience consisted of politicians and decision makers, civil servants and (not necessarily fellow) economists and students. The only comprehensible economic theoretical *Handbuch* was written after fifty years of research, and a second edition of *Grundriss* was being prepared when Schmoller was over the age of 75. *Grundriss* was meant to give a comprehensive, general and practically relevant outline of political economy. As we have seen, this was also the aim of Aschehoug's *Socialøkonomik*, and to continue the similarities, Aschehoug's magnum opus in economics was written between the age of 81 and 86. Furthermore, immediately after the last volume, a revision was begun, only to be interrupted by the death of Aschehoug two months later in January 1909.[54]

The purpose of *Grundriss*, as well as of *Socialøkonomik*, can be pinpointed thus: 'Schmoller's ambition was to make economics interesting and relevant, useful for practical purposes in politics and business, and therefore critical of the received university doctrines in economics. As Marshall, in Cambridge, who shared his concerns, he tried to reorient the economic profession from within with new approaches to research and instruction.'[55] And Schmoller writes himself in the preface to *Grundriss II*,

> However incomplete my *Grundriss* may remain, however little it may satisfy the theoretical economist or the individual historian, the effort at a general synthesis is not superfluous and not unfruitful. It had to be undertaken by an economic historian, one who has always considered it a false charge against himself that he was striving for description, not for a general understanding of the laws of economic life. Only with such a representation created from the whole can one serve the greater purpose of all scientific understanding. I do not pride myself too much on my work when I say that I have written it in the service of the leading economic ideas and trends of our time and of the ideals which rule my life. Without coming too close to other fields, I believe I may say that it is clear that a *Grundriss* of economic theory has been written by a scholar who is as much an historian of constitutional, administrative, and economic life as an economist, who has followed the process of psychological, social as well as economic development, and who, with the far greater means of present-day economic history, has attacked the work which Roscher began fifty years ago.[56]

Aschehoug says the following in the postscript to his *Socialøkonomik*: 'My aim has been to include and analyse all the new, relevant theories, literature and jurisprudence that are relevant to economic thought.'[57] Although he never explicitly states that he is 'a historian of constitutional, administrative, and economic life as an economist', this is clear from the very first chapter of his work.

Generally there are many similarities in the structure of *Grundriss* and *Socialøkonomik*.[58] Only a few points will be made to illustrate some important differences and similarities. The second chapter of *Grundriss* consists of nine sections. The seventh and eighth sections give an overview of ethics and how it has evolved and been perceived over time. The ninth section presents the interdependence between the natural and ethical elements in society on the one hand and social institutions on the other. Schmoller investigates these issues in more detail than Aschehoug. The sixth section outlines the formation of social classes, stressing the psychological mechanisms that lay underneath. This is not a separate topic in the work of Aschehoug. The forth section is called 'The evolution of economic life in general'. The second section describes the class struggle in space and time and how changes are brought about by government, law and legislation. A comparable perspective is not found in Aschehoug, although he has a chapter called 'Law and economics' and another called 'The individual and the state', and he also looks at what he calls the 'social combat' in connection to the later development in labour unions and so forth. To summarize, although the chapters may vary in the order in which they are presented, all issues are covered by both authors, except that Schmoller underlines the class struggle to a greater extent. *Grundriss* is, like *Socialøkonomik*, an encyclopaedic work. For each section, Schmoller presents the history, a current picture, a theoretical analysis and a recommendation for economic policy.[59] Aschehoug does the same, although his policy recommendations are not always as prominent.

Psychology is the key to understanding human economic behaviour. Thus, the economic historian was turning into a 'scientific economist', if one uses Schumpeterian (but not mathematical) terms, simultaneously including economic theory, statistics, economic sociology and economic history in their work. Schmoller also added two more dimensions to his analysis: psychology and policy implications. Schmoller states in *Grundriss* that 'psychology is the key to the humanities as well as to political economy'.[60] Aschehoug comments, 'The forces which economics must deal with belong also to the psychological world [as opposed to the mechanical or utility-driven world].'[61] Shionoya points out what Schmoller means about ethical determinants: self-interest was not the starting point of historical economics, rather it included looking at how the individuals in a community shared common values, based on their culture, history and traditions.[62]

The reception of *Socialøkonomik* was examined in Chapter 5, and at this point some comments about the reception of *Grundriss* will be mentioned. The reception of *Grundriss* varied. Some praised its enormous, encyclopaedic scope, describing it as a 'rewarding lesson', others criticized the lack of theoretical and abstract analysis. Broadly speaking, the different reviews all admired the detailed, varied and synthesized presentation of economics that Schmoller had been able to integrate into a coherent system. The critique, on the other hand, often focused on the lack of deductive methods and scientific theories. H. W. Farnam wrote a review, 'Schmoller's Grundriss', in the *Yale Review* just after the publication of the first volume, drawing attention to an important aspect of *Grundriss*: 'For one who desires a comprehensive review of economic history and of the growth of economic institutions in the evolutionary spirit, no better work can be found than the present volume.'[63] Thorstein Veblen proclaimed that it was 'an event of the highest importance in economic literature', and Balabkins says that 'Schmoller was very cautious in his language and mode of expression. He probably was a typical "on the one hand, and, on the other hand" economist'.[64] This just gives a small flavour of some of the more positive comments that were made.

Schmoller and Aschehoug: A Comparison

Reginald Hansen, a Schmoller scholar, has written a comprehensive article in *Handbook of the History of Economic Thought: Insights on the Founders of Modern Economics*.[65] He lists a couple of statements about Schmoller in order to analyse them and thereby re-evaluate the contributions of Schmoller's work. In order to compare the position of Schmoller to the position of Aschehoug, the relevant statements that Hansen makes about Schmoller will be used in comparison to Aschehoug: their personal background and career, their interest in historical method and statistics, the combination of science and policymaking with some comments on economics in general, and the impact of the Verein für Sozialpolitik and Statsøkonomisk forening, and *die soziale Frage*.

Personal background

Schmoller was slightly younger than Aschehoug; he was born in 1838 and died in 1917. He was, like Aschehoug, partly raised by his grandfather's family, also losing one parent early in life. The intellectual influence of the family ancestors was important – Schmoller's ancestors being scientists, Aschehoug's being parsons and local administrators. Early in his life, Schmoller was interested in statistics and worked in the office of his father, dealing with taxation and finance, before entering the University of Tübingen. He studied law, history and philosophy in addition to natural sciences and mathematics. Aschehoug enrolled for law studies at the University of Oslo and at an early stage started working with statistics. Schmoller's doctoral thesis was closer to economics – a historical analysis on the economic opinions prevailing during the reformation period.[66] Aschehoug, on the other hand, travelled to England after his graduation in law in order to learn about commission works and economic practices.

Schmoller was liberal in his early years and he later became conservative. He spent much time in his youth studying economic and institutional-administrative history. Aschehoug spent his early years working at the university, in combination with governmental assignments and commission work. In terms of political views, they were both liberal and conservative, but both rejected the maxims of laissez-faire. The historicist way of thought had an immense influence on both of them, and Aschehoug and Schmoller, like most practicing economists, accepted the need to 'contextualize' economic behaviour and the value of historical research.[67]

Statistics: An important instrument for historical research

Schmoller was clearly interested in statistics. As Hansen summarizes:

> Schmoller needed a thoroughly different theoretical approach for his research as compared with the usual access of historians to data. Individual facts, appearances

and events were only of interest or priority when presenting, confirming or falsifying regularities of consequences affecting economic life. The causal consequences of interconnected elements in society showing similarities even though limited to regional or local districts and periods continuously raised his attention. And he endeavoured to furnish findings with statistical data.[68]

Schmoller's effort to achieve suitable statistical equipment for scientific social research was a lifelong project. He spent the 1860s developing his historical methodology, investigating institutions, using historical research to uncover what he called *bestimmter wirtschaftlicher Kulturzustand* – not generalizing, but finding similarities and patterns in defined periods of similar cultural circumstances. Detailed analysis (*Detailuntersuchungen*) was important in developing an understanding of economic activity, restricted both in time and scope so as not to lose control. Karl Popper would call this a 'practical technological approach'.[69] In 1848 after his trip to England, Aschehoug wrote a review of an article called 'Norges statistik' (Statistics of Norway) by M. B. Tvethe, in which he underlines the purpose of statistical analysis, namely to uncover the causes of historical developments. He further claims that new explanations will be found over time when facts can be related to each other: 'Facts must be seen in relation to each other before it is possible to get a clear understanding of their meaning.'[70] Historical analysis was not only a description of what had been, rather the purpose was to unveil causes and relate them to present conditions. In his own statistical work from 1848, 'Om Norges folkemængde i 1664–1666' (About the Norwegian population in 1664–1666), Aschehoug presents a historical-demographical analysis evincing his command of statistical information. In this article he proposes three objectives for demographical analyses: they should contribute to an understanding of historical events; help to understand and judge historical internal, national affairs; and they should, first and foremost, facilitate an economic comparison between historical and contemporary circumstances.[71] History and statistics should then both be auxiliary disciplines to economics as they are both able to make comparisons over time. Aschehoug was for some time a professor of statistics, combined with law and economics, and during his early career he worked closely with the renowned founder of Norwegian sociology, Eilert Sundt (1817–1875). The importance of Aschehoug as a statistician may have been underestimated, and a revaluation of his contribution would be worthwhile, although his work is mentioned in Lie and Roll-Hansen's history of Norwegian statistics from 2001.

During the same period, Aschehoug busied himself with active commission works, juridical treatises and statistical works. His huge efforts to establish a history of law and constitution ended with his three important works, *Norges offentlige rett* (1875–85), *Statsforfatningen i Norge og Danmark intil 1814* (1866), and *Den nordiske statsret* (1885), which are still well known in the law faculties of Norwegian universities. These books are not only juridical, but, to a great extent, historical. In a way, Aschehoug gained knowledge by practical experience during this period of his life, whereas Schmoller dug into statistical analysis and methodology as a scholar. Aschehoug could not work only as a scholar – the Norwegian milieu was too small – and all able intellectuals had to be used in politics, in official commissions and in general public debates. To clarify the picture, this group amounted to just a couple of thousand people in Norway by 1850.

When it comes to Schmoller's interest in establishing sound statistical equipment for scientific social research, this can be compared with the efforts of Aschehoug. The statistical bureau of Prussia was a nexus in earlier times; Schmoller drew extensively from the ideas of his 'mentor' (to quote Grimmer-Solem) – the director of the bureau, Ernst Engel. For a period of time, Aschehoug worked for the Ministry of Finance before he returned to the university in 1852. His ministerial experience made him a valuable member of different commissions, where he used statistics extensively and worked together with Sundt – Sundt being the sociologist and Aschehoug the economist. Later, Aschehoug also contributed greatly to the foundation of SSB in 1876.

Both Aschehoug and Schmoller had a pragmatic, empirical inclination, using statistics in order to understand the development of society, finding the foundations of knowledge through empiricism and realism. Historical insights were used as a critical and analytical tool. Combined with statistics, it could be applied in practical economic problem solving.

The combination of science and policymaking: The core of economics

Schmoller worked behind the scenes, just as Aschehoug did after leaving politics in the early 1880s. They both lived and worked in countries that from one perspective were similar: the preoccupation with practical concerns and the required statistical and empirical research, which was focused in order to solve policy issues. In the last part of the nineteenth century these countries needed applied economics, not debates about general theories and economic laws. As time went by, this changed, due to the Austrian scholars and to the development in British neoclassical theory. The need to establish a separate discipline of economics, to discuss the theoretical foundation of economics, and to find the tools to use became predominant, first in Germany and a decade later in Norway. It should be added that the history of economic ideas can be seen as a pendulum movement, continually evolving in close connection to political, legal, social and material circumstances and developments. The image of economics as a *situated science* is depicted by the Austrian Otto Neurath (1882–1945): 'It is a ship on a perpetual journey where the sailors are forced to make unending repairs and adjustments without the luxury of a dock; economics is always engaged with unending, changing problems, and the hope of an ultimate authoritative foundation has proven illusory.'[72]

In 1911 Schmoller had modified his position in the *Methodenstreit*, claiming that economics had to use both an inductive and a deductive method. This was, according to Balabkins, a careful modification of his initial rigid insistence on the primacy of induction. In 'Volkswirtschaft, Volkswirtschaftslehre und methode', published in the *Handwörterbuch der Staatswissenschaften* in 1911, Schmoller suggests the following steps to a proper economic analysis, the collection of data and the evaluation of them: '1) observe and record observations; 2) describe observed material according to statistical methods by way of a sample of monographs using historical methods; 3) define and classify the material in hand; 4) attempt to isolate causes via causal analysis; and 5) formulate regularities and possible empirical laws.'[73] In this new version Schmoller distinguishes between objective and subjective value judgements. Hagemann points out that Schmoller 'never intended to make subjective ones based on class or party interest as necessary for scientific research, but that he wanted the success of objective ones on which great communities, nations, eras or the whole cultural world depend, over and above the lopsided ethical and political ideals which prevail in economics'.[74]

An important point is also made concerning Schmoller's views on normative approaches to economics. Backhaus claims that Schmoller fully agreed that personal convictions and scholarly analysis should not be confused, but that he firmly believed that values were important in economics, particularly in political economy. Because the knowledge that is being produced is composed of intellectual understanding and practical purpose – where ultimately the aim has to guide the intellectual endeavour – economic theories are, however, tools and not end results.[75] Backhaus adds that 'Schmoller was interested in developing theoretical constructions which were fit to capture an economic phenomenon in its historical dimension, theoretical structures that are at the same time, apart from the economic essence, also able to accommodate the relevant historical, sociological and political theories and facts bearing upon the economic phenomenon.'[76] Young economists should acquire knowledge in many fields, in order to be able to understand the interdependency between economics and other areas of human life. If possible, they should travel, learn languages, law and administration, as well as acquire a sense of practical life. Both Aschehoug and Schmoller may then be said to fulfil these requirements; Aschehoug travelled to England, read French, German, English, and the Scandinavian languages, worked for some time with administration and practical policies and was a professor of law, statistics and economics.

From Schumpeter's article 'Gustav von Schmoller und die Probleme von heute', Schmoller's program is described in this way:

If you want to understand the specific situation in which a particular economy happens to be at a certain time, and if you want to suggest something relevant about its current problems, then *everything that in theoretical economics is taken as given, assumed to be invariant and ignored in the course of analysis becomes the main subject of investigation and focal point of interest.* These data include the particulars of a nation's economic environment, the endowment with natural resources, capital and machinery, the position in international trade, the social structure, size, composition and distribution of the social product, and the economic and political constitution. In this case, *the collection of facts and figures becomes the paramount task, completion of which is a precondition for further research.* The second task is to *put all this information together in a definite order, in order to make it accessible.* Once these two steps have been made, a number of important questions are ready to be answered. The first and the second task can never be quite completed, work on them progresses as the available material is being used and as new methods are developed for data collection and use. Soon, *there arises a need to analyse the technical relationships,* the real behaviour of social groups and individuals, the constitution and functioning of social institutions such as the state, property, commercial law, etc. *The sum of these analyses forms the sociological and economic knowledge of a period, and one can try to forge this knowledge together into a provisional system.* It is important to note that Schmoller has actually worked his way through all the stages of this program, and therein lays his greatness. [My emphasis][77]

This paragraph by Schumpeter is important, and some of the main points are almost identical to Aschehoug's own presentation in chapter 2 of *Socialøkonomik*. The importance of not starting out with *a priori* assumption is also an echo of Aschehoug. Schmoller does not only describe, he prescribes as well. Economics has to be useful and answer practical questions. As with Aschehoug, the sharp division between positive and normative economics does not exist. They both appear to combine methods: 'As a matter of fact, Schmoller's "oughts" are not the "oughts" of welfare economics. He arrives at policy prescriptions by enriching the analysis sufficiently with historical, institutional, political, fiscal, and cultural data such as to impose constraints on the set of available solutions.'[78]

Backhaus sums up by saying that Schmoller's 'oughts' can be interpreted as a continuous process where qualitative and quantitative data are being analysed and finally narrowed to form coherent and usable solutions. Further, Schmoller's historical approach presupposes a balance of different methods, not only one over the other. In chapter 3 of the first volume in *Grundriss*, Schmoller discusses method, stressing the importance of abstraction for any meaningful observation and warning against circular causations. He is also sceptical about methods isolating economic variables from other social phenomena; this must be done with great caution. Disciplines that might be used to facilitate economic analyses are statistics, history, sociology and, above all, psychology, which he believed to be the key to all the humanities.[79] Both the inductive and the deductive methods should be used, mathematics already being completely deductive: 'Simpler sciences, like mathematics, mechanics, and astronomy, have already become almost completely deductive, whereas the simplest phenomena of economics do not lend themselves successfully to purely deductive treatment.'[80]

Schmoller makes a distinction between values and the statement of facts and causal relationships, and he recognizes the need for both induction and deduction. He believes that economics should not be based on simplified statements, but rather on empirical investigations. The close connection between perceived problems and the task of economics to broaden understanding in order to find appropriate solutions is clear. Schmoller says the following about method and the statement of facts versus values:

> Induction and deduction are the two means used to establish individual facts, causality and teleology are the two means to bring these individual facts into a broader connection. Through deductive conclusions causal connections can also be proved, but in the main the deductive method finds its application in teleology. An inductive establishment of facts can be important for a teleological viewpoint, although induction is mainly an aid for causal explanations. In teleology imagination and fantasy are indispensable, in causality reason and judgement are what matter. [...] True greatness in science is not possible without teleology, without a rich imagination. The devious path of causality is narrowly rooting through the dust, only seeing atoms and never a whole. [...] The devious path of teleology is strange illusions and fantastical mysticism, which by disregarding honest, assiduous research, has the pretence of having explained the world through a few catch-phrases, pictures or categories.[81]

Schmoller links his views on the origins of institutions with the idea of justice in political economy in an article from the 1881 edition of the *Jahrbücher für Gesetzgebung, Verwaltung und Volkswirtschaft*. According to Hansen, he used the broadest concept of institutions possible: 'the total of habits or behavioural patterns and moral norms, of customs, traditions and the law, all re-enforced by common behavioural standards in which people conduct life'.[82] The core of political economy was the institutions, made up by human feelings, actions, customs and laws in a historical process. The institutions had to be in accordance with the leading beliefs of justice by the public.

As already mentioned, Morgenstierne wrote a review of the first part of *Socialøkonomik* in *Statsøkonomisk Tidsskrift* in 1902.[83] He specifically mentions Aschehoug and the German historical school: 'His whole scientific position and methodical approach shows an affinity and sympathy towards the German historical school. [...] He shows himself most competent in the contemporary methodical approach in economics, as well as showing a deep understanding of the interconnections between economics and other parts of society.' Aschehoug himself comments, albeit quite vaguely, on the relationship between the individual and society, not really being as harmonic as this quote might indicate: 'As a matter of fact, there should be no insurmountable antagonisms between the true interests of society and the individual, because the relationship between them is ruled by a strong interaction, which in time, to some extent, removes the disharmonies.'[84] And Schmoller makes a similar comment: 'The idea that economic life has ever been a process mainly dependent on individual action – an idea based upon the impression that it is concerned merely with methods of satisfying individual needs – is mistaken with regard to all stages of economic civilization, and in some respects it is more mistaken the further we go back.'[85]

Both of them comment on John Stuart Mill and natural laws. Schmoller in particular criticizes his method. Mill wrote that experiments were not possible in any of the social sciences and that political economy rested on principles or 'laws of human nature' obtained by introspection. Aschehoug mentions Mill as well, stating that it is impossible to derive natural laws from human individuality or the cultural and historical aspects of society. It is misleading and inaccurate to refer to economic theories as natural laws. Bruno Hildebrand once said, 'Do not miss the opportunity, be it now or later, to devote the largest part of your studies to England; it is the real academy for economics and offers endlessly more than France or Switzerland.' Grimmer-Solem adds that this was probably a reference to British social reform, because that same year Hildebrand had written that economics was not to concern itself with seeking natural laws, but rather with the investigation of change and economic development, from which the 'foundations and the structures of contemporary economic civilization could be discovered, as well as the tasks whose solution was reserved for future generations'. According to Grimmer-Solem, this statement draws a link between empirical investigation and problem solving.[86]

Grimmer-Solem further states that

the early writings of Schmoller [...] were less explicit [than those of Brentano] on the place and role of history in his methodology. Indeed, it too was a source of empirical facts. [...] What is undeniable is that both Schmoller and Brentano believed that inductive empiricism was a guarantee of objectivity, a way to overcome "partisan economics" and thereby build towards a truly scientific study of economy and society. More importantly, the economics of Schmoller and Brentano, as that of Adam Smith, were closely and directly linked to a moral philosophy and a view of social progress.[87]

The impact of the Verein für Sozialpolitik: General debates, die soziale Frage, trade policies

Along with the institutionalization of economics at universities, the foundation of learned journals and the establishment of economic associations were an important stepping stone in the professionalization process in both Germany and Norway, as well as in other Western countries during the second half of the nineteenth century. According to the comprehensive article by Harald Hagemann on the Verein: 'The Verein was founded by a group of social reformers [*Kathedersozialisten*] who were opposed both to the laissez-faire positions of the Manchester school, which in Germany was represented by the Congress, and to the revolutionary ideas of Marxism.' He adds that these two positions were the extremes and that the critical juxtaposition between capitalism and socialism was reflected in controversies between 'liberals' and 'conservatives' with regard to social policies.[88] Schmoller was in between these polar opposites, and while he was chairman (1890–1917) the Verein was engaged in a two front 'war': against the reactionary industrialists and against the revolutionary Marxist position within the German social democrats who, in Hagemann's words, rejected cooperation with 'bourgeois' social reformers and denounced the professors as *Zuckerwassersozialisten*.[89]

Balabkins makes a general comment saying that Schmoller rejected the classical school of economics, as well as Marxism, as too speculative because both schools of thought had neglected to do the preliminary 'groundwork' on the historical, social and institutional phenomena. The schools were actually the twin offspring of the same speculative rationalism.[90] Economic activity must be studied in a changing society wherever it takes place. This is also apparent in the comments Aschehoug makes about Marxism in Volume I of his *Socialøkonomik*.

The Verein für Sozialpolitik was officially founded at a conference in Eisenach on 13 October 1873 after a preparatory meeting in Halle on 8 July in the same year and a conference on *die soziale Frage* (the social question) in Eisenach one year earlier on 6 and 7 October 1872. In the invitation to the congress in Eisenach 1873, Schmoller wrote,

> The undersigned are men of all political parties, who have interest in and moral-ethical pathos for [the social] question and believe that absolute laissez faire et laissez passer is not the right thing in terms of the social questions […]. What the undersigned hope to achieve through this conference is to draw diverging opinions together, to forge agreement at least on the most burning points of the social questions.[91]

Although the Verein's *raison d'être* was social policy, a decision was made in 1881 to refrain from taking an 'official position' on policy issues in order to avoid political influence, and instead concentrate on scientific and scholarly issues. But Schmoller regarded the whole activities of the Verein as research, functioning as preparatory work for public policy, which is obviously also the case for the Statsøkonomisk forening. In chapter 5, the statutes are quoted and the activities of the association are explored, and the conclusion is that the Statsøkonomisk forening was aiming at a similar purpose to the German Verein, and many of the topics that were discussed and presented are alike. The Norwegian association had members from politics, bureaucracy and private industries in addition to the scholars. The political influence is clear, although the association worked more indirectly through participation in commissions and in politics, without making explicit policy proposals.

According to Hagemann, it is a widely held opinion that it took decades for the Verein to mutate from a forum of agitation for social policies to a politically neutral scientific organization, although from the beginning the Verein published scientific works.[92] Backhaus adds that in order to see this, 'we not only have to consider that the early history of the Verein für Sozialpolitik can indeed be described as a struggle between two different orientations in economics', recognizing that the policy debates were usually on the agenda when a wider public met, whereas scholarly issues were discussed in the smaller committee.[93] The scientific articles also became part of *Statsøkonomisk Tidsskrift* during its first decade of publication.

Like the Norwegian association, the German Verein had many scholars among its members, including Lujo Brentano, Johannes Conrad, Bruno Hildebrand, George Friedrich Knapp, Wilhelm Roscher, Gustav Schmoller, Adolph Wagner and Ernst Engel.[94] Albert Schäffle was the only one that never became a member of the Verein.[95] Though this may appear to be a *Professorengremium* (body of professors), only one sixth of the members were professors. However, they had a two-thirds majority in the 'standing committee', in which most of the important work was done. A similar pattern is found in the Norwegian Statsøkonomisk forening.

Schmoller wrote volumes about economic, political and social affairs, and sought throughout his life to influence events. The impact on active politics of the 'joint' Verein and *Jahrbuch für Gesetzgebung, Verwaltung und Volkswirtschaft im deutschen Reich* was substantial. According to Grimmer-Solem, the Verein was the most important private fact-finding body within the empire and the first economic policy-oriented association in the world.[96] The *Jahrbuch* was founded in 1871 with Brentano as editor. Later (in 1877) it became the leading journal of the younger historical school, and in 1913 it was renamed *Schmollers Jahrbuch* and was regarded as the scholarly journal of the Verein.[97] The scholarly work of the Verein was published in the *Schriften des Vereins für Sozialpolitik*.

As already mentioned, the Statsøkonomisk forening was founded in 1884 with a somewhat broader mandate: 'by lectures, discussions and publishing of papers and scientific works, to contribute to the enlightenment of issues of importance to political economy and social questions'. But the broad invitation and profile of members can also be found in Norway (see Chapter 5). The association was open to all people interested in economics, and the number of members increased substantially during its first years of existence. The aim of the Verein, summed up in the words of Schmoller, was to bring about greater equality and therefore greater integration of the labour class into 'the organism of society and state [leading to] an ever growing share of the population partaking of the higher goods of culture, *Bildung* and wealth'.[98] The aim of the Norwegian counterpart was not as explicitly social, although the first lecture held by Hertzberg was called, 'Statssocialismens Theori', and social questions were often on the agenda, but were not the association's *raison d'être*. One common element that was important was the *Bildung* (enlightenment) of the general public.

The Norwegian discussion about trade policies follow in Chapter 11. Trade was also an issue in the German Verein. Free trade was at its peak in Germany the same year the Verein was founded. Hagemann shows in his article about the activities of the Verein that Schmoller was in the 'centre', describing his position on the free trade question in the 1879 Frankfurt conference as follows:

> Schmoller put the free trade and protectionist policies of the larger nations in comparative perspective, 'demonstrating' that the character of trade policy is not a matter of principle but a matter of practical value in the main political or economic upswings and downswings of nations, to conclude that in the current situation of the German economy (in which industry still suffered from the wake of the 1873 crisis, agriculture had to face strong competition from cheap corn imported from overseas since about 1876, and, as a result, the state suffered from insufficient tax income), protective tariffs are an adequate policy.[99]

In his youth, after the French-Prussian trade agreement, Schmoller had written, anonymously, a pamphlet called *Der französische Handelsvertrag und seine Gegner*, in which he strongly argued and favoured a liberal trade policy. The same comments that were made about Aschehoug's change in position (see Chapter 11) were also made about Schmoller's. He was accused of changing principles and of 'revising his earlier arguments'. In Norway, Aschehoug was supported by his fellow scholars, whereas in Germany, Schmoller caused turbulence, which resulted in the Verein wanting to abstain from final votes on sensitive policy issues in all future meetings (1879). Furthermore, the Verein oriented itself towards more scientific issues and more neutral topics of discussion. Hagemann comments that the Verein entered a long period of social conservative dominance. Schmoller became the chairman in 1890 after Erwin Nasse, a position he held until 1917.[100]

One of Schmoller's main topics of interest is *die soziale Frage* or *die Arbeiterfrage* (the labour question). Many of his concerns may also be found in Aschehoug's text. The Arbeiterfrage was important to Aschehoug, but was more pressing for Schmoller. One reason is probably the difference in urgency and the way these questions were handled in Norway as opposed to Germany. The close connection between morality and economics in Schmoller's work is also present in Aschehoug's, an example of which is included in Chapter 9 of this book. He comments on the ethics and social questions in *Socialøkonomik* saying that: 'the changes [during the nineteenth century] were irresponsible to such an extent that they had to be treated. The so-called social question was brought to the agenda.'[101] But Aschehoug sees this as more of a general development, connecting it to several traditions, but also explicitly arguing for a social amelioration and a bettering of working conditions.

When it comes to social questions, Schmoller recommends using the institutions as a way of safeguarding the necessities of life for all citizens. Educational efforts, insurance systems, pension schemes, health improvements and so forth are measures that must be used in order to better living conditions for the poor and the labour class. The institutions should be the framework in which economic activities are conducted: 'the total habits or behavioural patterns and moral norms, of customs and traditions and the law, all re-enforced by common behavioural standards in which a person conducts life'.[102] Hansen points out that he does not know of any item in today's German social market economy, with the exception of the *Pflegeversicherung* (old-age care insurance), that was not demanded as necessary or advisable in articles Schmoller wrote as early as 1864 and 1865 in the liberal periodical *Preußische Jahrbücher*.[103]

Social policy was a precondition for social balance and progress, and *Sozialreform* (social reform) was the way to obtain social welfare. At the time, Schmoller's essays in the *Preußische Jahrbücher* were greatly influencing the foundation and the main programme of the Verein für Sozialpolitik. The articles pointed out that the social problems were a result of the preceding transition from a traditional agrarian society to an industrial society as a consequence of the technical revolution. The rise of an industrial labour class of proletarians, and an increasing population in the cities, resulted in a lack of appropriate housing and in generally poor living conditions. Schmoller recommended the use of technical progress through increased utilization of machinery in order to improve the wealth of all citizens, but believed that the 'natural harmony' thought was utopic, unless there were accepted institutions regulating the behaviour of individuals. He believed that the key to maintaining balance and ameliorating welfare was the reform of the institutions.[104] The practical recommendations he proposed were the establishment of trade unions, a provision of an insurance system containing accident insurance, old-age insurance with an old-age pension scheme, invalidity insurance, health insurance and unemployment insurance. The suggested institutions should be the framework in which economic activities could be employed.[105] Furthermore, Hansen adds, Schmoller was not suggesting direct market interventions, he believed in competition and liberalism as a basis for the economy.

Aschehoug's position and views on social policies are presented in Chapter 9, and the similarities with Schmoller are clearly visible. If it were to be summed up in one sentence, it would be that the two seem to have the same basic personal belief and that they share the same approach, although adapted to their respective contexts.

Conclusion

Schmoller and his colleagues had a substantial influence and impact on other economists throughout Europe, and with this analysis it is clear that this also includes Norway. However, the influence was also reciprocal, especially from their travels and readings of texts from countries like Britain, France and Switzerland. The international influence also affected Aschehoug and his colleagues, while the reciprocity was more difficult due to their text being mostly written in Norwegian. Although the political leanings of the different German economists are not discussed specifically, Schmoller and his colleagues can be said to 'forge a new, far-sighted' liberalism.[106] As shown earlier, the Norwegians were mostly conservatives, but were also continuing the liberal Norwegian heritage. There are many similarities between the Germans and the Norwegians, particularly with regard to the apparent British influence. If any conclusion should be drawn, it must be that Aschehoug and his fellow economists had their own empirical and historical heritage, but that the German historical school reinforced this tradition and brought new insights both to the methods and especially to the commonly shared social questions.

The German historical school had the dislike of the deductive method and the laissez-faire conclusions of Smith, Ricardo and Mill in common.[107] They argued that there could be no scientific laws separate from politics, customs and the legal system. The economists should study history in order to understand, analyse and conclude on economic issues and policies.

The most important difference is the force of revolt and the strength of the several debates concerning the German historical school, its method and its members. The need for reform was larger and more present in Germany than in Norway and driven through with greater urgency. This cannot be found in the Norwegian debates, except for the small dispute about method in the 1890s. A last point might be that the most intense German debates took place about ten years earlier than what might be regarded as the Norwegian discussion. A greater clarity and understanding of the issues was the backdrop, and it was therefore conducted without any great misunderstandings. Menger's new comments (see above), and the publication of Marshall's *Principles* might have been other clarifying elements. Menger had sought to demonstrate that economic law existed, and Schmoller had rejected the laws as useless. Eugene Böhm-Bawerk, a the pupil of Menger and well known in Norway, wrote in a review of Menger's *Untersuchungen* that he doubted the possibility of exact theory divorced from reality or that such laws could lead to a final understanding of reality.[108] Grimmer-Solem also points out that the rather striking affinity of Böhm-Bawerk's policy views with those of Schmoller was an indication of a shift in opinion.[109]

The touch of reality, the tangible effects on policy of economic research and work was of equally paramount importance in both countries. As shown in the comparison of Aschehoug and Schmoller, they both influenced politics in many ways and both underlined the same point about the compulsory 'usefulness' of economics over and over again. It may be stated that their insights into the social complexity and the need to build economic research on empirical and statistical analyses were valuable.

Gide and Rist wrote that the German historical school had 'collected an impressive amount of first class empirical facts', but had not 'succeeded in raising a castle with harmonious proportions'. A sombre conclusion is found in *The New Palgrave Dictionary of Economics*, in the article on Schmoller by Bertram Schefold, who wrote the following:

Today there is a general agreement about the rather unlucky influence of Schmoller on the development of economic science in Germany: it contributed to the standstill of economic theory development for almost half a century in Germany. Neither Schmoller nor his students had fulfilled their intentions to build a new theory based on the historical material they had collected, even if these facts were most valuable.[110]

Indeed, the historical economists were practical idealists who believed, like Adam Smith before them, that economics addressed questions bigger than satisfying the wants of commodity-trading individuals; it was a policy science concerned with the sources of national prosperity, a science of progress that unavoidably contained an applied ethical component. And Grimmer-Solem adds dryly that 'if the historical economists can be blamed for falling short of their ambitions, they cannot be accused of inaction, impracticality, or irrelevance'.[111]

To conclude, Schmoller's favourite phrase may be quoted: 'Aber, meine Herren, es ist alles so unendlich compliziert' (However, gentlemen, this is all infinitely complicated).[112]

Chapter 7

ALFRED MARSHALL: ASCHEHOUG AND THE ADOPTION OF MARGINAL THEORY

The Importance of *Principles*

Another huge influence on Aschehoug, namely the publication of Alfred Marshall's (1842–1924) *Principles of Economics* in 1890, is important in understanding his work. It must be remembered that he was the first Norwegian economist who had a clear ambition in understanding, presenting and incorporating marginal theory in his analysis. It was an event which contributed to the evolution of political economy into economics, sending a signal that it was as much a formal science as physics, mathematics or other precise bodies of knowledge.[1] But Skousen adds, 'Later in life, Marshall was to regret this attempt to scientize economics, suggesting that we are still greatly ignorant of economic behaviour, but the die was cast. Economics would soon become a social science second to none in rigor and professional status.'[2] *Principles* is the single most quoted book in *Socialøkonomik*, which makes it worthy of further investigation. What did Marshall write that was so important to Aschehoug, and how did he follow or use the theories of Marshall? The clue lies in the prefaces, Book I and the appendices, and more obviously Book V. As Marshall wrote himself in 1920, 'But of course economics cannot be compared with the exact physical sciences: for it deals with the ever changing and subtle forces of human nature.'[3] The marginal revolution was already ongoing long before the first edition of *Principles* and other authors were well known to Aschehoug, but Marshall was the first, according to Aschehoug, to explain marginal theory correctly. The article Aschehoug wrote about marginal theory is probably the most theoretical of all his economic papers. It is not just an adaption of Marshall; he produces many of his own mathematical, graphical and theoretical explanations of the value-building process, the different elements to be considered in this process and relates it to what normally happens in the market. In *Socialøkonomik* he has skipped the diagrams and most of the equations, probably to make it easier to understand.

Mark Blaug stated in 1973, 'The success of the marginal revolution is intimately associated with the professionalization of economics in the last quarter of the nineteenth century.'[4] The early 1870s – especially 1871 – marked the period that three economists independently discovered the principle of marginal utility, at the time when Aschehoug had started concentrating on economics. This so-called 'marginal revolution' also meant that the paradox of value, which had been a topic of much controversy since Smith and Ricardo first posited the problem, was to be resolved. Aschehoug worked out an independent position, but struggled for a long time with the issues of value and marginal utility. He regarded the value-building process as a synthesis of the offer as well as the utility, both being necessary elements in understanding the value.

The late economic historian Earl Beach has some interesting observations about Marshall. He states that: 'Marshall's economics is not understood in one reading. His interest in realism is not being appreciated.'[5] And further, Beach sees two sides to Marshall: on one side he is successful in his theory of supply and demand, and on the other he tries to marry economics with history. The failure, according to Beach, is that the former theoretical contribution was to some extent overemphasized at the expense of the latter.

Beach asks some valid questions: What is economics? What is needed for its analysis? To what extent does economics differ from the natural sciences, and how should our approach differ from theirs?[6] He suggests that a broader reading of Marshall could be the answer, not only focusing on the famous Book V, but reading the prefaces, the first chapters and the appendices of *Principles*. This is exactly what Aschehoug does, and probably why he was so satisfied with Marshall's work.[7]

There are two obvious elements in *Principles* that caught Aschehoug's attention: firstly, the general view of economics; and secondly, the adaptation of the theories of Menger and Jevons, namely the theory of value. He integrates marginal theory into a broader picture, and this way of seeing marginal theory appeals to Aschehoug's own struggle with the so-called marginal revolution that gradually changed economics during the last decades of the nineteenth century. Oscar Jaeger wrote in 1911 that before Aschehoug started out his *Socialøkonomik* project for a third time he attended to the particular problems of marginal theory. He focused especially on revenue (*avkastning*) and income (*inntekt*), as well as the history of value and price theory, published in two monographs in *Statsøkonomisk Tidsskrift* from 1900 to 1902. The index shows that most of the paragraphs are included in *Socialøkonomik*, namely in chapters 30 to 32, chapter 35, and chapters 56 and 57.[8] *Socialøkonomik* includes a deeper and more extensive presentation, but the article 'Værdi og prislærens historie' includes a broader presentation of the history, as well as the diagrams and equations mentioned above. Aschehoug references his own paper whenever necessary, and sometimes in order to avoid repeating himself. The similar chapters already mentioned are not complete copies in *Socialøkonomik*, but they treat the same topics. In this chapter, *Socialøkonomik* will be used, as it is the most recent and most extensive presentation of marginal theory by Aschehoug.

Sæther and Hanisch write in their analysis of the reception of Marshall in Norway that: 'Aschehoug strongly believed that economic theory could be used to solve present-day economic and political problems. However, he had, for several years, been unsatisfied with economics as presented by the classical and, indeed, neoclassical economists. Like Schweigaard, he was particularly dissatisfied with its practical application.'[9]

They further claim that the early drafts of *Socialøkonomik* from the early 1890s show that Schmoller and Menger had a prominent place, but that Aschehoug was not satisfied with his presentation. He was certainly aware of the publishing of Marshall's *Principles* in 1890, and Marshall becomes the most important economist in the final version of

Socialøkonomik (1903–1908), quoting him more than one hundred and seventy times.[10] Sæther and Hanisch conclude that:

> At the age of 80, he started work on a final version. With Aschehoug's comprehensive use of Marshall's works, there was a substantial shift from German to English influence. […] Alfred Marshall was well known in Norway since the publication of his books *Economics of Industry* and *The Pure Theory of Foreign Trade* in 1879. His attempt, in *Principles of Economics* (1890) 'to present a modern version of old doctrines', was well received. Aschehoug thought Marshall had succeeded in his attempts and he made the study of Marshall's *Principles* compulsory for his students.[11]

Aschehoug did not solely use *Principles* throughout *Socialøkonomik*. Other books and reports that Aschehoug uses include: *Third Report of the Royal Commission on Trade Depression* (1886); *Royal Commission on Precious Metals, Final Report no. 9633* (1888); *Report of the British Association for the Advancement of Science* (1890); and *Elements of Economics of Industry*, second edition (1894) (in this last book, he gives a clear and comprehensive presentation of workers' associations).

One other quote from Marshall concerning capital as a production factor (not treated here) is taken from a treatise called 'Distribution and Exchange' in the *Economic Journal* (vol. 8). Further, Aschehoug states that he uses Böhm-Bawerk's general view of production capital, and he remarks that both Schmoller and Marshall mainly agreed that it is necessary to use different terms in order to treat capital correctly (production capital, consumption capital, etc.).

Aschehoug uses the fourth and fifth editions of *Principles*. The initial chapters include Marshall's broader views of the method and scope of economics. Aschehoug agrees with Marshall on a number of points such as the usefulness of statistics, the use of certain definitions (e.g., economic goods), socialism and the cooperative. But the largest part of Marshall's presence in *Socialøkonomik* is related to marginal theory. Aschehoug extensively built all analysis concerning price and value on Marshall, as well as his analysis of capital income, rent and money. He agrees with Marshall on the fourth production factor – the entrepreneur – and elements from Marshall are included when he looks at entrepreneurial income and the role of the entrepreneur. Finally, he uses Marshall again in his discussions on labour.

A few words about Marshall will provide a general picture of him. He was a Cambridge professor, interested in mathematics and philosophy. John Stuart Mill influenced him, but Marshall developed Mill's thoughts and studied price setting and gradual small changes. He did not see labour as the determining factor in the exchange value of goods. This value was determined by the satisfaction of consumers or the utility it represented, thus his perspective was that of demand and utility, and how the suppliers adapted in a market situation (i.e., the classical supply–demand equilibrium). Hanisch and Sæther give a short and precise description:

> The Classical School had claimed that the value of a good, its price, was determined by labour costs. The Austrian school took the opposite extreme viewpoint and claimed that the value was determined by marginal utility alone; the cost of production had no significance. Aarum [and, it should be added, Aschehoug] followed Marshall and claimed that the truth was somewhere in between. The interactions of demand and

supply in the market worked like a pair of scissors: neither blade cut without the presence of the other. Demand and supply simultaneously determined price and quantity. Market equilibrium became a key concept.[12]

Marshall is considered to be one of the founders of neoclassical economics, where the central elements were, and still are, marginal perspectives.[13] The marriage of supply and demand for the determination of value is the key concept in *Principles*, something that was clearly appreciated by Aschehoug, who in Marshall finally found the guide to marginal theory. The focus is on consumer behaviour, and the theories are based on mathematical analysis. Equilibrium is not only static, but can also be used to illustrate dynamic situations with uncertainty, imperfect competition and nonrational decision making.

The Norwegian economist Agnar Sandmo presents Marshall's ideas in his book *Samfunnsøkonomi: En idéhistorie* from 2006 (now in an English edition: *Economics Evolving*), where he mainly concentrates on the marginal theory of Book V of *Principles*.[14] He also includes a small biography and mentions that 'it is interesting that a person with such an extensive training in mathematics should claim that mathematics could be useful, but only if it was possible to express it in plain English'.[15] He comments that there is more to Marshall than Book V, and he partly follows this train of thought further in his presentation. I owe the references to J. M. Keynes's presentation of Marshall to Sandmo.

Marshall and Aschehoug on the Method and Scope of Economics

Firstly, a few comments on what Aschehoug says about method and how he uses Marshall will show why Aschehoug found a special interest in him (further analysis of his method is found in Chapter 5). On the question of the inductive and the deductive methods, Aschehoug finds an ally in Marshall, agreeing that both methods are necessary and that they have to be used over and over again in order to develop the economic theory. The uncertainty of causes and effects and of historical facts is another common point.[16] He extensively refers to the prefaces, first chapters and appendices from *Principles* (fourth edition from 1898) in the first volume of *Socialøkonomik*, published in 1903.

Aschehoug states that economic activity is divided into the production, sale (*omsætning*), distribution and consumption of economic goods. He says that there are several authors that don't adhere to this, but that Marshall agrees to it, even though he emphasizes the importance of consumption.[17]

In the opening chapter, Aschehoug describes equilibrium by stating that general equilibrium is purely a thought experiment, and that forces will always work to alter the situation. The description may be used for all different interactions of economic forces, like market prices, rent and wages. He borrows the description from the first three chapters of Book V of Marshall's *Principles*.[18]

Marshall's *Principles* is his most influential book. Published in eight editions, Aschehoug used, as mentioned, the forth and the fifth editions, although he does not specify which edition he uses each time he quotes Marshall. However, in the first volume we can be absolutely sure that he used the fourth edition.[19] Marshall argues that the central idea of economics is that of a living force and movement. It is a science of slow and continuous growth. He states that his *Principles* is

> an attempt to present a modern version of old doctrines with the aid of the new work, and with reference to the new problems, of our own age. [...] In accordance with English traditions, it is held that the function of the science is to collect, arrange and analyse economic facts, and to apply the knowledge, gained by observation and experience, in determining what are likely to be the immediate and ultimate effects of various groups of causes; and it is held that the Laws of Economics are statements of tendencies in the indicative mood, and not ethical precepts in the imperative.[20]

The spirit of applying mathematical methods was in the air when Marshall dedicated himself to economics during the late 1860s. Cournot's *Principes mathématiques de la théorie des richesses* (Research into the mathematical principles of the theory of wealth) came as early as 1838, and Marshall writes in the preface of his first edition of *Principles* that:

> Under the guidance of Cournot, and to a lesser degree of von Thünen, I was led to attach great importance to the fact that our observations of nature, in the moral as in the physical world, relate not so much to aggregate quantities, as to increments of quantities, and that in particular the demand for a thing is a continuous function, of which the 'marginal' increment is, in stable equilibrium, balanced against the corresponding increment of its cost of production. It is not easy to get a clear full view of continuity in this aspect without the aid either of mathematical symbols or of diagrams.

Marshall was careful not to include too many mathematical and diagrammatic proofs in his book – not because it was too difficult to understand, but because he didn't want to make economics too abstract.[21]

Mathematics played a minor role in this period among Norwegian economists and was not a widely used tool among economists before the time of Ragnar Frisch. Aschehoug himself was not a mathematician and, as mentioned, he did not include any diagrams in his *Socialøkonomik*, although both equations and diagrams that explain the basic theory can be found in the first part of the article 'Værdi- og prislærens historie' in *Statsøkonomisk Tidsskrift* from 1900, implying that Aschehoug was well aware of the mathematical foundation of the theory. Aschehoug managed to change the attitude towards mathematics; he pointed again and again to Marshall's graphical presentation.[22] Mathematics should be appropriately used and results should be possible to explain in written language. As mentioned in the analysis of method, Aschehoug is positive towards the use of mathematics, but he underlines Marshall's point by saying that mathematics is not trustworthy in the analysis of complex phenomena, meaning that when too many assumptions have to be made, the mathematical answers will be clear, but too simplified.[23] Marshall says,

> The chief use of pure mathematics in economic questions seems to be in helping a person to write down quickly, shortly and exactly, some of his thoughts for his

own use: and to make sure that he has enough, and only enough, premises for his conclusions (i.e., that his questions are neither more nor less in number than his unknowns). [...] The use of the latter [diagrams] requires no special knowledge, and they often express the conditions of economic life more accurately, as well as more easily, than do mathematical symbols; and therefore they have been applied as supplementary illustrations. [...] The argument in the text is never dependent on them; and they may be omitted; but experience seems to show that they give a firmer grasp of many important principles than can be acquired without their aid; and that there are many problems of pure theory, which no one who has once learnt to use diagrams will willingly handle in any other way.[24]

We owe several valuable suggestions to the many investigations in which skilled mathematicians, English and continental, have applied their favourite method to the treatment of economical problems. But all that has been important in their reasoning and results has, with scarcely an exception, been capable of being described in ordinary language. [...] The book before us would be improved if the mathematics were omitted, but the diagrams retained.[25]

Marshall was quite cautious of his own use of mathematics. Beach states that Marshall's simple abstractions are merely for instructional purposes.[26] When carefully reading the prefaces, this becomes obvious. Marshall himself highlights Book V, but in the eighth edition he writes, 'The theory of stable equilibrium [...] when pushed to its more [...] intricate logical consequences [...] slips away from the conditions of real life. [...] The stable theory of equilibrium is only an introduction to economic studies; and it is barely even an introduction to the study of progress and development of industries which show a tendency to increasing returns.'[27]

Wilhelm Roscher, according to Beach, was a strong influence on Marshall. Marshall was attracted towards the new views of economics taken by Roscher and other German economists, but the analytical methods of the historical economists were not sufficiently thorough to justify their confidence that the causes, which the historical economists assigned to economic events, were true causes. Marshall struggled as much with the interpretation of history as with predictions of the future. To remedy the shortcomings, he closely studied practical business life .

Marshall wrote, 'The work of the economist is to "disentangle the interwoven effects of complex causes", and therefore general reasoning is essential, and a combination of the two sides of the work is *alone* economics *proper*. Economic theory is, in my opinion, as mischievous an imposter when it claims to be economics proper as is mere crude unanalysed history.' This is Marshall's combination of theory and observation. In fact, Marshall was very supportive of historical methods and shared the historicist-institutionalist criticism of the assumed universalism of the deductive method, one of the main faults Marshall found in Ricardo.[28] According to Marshall, Ricardo had believed too much in the deductive method and was led astray. Marshall himself relied heavily upon historical statistics in *Principles*, including copious historical information, examples and analyses. The attempt to combine comparative statistics with the evolutionary analysis of institutions was common, Aschehoug being a clear example.

Marshall certainly placed economics as a subject on the curriculum. Beach asks his readers to be aware of the fact that Marshall recognized the importance of history in the study of economics. Marshall had spent some time in Berlin, where he was particularly interested in the German economic historians, and from Schmoller he took the phrase 'walking on two feet', a job which, according to Beach, Marshall did much better than Schmoller.[29] The early editions of *Principles* contain extensive historical material, which was later put in the appendices. As already mentioned, Aschehoug worked mainly with the first up to the fifth editions, where these pages are still in the introductory section and thus easily emphasized. Marshall himself stated that he was not trying to write history, but was rather seeking material for the building of good economic analysis, which is exactly how Aschehoug perceives the process.

Again, Aschehoug reminds us of how theory should be used, always making a parallel to the real world in order to make sure one does not forget all the other elements that might come into play in day-to-day decision making. In a way, the opening paragraphs of Marshall underline the same precautions that should be taken in the use of economic theories. For instance, he writes about economic laws, 'It is sometimes said that the laws of economics are "hypothetical". Of course, like every other science, it undertakes to study the effects which will be produced by certain causes, not absolutely, but subject to the condition that *other things are equal*, and that the causes are able to work out their effects undisturbed. [...] The action of the causes in question is supposed to be isolated.'[30] According to Marshall, the laws of economics can be compared with the laws of the tides, rather than with the simple and exact law of gravitation. The reason is that the actions and needs of men are so varied and uncertain, that the best statements of tendencies, which one can make in a science of human conduct like economics, must inevitably be inexact and faulty. Life is human conduct, and the best we can do, says Marshall, is to formulate well thought-out estimates, or provisional laws, of the tendencies of human action.[31] He further states that there are no hard and sharp lines of division between those social laws that are to be regarded also as economic laws and those which are not.

Economics: Theory and Praxis

Beach mentions that Marshall had extensive practical training in commissions, government work and writing submissions during his time in the United States. This must have made him acutely aware of the close connection between economic theory, historical facts and current economic activity.

Due to the bias of the famous scissors of supply and demand, which had taken up all the attention of later economists, seeing this as Marshall's (only) contribution, the overall approach to economic science and to economic problems was lost along the way.[32] Marshall wanted to 'produce a balanced overall picture of the economic system with due weight given to historical and institutional factors', and the formative influences of Marshall included German idealism, Spencerean evolutionism and the utilitarianism of Bentham and Mill.[33] Marshall defended and supported historical work, and he considered deductive theory and the historical approach equally essential. He also defended capitalism, but he understood that its defence required measures to correct inherent problems.

Some quotes from Marshall that correspond to the general method and scope of economics, can also be seen in the first two chapters of *Socialøkonomik*. Economics is concerned with solving practical problems, laying down rules, which may be a guide in life. In fact: 'Economic laws and reasoning are merely a part of the material which Conscience and Common-sense have to turn to.'[34]

One of the good things about Marshall, Keynes states, is that he arrived very early at the conclusion that pure economic theory is not worth much without the useful and practical application of it to the interpretation of current economic life, which of course requires a profound knowledge of actual facts.

> The change that has been made in the point of view of Economics by the present generation is due to the discovery that man himself is in a great measure a creature of circumstances and changes with them. The chief fault in English economists at the beginning of the [nineteenth] century was not that they ignored history and statistics, but that they regarded man as so to speak a constant quantity, and gave themselves little trouble to study his variations. They therefore attributed to the forces of supply and demand a much more mechanical and regular action than they actually have. Their most vital fault was that they did not see how liable to change are the habits and institutions of industry.[35]

As discussed earlier, Aschehoug gathered extensive practical experience himself before he wrote about economics. His purpose and aim is very much in line with Marshall when it comes to these general opinions about economics, and can also be seen when he explains marginal theory in detail.

Another point is the importance of ethical forces, something Marshall discusses quite substantially in his preface, and which is important to Aschehoug. Marshall does not adhere to the 'doctrine of the economic man', who is 'under no ethical influences and who pursues pecuniary gain warily and energetically, but mechanically and selfishly'.[36] Aschehoug himself discusses ethics in his chapter about the interface between economics and other sciences, where ethics is the most important aspect of human behaviour.[37] And one thing is for sure: 'Between true morals and sound economics there is a deep understanding.'[38]

In the 1920 edition Marshall writes, 'It is strong proof of the marvellous growth in recent times of a spirit of honesty and uprightness in commercial matters, that the leading officers of great public companies yield as little as they do to the vast temptation to fraud which lies in their way.' This is thoroughly treated by Aschehoug whenever he comments on entrepreneurs (see comments later in this chapter).

Keynes says about Marshall that he never departed explicitly from the utilitarian ideas that, in Keynes's view, had dominated the generation of economists that preceded him. And he adds that it is remarkable with what caution Marshall goes far beyond Sidgwick and is the polar opposite to Jevons. Further, Keynes finds no passage in Marshall's works in which he links economic studies to any ethical doctrine in particular. Rather, the solution of economic problems was for Marshall not an application of the hedonistic calculus, but a prior condition of the exercise of man's higher faculties.[39] Marshall writes the following about the possibility of progress:

> [It] depends in a great measure upon facts and inferences, which are within the province of economics; and this it is which gives to economic studies their chief and their highest interest. [...] The question cannot be fully answered by economic science. For the answer depends partly on the moral and political capabilities of human nature, and on these matters the economist has no special means of information, he must do as others do, and guess as best he can.[40]

In retrospect, Keynes quotes the following statement from Marshall describing how ethics influenced his economics:

> From Metaphysics I went to Ethics, and thought that the justification of the existing condition of society was not easy. A friend, who had read a great deal of what are now called the Moral Sciences, constantly said: 'Ah! If you understood Political Economy you would not say that.' So I read Mill's *Political Economy* and got very excited about it. I had doubts as to the propriety of inequalities of *opportunity*, rather than of material comfort. Then, in my vacations I visited the poorest quarters of several cities and walked through one street after another, looking at the faces of the poorest people. Next, I resolved to make as thorough a study as I could of Political Economy.[41]

Marshall underlines his own humble stand towards the end of his life: 'The more I studied economic science, the smaller appeared the knowledge which I had of it, in proportion to the knowledge that I needed; and now, at the end of nearly half a century of almost exclusive study of it, I am conscious of more ignorance of it than I was at the beginning of the study.'[42] This resembles the comments Aschehoug makes himself in the last volume of *Socialøkonomik*, where he admits that 'the reason [for all the time] it had taken to complete the work was that I wanted to include the important developments in economics, and so much is happening, it's almost overwhelming'.[43]

Keynes describes Marshall as 'belonging to the tribe of sages and pastors', and like them, 'endowed with a double nature', being a scientist, too.[44] The paradox, Keynes later says, is perhaps that the master economist, like Marshall, must possess a rare combination of gifts; he must be a mathematician, historian, statesman, philosopher; and he must contemplate the particular in terms of the general, and touch abstract and concrete in the same flight of thought. And as Keynes wisely puts it: 'He must study the present in the light of the past for the purpose of the future.'[45] Marshall possessed many of these qualities, but first and foremost he was a historian and a mathematician. Aschehoug's combination was law and economics, but also statistics and history, which made him, like many of his contemporaries, including Marshall, a holistic scientist.

Marginal Theory

The mainstream of economics accepted and encouraged historical and statistical research and favoured economic reforms. Marginalism was widely accepted as one element of theory but was actually practiced by a relatively small group of economists at the turn of the century. The fuller picture of economics, however, was much wider and even further away from the conventional picture.[46]

Beach summarizes, 'For Marshall, economic progress is the "high theme" and an understanding of the theory of value is an essential step along the road to understanding how economic progress takes place. The concept of equilibrium is a tool to be used with care in analysing these questions.' Edgeworth says about *Principles* that 'the new light thrown on Cost of Production enabled one more clearly to discern the great part which it plays in the determination of value; that the classical authors had been rightly guided by their intuitions, as Marshall has somewhere said, when they emphasized the forces of supply above those of demand'.[47] In Keynes's words,

> The general idea, underlying the proposition that value is determined at the equilibrium point of Demand and Supply, was extended so as to discover a whole Copernican system, by which all the elements of the economic universe are kept in their places by mutual counterpoise and interaction. The general theory of economic equilibrium was strengthened and made effective as an organon of thought by two powerful subsidiary concepts, the margin and substitution.[48]

Marshall also introduced the time element, but said himself in the first edition that, 'for the element of time, which is the centre of the chief difficulty of almost every economic problem, is itself absolutely continuous'.[49]

First and foremost, it is interesting that Aschehoug clearly has read all that he could about marginal theory. He not only uses Marshall, but frequently makes points coming from Menger's *Grundsätze* (1871), Jevons's *Theory* (1871), Lehr's *Grundbegriffe* (1893), Böhm-Bawerk's works, Pantaleoni's *Pure Economics* (1898), Wicksteed's *Alphabet* (1888), Gossen's *Entwicklung der Gesetze des menschlichen Verkehrs* (1854), Fischer's *Mathematical Investigations in the Theory of Value and Prices* (1892), and Wieser's *Natürlicher Werth* (1891), to mention the most frequently used economists. That Aschehoug himself believes in the basic ideas of the marginal value theory is quite clear when, in paragraphs 9 and 10 of chapter 32, he defends it against the objections of Lexis and Nicholson and refutes their criticism.

When summing up the teachings of the classical school, Aschehoug draws a line from Adam Smith to David Ricardo and then to John Stuart Mill. He mentions that Say emphasized the utility of the goods as being most important to decide the exchange value (*bytteverdi*), meaning that the buyer will have more influence on the price than the seller (or producer).

With Mill, the picture becomes clearer, and Aschehoug states the well-known theory of price determination explained by supply and demand.[50]

However, he explicitly criticizes the shortcomings of the classical school when it comes to explaining the theory of value. Firstly, they underestimated the quantity when they described the utility of an economic good. Secondly, the underlying causes of the production cost were not sufficiently analysed. Thirdly, the impact of time was underestimated. And lastly, utility and production costs were not brought together in a comprehensive theory. Ricardo's theory focused too much on production cost, whereas Say emphasized utility too much, both being one-sided.[51] In his 'Værdi- og prislærens historie', Aschehoug illustrates the controversy between Ricardo and Say, quoting Ricardo's critique of Say in a letter to Malthus, and pointing out how Jevons later criticized both of them.[52] Walras, together with Jevons, are representatives of what Aschehoug calls the new mathematical theory in economics, the theory of marginal value that started in the 1870s. The main principle was to show that individuals made decisions based on their individual utility. Aschehoug traces the development of this thought to Nicholas Barbon (1640–1698), who wrote about this in his *Discourse of Trade* that was published as early as 1690. The theory of value quickly became popular, notably through Marshall and his *Principles* from 1890, but French economists like Gide, Maurice Block and Leroy-Beaulieu have also embraced the theory. Leroy-Beaulieu and Colson have, according to Aschehoug, managed to produce presentations of the theory without algebraic formulas and diagrams, something that must have been difficult given the texts of Walras. Another interesting observation that comes to mind is that Walras was only available in French. Aschehoug must have been able to read French and understand the difficult mathematical theory that was outlined, which Agnar Sandmo states was not common.[53]

In general, Aschehoug often refers to Walras when he talks about mathematics. For instance, he quotes Walras when he discusses the claim that economics is just the mechanics of utility or the mechanics used to find equilibrium or movements from one state of equilibrium to another. For Aschehoug, economics is neither a mechanical science, nor a psychological science, so Walras's definitions are too limited. Aschehoug also makes an interesting point by saying that Smith's and Say's definitions have been thoroughly criticized by Walras in his *Éléments d'économie politique pure*, which is not surprising considering the different views of Walras and Say. It appears that Aschehoug takes Walras's theories into account when it comes to discussions about value and marginal utility, but that he uses and discusses Marshall much more frequently throughout *Socialøkonomik*. It might be the case that Aschehoug considered Walras's theories too abstract and that reading him was, for most people, too difficult. Aschehoug's own position is clearly much closer to Leroy-Beaulieu, who opposed the mathematical method, than to Walras.[54] This is not to imply that Aschehoug did not accept mathematical analysis as a part of economics. As was his habit, he discusses the pros and cons, and stresses that a belief in mathematics as a tool that can provide conclusive answers would be misleading. The more complex an issue is, the more dangerous it is to rely on mathematics to resolve it.[55]

A short description of the main points Aschehoug makes shows that he sees value as the main way of evaluating goods that have no cost of production, like natural resources or land. But generally there will be costs of production or a sacrifice in some way, and these costs must be considered in the following way: there is a limit to how much one is willing to sacrifice in order to produce a good. Through this evaluation of costs and sacrifice, the value of a good is decided as well as the comparison to the production of other goods, hence the marginal value. The marginal value must reflect the cost of production by comparing it to the cost of production of other goods with the same means of production. But according to Aschehoug this reasoning lacks one point: it must be clear what decides the value of the marginal product. It is not necessarily the utility itself, but also the sacrifices that are needed in the production process. Means of production that cost – like labour, capital and production sites – can always have an alternative usage, and they will always be used the way the owner (the entrepreneur) finds best in the given circumstances.

In the early 1870s, marginal theory was introduced, and Marshall's *Principles* made sure that the theory gained currency.[56] This theory showed that it was the subjective utility that decided the economic action and thereby the exchange value.[57] By 1900, the marginal value theory had become mainstream, and most authors adhered to it completely or at least to its basic ideas. In the last category, Aschehoug mentions the Germans Wagner, Dietzel and Schmoller, commenting that Schmoller in his *Sitzungsberichte der Preussischen Wissenschafts-Academie* had printed parts of his lectures concerning the theory of value in which he says that supporters of the theory overestimate its importance, even though he admits that it is better and more to the point than that of the classical school.

Aschehoug comments on Jevons that he probably overreacted in his condemnation and criticism of Ricardo and Mill. The main postulates of the classical school are still valid:

1. No need has economic meaning unless it brings forth economic actions, positive or negative.
2. An object must be believed to satisfy a need in order to have economic value.
3. A need must, in order to get economic meaning, be subjective and concrete, and be felt by one or many defined people at a definite occasion. It will be he or them that will estimate the value of the object.
4. All needs can be temporarily satisfied, either completely or partially.
5. A need ceases to be economically active, not only when it is satisfied, but when the satisfaction is secured by the acquisition of the necessary means.[58]

Aschehoug explains the general postulate of marginal theory much like Marshall does. He also points out the different uses of the term marginal, showing that the Norwegian term comes from the German *Grenznutzen*, Scandinavian *grensenytte*, the English term quickly became *marginal utility*.[59] In explaining this, Aschehoug uses examples (such as the analogy of water) from Menger's *Grundsätze* and Böhm-Bawerk's *Kapital*.

Marshall's *Principles* Book III, chapter 5 ('Choice between Different Uses of the Same Thing: Immediate and Deferred Uses'), paragraph 1 states, 'If a person has a thing which he can put to several uses, he will distribute it among these uses in such a way that it has the same marginal utility in all.' This principle is valid says Aschehoug, but he adds that: 'In real life, which will be the chosen solution depends on the actual circumstances, the individual himself and if the quantity of goods can be divided. The teachings must be understood with the obvious reservation that each will organize their economy, presumably following a sensible plan.'[60] A reduction or an expansion of production will be considered by analysing the marginal value and the marginal offer (including costs and sacrifices), and the level will be where it is not economically viable to either increase or decrease production.[61]

In chapter 32, Aschehoug expands the marginal utility discussion from the isolated household (chapter 31) to the marginal utility of the exchange economy (*bytteøkonomien*). In discussing exchange, Aschehoug uses the postulate of Menger and says that 'there must be a difference in the trading value each party attributes to the object in order to continue exchanging'.[62] This sentence is only a general principle, not an absolute rule. In real life, many other aspects will count. The true value of this postulate is only that one should try to organize one's consumption so that one's needs are satisfied in the best way possible.[63] Aschehoug also comments on the exchange value in monetary markets, where value is decided both by cost and utility.[64]

The economy is not only a state or condition, it is a dynamic activity, which brings Aschehoug to the analysis of production cost. The value of a commodity is not only decided by its usefulness in satisfying needs, but also by its production cost. He tries to answer two questions: what is understood by production costs and how are they related to the value of a commodity? Although many earlier theories have been incomplete, it all falls into place with marginal theory and Marshall's *Principles* Book V, where he points out that production costs are both the value put in by work and the costs of the entrepreneurs.[65]

Aschehoug spends time going through all aspects of production costs, but it all leads up to general theorems of marginal utility. Marshall's influence is also clear in this discussion, because he compares the statements of the Austrian school, namely Böhm-Bawerk, Jevons and Philippovich, to those of Marshall. This is especially clear in the discussion of the measurement of the value of economic goods.[66] After presenting the theory of Wieser from his thesis in *Annals of American Academy of Political and Social Sciences* (1892), repeated in the article 'Grenznutzen' in Conrad's *HWB* (second edition) and the theory of Böhm-Bawerk in his *Kapital und Kapitalzins*, he concludes that Marshall's theory is correct.[67] Marshall claims that one has to look at the basic principle in economics; a product can have an exchange value and be sold, not only if it covers a human need, but also if the product is scarce, meaning that it is not so abundant that anyone could acquire it without any effort. Aschehoug adds that the value of the product has a double base, the use of it brings about a satisfaction and the production of it takes an effort of some kind.[68]

The principle of applying different production factors lies in the marginal utility theory. To clarify the core of all exchange, Aschehoug quotes Marshall's *Principles* from his Book VI:

> To sum up the whole in a comprehensive, if difficult, statement: Every agent of production, land, machinery, skilled labour, unskilled labour, etc., tends to be applied in production as far as it profitably can be. If employers, and other business men, think that they can get a better result by using a little more of any one agent they will do so. They estimate the net product (that is the net increase of the money value of their total output after allowing for incidental expenses) that will be got by a little

more outlay in this direction, or a little more outlay in that; and if they can gain by shifting a little of their outlay from one direction to another, they will do so. Thus then the uses of each agent of production are governed by the general conditions of demand in relation to supply: that is, on the one hand, by the urgency of all the uses to which the agent can be put, taken together with the means at the command of those who need it; and, on the other hand, by the available stocks of it. And equality is maintained between its values for each use by the constant tendency to shift it from uses, in which its services are of less value to others in which they are of greater value, in accordance with the principle of substitution.[69]

In order to clarify the point, Aschehoug brings in arguments and examples from Böhm-Bawerk's *Kapital* and Edgeworth's comments in the *Economic Journal*. The conclusions he draws show a critical review of the different hypotheses in marginal utility theory. He also finishes his analysis by stating that the marginal value of the product is found in the point where the marginal cost of production equals the marginal utility of the product. And thereby the two parts of the theory, marginal utility and marginal cost, are united.

Market prices of the means of production fluctuate around an equilibrium point. Deviations happen all the time and movements towards equilibrium may be slow. This point of equilibrium, explains Aschehoug, is not unchangeable. It may change very quickly due to a new law, a tax or the lack of means of production. But the equilibrium point is always present somewhere as long as competition is free on both sides of supply and demand.[70] Later he points out that the movement might leap forward – *per saltum* – due to the same forces. The changes can be scientifically explained mathematically, but in practical life, producers must try to observe their environment as best as they can, and then choose to try out different prices and/or quantities.

As always, Aschehoug asks the question about the practical use of the theory. He says that many of the terms in the marginal utility theory are easy to understand and give an intuitive association with practical economic activity. It would have been easier to understand and adapt the marginal theory if a product could only have been produced by a set means of production or if a certain production only produced one product, but neither is the case.[71] Aschehoug observes that the complexity of, and the rapid changes in, daily economic activity make it difficult to estimate exactly, which is why the theory of value must simplify and thereby may lose sight of important factors influencing the result. Marshall operates with the term 'normal value', and it seems that Aschehoug accepts this as the best possible estimate of value.[72]

'The circumstances on which the supply and demand graphs are based will never occur in real life. It is only a guide to the thought. [...] It is, though, an aid for understanding [...] and the price determination can be shown graphically, but to those other than mathematicians, the theory will not be easier or more explanatory.'[73]

Other Selected Topics: Entrepreneurs, the Cooperative and Labour

As mentioned in the introduction, Aschehoug uses different papers and books written by Marshall. Traces can be found on nearly every page of *Socialøkonomik*. Since both entrepreneurs and labour will be discussed later, a few comments from Marshall chosen by Aschehoug will be included here.

The entrepreneur is important to both economists, and Marshall calls them the 'captains of industry', the instruments of change and development. Their importance in the development of the industrial revolution must be recognized and Marshall was appreciative of the contributions of such people. Aschehoug mentions the *business ability* as a fourth production factor, mentioning Marshall as one of the economists that uses this distinction.[74] Beach further states in his article that 'an important part of [Marshall's] answer [as to how a country achieved its economic status and where it would go] was entrepreneurship in the form of businessmen, those ceaselessly striving, calculating people of the modern world'. And it is 'particularly interesting that Marshall sensed a strong trend for improvement in morality among able businessmen'.[75] To Marshall, the entrepreneur – through competition, private capital and free markets – was necessary in order to raise living standards and better conditions for as many as possible; this perspective is a further development of Smith. But Marshall also favoured the slowing of population growth, education for the poor, self-help for the working classes, cooperation and education (see Aschehoug on these issues in Chapter 9), and encouraging cooperative communities. The free market should be regulated and competition should be managed. As Aschehoug also did (see Chapter 9), Marshall favoured the eight-hour workday, but contrary to Aschehoug he feared the labour unions.

The entrepreneurial role is important in a capitalistic economy, something both of them underline. That is the problem with the cooperative. It seems that they both think that it is a good idea, but that it is difficult to have sustainable cooperatives in practical business. Aschehoug chooses to quote in length the views of Marshall in his chapter 28 on the subject. He calls § 19 'Marshall's judgement over the future of the cooperatives'. How quickly the cooperative will grow depends on the development of largely civilized people. Aschehoug uses the arguments of Marshall in order to explain the future of the cooperative, calling him one of the most esteemed and sober contemporary authors. Marshall treats cooperative associations as ideal, where the members are the entrepreneurs and the superiors of their managers. They will have the best opportunities to overlook the operations, steer it and discover any erroneous behaviour. The members will feel responsible, because it is in their honour and economic interest. But there is one huge problem with these idealistic associations: the workers may well be unfit to be the superiors of their managers. A cooperative will never be as efficient and as well managed as an ordinary business. Aschehoug quotes Marshall: 'Enough has already been said to show that the world has just begun to be ready for the higher level of the work of the cooperative movement, and that different proper organizations will become more successful in the future than in the past.'[76] It seems they are both sceptical about human ability to conduct business in a cooperative due to the shortcomings of human nature.

The analysis of Aschehoug and his perspectives on labour are included in Chapter 9. Here I will include just a few comments on what Marshall says and what comments Aschehoug has about it in the chapter called 'The final distribution of national income'.[77] The comments from Marshall are being used in paragraphs 7, 8 and 9, namely: 'The common interest between the productive classes of the society', 'The double competition between them about the distribution of income', and 'The marginal theory's answer to the problem of income distribution'.[78] The purpose of the chapter is to discuss the strengths of the relations between the different participants in the production of national income, namely entrepreneurial income, capital rent, ground rent (*grundrenten*) and labour wages. The general observation is that a just distribution must be that all participants in the economic activity of society must keep the part of the income that corresponds to their contribution in generating the income. After a couple of pages where Aschehoug discusses the shortcomings in Ricardo's theory, he includes Marshall's contribution. Marshall writes in his *Principles* that 'the national dividend which is the joint product of all the agents of production, and which increases with the supply of each of them, is also the sole source of demand for each of them'.[79]

Furthermore, it is often the case that the interests of the different classes in society do not coincide. Firstly, there is competition in the use of the means of production (substitution), and secondly there is competition between the same means of production in order to get the best employment, for instance between workers, between different projects that need capital and so forth. Then we have marginal theory: 'Just as in all other economic competition, the law of marginal value is ruling the competition of the distribution of national income. The understanding of the implications of marginal theory has more than anything brought about a deeper and clearer understanding of distribution and dismissed many old disputes.'[80] Aschehoug mentions that Say demonstrated the influence of marginal value on different classes of income, further than Von Thünen had developed this thought in his *Isolierter Staat*. The contemporary theory is presented by Carl Menger in his *Volkswirtschaftslehre*, in the *Kapital und Kapitalzins* by Böhm-Bawerk, by Wicksell and Pantaleoni, and of course by Marshall. The marginal theory presents a more differentiated picture of the distribution of income than earlier attempts to understand this complexity.

The distribution of value between the means of production is decided by each comparative marginal value. In order to explain, Aschehoug quotes a sentence apparently added by Marshall in his fifth edition: 'Marginal uses do not govern value, but are governed together with value by the general relations of demand and supply.'[81] Aschehoug adds at the end of the paragraph that even if you know these general statements about income distribution, the use of them in real, practical business life may be quite complicated, because there are many circumstances that should be considered, and they may be difficult to distinguish and balance.

Marshall wrote in his sixth edition of *Principles*, one year after the death of Aschehoug, something that could have been taken right out of *Socialøkonomik*. He comments on the classical school of Ricardo and their belief in the deductive method, which caused them to

> speak of labour as a commodity without staying to throw themselves into the point of view of the workman; [...] they therefore attributed to the forces of supply and demand a much more mechanical and regular action than is to be found in real life; and they laid down laws with regard to profits and wages that did not really hold even for England in their own time. [...] [They] did not see that the poverty of the poor is the chief cause of that weakness and inefficiency which are the causes of

their poverty: they had not the faith that modern economists have in the possibility of a vast improvement in the condition of the labour classes.[82]

It may then be said that the influence of Marshall in the last work of Aschehoug was substantial, and brought Aschehoug somewhat closer to British thought than he was before 1890. It is clear that Aschehoug embraced Marshall, reading him carefully and integrating his marginal theory in his own picture and structure. They both shared the same overall view on economics, which is probably why Aschehoug was so satisfied with the publication of *Principles*. They never met and never wrote. Aschehoug was among the established, old Norwegian economists, Marshall was the modern thinker. But Aschehoug was not old-fashioned when it came to Marshall; he was progressive and modern.

In order to sum up the views that Frisch held about Marshall, the article by Hanisch and Sæther, 'Alfred Marshall in Norway', can be quoted. This shows that the development in economic thought was gradual, and that the reception and use of Marshall continued for more than a hundred years up to the late 1990s, being firstly introduced and well treated by Aschehoug. The article states that Frisch took up the tradition from his predecessors, Aschehoug and Aarum, and used Marshall's *Principles* as his main textbook, in particular Book V – according to Frisch the central part. Frisch further supplemented the Marshallian theory with a compendium of notes, *Grunnkurs i økonomisk teori* (Notes on economic theory) in 1939, where he wrote in his preface that he considered Marshall's *Principles* to be the best textbook ever written in economics: 'The most valuable aspect of Marshall's presentation is the richness of his details and his taste for the connection between theory and practice.'[83] Eleven years later, in 1950, he reviewed Marshall's theory of value in a 30-page article in the *Quarterly Journal of Economics*, and as an echo of Aschehoug he wrote,

> Like all human work, Alfred Marshall's theory of value had its definite shortcomings. [...] Despite these shortcomings, and despite all the changes in economic conditions and economic policies that have come about since Marshall wrote his theory of value, this theory still holds its own. It contains elements about which no economist can afford to be ignorant however 'modern' he claims to be.

He ends the article by saying, 'This presentation has sought to outline and systematize the reasoning in Marshall's Book V. Only its general features have been considered. To appreciate the wealth of detail one must study the book itself. *What is most valuable in Marshall's work is the way in which he succeeded in combining the theoretical and the concrete.*'[84]

The theory of value may be said to have been properly introduced by Aschehoug in his article 'Værdi- og prislærens historie' in 1900–1902 and elaborated in *Socialøkonomik*. Although not from Aschehoug but directly from Marshall, the main principles of the theory were still to be found in my curriculum of economics in the late 1980s in Norway, but the emphasis on the practical, as well as the broad, understanding of economics that is being expressed in both Aschehoug and Marshall was lost. Marshall is remembered for the extremely influential principles of supply and demand, the determination of price, the cost of production, and the equilibrium in the short and long run, all which can be found in any textbook of microeconomics today, when presentations of the theory of individual consumers and producers are done. In this respect, Marshall transformed political economy into the science of economics.

A last question may be asked: did the marginal theory influence Aschehoug's economic thought in general? Clearly, it is the single most difficult topic to handle, the one that takes Aschehoug a couple of years to digest, and that postponed the publishing of *Socialøkonomik*. Aschehoug tried to follow the developments, and probably at some point had to stop in order to conclude *Socialøkonomik*. According to his colleague, Aarum, Aschehoug managed to understand the theory well and even had his independent explanation of it. As mentioned earlier, Thorstein Veblen found his article 'Værdi- og prislærens historie' very interesting, complementing its 'compact form and concise presentation, together with an easy and graceful touch and the absence of any attempt to follow the inquiry out exhaustively at any one point.'

It can only be speculated, as Veblen also states, how Aschehoug could have developed the theory further, had he lived longer. Veblen's praise may conclude this chapter: '[Aschehoug] shows such wide and intimate familiarity with the literature of the subject, and such sympathetic, and at the same time critical, appreciation of the many writers and points of view, as to leave the reader with a hearty regret that Professor Aschehoug has not chosen to deal more exhaustively with his subject.'[85]

Chapter 8

THE FRENCH INFLUENCE: ADOPTING SAY AND REFUTING SOCIALISM

The third and final international influence on Aschehoug to be analysed in this book, that of the French, will be the topic for this chapter. Even though the French influence on his economic thought was not central, it was nevertheless substantial. More than one hundred and thirty different French authors can be found in his author index. A brief re-examination of Aschehoug's own research position, which it is important to understand while reading *Socialøkonomik*, will be followed by a more thorough analysis of Aschehoug's work in order to outline how he used, and was influenced by, French economic, social and political thought. This chapter will show that he mostly found it useful for historical, philosophical and ideological purposes, and as a means to explain his own ideas. It is more often commented on in historical outlines rather than in concrete discussions of economic issues and definitions.

His first sources were from as far back as the eighteenth century, and his comments on the physiocrats and on Turgot will begin this analysis, continuing with the nineteenth century, and two different French traditions or schools of thought. The first is the well-known French liberal school, sometimes referred to as the 'Paris group'. This school is represented by economic thinkers such as Jean-Baptiste Say, Michel Chevalier, the two brothers Paul and Anatole Leroy-Beaulieu, Charles Dunoyer (1786–1862), Frédéric Bastiat, A. E. Cherbuliez, Maurice Block and Pierre Emile Levasseur (1828–1911). The other tradition is characterized by thinkers associated with socialism, who are not necessarily economists. Examples include papers written by Pierre Joseph (1809–1865), Henri de Saint-Simon (1760–1825), Louis Blanc (1811–1882) and Charles Gide (1847–1932).

This chapter will follow Aschehoug's own work and therefore start with the historical analysis he presents in his first volume, in which we find by far the greatest French influence and inspiration.

Aschehoug and Economics as a Historical Science

It is important to bear in mind that Aschehoug was also a historian, and this is reflected in his legal and economic works. But he was by no means only interested in history, as such. He wanted to base his knowledge and visions of the future on an understanding of history. His historical research was not conducted only to produce an outline of history.

Aschehoug also wanted to enlighten the knowledge and understanding of his own age by conducting a survey of historical circumstances. Aschehoug understood economics as both an empirical and a theoretical science. It was the interaction between theory and empirical studies that was important.[1] Both history and statistics became useful and important tools in his research.

He believed scientific results could be used as guidelines for practical decision making. Knowledge of the past was used for contemporary political decisions. He saw history as a science in which causes, connections and consequences could be revealed: 'Historical events create a huge coherent whole, so that one event has its causes in previous events.'[2] His belief in history as an ongoing process of development is clear: 'The development and progress of society bring about a deeper understanding and insight among its citizens and thereby increases their understanding of society's institutions.'[3] Aschehoug, being both a professor of law and of economics, was a clear proponent of the view that the degree of the rule of law in any given society is the measurement of that society's development.[4]

Later in life, Aschehoug's belief in the progress of history diminished. He had finished his political career in 1882 and had turned all his attention to scientific work. He had a deeply deterministic view of both his own individual life as well as of historical development. In *Stortingstidende* (vol. 29, 1880) he writes,

Most of us meet at the Storting with a developed view of politics. It is a result of many years of practice and considerations that have almost become a part of one's personality, and is therefore difficult to let go of. Nevertheless, a man's views may change, not by talks, but by viewing results and experiences, by new considerations, new observations brought about by historical events and developments. Only by this process will a man change his views, not by oratorical skills.[5]

Aschehoug's first chapter of *Socialøkonomik* discussed in Chapter 4 underlines his approach and views of economics as well as his use of history in his research. The first part, consisting of two chapters, is devoted to the term 'social economics'.[6] Already in these opening lines, Aschehoug brings in many different thinkers and perspectives. He outlines the whole of theoretical economic history and discusses different uses of the terms and definitions of key economic concepts. He points out the scope and goal of the economic discipline and states that it has throughout history been defined very differently.[7] One of the first French economists he refers to is Maurice Block and his *Progrès de la science économique* from 1890. In many respects this was an overall synthesis of economic thought, just like Aschehoug's own *Socialøkonomik*. To illustrate the differences, Aschehoug typically starts by quoting Smith's definition of economics as the 'theory of the wealth of nations, its nature and causes'.[8] He then broadens the definition by saying that Jean-Baptiste Say and later thinkers have defined economics as the theory of producing economic goods (production), circulation, distribution or repartition and consumption.[9]

Aschehoug's own position is clearly stated when he says that if one has a theoretical approach in the study of economics, and sticks to theory only, then economics become just that, 'only a theory'. It is important to Aschehoug to outline the tasks of economics, and he has a few interesting arguments concerning theoretical and practical approaches, incorporating the French debate about these issues.

> These issues have also been discussed in France, where a few authors have divided between economics as a theoretical and as a practical science (Corcelle-Seneuil, Cherbuliez, Maurice Block among them). But most French economists have viewed economics as both theoretical and practical, and by doing so their accounts and presentations are more interesting and relevant (Leroy-Beaulieu and Gide have written excellent examples which show how true this is).[10]

Aschehoug aligns this point with his conviction that 'Economic theorems that have never had or that can never have any practical use are empty thought experiments. The tasks of economics will always be practical.'[11] It is clear that Aschehoug wants to show that economics is much more complex than simply 'the mechanics of self-interest or utility or that economics is a mechanistic approach to economic equilibrium and movement', which Aschehoug believes is a Walrasian way of defining economics.[12] Economists gather information from statistics and mathematics, but also to a great extent from the 'psychological world'. This premise is clearly embraced throughout *Socialøkonomik*.

Aschehoug continues his first chapter with a discussion of the method, theory and system of economics, which reveals the same dichotomy as when he explains the inductive or empirical method and the deductive method (see Chapter 4). Most economists since Adam Smith have used both methods, but to different extents. Aschehoug himself adheres to historical research as well as to statistics in economic theory, referring to, among others, Leroy-Beaulieu's *Traité*. At the same time, he underlines the importance of the deductive method and mathematics in the development of economic theories, notably for the theory of value (see Chapter 7).

The Physiocrats, Quesnay and Turgot

Socialøkonomik is a brilliant example of how Aschehoug believes that economic theory should be understood and presented. His second chapter starts with economic history. He makes wide-ranging and thorough use of his sources, and presents and comments on historical facts. He starts with an outline of economic thought during antiquity and medieval times. Among the French historians and various intellectuals, he uses Levasseur (1828–1911), d'Avenel (1855–1939), Block (1816–1901), Cauwès (1843–1917) and Rambaud (1842–1905), as well as many British and German writers. He then continues with a presentation of mercantilism as an example, not of an economic theory, but of a practical, commercial political system.[13] The core of mercantilism lies in its balance of trade principles (i.e., that the global volume of international trade is unchangeable and that the prosperity of a nation is dependent upon its supply of capital).

Colbert developed the mercantilist system during his political career in the 1660s to the 1680s in France. Mercantilist thought had a long tradition in France, and Aschehoug recommended Fagniez's *L'économie sociale de la France sous Henri IV* and *Documents relatifs à l'histoire de l'industrie et du commerce en France* as brilliant presentations of French mercantilism. Colbert's economic policy was, according to Aschehoug, to 'strengthen the large industries and factories, even if this happened at the expense of smaller industries and crafts'.[14] Colbert's decrees on customs from 1664 and 1667 served as useful examples for many countries during the seventeenth century. Customs were high, and conditions and regulations for production were outlined in detail. Aschehoug does not say whether this made French industry successful, but he notes the substantial disagreement of later authors. According to Aschehoug, it is Levasseur that gives the most impartial and reasonable analysis of French mercantilism.[15] He then departs from the French influence and comments on the later mercantilist opposition.

Chapter 23 in Aschehoug's *Socialøkonomik*, 'The individual and the state', is important with respect to French influence and thought. This chapter outlines the public part of the legal system, meaning the organization of the state and its institutions and laws. As usual, Aschehoug provides a historical overview and refers to an impressive amount of literature. After going through different opinions of the purpose of the state, he sets forth his own views:

> The purpose and justification of the state lies in its ability to work for human society. [...] The purpose of the state cannot go further than its means permit. [...] But the question of how much influence the state should have, how large the authorities are, and which ends the state should serve, are still being discussed. This is of utmost importance for the practical relevance and importance of economics.[16]

By the time Aschehoug wrote *Socialøkonomik* he had been a member of the Norwegian parliament for more than thirteen years. Many of the comments and opinions that Aschehoug expresses in his *Socialøkonomik* clearly spring from his personal experience in practical politics and as a member of many commissions. Aschehoug states that the battle for freedom of the individual from the regency of the state had taken a long time in many countries, and that economic freedom has to be prepared politically. Before the French revolution political and economic freedom went hand in hand. Ten years before Quesnay wrote his thesis, Montesquieu had claimed political freedom in his *L'esprit des lois* (1748), but Aschehoug says that he didn't consider economic freedom and characterized him almost as a mercantilist. He further points out that reforming public administration was not one of the goals of the physiocrats, and that they 'supported absolute monarchy and hoped by their "wise advice" to move the king in favour of economic freedom'.[17] The French Revolution turned all this upside down, and Aschehoug claims that the basic ideas for the revolution can be found in Rousseau's texts, especially in *Le contrat social*. The author Benjamin Constant defended the constitutional system in France after the Napoleonic restructuring of the state. After the establishment of the new constitution, Toqueville published his famous texts about the development of modern democracy in 1830. Aschehoug comments that: 'Both these outstanding authors [Turgot and Constant] didn't like the public interference in private, individual freedom. Firstly Toqueville developed how and why the modern democracy is unavoidable, and secondly what dangers it may give rise to, and finally what measures can be taken to restrain the downsides.'[18]

The French influence continues in Aschehoug's discussion of the physiocrats, a French economic school of thought developed during the eighteenth century. The mercantilist system had heavily diminished economic freedom of action, and Aschehoug thought that it had created more damage than gain. The opposition to mercantilism started just after 1700, described by Aschehoug as an 'intellectual revolt, first economic and later political'.[19] In his own words:

> It started in 1706 with Vauban's critique of the tax system (*Dîme royale*), which was picked up by Boisguillebert, who in his *Détail de la France* (1707) demanded freedom of trade and industry. But enduring influence on public opinion came later with the physiocratic school of thought, founded by the doctor Quesnay, whose writings came out between 1756–1768.[20]

Ronald Meek defines the main line of physiocratic thought in his book *The Economics of Physiocracy*: 'Wealth is the fruit which comes from the land for the use of men; the labour of man alone possesses the capacity to increase wealth. Thus the more men there are, the more labour there will be; the more labour there is, the more wealth there will be.'[21] This is in line with Aschehoug's own definition. Aschehoug further points out that the physiocratic school developed in two directions; Quesnay belonging to one, Turgot and Gournay to another. The physiocratic school of thought had both a juridical-philosophical and an economic side. Its legal thought was based on natural law inspired by Grotius, Hobbes and Locke. Its principal thought was that 'all human beings were subjects of law. And this was the innermost thought of the system.'[22] The state could, through its legal system, reduce the freedom of action of every individual human being and also impose obligations. But these obligations could only be real through a voluntary agreement, the so-called commonwealth.

Quesnay was an opponent of both mercantilism and of the French central state policy.[23] Aschehoug describes his point of view in this manner: 'People, he says, are subject to a double legal system, the natural and the positive. The natural laws are deduced by human reason, its nature and its plan. These laws are the most useful for human co-existence. The only purpose of positive law is to ensure natural law.'[24] Quesnay adhered to the idea of the legitimate, enlightened, absolute monarchy based on the Hobbesian commonwealth. The social contract was not agreed without securing natural rights – first and foremost individual freedom.

The main economic influence of the physiocrats came through their views on agriculture and this sector's importance in the economic system. For Aschehoug, this was the most peculiar part of their theory. The importance of the production of raw material afforded agriculture a dominant position in the economy. On the other side, the French mercantilists had underrated agriculture, and Aschehoug sees the physiocratic's overrating as a natural reaction.[25] The theory of agriculture was the core of physiocracy, just as the balance of trade was the core of mercantilism. The physiocrats thought that agriculture, fishing and mining were the chief activities that produced wealth, while trade and industry were unproductive. Industry was important, but had only a secondary position in the economy. The physiocrats believed that if the farmer owned his land, he could keep the surplus of his production. Agricultural production would provide – *un produit net* – but this would not be the case for industry and trade. Therefore, industry and trade could not increase the wealth of society.

In his chapter about wages, Aschehoug gives an account of how they are determined, and he starts with a historical account of how wages were introduced and decided.[26] Beginning with the physiocrats, he claims that wages had their origin in the physiocratic theory of production. The physiocrats claimed that agriculture and other raw material production gave a net surplus, while only industry and trade could replace their production costs.[27] On Turgot's theory Aschehoug writes,

> Turgot seemed to me the first who tried to create a concept of the distribution of society's surplus production. As a physiocrat, he naturally thought that wages and interest on capital could not exceed a natural low level, and he based this on his practical experience as well. It was well known that interest on capital had diminished, and Turgot thought that it could not rise higher than to encourage a sufficient level of saving.[28]

In Turgot's age, wages were low in France, but probably sufficient to sustain a minimum standard of life. According to Turgot, a rise in wages was inhibited by the harsh competition between workers. Aschehoug points out that this theory of wages disappears when Adam Smith introduces his theory.

The physiocrats divided society into three classes: landowners, peasants and all others. The peasants were the productive class and consequently supporting the two other classes. The others (e.g., traders, craftsmen, workers, etc.) were sterile in the sense of being nonproductive. Since the landowners ultimately gained the surplus of the agricultural production, the physiocrats proposed a direct tax – *un impôt unique*. Even though Aschehoug finds the theoretical foundations curiously weak, he nevertheless points out that the physiocrats were the first to treat society's economy in a scientific manner. Both as an economist and as a professor of law, he thinks that the physiocrats' contribution was crucial to later economic thought. He writes, 'They brought economics into contact with the legal system. This had a great and permanent influence on both disciplines.'[29] The physiocrats wanted to reduce the power of the state. According to them, the main purpose of the state should be to protect the country against internal and external threats and protect the land and property of the inhabitants. Everyone should care for their own well-being, and this should be reflected in the economic law system.

Aschehoug attributes the famous saying 'laissez faire, laissez passer' to the physiocrats. It had for a long time been credited to Gournay, but the influence of the physiocrat Turgot is palpable.[30] Gournay, as well as Turgot, wanted full economic liberty and competition, meaning freedom of trade and the demolition of guilds and monopolies. As a consequence of this postulate, Louis XVI dismissed Turgot as an economic advisor.[31] The main lesson Aschehoug draws from the physiocrats is their introduction of an economic theory in which the legal system and economy are viewed together. He also sees the physiocrats as the forerunners of liberal economic thought, even though he doesn't adhere to their production and creation of wealth principles.

Positivism and Comte

Before looking at the French liberal school that constituted most of the French influence on Aschehoug's thoughts, his comments on positivism and what Aschehoug calls the 'ethical direction', which mostly concerns Sismondi, will be discussed. Aschehoug sees the positivists as a real French historical school.[32] Auguste Comte was the founder of French positivism, and he published his main work, *Cours de philosophie positive*, between 1830 and 1842.[33] His main philosophical thesis is based on mechanical physics, in which descriptions and explanations of causes, the establishment of hypotheses from observations, and lastly a verification of them by experimentation are the ideals. Comte built his whole system on these kinds of physical laws. He transferred the ideals of the natural sciences and physics to human society.[34] He called his science 'sociology' and it covered all human activity, not only economic.[35] Society is the core of Comte's teachings, not the individual.[36] The basis of sociology can be found in both human biological nature and in historical conditions. Comte divided society into a static and a dynamic part. The static part was described through historical experience, while the dynamic part examines laws of changes in society, and thereby tries to understand and describe the development and evolution of society.

Comte's maxim 'Science, d'où prévoyance; prévoyance, d'où action' might serve as a motto – science being the key word, as opposed to philosophy – and one is reminded of the German philosophy article by Schweigaard discussed in Chapter 3. By the *fin de siècle* a reaction against positivism had set in, creating a sceptical environment reminiscent of the more pragmatic Aschehoug. The turn to concrete facts, statistics and empirical knowledge is also embedded in the ideas of realism, growing stronger as the century proceeded. The second half of the century bore the idea of evolution: 'A dynamic positivism has displaced the older static positivism', as the French philosopher Alfred Fouillé said in 1896.[37] But, importantly, positivism was still hanging around by the *fin de siècle*, and this was the still the case very near to its flood tide. Many thinkers, among them Aschehoug, still expressed confidence in reason as a means to achieve progress. But it was also a moment of uncertainty, of unprecedented openness, as Aschehoug expresses in the last chapter: 'The doubt about the economic future of humanity is in the raw material production. It is a possibility that it will become insufficient to cover the need. [...] It might be easier facilitated by new technical inventions [...], but if one could hope for such inventions, it could not be foreseen with certainty.'[38] As Baumer states,

> Human nature simultaneously began to look less rational, knowledge more subjective and elusive, and history less predictable and understandable. The overall trend in thinking toward a more chancy universe, subject to change without end or ends. It was a trend only, but it was a trend with a future. To repeat, the *fin de siècle* represented neither a unified nor a dominant mode of thought. It remained closely within the larger world, still potent, of Enlightenment expectation.[39]

I believe this pinpoints the position of Aschehoug, coinciding with his own path of life, from an optimistic youth, believing in progress, and gradually growing and developing his thoughts along with the century, until the *fin de siècle*, and his own termination, both literally and professionally.

Aschehoug points out the similarities of the German historical school and Comte's description of human development. Comte described human development as a dialectic exchange between the egoistic, self-interested human drives and the altruistic, sympathetic drives. He claimed that social development was caused by a refinement of the human intellect, and that altruism outweighed egoism. Aschehoug quotes Comte in French, describing how reform happens through the development of human opinion, followed by morality and finally the institutionalization of this morality in society.[40] Aschehoug devotes serious attention to Comte's thought, and he also compares positivism and Hegelianism, observing that was Hegelianism based on abstract thought, while positivism was based on concrete facts. Yet Aschehoug still sees similarities in the fact that both afford greater value to the society than to the individual, and that both doctrines have an optimistic view in seeing development as progress. Reviewing Aschehoug's comments it's clear that he has a thorough knowledge of philosophic theory. He points out that Comte soon gained adherents in a small circle of 'outstanding thinkers', both in France (Littré) and in England (John Stuart Mill), but that the general dissemination of his thoughts were due to Charles Darwin.[41]

Economics held its position as a separate science in spite of Comte's sociology. Yet Aschehoug valued several aspects of Comte's thought: 'It is due to Comte that attention was drawn to the different connections between sciences concerning different aspects of society. This has contributed to a greater attention to studying similar sciences while studying, for instance economy, law or history.'[42]

After Comte, sociology developed in several directions, among them an evolutionary biological direction in which the goal was to build on the notion that society was an organism. Fouillé is mentioned as a French representative that wanted to build a sociological system on a biological basis. He saw society as an organism, but at the same time admitted that society was created by human will – what he called a contractual organism. Aschehoug followed sociological thought and writings all through his life, and concludes by saying, 'Sociology had not yet brought great benefits to economics, which could not be expected of this relatively new science. The benefit of the sociological school lies in the publishing of interesting articles in their reviews.'[43] This demonstrates Aschehoug's interest, but also shows that sociology as a discipline had not yet become important. What he does not say is that sociology was embedded in his own thought, and to Aschehoug it was probably unnatural to separate sociology and economics.

The Ethical School in French Thought

The ethical school in French thought mostly involves Sismondi. Aschehoug had during his career been a participant in several public commissions in which the relationship between economy and ethics was central, among them the Poverty Commission and the Smallholder Commission.[44] While working in these, Aschehoug was able to test out scientific theories and their practical application. Aschehoug takes the scientific position when writing *Socialøkonomik*. He accounts for the establishment of the division of ethics and economics at the time of the works of Adam Smith. He mentions three possibilities for thoughts about improvements for all (including industrial workers). The first is the improvement of working conditions based on the law and structure of the current society, the next is a swift change to conditions in society (the ideal of socialism), and lastly the socialists of the chair (*Kathedersozialisten*) who didn't wish to change society by revolution but by evolution. Aschehoug puts Sismondi in the first category, and describes him as a particularly interesting thinker, especially as a historian, giving a thorough and updated analysis of Sismondi's thought.

As an economist, Sismondi was affiliated with the classical school, but he broke off this affiliation when he published his main work *Nouveaux principes d'économie politique* (1819).[45] Aschehoug formulated Sismondi's philosophical question to the classical school like this: 'How can it be that wealth is all and humans absolutely nothing?'[46] The question expresses Sismondi's central thesis that wealth is just a means, whereas humans are an end. Sismondi insisted that economic science studied how to increase wealth too much and how to use that wealth to create happiness too little. Aschehoug also comments on Sismondi's theory of economic cycles, especially his thoughts on the conditions for workers and for small entrepreneurs. Sismondi objected to an economic theory that was based on laissez-faire, and he wanted the state to interfere and compensate for the negative aspects of free competition (especially for the workers). It was important to take care of the workers who became ill or unable to work. In this case, Sismondi was a forerunner for the aforementioned German socialists of the chair.[47] Aschehoug faced similar questions in his work for the Poverty Commission. Aschehoug displays his in-depth knowledge when describing the development and the often poor conditions for workers and small entrepreneurs. Neither Sismondi nor Aschehoug wanted to change society dramatically, and they both saw that property rights and the necessity of interest on capital were important principles, even though Aschehoug claims that this is in conflict with Sismondi's basic thoughts. He also says that Sismondi mistakenly followed Smith by assuming that work is the only source of wealth. Since Sismondi didn't deal with the consequences of this, Aschehoug states that Sismondi was not a socialist. It is clear that Aschehoug was interested in Sismondi's teachings, and he claims that Sismondi 'increased awareness of the fact that something was wrong in the relationship between ethics and economics, the latter clearly closed its eyes to the former'.[48]

The French Liberal School

Aschehoug was inspired by the French liberal school in many cases, but before reviewing this, a brief mention of the transition from the physiocrats will be made. Adam Smith is naturally central to the classical school of economic thought. Yet Aschehoug uses references and arguments from French thinkers, even though the production theory of the physiocrats was pushed aside by Adam Smith fairly quickly. Aschehoug doesn't ascribe this to a critique of the physiocrats, but to the fact that Adam Smith's theories were superior. As already mentioned, Aschehoug points out that Smith's theories had similarities to Turgot's, but as a result of the discovery of Smith's *Lectures* it was proven that the two developed their thoughts in parallel. The physiocrats also influenced Smith, but he especially denounced the basic physiocratic thought about the wealth of a society only deriving from agricultural and other raw material production. In other cases, he approved of their principles, notably: 'The introduction of complete justice, complete freedom and complete equality is the easiest way to ensure wealth and prosperity for all classes in society.'[49]

Aschehoug sees many of the French thinkers and economists in the French liberal school as followers of Adam Smith. Among them we find Say and Bastiat, but also others like Chevalier, Cherbuliez, Courcelle-Seneuil, Leroy-Beaulieu and Block. The last part of Volume I of *Socialøkonomik* is called 'Economic activity seen as a whole'. This title also underlines Aschehoug's thought. When defining the term economic goods, he starts with the etymology and points out the differences in French, German and English. About the French concepts he says, 'The French language has the words *richesses* or *biens*, the last one similar to our "economic goods [*økonomiske goder*]". By *biens* it is assumed that the described things are assets, and thereby a few authors have been inclined to use this term, nevertheless the term *richesses* is still the most common.'[50]

For instance, Say thought that immaterial services were economic goods, and for a long time this view was held by followers such as Block, Leroy-Beaulieu and Gide. This kind of analysis of concepts shows that Aschehoug's knowledge was both broad and deep, and that he was able to employ his insight even with respect to small details and nuances.

Before commenting on Aschehoug and Say, a brief review Aschehoug's use of French liberal thought in terms of the relationship between the individual and economics will be included. He observes that Say had the same modest views as Adam Smith concerning the role of the state in relation to private economic affairs. He points out that successful British free trade hugely influenced French theoretical thought. One could say that individual freedom was a principle no one contested in economic thought. The most extreme representatives for this individualism in France were Charles Dunoyer (*Liberté de travail*, 1835), Joseph Garnier (*Traité d'économie politique*, 1860) and, above all, Frédéric Bastiat (*Harmonies économique*, 1850). Aschehoug compares these thinkers to the British liberal equivalent, the Manchester School, which had been criticized by the German 'socialists of the chair' (*Katheder Sozialisten*). What made the French liberals so eager to maintain individual economic freedom was, according to Aschehoug, probably fear of the socialist goal of putting all economic activity under state control. Aschehoug himself doesn't seem so afraid of this fifty years after the February Revolution of France, and he finishes by saying that this fear did not have much practical or political influence.[51] He also states that France is a country that sticks to the principles of individualism and economic freedom. He observes that a few outstanding authors, such as Molinari and Guyot, were hostile to all public interference in economic activity unless it is necessary to prevent a violation of the freedom of other individuals.[52] According to Aschehoug, more recent French thinkers of the time adopt a more moderate position, but are generally negative towards public interference. Among them we find not only economists like Leroy-Beaulieu, Block and Colson, but also philosophers in the jurisprudence tradition like Beudant, Boistel and Henri Michel. But France has changed as well, Aschehoug remarks. By the end of the nineteenth century, French economic policy was to promote the interests of the society at the expense of individual interests and freedom, and he refers to the introduction of a strongly protectionist customs system, as well as other restrictions in working conditions, and other humanitarian interests.[53]

Jean-Baptiste Say's ideas in *Traité d'économie politique* (1803), and later in *Cours complet d'économie politique pratique* (1828–29), in which Say further developed his economic thought, are characterized by Aschehoug as especially elegant and clear presentations. Aschehoug is therefore much more positive towards Say than many of his contemporaries, who tended to overlook him. Aschehoug generally thought Say was more positive in his basic view of economics than thinkers like Ricardo and Malthus. Aschehoug comments that German economists often disregarded Say, but that John Stuart Mill, for instance, called him 'a clear thinker and skilful expositor'.[54] The influence of Say on Norwegian economic thought is well documented in an article by Ib E. Eriksen and Arild Sæther about the entrepreneur, and in Sæther's 'Jean-Baptiste Say's Influence in Norway'.[55]

Aschehoug points out that Say was able to present a coherent vision of economics and that his theoretical contribution was substantial, including his concept of economic goods.[56] Say claimed that economic goods should include immaterial work, and he also made an important division between capitalists and entrepreneurs. Moreover, Say pointed out the importance of utility for the concept of value. Say correctly noted that the value of goods and services is ultimately determined by utility. If there is no demand or need, it does not matter how much labour one has put into it, the value will not increase.

When Aschehoug comments on the historical school, he mostly focuses on jurisprudence and philosophy. Since the historical school had its centre of gravity in Germany, not many French thinkers are discussed. All the same, he makes a point concerning Say's lack of historical insight: 'Say obviously lacked a sense of history. He didn't appreciate Smith's historical analysis and research, and he dismissed a defence of older ideas by saying that they were no longer relevant.'[57] Even though Aschehoug observes that Say makes a distinction between the theory and the practice of economics, and that he admits to the relevance of historical knowledge for practical economics, Aschehoug still thinks that historical knowledge is relevant and essential to the theory of economics. In his discussion throughout Chapter 8, Aschehoug makes this point repeatedly. He also notes that there were deep discrepancies between the German historical school and the French liberal school. Aschehoug concludes that history doesn't interest the French liberals, while the French positivists were deeply interested in this area.[58]

In the second volume of *Socialøkonomik*, Aschehoug presents the different definitions of national wealth and national income. He points out the discrepancies in how they are defined using Smith/Ricardo and Say as examples of two different, extreme definitions. Say stated that the national net income was equal to the national gross income, but Aschehoug corrects both the Smith/Ricardo and the Say definitions by saying that the national net income is the national gross income less the value of raw materials used in the production and usage of fixed capital, such as machinery and what he calls 'basic property' (*grunneiendommer*). He further states that private economic activity must also be included in national income, a view he shares with other contemporary economists.[59]

The next section deals with production and acquisition. Aschehoug asks what the term production involves. He uses Say's definitions to illustrate different questions such as: What is being produced? Are the products useful (meaning that the production is useful)? Is it enough to say that the product is useful, or must it also be valuable? The answer is that it is value that is being produced, an answer acclaimed by many authors. Already at the beginning of the nineteenth century, Say had mentioned all the different aspects that Aschehoug presents. In his *Traité*, Say writes, 'La production est une création d'utilité' (production is to create utility). In the same work he also writes that 'produire, c'est donner de la valeur à une chose' (production is to give value to something), which he quickly explains in detail: 'La valeur qui en resulte n'est que la mesure de cette utilité' (the value that is created is then a measure of the utility). Later in the French liberal tradition both Bastiat and Leroy-Beaulieu claimed that economic activity created value.[60]

Say was the first to make an important distinction concerning entrepreneurs (*driftsherrer*), which was important to Aschehoug. In his *Traité*, Say differentiates between entrepreneurs and capitalists, and Aschehoug points out that this was long before this distinction gained a foothold in English literature. The distinction is important. Say understood the entrepreneur as someone who ran an economic activity at one's own expense. The owner of the activity was then directly influenced by both gains and losses. Aschehoug claims that Say used the term 'entrepreneur' in its widest sense, because everybody working at one's own expense was considered an entrepreneur. Their income was partly a direct salary and partly an entrepreneurial gain.[61] A further discussion of the importance of the entrepreneurs to Aschehoug is discussed in Chapter 10.

Volume III of *Socialøkonomik* begins with few references to French thought, and the references are mostly made when it comes to the definition of different terms and statistical information.[62] One example of French influence is found in Chapter 75, concerning the exchange value of money. Aschehoug says in § 14. 'J.-B. Say has in a famous chapter of his *Traité* called attention to the fact that all trade is really barter trade, even though it involves money.'[63] Say's logic is as follows: a sellable object is sold; either it's a thing, a service or a right, and only with the income is it possible to acquire other useful objects for oneself. Any income is quickly turned into a new purchase price; therefore money is just a facilitator in this barter. It is sufficient that the seller gets enough money to afford what he needs. Say's reasoning is accumulated and generalized for the demand and supply in society as a whole. A society's general demand equals the society's general supply. Aschehoug comments on Say's reasoning by saying that the argument is weak, and he points out that it is not certain that the supply and the demand are equal – the supply can be greater than the demand and vice versa.

Furthermore, Aschehoug comments on trade policies and includes a few French references, among them Colson's *Cours d'économie politique* (1903), one of the most recent French commentaries on trade policy at the time. Aschehoug states that Colson follows a long French tradition and defends free trade, and Aschehoug himself sees the contemporary discussions about foreign trade as ferocious.[64] In paragraph 2 Aschehoug writes, 'It seems like the idea of free trade should in the end win in the civilized world's trade policy with its promise of great advantages both for world peace and prosperity.'[65] But the promise and free trade progress was short lived, as Aschehoug subsequently explains, using the US and Russia as examples of protectionist behaviour in international trade. He also points out that continental Europe, Germany and France had changed their trade policy to be more protectionist. A couple of French voices in this debate are mentioned, namely Thiers and De Broglie. Aschehoug himself doesn't applaud the protectionist wave and comments that several statistics have shown a decrease in growth.[66] These issues are discussed in further detail in Chapter 11.

When Aschehoug deals with questions about different forms of economic revenue, both capital revenue and income, he also discusses misunderstandings between capital revenues and entrepreneurial revenue and income (*driftsherreinntekt* and *driftsherregevinst*). Aschehoug divides society's net income as follows: ground rent (*grunnrente*), interest on capital or revenue, income and entrepreneurial rent and income. The French influence is seen mostly through Say, but also through more recent writers like Leroy-Beaulieu and Gide, as well as Garnier and Courcelle-Seneuil, who thought that entrepreneurial income was mostly a payment for work.[67] As usual, Aschehoug shows a thorough historical knowledge about the evolution of interest on capital. The justification of interest on capital has been discussed since antiquity, and Aschehoug finds various religious, linguistic, political and economic explanations for it. The debate about interest was not concluded with Adam Smith, it reappeared when the socialists entered the stage in the mid-nineteenth century. As a curiosity, he mentions in a footnote the socialist Proudhon's belief that interest on capital could be abolished by removing money and establishing banks that exchange products according to an estimated value, and where customers could have interest-free loans. Aschehoug dismisses this theory as 'naturally wrong'.[68]

Aschehoug also attacks the socialists' scientific thoughts about interest on capital. It is clear that he strongly disagrees with them, something that is quite unusual throughout *Socialøkonomik*. He goes on to explain the fairly recent theories of Senior, Böhm-Bawerk and Marshall, and notes that the French liberalist Bastiat follows Senior, who wrote that the productivity of work was dependent on a sufficient supply of capital.

Frédéric Bastiat was one of the protagonists of the French liberal school. His controversial pamphlets and writings from the mid-nineteenth century against customs protection and socialism gained a lot of attention. His main work *Les harmonies économiques* came in 1850. Bastiat argued that the development of society leads to economic prosperity and welfare. He also thought that individual interests were in harmony with the interests of society, which Aschehoug explains with Bastiat's 'concept of value'.[69] Bastiat also fought for free trade, and he believed that the state should not interfere with the economic liberty of individuals. Aschehoug was clearly positive towards Bastiat and his way of thinking during the 1850s.[70]

Aschehoug quotes a passage from Bastiat's *Harmonies économiques* about interest on capital and adds that several later French economists like Levasseur and Cauwès followed Bastiat's views:

All in all Bastiat followed Senior and found, like him, that accumulation of capital is a sacrifice (privation) or at least a delay of the immediate utility the consumption of the capital good could give. But Bastiat argued more strongly than Senior that the capitalists' use of the capital good in production would increase the value of the capital good. His idea was that by providing capital for use in production for consumption, the capitalists served the entrepreneurs as well as the consumers. This service would oblige a return service, which means that the capitalist would have a legitimate claim for interest on capital.[71]

When it comes to the rate of interest on capital (*rentefoden*) Aschehoug uses Leroy-Beaulieu's views from his *Répartition des richesses*. Whether society would benefit from high or low interest on capital is an old question of debate. Leroy-Beaulieu had presumed that a decrease in the interest on capital would lead to a certain equalization of the economic conditions of the different social classes. A low interest on capital would make it more difficult to acquire and possess huge fortunes, and even the middle class would not be able to live on interest on capital alone. Aschehoug says that this train of thought 'has some truth in it, but there are certain claims to be analysed'.[72] Aschehoug demonstrates with some practical examples; for example, he states that the interest on capital in France is still not allowed to be higher than 5 per cent, and that Cauwès defends this practice. Say had also written in his *Traité* about the historically low rate of interest around 1812, and that it was thought that a low rate of interest would produce general welfare, whereas the situation in 1812 was the opposite. It was not until 1815 that interest on capital mirrored economic performance and rose and fell with economic activity throughout the nineteenth century.

Aschehoug also comments briefly on labour income. He states that any contract or agreement for paid work is commerce. He continues and says that several authors have touched on the thought that the worker is really a co-owner of what is being produced through the labour income, and ultimately the owner of the product or service that the labour has produced. By transferring the part of the product he has produced to the employer, the labourer is in fact the real owner of the product. Aschehoug finds traces of this in Say's works, and naturally in the works of Proudhon, but more surprisingly also in the work of the liberal thinker Leroy-Beaulieu. Leroy-Beaulieu claims in his *Traité* that the 'lease of work' is a kind of 'association à forfait', which indicates an agreement to purchase the product being produced. This is all wrong according to Aschehoug. There is no transfer of property rights. The working contract is voluntary and both parties must have an understanding of the mutual benefits in the agreement, or they would forget it.[73]

In the two last parts of volume 4 Aschehoug reviews the use of economic goods. He looks into consumption and concludes that, even though the mercantilists and physiocrats were concerned with this question, generally earlier theories had not sufficiently considered it, and Adam Smith mostly considered production. This has changed. The first to consider consumption separately is Say in his two works *Traité* and *Cours complet*. Aschehoug points out that this was necessary because Say was looking into the taxation of consumption.[74] There are few references to French thought later on in the chapter, but when it comes to luxury, Aschehoug comments on the French writings of the Belgian Laveleye (1822–1892), who claimed that luxury consumption was despicable and useless, and also required great production capacity. Later research, including by Leroy-Beaulieu, is not as hostile. Aschehoug thinks that luxury consumption must be considered historically. He mentions the well-known protests from Rousseau and the equally well-known supporters Voltaire and Hume. The discussions could easily become moralistic, but Aschehoug turns away from this train of thought and analyses what considerations should be made concerning the necessity of the consumption of luxury goods and whether it is useful or not to produce them following Leroy-Beaulieu and Roscher's works.[75] Even though he claims not to consider the subject of luxury philosophically, his concerns with respect to this show his analysis is more than just a strict economic analysis. Aschehoug is clearly concerned about moral questions, but he is realistic and doesn't want to abolish luxury as such.[76]

Aschehoug is most clearly influenced by Jean-Baptiste Say. The other French liberals are mentioned and used to underline points, but when it comes to theoretical discussions, it is Say's position that is most commonly appealed to and discussed.

Aschehoug and His Comments on French Socialism

Aschehoug gives much space to the socialist tradition. Naturally, he explains and comments on the thoughts of Marx, but there are also references to French socialists. The most important figures of French socialism are Henri de Saint-Simon, Charles Fourier (1772–1837), Louis Blanc and Pierre-Joseph Proudhon, the latter two having had most influence on the socialist sciences in France. Aschehoug starts with a brief summary of different socialist projects, some of which are utopian. Socialist thought has a long tradition in France, and Aschehoug draws the line back to Rousseau: 'The seeds in the literature are found in Rousseau's works. [...] He argued against all unequal distribution of wealth and thereby prepared the mind for socialistic ideals.'[77] Aschehoug further claims that theories against the old regime were first established and gained a foothold in France.

According to Aschehoug, Saint-Simon was the first important socialist in France. His main principle was to concentrate all power (including economic) in the state. The wealth created by economic activity was to be distributed by public authorities. Aschehoug quotes the Saint- Simon manifesto, but comments that no references are made to how the hierarchy should be composed or who should have the responsibility or be employed.[78] Gerschenkron has a few interesting observations about the influence of Saint-Simon on economics, some are found in the thought of Schweigaard. It could be argued that Saint-Simon was in reality far from being a socialist; that in his vision of an industrial society he hardly distinguished between labourers and employers; and that he considered the appropriate political form for his society of the future to be some kind of corporate state in which the 'leaders of industry' would exercise major political functions. But, as Gerschenkron adds, the Saint-Simonian doctrines incorporated a good many socialist ideas, including the abolition of inheritance and establishment of a system of planned economy designed to direct and to develop the economy of a country.[79] Saint-Simon is often labelled as a utopian socialist, wanting to abolish private property rights and to organize society into cooperatives. Nevertheless, Saint-Simon stressed industrialization and the role of the banks as instruments for the organization and development of the economy. The question is then as follows: why was the socialist garment draped around an essentially capitalist idea, and in France adopted by the most successful capitalist entrepreneurs? Gerschenkron points out the friendship between Saint-Simon and J.-B. Say, saying that Saint-Simon was never adverse to the ideas of laissez-faire policies, and that another follower, Michel Chevalier (1806–1879), was the co-author of the famous Franco-English Treaty of Commerce from 1860. The French problem was that the ideologies of laissez-faire did not fit a 'spiritual vehicle of an industrialization program'.[80] The Saint-Simonian faith in a golden age lying ahead of mankind appealed to even the most daring and innovative entrepreneur, even more than a general belief in mere profits.

The general ideas of Saint-Simon were continued in France by others including Cabet, Considérant, Fourier (considered a genius by some and a lunatic by others, according to Aschehoug), Proudhon (a brilliant dialectic, but devoid of all practical sense) and Louis Blanc (a socialist leader, wrongly accused of responsibility for the failure to establish national factories).[81] Blanc also wanted to centralize all property rights relating to physical machinery in a gradual process, and in 1839 he published his famous article 'L'organisation du travail'. In this article Blanc outlines the principles that would later become the foundation of his political career. The article focuses on working conditions in which competition makes the weakest the losers. He demanded an equalization of salaries and that each person should receive according to their needs and give according to their capabilities ('à chacun selon ses besoins, de chacun selon ses facultés').

Aschehoug continues his analysis by reviewing the ideas of Karl Marx, which naturally form an important part of the socialist ideas that became popular in the mid-1840s and 1850s. Erik Reinert has referred to 1848 as a turning point – 'the 1848 moment' – which may underline Amundsen's remark:

> 1848 produced three important books all critical of the economic order legitimised by Ricardian economics: Karl Marx and Friedrich Engels' *Communist Manifesto* (Marx was so radical that he was forced to flee Germany for England), Bruno Hildebrand's *National Economics in the Present and in the Future* (Hildebrand was a liberal who had to flee Germany for Switzerland in order to escape the death penalty), and John Stuart Mill's *Principles of Political Economy*. From completely different political angles, all three books attacked the mainstream economics of the day for suffering from the same weaknesses of which we [Reinert's argument] accuse today's mainstream. By attempting to make economics a much more accurate science than it merits, mainstream economics has created economic disasters: both financial crisis and poverty in the periphery. All three 1848 books understood that national wealth required industrialisation.[82]

Jules Guesde (1845–1922) later became a follower of Marx. He belonged to an association that was called the 'possibilists', because they only wanted to implement reforms that were possible in the current society. Of the more recent French socialistic thinkers, Aschehoug mentions Benoit Malon (1841–1893), who published *Le socialisme intégral* (1891). Malon states that the socialist goal is that not only land, but also all means of production should be either owned by the state or under state control. Aschehoug sees Malon's proposal of how this should be implemented as the most interesting part of his theory. Malon drew attention to the cooperatives and the workers unions as a means of educating the masses and teaching them how to control their leaders, both in economic and political matters. He proposed that a ministry of work should be established and given the job of finding industries that could be taken over by the state, and also be in charge of the industries and activities that would be owned by the state. Malon also wanted high taxation of what he called 'stock games'. He wanted to forbid the establishment of shareholder companies and the issuing of private bearer bonds. Furthermore he wanted to nationalize the French bank, and make the state take responsibility for all kinds of insurance business, railways, mines, machinery workshops and so forth. Malon also accredited an important role to the municipalities in this socialist society. Without agreeing to the socialistic ideas, Aschehoug was clearly positive towards Malon, seeing him as a socialistic theorist who had presented a plan for implementation.

Two other socialist thinkers are used by Aschehoug, mainly through references to their works: Christian Gide and his *Principes d'économie politique* and Paul Cauwès with his *Cours d'économie politique*, both published in 1893. Aschehoug clearly has knowledge of their texts, and they are used all the way through Volume I of *Socialøkonomik*, especially to illustrate historical information. They are often used together with two liberal thinkers, Anatole Leroy-Beaulieu and Maurice Block, to demonstrate differences between socialistic and liberal views. Even though the brother of Anatole, Pierre Paul, was an economist (who after 1880 followed his father-in-law, Michel Chevalier, as the leader of the economy chair in the Collège de France), Aschehoug mostly uses Anatole as a historian. Nevertheless, Aschehoug is generally critical of French socialist thought. His main objections are that he is unsure about whether socialism would procure all the wealth and prosperity it claims it would, and how such a system would be implemented. The socialist project is 'an impractical thought' for Aschehoug.[83]

When Aschehoug comments on property rights he maintains that this is one of the most controversial principles in society.[84] Aschehoug's view is clearly exhibited in all the references he uses. Among the French economic thinkers we find Thiers, Gide, Cauwès, Leroy-Beaulieu and Boistel. Aschehoug presents himself as a neutral voice in this debate by giving the views of all the different economic schools of thought. Only after commenting on Proudhon's views does he state that he has now reviewed all the different views concerning property rights and, although some thinkers will abandon this principle, Aschehoug feels confident that property rights is a viable principle.[85] And as the example of Proudhon will show, Aschehoug reviews a wide variety of arguments before his own views are expressed.

Generally, Aschehoug is somewhat sceptical about the changes to the current social order the socialists want, especially with respect to the practical possibility of implementation. He reveals his scepticism when reviewing the ideas of the extreme socialist, the first leader of the anarchist movement, Pierre-Joseph Proudhon. Proudhon was the first declared anarchist in France. In 1840, he published a small pamphlet named *What is Property?* (*Qu'est-ce que la propriété?*), and he answered that property was theft ('La propriété c'est le vol'). The pamphlet contains sharp criticism of the existing social order, especially the unfair position of workers. Proudhon identifies three sources of authority in the modern society: the state, the church and the capital. He was a determined opponent of all three. Aschehoug is naturally sceptical, but he credits Proudhon for his intellectual creativity and originality of thought, but not his attempt to create a new society: 'It cannot be denied that Proudhon came up with many new and interesting thoughts, or that he explained old thoughts in a new fashion. But when he started to explain how economic activity should be organized voluntarily, meaning without support from the state and its authority to enforce law and order to secure the supply for the needs of society, it all went wrong.'[86]

Aschehoug further sums up by saying that 'Proudhon finally realized that the ideals of anarchism were utopian, and that the only realistic way was to establish a "federation", meaning cooperation between autonomous local municipalities'.[87] In the words of Proudhon, private property constituted theft. Employing a revised version of the old labour theory of value, Proudhon argued that land, precisely because it was not produced by labour, should revert to the community. In modern industry, on the other hand, everything was produced by the labour of all; hence industry, too, belonged to the whole body of labourers.

Concrete French economic theories are not discussed in detail in Volume II of *Socialøkonomik*, but Aschehoug continues to use statistical sources and examples of theories to illustrate his points. As an illustration, we again find Proudhon and his theory of 'value antonymy' in Chapter 39, 'Task and results of the economy'.[88] Aschehoug states that if it is correct that only goods that have a barter value are economic goods, then the task of the economy is not to augment economic goods, but to increase value. He then gives an example of overproduction and price reactions:

> Because of what has already been mentioned, [Proudhon's] understanding of value contains an inconsistency. This postulate is called Proudhon's postulate because it came from him. He said that 'because we all live only by work and trade, we become richer the more we work and the more we trade. Each has to produce as much as possible. All well and good. But the problem is that when work and production increases, the prices of the goods decrease and this reduces their barter value.'[89]

Aschehoug points out that Proudhon's theory of value contains a mistake that was exposed when the new theory of marginal value was launched. Proudhon was not aware of the difference between production value and barter value, and neither did he make a distinction between warehouse marginal value and total value. If the quantity of a product increases, the marginal value and marginal utility of the product will be reduced, other circumstances being equal. As a consequence, both the barter value and the utility value of the product decrease. If the increase is large enough to cover the whole demand for the product, then not only does the barter value disappear, so does the utility value. On the other hand, if one looks at the whole picture, meaning the total value and total utility value of the product, the result is that both values increase when the supply increases, and the highest value is reached when the warehouse is full and the supply is sufficient to cover all demand.

To sum up Aschehoug's view, the important point is that a country should have as many warehouses full of products to cover as many demands as possible. The issues of debate are, as in many cases, the difference between the individual's (producers) and society's (consumers) interests. The producers will want to produce as much as possible to get the highest revenues because it is in their interests to satisfy as many needs as possible. On the other hand, a society will be interested in meeting as many needs as possible for the largest number of individuals living in the society. The barter value has two different functions: it decides how large the supply of a product should be for each person, and secondly, what kind of products should be produced and in what quantities. The going price is normative and indicates if the supply is too large, sufficient or too small compared to the supply of other products. In both cases, the suppliers are more likely to change the supply or alter the supply to smooth out disharmonies. Correct assessing of the barter value of a product is a prerequisite for a sound economy. Aschehoug's conclusion is that barter value more successively regulates production than distributing the supply necessary to meet each demand.[90]

Conclusion on French Influence

The French influence throughout *Socialøkonomik* was most valuable in terms of historical, philosophical and partly sociological analysis. The French traditions are used to describe a wider and more detailed analysis of economic activity. Furthermore, Aschehoug read French and, together with his thorough historical education, this enabled him to use a broader variety of sources and texts, which in turn provided him with a deeper and more thorough understanding of economic activity in society.

Aschehoug the politician is apparent in the final part of *Socialøkonomik*. One of his last themes is 'The inequality of economic wealth', and he starts by explaining the principles of the classical school and its pros and cons for society. He also states that the classical school does not want too much inequality. The French economist Leroy-Beaulieu mostly followed the classical school, whereas the French socialists naturally deviated from these views. Yet most authors find themselves somewhere in between these two extremes, even though Aschehoug underlines that there are substantially different views concerning justice and distribution, and that these differences result in different economic theories. Aschehoug also touches on questions about the legal system of modern society and asks whether it creates rising injustice or rising inequality in the distribution of income and wealth. By looking at the most developed countries, Aschehoug tries to explain that there are no clear connections between capitalistic societies and great inequalities. On the contrary, his statistical examples show that the distribution of goods has greatly improved, wealth is higher and the general standard of living has risen.[91]

In the next chapters specific topics in Aschehoug's work will be analysed which are relevant for contemporary economic discussions. Firstly, two of his four production factors, labour and the entrepreneur, will be discussed; secondly, the trade policies that were discussed in Chapter 3 will be analysed further; and finally, a presentation of Aschehoug's views on economic crises will be included.

Chapter 9

VIEWS OF LABOUR IN THE WORK OF ASCHEHOUG

Different dimensions in the debate on labour and work are used by Aschehoug to present the general approach and ethics embedded in his economics.[1] The main findings can be summed up as follows: Aschehoug represents a 'multidimensional' economics, giving a broad, nuanced picture that draws on economics as well as psychology, philosophy, sociology and other human sciences. As a consequence, workers are not considered merely as production factors, but as human beings having human needs. Balabkins underlines exactly the same point in his discussion about the German/Austrian economist Albert Schäffle – one of Aschehoug's contemporaries who had almost the same lifespan. Balabkins points out that Schäffle 'brings into a wider perspective that economics is a science about the complex living organism called *Homo sapiens*. [...] The human being was not a commodity.'[2] Furthermore, he describes Schäffle as being 'not a typical contemporary one-dimensional mathematical economist, possessing statistical prowess but lacking erudition in economic history or geopolitics, or rudiments of sociology'.[3] Though none of Aschehoug's contemporaries could be considered one-dimensional, the trend towards a specialized scientific mathematically based economics was on its way.

In the following discussion, views on labour will be used as examples to demonstrate that Aschehoug the economist favoured 'economics with a human face'. A warning can be discerned in Aschehoug's text on work: 'Follow my advice! Otherwise, labour productivity will be affected negatively, your nation's competitive advantages reduced, and the quality of life of workers negatively affected. And last but not least, the moral standards of society deteriorate.'[4]

His Background Shaping His Beliefs and His Ethics

In order to understand Aschehoug's approach, it might be interesting to see what kind of position he takes on philosophical questions, what he believes in, and what might be the basis of his thought on work in general, as well as the worker himself.

Aschehoug was a conservative. He belonged to the conservative political party and became its leader after Anton Martin Schweigaard. He started out as an academic expert working in commissions at the same time as being at the university. After his political career, he became a full-time professor, but all the time remaining tightly connected to political debate. He brought forth his arguments in many articles, meetings and scientific works, but not in parliament directly. He also became aware of the issue of working conditions and other challenges facing society during his many assignments for the Norwegian government, and through his works in economics during the last part of the nineteenth century. He was well acquainted with political and economic debates, not only in Scandinavia, but in Northern Europe as well – Germany, England and France being the prominent countries.[5]

His family background had taught Aschehoug about the real problems and lives of Norwegian farmers and later also industrial workers. Aschehoug was an industrious man, working hard all his life and admiring others with a strong work ethic. Seip mentions in her doctoral thesis about him that his moral ideal was not that of a dandy, the country boy wanting to impress the sophisticated boys of the capital city, but he rather had an admiration for 'people who worked, who had a plan in life and who were able to abstract the daily life from their thoughts'.[6] This comes from a youth, 18 years old, and clearly shows that he admired intellectual work, the kind that he would occupy himself with for the rest of his life. His health was at the time in a poor condition, and he had to follow a physical regime to recover, which he eventually did.

Neither was Aschehoug religious – being a pastor's son had given him knowledge of the life of ordinary people, the peasants and the poorly, as well as the local gentry, but it did not excite a religious calling. His personality had a strong realistic streak that was visible in all his enterprises. At the same time, he was not lacking idealistic values. In his youth he was influenced by Hegelian philosophy together with his friend and later colleague, the philosopher M. J. Monrad. Hagerup points out that Aschehoug probably had a deep religious personality, but that he kept these influences for his personal, private life, and remained a strong adherent of empirical facts and the positive reality of his intellectual, public life.[7] In a letter to his lifelong friend Henrik Helliesen (1824–1900) in 1841 he characterized himself as having a 'history of systematized selfishness' ('Geschichte des systematizierten Egoismus'), but in a letter three years later smoothed over this picture by saying that 'I have left behind my latest passionate ambitions, and I believe more in my own abilities, knowing that I can satisfy my requirements'.[8] Aschehoug must have been an ambitious young man, who quickly understood that hard work and confidence in his own abilities were more important than trying to impress fellow students or intellectual milieus.

Anne-Lise Seip makes an interesting comment in her discussion of Aschehoug's scientific beliefs. According to Seip, Aschehoug believed that social sciences could reveal that the laws of society were rooted in needs. The seeds of social and economic theories were planted in confrontation with the social problems of the eighteenth century.[9] Keynes writes about Alfred Marshall that 'it was only through Ethics that he first reached Economics', and Marshall himself had said that his growing concern for the conditions of society had lead him to study economics. Aschehoug probably felt the same concerns that quite a few of his contemporary economists did.[10] He used his historical knowledge to inform his understanding of the present, and economics became, in combination with history, the most important way to understand society. It is also mentioned by Balabkins that Schäffle was greatly praised by Marshall in his *Principles of Economics*. Like Aschehoug, Marshall was fluent in German.[11]

From early on, Aschehoug became interested in the material conditions for a healthy social and mental life. The interaction between material and economic conditions and the insight of intellectual analysis was the driving force for civilization. Seip comments that he had an overall leaning towards seeing material conditions as more important than the role of the intellect.[12] She further says that this lead to an understanding of historical conditions through material lenses, which weakened the moral and intellectual considerations, even though he generally believed that societies progress towards civilization.[13] The report of the Poverty Commission in 1856 underlines this view: 'The labour class are what conditions have made them.'[14] But is this the true picture of Aschehoug? Reading the later revision of *Socialøkonomik*, it seems clear that Aschehoug must have had, or at least developed, a much more nuanced understanding of the 'labour class'. The next paragraphs will underline this argument.

Some remarks about the early work of Aschehoug in the Poverty Commission might shed light on working conditions in Norway in the mid-eighteenth century, fifty years before the publication of *Socialøkonomik*. The poverty problem was considered mostly a farm worker problem, in Norway as well as in other European countries. The structural changes in farming had created a farm worker proletariat that often lived in poor conditions. The work of the Smallholder Commission a few years earlier had already pointed out the close connection between poverty and the smallholder's economic situation. The problem of poverty had a more prominent position, and was subject to a more thorough statistical and theoretical analysis, in the work of the Poverty Commission. Aschehoug was the first collector of statistical data, having claimed during the work in the Smallholder Commission that it was difficult to even tell 'whether poverty was increasing or decreasing'.[15] Economic analysis showed that general welfare had increased, quite the opposite of what was expected. The Poverty Commission concluded, after seeing the results, that even though most people were better off, the gap had widened and the situation for the lowest ranking workers had become worse. Aschehoug gradually came to understand that the distribution of wealth had to be organized differently in order to ensure a sustainable life for the poorest. In the 1850s, Aschehoug believed in economic development in order to create welfare, and he thought that a development towards a more civilized society would eventually help the labour class to become more industrious and more frugal. In a way, improved moral conduct was considered a consequence of civilization. Aschehoug did not, during his commission work in the 1850s, suggest any moral constraints or advice to be followed by the labour class. He believed in the Malthusian argument that they would understand the right behaviour, and wait to marry until their personal economy could afford children. This might be why Seip, as mentioned earlier, regarded Aschehoug as someone who had had an overall leaning towards seeing material conditions as more important than the role of intellect.

In the late 1860s, Aschehoug was again confronted with poverty and social problems, and instead of explaining the condition of the poor in terms of economic conditions, he put forth a moral explanation: 'It was basically [...] a moral evil, not economic.'[16] He continues by referring to the practice of early marriage among the poor and the high birth rate. The age of marriage had fallen and, at the same time, material needs had risen: 'They live from hand to mouth, have little income, no means, and they marry too early; at the same time, their needs increased. [...] This was the main cause of poverty.'[17] When economic growth no longer could be trusted to increase the welfare of the poor and supply work for all, Aschehoug faced a dilemma. How was it possible to improve moral standing or to ensure jobs when economic growth was not continuous but fluctuating, and how should the poor be helped? The dilemma was international; all Western European countries faced unemployment, economic crises and poverty problems. Politicians and economists, Aschehoug being no exception, gradually came to distinguish between the undeserving poor, often synonymous with the unemployed, and the poor who were unwilling to work and therefore had brought it upon themselves. The German influence, through the foundation of Verein für Sozialpolitik, could be seen during the last decades of the nineteenth century in Norway. However, Aschehoug's position changed from a preoccupation with morals in 1869 to the position that can be seen in *Socialøkonomik*, which is the position that will be treated in detail here.

In the late 1880s, Aschehoug debated the question of the division of the national product in a meeting of the Statsøkonomisk forening. The author of the paper that was being discussed was the manager of the Central Statistical Bureau, Anders N. Kiær. He had presented his thoughts about the development and outlook of the national economy.[18] Aschehoug started his comments by stating that his outlook was somewhat more positive than that of the author.[19] He questioned the conclusion that there were pressing times ahead and a worsening outlook, and asked inquisitorially, 'Is this true for all? Maybe for the entrepreneurs and the capital owners, but not for the workers.'[20] He also remarked that the members of the Statsøkonomisk forening had gradually come to see this, since he had defended this view in the meetings for some time. He also drew on European experiences saying that 'it is really a large change in the division of income and wealth in the civilized countries [of Europe], because the entrepreneurs and the capital owners get a lesser share of the dividends, while the labour class gets a larger one'.[21] And if this were true, no one would be entitled to say that times are worsening for society as a whole. He added that there were clear signs of continued consumption and production, contrary to Kiær's more pessimistic overview. Another debater, Overrettssagfører Bruun, agreed that the workers were better off, but he took the static position and claimed that higher salaries must lead to a decrease in the income of the entrepreneurs. Aschehoug finished his discussion by saying that the change in income distribution would continue in favour of the working class, but that society as a whole would produce more and consume more, resulting in improved overall welfare. This would be due to technical and educational progress. He also believed that entrepreneurs and capital owners would get their dividends, because they could not survive with losses for a long period of time. This was also important for the labour class – bankruptcy would only lead to unemployment.

About Working Contracts and Salaries

Aschehoug defined four production factors: capital, natural resources, labour and entrepreneurs. Aschehoug explicitly underlines that labour cannot be juxtaposed with nature and capital as a production force. Human labour is both a service and a production force, whereas capital can only be a means of production, not a force in itself.[22] He also outlines the different views on labour and the working class, saying that initially only manual labourers were perceived as members of the working class.

Workers who were being employed with immaterial labour were considered part of another class. Aschehoug points out that the distinction is difficult to make, because many workers are skilled and have substantial education, even though their work could be considered as manual or physical. The real social difference lies in the size of the salary.[23] Another difference is whether the worker is employed and has agreed to a contract with certain working conditions, or if the worker is self-employed. In the first case, the salary should be determined voluntarily in the agreement between the employer and the employee.[24] Ideally, both parties will of their own free will sign a working contract, and they would both find it worthwhile to agree to the conditions, or else not sign. The employer bears the risk of the production, and the employee will get his pay according to his contract; even though the employer may be running his business with losses, the employee will normally get his pay while other creditors must wait. Of course there is always the risk of bankruptcy and unemployment, but for workers the greatest risks are accidents and disability.

Aschehoug, being fascinated by technological improvements and focusing strongly upon entrepreneurship, considered competition based on the suppression of wages an anachronism, but realized that this idea still prevailed in his time: '[In older times] one thought that low wages were a prerequisite for cheap production and thus export industries; a notion which to some extent still prevails in the business world.'[25] As discussed above, seeking competitive advantages in cheap labour is currently a major strategy of companies, cities and countries producing for the world market.

Aschehoug recommends that workers' wages should be high enough to secure reproduction and sufficient to ensure the development of skills. Furthermore, he claims that fulfilling the needs of workers and their families increases aggregate demand and therefore creates growth: 'Well-paid workers are more content, and more eager in their work. They are not only producers, but constitute the majority of consumers. The higher their wages, the higher their buying power, and thus a market for all the goods they consume can be secured. This benefits those who produce these goods.'[26] This point is also made in Aschehoug's discussion of salaries: 'Workers are more efficient in countries where salaries are high in relation to the working hours, and entrepreneurs get more output for the same amount of money than in countries where the salaries are low.'[27] The statement is followed up by a partly moral recommendation of the right use of the increased salary, and a warning that salaries should not be increased too quickly, something that would lead to a moral as well as a general decay (drinking being the worst).

When discussing different types of salaries, such as fixed salaries and piece-rate pay, Aschehoug clearly takes the side of the worker, listing all the inconveniences and downsides of the 'harsh' and often exploitative piece-rate system. If it should be used, it must be as a result of an agreement between the employer and the employees, where both parties agree to the conditions. Recent investigations had shown a more positive attitude towards the system, including that of the workers, if it is applied properly. Aschehoug sees this as a result of the tighter connection between employers and the emerging labour organizations.[28] Another principle that was gaining ground at the time was the acceptance of salary increasing with seniority. Fifty years earlier, Aschehoug had had a more positive view towards the piece-rate system, and claimed that it would have a beneficial influence on the morale of workers, enhancing their motivation. The movement in Aschehoug's thinking away from this position is probably due to his experience in politics hence, and the general development in the formation and organization of the workers unions and employer organizations.

Most important for Aschehoug is to enable the workers to rent or acquire better housing and to ameliorate the daily lives. While discussing the size of salaries in general, Aschehoug makes some interesting points about what an increase in salaries could lead to.[29] The workers could reduce their working hours, daily or as an extra day off, or they could work as before and use the extra income to buy a house, save money and so forth. They could also rent better housing, buy more nutritious food and set up a family at a younger age. In a discussion at the Statsøkonomisk forening in 1896, Aschehoug commented on a presentation about customs and underlined that customs that made grain and animal food more expensive were not recommendable, as it would make the working class worse off and thereby the whole economy.[30] Housing receives a thorough analysis in chapter 47 of *Socialøkonomik*. Adequate, affordable housing should be made available, although Aschehoug seems to believe that private enterprises should build them, and that public loans and financing should contribute to the capital that is needed. Participation in cultural activities should be stimulated through the system of general and public education, *folkeskolen*.

Another aspect of Aschehoug's beliefs is how education can influence the size of the salary. Usually, the salary will be increased in proportion to improved education. However, education can be a blessing in itself. Aschehoug observes an increased application for general education as well an improvement in teaching programmes. Inconvenient and disagreeable work should be better paid (though it is often not the case); the same goes for unhealthy working conditions, and likewise dangerous work. Positions that command extra trustworthiness and honesty deserve higher salaries. To the modern reader, all of this seems accurate and well observed, but when it comes to explaining the salaries of women, Aschehoug must be described as old-fashioned. He concedes to lower payments for women, and the reasons he gives (mostly connected to gender differences) are antiquated and outdated.

When it comes to the ownership of the production output, Aschehoug is clear: 'The workers contribution is the work itself, not the product outcome.'[31] On the other hand, he conveys fairly modern views when he outlines the pros and cons of a salary system based on the results of the business operations. In line with what might be considered a modern experience, employee participation and ownership can lead to a greater commitment, but fixing the levels of profit sharing, and at the same time having a long-term perspective, is a difficult balance. Salary systems known as the 'sweating' system and the contract labour system do not get much sympathy from Aschehoug.[32] It might be profitable for employers in the short run, but can easily be ruinous for the workforce. To summarize, Aschehoug has a balanced view on salary systems and how they influence workers. Very often he takes on the workers perspective and clearly understands their claims and objections. The account he gives is strikingly modern and thoroughly thought through.

Aschehoug and the Arbeiterfrage: Laws and Regulations

The flip side of worker specialization is that many workers had to endure bleak working conditions in the factories; Aschehoug calls this unworthy and deeply regrets its effects.

To ameliorate it, Aschehoug believes in public education and restrictions on working hours. Education would lead to a more flexible working population, as well as an individual stimulation both morally and intellectually. Aschehoug repeatedly comes back to the fact that humans cannot be seen as solely a means of production, even though this view can be observed in many economic presentations, some even trying to fix a price on an adult human – meaning the cost of upbringing and fostering to become a fully useful worker. Schäffle also shared this view on workers and work, stating that one of the flaws of the current political economy, among other things, was the exploitation of workers, and underlying many of the flaws was the 'social question' or 'die soziale Frage'.[33]

In his discussions about the specialization of work Aschehoug follows the arguments of Adam Smith. However, a hundred years after the *Wealth of Nations* and the industrial development during the nineteenth century, the down sides are also apparent, which of course they were to Smith as well.[34] Technical specialization often meant monotonous factory work, as well as limited technical skill. If workers were laid off, it meant that it could be difficult to find other occupations. A clocksmith's apprentice could not easily be a factory worker and vice versa. Women and children could also work in factories, but Aschehoug sees this as an evil of society that has to be remedied by laws. Lighter work and housework would be more appropriate occupations for them. Even though work in general by these groups would increase the output of production for society, Aschehoug does not recommend it.[35]

A particularly interesting point, as seen with contemporary eyes, is that Aschehoug recognizes the political agency of labour, which is striking when contemplating the negligence of this factor by many economists that came after him. New regulations that shape working conditions and wages are seen by Aschehoug not only as gifts from benevolent rulers, but may also result from 'pressures and demands from workers, namely, where the demand stems from a well-organized and large trade union'.[36] An example is the eight-hour day in Australia, though 'climate determinism' is a factor: 'Longer working hours – even outdoors – is considered almost unbearable in the Australian climate.'[37] Workers are collective agents that shape regulation, and thus the conditions under which investors invest and producers produce. Regulation of working conditions is a central concern of his; he thus recognizes the need to limit economic freedom and praises the efforts of the labour unions to shorten working hours and negotiate for better salaries.[38]

Aschehoug calls attention to the 'forces that are moving towards bettering the conditions of those without or of limited means', observable in new protection laws and labour insurance systems.[39] According to Aschehoug, these measures represent a small social revolution or reform, Germany being in the lead of the development in the *Arbeiterschutzgesetzgebung*.[40] The first measures to regulate working hours were taken by the factory laws in Britain from 1802. Norway introduced similar measures in 1892 – 'Loven om Fabriktilsyn' – which were followed by similar laws and systems.[41] The debates concern voluntary versus compulsory insurance and financing systems, and likewise, a public system based on taxes versus a private system based on taxes or insurance premiums. There is no doubt that Norwegian development at this early stage of social welfare was greatly influenced by both the German and the British experience.[42] Aschehoug tends to go for compulsory schemes, believing that voluntary schemes, being ideologically and morally preferable, are not practically obtainable. The classical division of costs is between the insured, the employer and the state. These questions were intensely debated during the ongoing publishing of *Socialøkonomik*. Aschehoug did not take an active part in these discussions, only following them at the Statsøkonomisk forening, which he also refers to in his presentation.[43]

Aschehoug's appreciation of human labour is beautifully described in the following: 'Humans do not produce to acquire "gold" but to get a decent life. [...] A proper economically organized consumption is the most useful employment of economic goods; because it will serve the maintenance, strength and development of the most precious of all means of production, namely human labour.'[44] The humanist perspective is also evident when he discusses the right to work. He acknowledges that the right to work is probably one of the most important claims a human can have, but at the same time who can give such a guarantee? Even though one recognizes that the state has a natural obligation to provide work to all able-bodied citizens, what could be done with all those who are unable? Aschehoug is clearly influenced by European, and especially German, developments in social politics and welfare. The Norwegian government had, during the last part of the nineteenth century, gradually come to comprehend the great social challenges that industrialization had created. As already mentioned, Aschehoug had been participating in this development as a politician and as a much used committee member. In a discussion at the Statsøkonomisk forening in 1892 on A. N. Kiær's paper 'About the economic value of humans', Aschehoug said,

> We have now touched a part of human life that has some economic interest [the cost of raising children], but which runs much deeper. What one has to be careful about is not to see the object [the worker] just from an economic angle. This will bring about huge difficulties because one operates with terms that are created for human activity that includes the acquiring and keeping of fortune, which do not fit, nor will fit, all parts of human life, and that disappear completely in the relationship between parents and children [...] and therefore I have never been able to attribute much weight to the argument about the production cost of raising children and the rentability of the upbringing.[45]

The right to work and questions of poverty are tightly connected. If a person is able to work, giving him the opportunity is the first priority. The goal is to get as many people working as possible, thereby reducing direct poor relief as much as possible. This could be seen as a blunt economic argument, but in his analysis Aschehoug clearly shows that this is not how he perceives it. When it comes to poor relief the state has an important role to play:

'It is now commonly recognized that the state must provide welfare services to needy classes that cannot be assisted otherwise. [...] The controversial issue is whether the state should support the needy who could have sustained themselves but have become unable, lost their work or cannot find occupation.'[46] The debate is then focused on how to treat unemployment and inability due to old age or disability. Despite the fact that Aschehoug mentions moral issues and the obligation everyone has to behave, he sees grim examples of people not seeking help because of the shame of asking for poor relief.

Old age and retirement pensions were being discussed in Norway around 1900, as well as in Denmark and in Germany. These issues were being discussed in relation to other labour and social measures, and no clear agreements were obtained during Aschehoug's lifetime. He mentions the ongoing discussions and points out that the premium system seemed to have an advantage over the fund system.[47] The other question of utmost importance was the establishment of a law of unemployment. An employment agency law was passed in 1906, as well as a general law of unemployment relief, which secured economic help during unemployment.[48]

What are the prospects for the labour class, and what has happened since the first classical economic texts appeared in the late eighteenth century? These are the questions Aschehoug asks after almost 2,200 encyclopaedic pages. The first wave of optimism was washed away by the writings of Malthus, Ricardo and James Mill, and even in the writings of John Stuart Mill. The next optimistic phase came with the French liberal school, being met by the pessimism of the socialist thought rising in the mid-nineteenth century. Fifty years later, Aschehoug places himself among the sober optimists. Better housing, better nutrition, better clothing and living conditions in general, better education and increased interest in social welfare systems are all contributing to the amelioration in welfare for the labour class. 'General education diminishes class differences through its development and extensiveness, and awakens and strengthens the consciousness about the equality of humans.'[49] Economic development will most probably continue, bringing even more welfare to the labour class. The general return on society's production can and will be increased, and it will be more evenly distributed, even though a total equality is neither possible, nor desirable.

Aschehoug lived during a period of time when the conditions of the labour class as well as state regulation were burning issues, as can be learned from his biography and his *Socialøkonomik*. Humanism pervades Aschehoug's writings on work, workers and the regulation of working life: 'Even the strongest of men is weak, if he is considered solely as a machine.'[50] And to underline the point: 'Previously, working hours have been too long in Europe. Both factory owners, landowners and farmers thought that workers could produce more the longer the working hours were. They now understand that this is incorrect.'[51]

Aschehoug contemplates the uncivilized past, when employers had such an instrumental view of workers: 'Previously, in olden times [...] even science tended to see manual workers as pure tools, and forget that they were humans, and constituted the majority of society.'[52]

Workers are Humans and are Subject to Diminishing Returns

According to Aschehoug, the need to work is ingrained in us all, and work is a sacrifice to the greater good of yourself and society. We *toil* – work may be unpleasant, but serves a greater purpose. We experience joy while working, and while working we may educate ourselves and explore our talents. Therefore, work has an important role to play in people's lives besides being a source of income. Aschehoug stresses that we are biological creatures: 'Only the bodily energy that is not needed to sustain life can be used for voluntary external work.'[53]

Workers are humans and humans are part of nature and therefore subject to diminishing returns: 'The labour power of every human being is limited. Nobody can yield beyond their capacity.'[54] Aschehoug attributes different capabilities to different 'races', and distinguishes between 'civilized' and 'natural' races. The stereotypes he describes survive in the present day: the British are very productive, the French artistic, Italians innovative and Germans highly skilled and disciplined and so on. The negative associations are strongly correlated to the uncivilized.[55] Labour is thus locally embedded; but on the other hand he stresses *individuality*. The capacity to work and human capabilities vary in a population; we find differences according to gender, age, physical strength and faculties. Some workers are thus more vulnerable than others and deserve a greater protection against exploitation; different needs pertain to different people. Older workers, women and children need special protection. He draws attention to basic nutritional needs, a topic which is seldom found in economic textbooks of the time. By scientific means, nutrition should be improved and sports encouraged, avoiding burnout. Productivity depends not only on the interest and energy of each worker, but also on circumstances beyond their control, such as the intensity of work. The human body needs rest; if over-taxed, nature will strike back: 'Finally, there comes the moment when the toil becomes unbearable, even impossible, and the need for rest irresistible.'[56] In this quote it is possible to grasp the fundamentals of Aschehoug's work on labour law. Workers should not be 'wage slaves', but be aided to decent lives with their families by limiting the number of working hours and having Sundays off. Workers are seen to be more than production factors, bodily carriers of labour power.[57]

Aschehoug's criticism of socialism starts with the misconception that work is just manual work.[58] Work is also immaterial work, and Aschehoug attributes the general civilization and development of society mostly to immaterial work, like technical progress, better organization of society, the progress of science and education and developments in jurisprudence. The belief in progress and in a positivistic philosophy shines through here, but he goes on to say that manual work is indispensable.[59] His critique also attacks the somewhat unreal socialist belief that work should only be about happiness and that work, according to Fourier, who he uses as an example, should be organized in cooperatives (*phalanstères*). As a realist, Aschehoug states that work can be, and often is, unpleasant. Work can be described as an equation: toil equals time multiplied by intensity.[60] The human concern continues in this description – what you may eat, drink, at what temperatures you can work, how much sleep and rest is needed, the living conditions, etc. Physiological investigations are used to underline the points, even down to how many calories are needed, showing both a concern and a fascination for the natural sciences. Immaterial work is no exception; you need rest, but also exercise, in order to be able to work. Your diet can vary, but you have to eat nutritiously, and Aschehoug argues that nutritious food should be made available to all. If it is too expensive, the salaries of the lowest paid must be raised.[61]

Qualification is another element that influences work; not only the toil, but the time spent and the investment the worker has made in order to perform well will alter the quality of the work. The equation now becomes work equals time, intensity and skills. Measuring intensity and skills might be difficult, but time is measurable. Therefore Aschehoug spends much time discussing working hours. Outlining the formation of the decision of working hours, he soon enters the contemporary debate about the length of the working day. Few people will be able to work for more than 12 hours. 24 hours should be divided between work, sleep and other activities. If the time spent on working is pushed too hard, 'it leads to exhaustion. Life becomes dull and monotonous. One does not live only to work to create economic results, but to fulfil one's duties towards one's family, country and to develop oneself intellectually. These activities take time, and it has to be balanced against the necessity of work.'[62] Ideally the working day should be eight hours, splitting the day in three, eight hours sleep and eight hours for other activities. In Norway, this was established in the regulation of the working day in the public sector. To Aschehoug this was natural, as the state was the largest employer. The private sector had to a large extent followed, also because of the pressure from the upcoming labour unions. Officially the Norwegian eight-hour day law was not passed until 1919.

The close connection between workers and entrepreneurs can also be illustrated with an example of the eight-hour working day. Aschehoug claims that an eight-hour working day would diminish the fluctuations in the demand for labour, something that is equally good for workers as well as for entrepreneurs. The problem is, of course, the uncertainty when it comes to the output that is being produced and the level of salaries; is unemployment going down if the working hours are reduced?[63] The entrepreneurial argument that is being used against the length of the working day would make Norwegian companies less competitive internationally. Aschehoug understands this fear, but says that if all parties agree, it should be done: 'Experience has shown that the eight-hour working day has been introduced in enterprises with success for all parties, and this success is gradually encouraging others to introduce it through voluntary agreements.'[64]

On the subject of marginal utility and the considerations the entrepreneur will make when deciding what and how much to produce, Aschehoug notes that even Böhm-Bawerk has to admit that in some cases the worker can influence his own work and manage his own working hours, but when it comes to production and fixed employment, the worker has to follow fixed working hours and the working process. Aschehoug remarks that even though the worker cannot influence his working hours, he may influence the intensity and output and thereby also regulate his efforts and payment.[65]

Aschehoug, however, does not enter into a philosophical discourse on the peculiar character of labour power. Reducing workers or their productive capability to a mere commodity would go against his ethics. He seems to consider workers a 'physical, psychological and moral entity'. But Aschehoug reflects upon the labour market in his discussion on the merits of giving workers high wages: 'Work may, probably, be considered a commodity. Any clever man understands that it often pays to buy more expensive but better textiles, than cheaper ones of poor quality.'[66] It is worth noting that Aschehoug writes that *work*, not labour power, is a commodity, firmly locating him outside Marxist camps. And he explicitly distances himself from the socialist view of work. To socialists he attributes the view that only manual labour 'counts'. According to him, socialists underestimate firstly the value of immaterial and spiritual work, and secondly the immaterial work that is ingrained in any kind of manual labour. Since all tasks must be planned before they are undertaken, all workers need their brains: 'The workers doing so-called manual work degrade themselves if they consider themselves machines and attribute their economic importance to their muscles only.'[67]

Aschehoug considers the socialists' praise of manual work to be rooted in their understanding of the workers' crucial role in production. I might add that the socialists' ideological elevation of manual work should also be understood in terms of centuries of underestimation of its economic worth, and the glorification of spiritual work. But Aschehoug makes his point well; praising manual work is part of the socialists' identity-building project.

Conclusion

Aschehoug distinguishes between different forms of labour, thus underlying that each worker is unique and that economic activity must be analysed within its appropriate national or local context. Labour cannot easily be replaced between industries – most economic activity demands adapted knowledge. Workers are not considered production factors only, but seen as human beings having human needs. Aschehoug's views on labour as a production factor is clearly detailed and elaborated. He does not treat labour as a general, one-size-fits-all production factor.

Furthermore, he underlines important measures for better working conditions: eight-hour days, holidays, routine changes (if your work is monotonous), education, better housing and better nutrition. His participation in discussions at the Statsøkonomisk forening about the 'social question' underlines his and his fellow association members' efforts to ameliorate working conditions.

Aschehoug likewise wrote whole chapters on capital and on nature, which are not included here; capital and credit issues as a separate project are not within the scope of this book. However, the fourth production factor, the entrepreneur, will be the topic of the next chapter.

Chapter 10

THE ENTREPRENEUR: THE FOURTH PRODUCTION FACTOR

Before Aschehoug, the entrepreneur (*Unternehmer* in German, *driftsherre* in Norwegian) had a clear foothold in Norwegian economics. Looking back at the structure of Norwegian economic activity during the nineteenth century, it is not surprising that the theory of the role of the entrepreneur had a considerable impact on economic thought and economic policy. This chapter demonstrates that the idea of the entrepreneur as the fourth production factor came to Norway through the works of Jean-Baptiste Say, and that Aschehoug adopted his views and those of Schweigaard, and further developed these in his work. After Aschehoug, the idea of the entrepreneur as a fourth production factor gradually disappeared from textbooks. This was mainly because the role of the entrepreneur became that of the manager, henceforth just a figure in business economics and subsequently not a part of macroeconomic analysis. Another point of interest is that the theory of the entrepreneur is firmly grounded on the idea of private initiative and also on private ownership. With a reference to the kind of economic activity that a municipality would undertake, Aschehoug asserts that economic activities with the goal of making money should be left to private entrepreneurs. I believe this statement underlines what kind of perspective he had on the importance of this production factor.[1]

Schweigaard had emphasized the importance of management and, following Say, he split the national product between the four income sectors: wages, capital interest, rent and entrepreneurial income.[2] Aschehoug clearly demonstrates his approval of Say's views: 'The author who earned himself the greatest merit in the systematization of science was J.-B. Say, distinguishing between capitalists and entrepreneurs, and giving an extensive explanation of entrepreneurial activity.'[3]

There is a line of thought from Say through to Schweigaard and Aschehoug which views the entrepreneur as a separate and independent production factor, bearing his own production risks. Schweigaard followed Say and differentiated between salaries, entrepreneurial income, capital rent and economic rent (*grunnrente*); Aschehoug developed this further.[4] Initially, this could well be a farmer or someone who ran his own small business. The organizational talent is obvious, as well as the many decisions that need to be taken in order to produce and sell the right amount of goods in the market. If he receives an income that exceeds his costs, he has created an entrepreneurial income.

Say and the Entrepreneur

Jean-Baptiste Say published three works of importance for the Norwegian audience: the *Traité d'économie politique* (1803, Treatise on political economy), *Catéchisme d'économie politique* (1815, Catechism of political economy) and *Cours complet d'économie politique pratique* (1828–30, Complete course in practical political economy).[5] They were quickly translated into Norwegian, and also into Danish, but it appears that Aschehoug must have had copies of the French editions. In any case, the books were readily available.[6] Sæther claims that: 'With his books and these translations, Say had a strong influence on the development of political economy in Norway. As a consequence the role of the entrepreneur became an important feature in the subsequent teaching and writings on political economy.'[7] This is certainly true for the nineteenth century and the first decades of the twentieth century, with Say's economic arguments being used by both Norwegian business people and academics.

Underlying Say's analysis is the premise of private property, meaning property not controlled by the state. He believes that a productive economy must rest on private enterprise and private initiatives.[8] Nonetheless, Say underlines the importance of a strong state, securing a reliable legal system, in order for the economy to function properly.

The importance of the entrepreneur lies in the fact that it is his efforts which make it possible to produce value from the three other production factors – nature, capital and labour. In his *Traité*, Say differentiates between entrepreneurs and capitalists, and Aschehoug points out that this was long before the distinction gained a foothold in English literature. The distinction is important: Say understood the entrepreneur as someone who runs an economic activity at their own expense; the owner of the activity was then directly influenced by both gains and losses.

Aschehoug claims that Say used the term *entrepreneur* in its widest sense – anybody working at their own expense could be considered an entrepreneur.[9] Their income was partly a direct salary and partly an entrepreneurial gain.[10] Say made a clear distinction between the 'profit of the entrepreneur' and the 'return on capital'. Later Schumpeter wrote in his *History of Economic Analysis* from 1954 that Say 'was the first to assign to the entrepreneur per se a definite position distinct from the capitalist in the economic process. His contribution is summed up in the pithy statement that the entrepreneur's function is to combine the factors of production into a producing organism.'[11]

In his *Traité d'économie politique*, Say writes,

It may be remembered, that the occupation of adventurer is comprised in the second class of operations specified as necessary for the setting in motion of every class of industry whatever; that is to say, the application of acquired knowledge to the creation of a product for human consumption. It will likewise be recollected, that such application is equally necessary in agricultural, manufacturing, and commercial industry; that the labour of the farmer or cultivator on his own account, of the master-manufacturer and of the merchant, all come under this description; they are the adventurers in each department of industry respectively. The nature of the profits of these three classes of men is what we are now about to consider.[12]

It very seldom happens that the party engaged in the management of any undertaking is not at the same time in the receipt of interest upon some capital of his own. The manager of a concern rarely borrows from strangers the whole of the capital employed. If he has purchased some of the implements with his own capital, or made advances from his own funds, he will then be entitled to one portion of his revenue as the manager, and another as capitalist. Mankind is so little inclined to sacrifice any particle of its self-interest, that even those who have never analysed these respective rights know well enough how to enforce them to their full extent in practice. Our present concern is to distinguish the portion of revenue that the adventurer receives as adventurer. We shall come to see what he, or somebody else, derives from his role as capitalist.[13]

As we will see, the two quotes from Schumpeter and Say above are examples of the principles that were used in Schweigaard's lectures; Schweigaard uses the same division of net income as Say, as does Aschehoug in *Socialøkonomik*.[14] Furthermore, it is only Say who makes this distinction between entrepreneurial gain and capital gain, and it is interesting to note that this was accepted and adopted in Norway, and that Aschehoug was among the few who argued for entrepreneurs to be a separate production factor.

Schweigaard Following Say in Norway

The first Norwegian economist to treat the entrepreneur systematically was Schweigaard. There were other economists before him, like Christen Smith (1785–1816), Gregers Fougner Lundh (1786–1836) and Jacob Aall (1773–1844), who was an entrepreneur himself, but none of them had the same impact.[15] Even though Schweigaard's written works were not assembled and published before 1904, from the early 1840s they were well known through his lectures. Schweigaard had already accentuated the same points in his *Ungdomsarbeider*, which were clearly known to Aschehoug in 1846, since Aschehoug at that time was attending Schweigaard's lectures as a student. In *On Production*, Schweigaard writes the following:

> The yield of human labour is not only dependent on its strength and endurance, but also to a substantial degree on the insight which leads it, and of the freedom from disturbing influences where it is carried out. This can be clearly seen when a business becomes more complicated, its management must then be handed over to a special manager, who does not participate in physical work and yet whose activity in the strict sense is productive, since the success of the business in the main depends on him.[16]

Schweigaard emphasizes how entrepreneurs influence the division of labour and the composition and accumulation of capital. Capital accumulation and diversity in economic activities make society more complicated, and to organize it all is not possible, 'without the contribution of people, who are equipped with greater insight and abilities and therefore can claim a greater part of the proceeds'.[17]

According to Sæther, Schweigaard's views about what is productive also depart from the standard views among English classical economists.[18] As Aschehoug later does, Schweigaard adheres to the views of Say and separates entrepreneurial profit from capital interest as an income category in itself.[19] Furthermore, Schweigaard follows Say and differentiates between salaries, entrepreneurial income, capital rent and economic rent (*grunnrente*), which Aschehoug then develops further.[20]

He dedicates a small chapter to entrepreneurial income, in which he explains different types of entrepreneurial business. In the case of Norway, the shipping industry, as well as trade and farming, are obvious examples. The view is that entrepreneurial gain exceeds capital rent and comes from the business talent of the entrepreneur in running his affairs. It is, therefore, a payment for his talent and his work, and cannot be seen as a salary. The size of the gain is closely connected to the capital employed, because the entrepreneur does not need to own this capital, it can be partly borrowed in order to develop his business further. Schweigaard also mentions economic crises in relation to entrepreneurs, saying that businesses that are going well will usually attract newcomers, which will eventually lead to an overproduction and a downscaling before it restarts.[21] This also points to the risk of losing money and the unpredictability of entrepreneurial income.

As will be explained later, Schweigaard agreed with Say about the impossibility of a general overproduction. What was overproduction in one industry was underproduction in another, since each commodity or service was offered in the market to be used in the production of another commodity or service. The problem of overproduction is therefore rather: 'disproportions between the different branches of production'. He also discussed the question of whether new machinery and tools could lead to an increase in unemployment. When this could be claimed to be the case, he thought that this was due to a mix-up between short-term and long-term effects. In the long run the economy would regain its equilibrium.[22]

As we have seen, Schweigaard clearly differentiates between the four different incomes: capital interest, ground rent, wages and entrepreneurial income.

Aschehoug Adopting and Developing Say's and Schweigaard's Theories

Say's views were made popular in Norway through the lectures of Schweigaard. Aschehoug adopted the entrepreneurial theory, both through Schweigaard, but also by reading Say himself. Sæther states that:

> Among the classics, his favourite is unquestionably J.-B. Say, whom he frequently quotes and whose economic definitions and theories he uses. He refers to Say more than 50 times. Among the moderns his favourite is undoubtedly Marshall, who he refers to more than 170 times and whose views he often finds support the views of Say. An investigation shows us that Aschehoug again and again accepts Say's views, particularly the ones where he emphasizes the role of the entrepreneur, and uses them to develop his own analysis.[23]

Aschehoug underlines the exceptional importance entrepreneurs have in contemporary economic activities – they are the 'captains of industry'.[24] In the competition between entrepreneurs it is always ability, not capital resources, that in the long run will 'secure the victory'.[25] Aschehoug emphasizes how entrepreneurs influence the division of labour and the composition and accumulation of capital. Capital accumulation creates a diversity of activities, which could not succeed 'without the contribution of persons who are equipped with greater insight and abilities and therefore can claim a greater part of the proceeds'.[26] Business talent or entrepreneurship is therefore perceived as the fourth factor of production: 'All things considered, I would say that most reasons given support treating business talent as a production factor in its own right.'[27] Abundant capital resources are, of course, important for a well-functioning and prosperous society; but in reality, personal capabilities or human resources are even more important in its development. If morality and jurisprudence are properly developed and adhered to, a society can rebuild quickly after setbacks like wars or economic crises. This view echoes Say, who claimed that 'a country well stacked with intelligent merchants, manufacturers and agriculturists has more powerful means of attaining prosperity than (other countries)'.[28]

The production capabilities of nature, human labour and capital are limited in isolation. However, the entrepreneur brings it all together: 'For them to be a force, they have to be present in a suitable proportion, of requisite usefulness and properly connected with each other. This is the duty of the entrepreneur, and this is the strongest defence for a system, which views business talent as a means of production next to nature, labour and capital.'[29] Aschehoug is being explicitly detailed in his description of the different tasks of the entrepreneur. An entrepreneur must make plans and decide what kind of economic activities should be started and kept going. Furthermore, he must organize his whole business – the set-up, the machinery, the employees – and make arrangements with his suppliers and his customers. The entrepreneur is also responsible for all calculations and budgeting, deciding what to be produced, in which markets, and at what prices.

The personal qualifications of a typical entrepreneur are as follows: 'sound judgement, equanimity, enterprise, staying power, strong will and the capability to survey many particulars and to be able to make fast decisions'.[30] From this it follows that organizational talent is crucial and it is this aspect of business ability that is most important. He further has to negotiate with 'the owners of land and buildings used, with the hiring or buying of these or other capital goods, with clerks and workers about wages, and with banks and customers about loans and granting of credits'.[31] The result is that entrepreneurs have an important influence on the distribution of the proceeds from production.

Aschehoug defines the science of economics as 'the theory of production, turnover, distribution and consumption of economic goods'.[32] Thereafter he stresses that the entrepreneur will normally own some part of the capital he has employed in his business, but emphasizes that in older times, with less-developed credit markets, it was normally the case that the entrepreneur owned a substantial part of the capital. Aschehoug continues:

Since the entrepreneur carries the risk for the business's outcome, it is possible that he, with the sale of its products, does not obtain the gross income that covers expenses. In such a case he suffers a wealth loss, and if he cannot later bring the firm on a better footing he will have to give it up. But if his operations go well and can deliver a profit above the cost of production, then this will be his net income.[33]

This net income can be divided into different parts, namely:

1. Remuneration for the work in the firm that the entrepreneur has personally carried out;
2. Remuneration for normal interest of the capital that he has employed in the firm;
3. Remuneration for the risk attached to the firm that he himself has taken over, irrespective of if he has insured against it;
4. Remuneration for the common business risk, that is, the risk which it is impossible to insure against; and finally,
5. The profit he can retain after he has calculated a reasonable remuneration for these personal production sacrifices.[34]

What Aschehoug does here is explain why the entrepreneur needs to be a fourth production factor – this factor is the 'glue'. He also explains why it is necessary to favour the entrepreneur separately from labour and capital. He even claims that, in fact, it is not capital but the personal ability and competence of entrepreneurs that is the most valuable asset in society, securing productivity and welfare.[35] Even after serious crises, such as wars, competent and technically skilled entrepreneurs will quickly assure society regains its previous level of welfare, as long as legal systems and morals are respected. It is interesting to see how much Aschehoug emphasizes private initiative and the utmost importance he believes it has in order to create a productive society.

Moreover, it is interesting to see what Aschehoug says about limited companies, which is the contemporary and modern way to organize private businesses. The emergence of larger business operations in limited companies (*Aktiengesellschaften/ aksjeselskap*) is also recognized by Aschehoug, even though smaller entrepreneurial businesses were more common in his lifetime. Therefore, limited companies and other modern ways of setting up enterprises with limited responsibilities are briefly approached in chapter 50 of *Socialøkonomik*. When smaller businesses become larger, the entrepreneur and the owner(s) may be different people. The entrepreneurial gain goes to the general assembly and the shareholders, because they bear the operational risk and will lose their capital if the company goes bankrupt, whereas the entrepreneurial income is paid to the general manager(s).[36] Aschehoug's model is based on the assumption that entrepreneurial profit will diminish when competition increases, but it will vary according to skills, entrepreneurial spirit and pure luck.

One of the most important conclusions to be drawn from this is that it appears easier to establish limited companies when the purpose is to raise larger sums of capital. These companies are not only important for production capacity, but they also influence the distribution of wealth and income.[37] But limited companies are inherently positive, especially those which are run by incompetent people and those which are potentially exposed to fraud and speculation of different kinds. Because, as Aschehoug, in my view correctly, states,

The manager of large companies [limited companies] doesn't have the same economic interest in the economic results of the company as would an entrepreneur who owns his business, and even less so if the company loses money. The larger companies acknowledge this to some extent and offer the manager a higher salary, but sometimes also a bonus (*tantieme*), based on the economic results for the last year. But it is not possible to know whether this system would ensure that the management of the limited companies will be as clever and efficient as the best private entrepreneurial companies. […] In companies where the many shares are distributed so that no shareholder has a great interest in the management, the company often lacks a good management.[38]

This demonstrates the dilemma of responsibilities and economic results. As Aschehoug states, owning a company and working hard for its success usually go hand in hand. The difficulties arise when the shares are widely distributed and the management become employees. Aschehoug acknowledges that encouraging professional managers can be done through bonuses, but making a sound motivational system for managers in limited companies is difficult.

It appears that the limited company model is best adapted to capital-intensive activities such as railways, banks, insurance companies and so forth. The Norwegian ideal of the entrepreneur didn't survive in the textbooks, but it was very much alive in the Norwegian industrial structure. As shown in Chapter 3, Norway had just a few large industries and most companies were small and run by entrepreneurs. The entrepreneur was in many ways the 'real' capitalist, the one who set up his own company and ran it himself, but on a smaller scale than the large (multi)national companies that came relatively late to Norway. The larger companies were often wholly or partly owned by the state, because of the lack of large private capital owners, but some large private capital owners were also present, for instance in shipping.

In Volume IV, section 8, entitled 'The distribution of the proceeds from economic activity', Aschehoug gives a clarification of some important concepts. Firstly he defines the science of economics as 'the theory of production, turnover, distribution and consumption of economic goods'. Thereafter he stresses that the entrepreneur would normally own some part of the capital he has employed in his firm, but emphasizes that with less-developed credit markets it was normally the case that the entrepreneur owned a substantial part of the capital himself. These forms of capital have two different functions: one being saved capital (to be invested) and the other productive or employed capital. According to Aschehoug, the reason why Adam Smith regarded entrepreneurs essentially as capitalists, and included their part of the proceeds from the business activity under the common denomination of profit, was because they were often owners of production factors. Capitalists may live off capital rent, but it is more common that entrepreneurs borrow most of the capital that they employ. The confusion between the different forms of capital is, in Aschehoug's opinion, the main reason why the general consensus has been that the conflict of interest is between capitalists (owners of saved capital) and workers.

Furthermore, according to Aschehoug, it is with the entrepreneurs that the workers are fighting for their wages.[39] In Aschehoug's view, there are four production factors, so he clearly distinguishes between capitalists and entrepreneurs, even though the entrepreneurs might own some capital like housing, machinery or other production factors. The point is that they are actively taking part in the production and they are indispensable to the production process. He concludes that 'society's net income will be distributed as land rent, capital interest, labour wages and entrepreneurial income'.[40]

In order to clarify this competition between workers and entrepreneurs, it will be shown that the distinction Aschehoug makes is also apparent in the German tradition (although the example below is from Pareto). Backhaus points out the German adaptation of the *Unternehmer* before Schumpeter in his article 'Unternehmer in Wirtschaft und Politik'. He says that, with regard to the theory of profit of enterprise, it is essential to note that entrepreneurs and investors certainly need not be identical.[41] Further, he quotes Pareto, who, in *The Mind and Society* from 1935, explains in detail the qualities of the entrepreneur:

> Some authors have, and are still confusing, two very different meanings of this term: ownership of savings and those people who live off the interest from their property and those who keep everything moving in the company: the entrepreneur. This confusion is really a major obstacle to the understanding of economic issues, and even a greater barrier to understanding social processes in general. Indeed, in pursuing these two different goals capitalists often have diametrically opposed interests. The opposition of those interests may be even larger than the traditional class antagonism between the proletariat and the capitalist. From an economic standpoint, it is only beneficial for the entrepreneur if the interest on the savings and the capital which he borrows is as small as possible. [...] Also, wage increases for the entrepreneur who runs a factory can only be unpleasant for a certain transitional period, as long as he is bound by existing contracts. [...] In these cases, the entrepreneur has the same interests as his employees, and both are in conflict with the owners.[42]

Backhaus continues to quote another German, Pierstorff (whom Aschehoug knew and also refers to) from his work *Die Lehre vom Unternehmergewinn* from 1884:

> [The entrepreneur] is a class of independent producers [...] setting up their own capital assets, as a rule, but also their own activities, by reference to and use of other means of production or capital assets. They produce economic goods and services on their own account, organize economic activity and conduct operational risks to achieve for themselves a moderate recovery of the produced material goods and services, the revenue or the generated income.[43]

This definition is, according to Backhaus, strongly leaning on the characteristics of the entrepreneurial function in economic development that had previously been taught by Schmoller and other representatives of the German historical school.[44]

Aschehoug believed that because property income and work income had been treated together, and not separately, the conflicts that can be seen are, strictly speaking, between workers of different kinds: the employees and the entrepreneurs (employers). The division of income between these two groups is one of the main challenges in economics.[45] The socialist view that all income should accrue to the workers that personally 'did the work', and that capitalists and entrepreneurs only made their property and other machinery at the disposal of production and did not contribute with their personal effort and sacrifice, is a misconception. Entrepreneurs are also working, as well as being capital owners. Aschehoug believes that entrepreneurial income provides remuneration for the able planning, implementation and management of economic activities. In addition, many authors stress the importance of the entrepreneur to society's economic activity, pointing out the interaction between entrepreneurial activity and economic development. In many cases it is the entrepreneurs that have directed this development.

Aschehoug claims that John Stuart Mill saw entrepreneurial income mainly as interest on employed capital, with some additional income for the entrepreneur's own work. Aschehoug states that all new authors, including himself, associate themselves with the German view. German authors such as Hermann, von Thünen, Mangoldt and Schäffle stressed that entrepreneurial income is the result of bringing together different production factors.[46] Even if it is a composite income, it is still a remarkable and independent income, which should be counted along with labour wages, land rent and capital interest. Aschehoug emphasizes that the entrepreneur also carried the risk for the firm's economic activity.

In his early comments on workers and the question of productivity, and interrelations between the workers and the entrepreneurs, he points out that the human factor is fundamental. Productivity was enhanced by developing human resources both morally and educationally. The workers should show 'consideration', 'frugality', 'order', 'industriousness' and 'dependability', as well as showing an 'interest in cultural life', 'capability' and 'generally enlightened behaviour', in order to be 'willing to learn, to be trustworthy and competent'. On the other hand, the entrepreneurs should be 'technically competent', 'technically and universally educated', 'have special insights' and 'be intellectually capable of running businesses'. They should also show 'frugality' and 'carefully invest their capital', but most importantly, they should be real entrepreneurs and show initiative and industriousness.[47] Aschehoug had read the works of Karl Heinrich Rau, who in 1833 published the second part of his *Lehrbuch der politischen Ökonomie*, the *Grundsätze der Volkswirtschaftslehre*, where he described the ideal qualities of the entrepreneur as being 'Kenntnisse, Efahrungen, Combinationsvermögen, Besonnenheit und Aufmerksamkeit, Festigkeit des Willens, Fleiss, Ordnungsliebe' (Knowledge, experience, the ability to combine resources, balanced and able to show attention, strength of character, industriousness, love of order), many of which Aschehoug repeats and underlines in *Socialøkonomik* fifty years later.

The functioning of society was not only a question of the workers efforts, it was just as much a question of a sound relationship between them and the entrepreneurs. Both parties had a common interest. I believe that this ideal of a close relationship between the workers and the entrepreneurs is at the foreground of Aschehoug's thought when dealing with these issues in *Socialøkonomik*. It may have been naïve to believe in harmonious economic development, but Aschehoug was able to face reality and the many challenges for workers, and likewise for entrepreneurs.

Aschehoug outlines the development of the Industrial Revolution, using it to explain industrial structure. He sees standardization as concomitant with technical progress, but reminds the reader about the importance of individual initiative. However, statistics show that the structure of Norwegian industry around 1900 was fragmented with only a few larger industries, the largest employing around a thousand workers. In 1890, only 23 factories had more than three hundred employees. Due to the dispersed habitation pattern in Norway, consumption in the national market did not allow for large-scale production without an international market (an argument that is treated in a later chapter). In addition, Norwegian capital resources were limited, and Aschehoug remarks that industrialization was still young, although many advances had been made during the previous 30 years (1875 to 1905). The rise in employees in factories was 40 per cent between 1891 and 1900; in small industries it was 26 per cent.[48]

Aschehoug raises the question of how the emergence of larger factories would influence the industrial structure of Norway. He sees technological progress as a paramount force in future developments, but he has no clear answer to the question of how mechanization and, above all, electrification will be put to use in different industries and what the impact of the structural changes between smaller and larger businesses will be.[49] When it comes to the opposite of the small entrepreneurs, the large trusts, Aschehoug concludes that the initial scepticism from the workers' point of view is entirely merited. But with the development of strong labour unions, he sees a appropriate check on the power balance. Even though Norway only had a few large industries, the *Sagbrugsforeningen* (Sawmills Association) being the most famous example, the trust and monopoly problems were smaller in Norway. In his concluding remarks on Norwegian industrial structure, he says that smaller industries will most certainly defend their place in the future economy. He also believes that the municipality and the state can run industries that will require large investments. In agriculture, still the most important industry around 1900, the individual entrepreneurs will continue to be dominant in the future.[50] Agriculture was important for a long time in Norway, but as industrialization developed during the first decades of the twentieth century, the sector gradually lost its importance. However, the ideal of the small, independent farmer still existed (as shown earlier).

Conclusion: What Happened after Aschehoug?

Finally, the pertinent question is: what happened to the entrepreneurial theory after Aschehoug?[51] There were still followers of his teachings living and working in Norway after his death. The closest contemporary economist was Morgenstierne, as well as the somewhat younger Jaeger, who in 1922 published his own work, *Teoretisk socialøkonomik* (Theoretical economics), and Aarum, who revised Aschehoug's *Socialøkonomik*. Morgenstierne became a professor in 1886, Jaeger in 1902 and Aarum in 1917. Morgenstierne views the entrepreneurs in the same way as Say and Aschehoug. He carries the risk of his business and assembles the productive forces, having an important function in society. He states that: 'The entrepreneur receives his gain in different way to those that render the productive forces, his gain is what is left when all the assistants have been paid. The amount that is left will then depend on whether the production has been economically profitable.'[52] Morgenstierne also introduces the term 'risk premium' as an element of entrepreneurial gain:

In many cases entrepreneurial gain will only to a limited degree contain a compensation for work. And when it is something that neither can be placed under capital gain or labour wages, what is it then? To be sure it is then the risk premium, which falls to the one that employs capital in an independent productive activity. When it commonly will be expected a greater result of own employment of capital then from borrowed, it is evidently a risk premium.[53]

Jaeger picks up the idea of a risk premium and the view of the entrepreneur as a risk taker, but importantly he does not count the entrepreneur as a fourth factor of production. He writes,

> The one for whose account the economic activity is operated is called entrepreneur. Entrepreneurs can therefore not only be the private producers, but also the state and a municipality. The characteristic of the entrepreneur is that he carries the risk that is connected with the business. This is shown by the fact that the so-called entrepreneurial gain, which is from land rent, wages and capital interest an essentially different income, always falls to the one for whose account and risk the business is carried out, and who therefore in return always must carry the entrepreneurial risk connected with the business.[54]

Aarum follows Jaeger and makes the division of the production between land, labour and capital. Aarum's view on the entrepreneur is in the Say tradition:

> The one that manages the activity, regardless of its objective, is called 'driftsherre' [Unternehmer, undertaker, entrepreneur]. The entrepreneur has the difficult task of planning and managing the firm and bears its risk, e.g., the judicial responsibility for its obligations, vis-à-vis other private persons or the public authorities together with the economic burden, which insist that he must carry the loss when the activity for one reason or another is not profitable or cannot cover its costs.[55]

He continues his argument and claims that the task of the entrepreneur, as such, comprises both the management of the firm and the bearing of its risk. In some respects more weight can be placed on one, and in other respects more can be placed on the other of these functions, but this does not mean that they are the only criteria for the term entrepreneur.

Sæther and Eriksen have analysed the further development of the entrepreneur in Norwegian as well as international literature. Their conclusions are that the entrepreneur gradually disappeared with Ragnar Frisch and the Oslo school of economics. Sæther and Eriksen further assert that the theory of the entrepreneur is not present in any of the international economic textbooks and that he became an *invisible man* in mainstream economics. They have analysed the economic textbook canon and find that microeconomic models predominantly study timeless static equilibriums. In their analysis they have found that the entrepreneur is present in the theories of Frederic Garver and Alvin Harvey Hansen, presented in the *Principles of Economics* (1928), a book that was widely used in the US before World War II. The entrepreneur has a major role also in the later second and third editions from 1937 and 1947. They see the entrepreneur as particularly important for the production of society, and in chapter 3 they state, 'The entrepreneur is the final coordinator of the factors employed, including even the salaried managers themselves. The going concern is under the final control of the entrepreneur, or group of entrepreneurs, and the ultimate decisions of management therefore are in their hands.'[56]

In a society with larger group companies, the entrepreneurs are 'the small group of stockholders who dominate the company, elect the directors and officers, and dictate the policies of the enterprise – these persons are the entrepreneurs'. In addition, in business the entrepreneur and risk taking are inseparable. The *Principles of Economics* was a standard textbook before the breakthrough of neoclassical theory. Sæther and Eriksen conclude that the entrepreneur disappeared both from Norwegian and international textbooks after the third edition of Graver and Hansen's *Principles of Economics*, some time during the 1950s. I may add that a quick look in textbooks from the 1980s and 1990s confirms that there are no traces of the fourth production factor, the entrepreneur.[57] The result may be a neglect of the importance of what I have referred to as 'the glue' between the other production factors. From Aschehoug's view, private initiative, skills and the personal ability and competence of entrepreneurs are the most valuable assets in society, securing a productive society and enhancing general welfare.

Chapter 11

TRADE AND CUSTOMS DEBATES FROM 1840 TO 1906

In Chapter 3, the Norwegian economic and political context in the nineteenth century was examined, and the main protagonist, Schweigaard, was presented. This chapter looks at the different trade and customs debates, focusing on those which followed Schweigaard's death in 1870. Aschehoug was central to many of them, as were his colleagues at the university, Hertzberg and Morgenstierne. The intention is to relate these debates to Aschehoug's final statements on trade and trade policies in *Socialøkonomik*. The conclusion that can be drawn is that Aschehoug and his fellow scholars believed in the principles of free trade, just as Schweigaard had before them. They were nevertheless concerned about the international protectionist development, especially from the 1870s onwards. And at the turn of the century, they felt compelled to admit that protectionist measures were needed in order to 'meet the international trade regimes'. Their main argument in favour of free trade was that, for a small open economy like that of Norway, free trade was of paramount importance for economic growth. But again, the debates show that pragmatic decisions were made, and above all, trade and customs were a general concern of the state and should not be left laissez-faire, but as the saying further goes, 'laissez-passer les marchandises' ('let the merchandise pass' – the origin is pointed out in Chapter 8).

The debates do not imply that the Norwegian economists were adherents of laissez-faire. As should be remembered from the summary of Schweigaard, laissez-faire was never accepted wholeheartedly in Norway. In general, Norwegian economists and politicians, including Schweigaard and Aschehoug, were both liberal and conservative, but they still rejected laissez-faire. One of the reasons why they have nevertheless been interpreted as laissez-faire economists by many historians until recently can be found in the work of Anne-Lise Seip and her husband Jens Arup Seip (who wrote who wrote several seminal Norwegian books in the 1960s and 1970s on nineteenth century politics). Rune Slagstad, the author of a more recent analysis of Norwegian political and historical development, comments on how Jens Arup Seip's interpretation of Aschehoug's ideological sympathies come from Aschehoug's travels to England: 'Aschehoug travelled to England to study modern liberal economics in practice. This has been used to prove the Norwegian turn towards British laissez-faire ideology.'[1]

Slagstad claims that Anne-Lise Seip has taken this as proof of the liberal preferences of Aschehoug, a train of thought that she follows all the way through her work and why she claims that so-called 'harmony-liberalism' came under pressure during the 1870s.

Slagstad underlines the fact that, even as early as 1848, Aschehoug appealed in his lectures for his students to follow a more 'Hegelian way', as opposed to the (general contemporary) view of Adam Smith's laissez-faire: 'The latest views on the state that had been developed were that it was not only a useful union, but that it was a necessary union of the external, manifested human intellect, an organism, a real individual, not equal to the physical individual, but parallel to it.'[2] It is clear that Aschehoug and his fellow scholars argued for the benefits of freer trade, because they believed in the economic benefits of trade. The actual development showed that domestic trade restrictions (between towns and villages) were abolished, thereby increasing the home market, whereas restrictions and protectionist measures followed the international wave of more liberalized trade during the mid-nineteenth century. The Norwegians kept the more liberal regime as long as they could, but eventually had to apply a more protectionist system. The analysis is concluded with the 1903 trade debate. The arguments that arose in this debate show their concerns and their positions.

Historical Trade Development in Norway: Theory and Reality

Schweigaard claimed, by using general economic arguments, that the laissez-faire doctrine was insufficient to explore the causes of national wealth. He argued that empirical and historical analyses had to be conducted and that other sectors of society had to be brought into the analysis in order to understand the workings of economics. He says, 'One would then find that the causes which have their origins in the religious, moral and political strata in society are more important than other premises for economic production in society.'[3] He mentions the factor of morality in British political and institutional superiority: 'among the conditions for a general distribution of welfare one finds morality, as well as superior political and juridical institutions being just as important as general conditions for utilizing the production forces'.[4] Keilhau, a Norwegian professor in economics (from 1935 after Oscar Jaeger), points out that the Norwegian and British development of free trade were parallel in many aspects during the mid-nineteenth century, and that Schweigaard was the driving force.[5]

Another important element in the debate is that Norway did not have any income taxes between 1838 and 1892. During this period, the customs policy was the whole tax policy and almost the full financial policy, with most of the income received by the state coming from customs.[6] According to Mestad, what Schweigaard meant when he talked about free trade was not a trade without any customs or taxes, it was a trade that was as free as possible within a reasonable framework, a compromise between the income to the state and as few obstacles for free trade as possible.

Aschehoug bases his analysis of the Norwegian trade development on Schweigaard's *Ungdomsarbeider* and the Danish economist William Scharling's *Handels og toldpolitik* (Trade and customs policy). The Norwegian trade regime was for a long time built on mercantilism. But even before the end of the union with Denmark in 1814, mercantilist politics were broken by a new law, introduced on 1 February 1797, which abolished the protectionist policies of the old mercantilist system, but retained a moderate protection for domestic industries.[7] Hertzberg had claimed that Albert Schäffle was the 'real' founder of the historical school, and Lykkja mentions in his thesis the influence of Roscher and Hermann on Norwegian thought, all underlining the importance of a regulatory state. Another German, Rau, had defended protection customs for industries in their emerging phases, which will be shown was a part of the Norwegian debates at the turn of the century (1903). This trade regime was kept for four decades, and new customs tariffs arrived in 1842 and 1860, both lowering tariffs and generally establishing a free trade system, but still protecting domestic industries.[8] This point is also underlined in the lectures of Keilhau. He claims that Norwegian economic policy, from 1814 to 1860, consistently followed a more protectionist path for domestic industries. Later, the level of protection was lessened due to the trade treaty with France in 1866 and by a parliamentary decision in 1873. The question of a protection custom was again discussed in parliament in 1881, though not resulting in any significant changes. Another important free trade treaty with Sweden came in 1874, but was abolished in 1895 (effective in 1897). Morgenstierne wrote an article in *Statsøkonomisk Tidsskrift* about the termination of the treaty in 1897, and as Aschehoug remarks, 'even the warmest adherents of free trade had to admit that Norway had to protect its industries from Swedish competition'.[9]

As mentioned before, shipping was crucial in Schweigaard's trade scheme, more so than growth through industrialization. The liberalization of European trade during the mid-nineteenth century was positive for Norway, and especially for shipping and transportation. Keilhau underlines this point in his lectures almost one hundred years later: 'The most distinctive trait of Norwegian economic development during the past 100 years or so is that our small country has been able to build one of the largest trading fleets in the world. [...] Free trade has, to a great extent, created the possibility for Norwegian shipping to be in a strong position.'[10] Ola Mestad calls the second half of the nineteenth century 'the first globalization period', corresponding to the huge growth in Norwegian shipping.[11] The Norwegian position concerning a freer trade was naturally positive due to the huge importance of its trading fleet, which not only shipped goods to and from Norway, but engaged in shipping globally. Even though transportation by land is generally the most important globally, shipping has historically been most important in Norway, and still is.

Trade, money and credit constitute a whole volume in *Socialøkonomik* (Volume III). The scope of this chapter is limited to his comments on trade per se, not his monetary and credit theories. However, Aschehoug also contributed a large article to *Statsøkonomisk Tidsskrift* on money and credit, and generally took part in many discussions concerning these issues. He was also one of the founders of the largest commercial bank in Norway, Den norske creditbank. The complete picture of international economics and trade must, of course, include monetary policies, but the scope of this work does not allow for an analysis of money and credit, which in another setting would be useful. In the following, what Aschehoug says about trade in general will be analysed.

Aschehoug relates theory to historical development in his presentation and analysis in *Socialøkonomik*. Originally, free trade was based on the theory of Ricardo: 'The teachings of the classical school were based on the comparative advantage of production. [...] International trade was originally barter trade [...] and the relationship between the production cost of the two goods influenced production in both countries. [...] A country must choose to produce the goods that give the most valuable output in relation to the production sacrifice.[12]

Aschehoug here quotes the main theories found in Ricardo's *Principles of Political Economy and Taxation* and John Stuart Mill's *Principles of Political Economy*. He continues his quote by mentioning recent discussions in Britain, France and Germany, displaying his thorough knowledge of international literature.[13] Thirty years later, Keilhau endorses Aschehoug's analysis: the free trade arguments are basically grounded in the theories of the British classical economists.[14] In his lectures, he emphasizes two points in order to explain the development of economic liberalism: a gradual liberalization of industries and the right of establishment, and a general breakthrough of free trade principles in international trade.

After having presented the basic principles of international trade using the comparative advantage theory, Aschehoug states that the current international trade situation looks different, pointing out that transportation is the vehicle for international trade, which is just what the Norwegian case shows. Goods must be transportable, and trade may include services as well.[15] Transportation gets a separate chapter in Aschehoug's analysis, connected to the general presentation of the means of production. The German term is *Verkehr*, and the Norwegian is *befordringsvirksomheden*, Aschehoug pointing out the natural basis for different means of transportation, even mentioning airborne transportation (aviation was still in its infancy in 1907). Transportation is vitally important for all domestic economic activity as well as for transactions between countries. The main point to highlight is that the cost of transportation is a part of the total production cost, so a reduction in it will lead to a lower total production cost. Better transportation possibilities also increase the size of the possible market for a product. For example, cheaper transportation made it feasible to export grain produced in Australia, the US and Russia, supplying the rest of Europe with cheap grain.[16]

A country's international trade is dependent not only on its natural industries or resources, but also just as much on the productivity of its citizens, their degree of civilization and their capital strength. Aschehoug underlines the importance of unhindered transportation, saying that neither laws nor trade restrictions should hinder trade. This free trade approach gained strength with the development of railways and steam ships, but soon met insurmountable obstacles. According to Aschehoug, the development in international trade leads to more similar jurisprudence among countries, especially when it comes to trade and industry laws (*næringslovgivning*) and shipping laws. Finally, Aschehoug saw the old dream of a peaceful coexistence because of trade come true, due to the rapid development of transportation, and communications now being an accepted task of statesmen. The same point is underlined in Keilhau's lectures forty years later.[17] As protectionist policies were adapted, this argument became weaker.

Aschehoug further claims that the growth in international trade had come about due to the progress of legal institutions and means of communication (transport), technical advances and general population growth. But of most importance was the building of the legal institutions (*rettsstat/Rechtsstaat*), which includes the legal security of making agreements, stock exchanges and monetary and credit systems.[18] The building of institutions was, as shown in Chapter 3, a crucial part of the Norwegian modernizing scheme.

Aschehoug sums up his position by explaining the main principles of free trade in the following way: the first premise is that the state should refrain from hindering free trade as much as possible, and only apply customs in order to secure income to the state (fiscal) or hinder consumption of damaging products such as alcohol and tobacco (cultural), and not to protect domestic industries. The main principle is that export of all kinds of domestic products must be allowed. Secondly, import customs can only be applied to products that cannot be produced domestically. Thirdly, if it is necessary to apply customs to imports due to fiscal or cultural reasons, then domestic production of the same goods must be either prohibited or tariffed as well. Internal, domestic customs barriers have been abolished, so the issue to be discussed is external, international trade. Aschehoug points out that the reason for using protection is purely political.

So, what does Aschehoug generally say about a protectionist regime? He firstly makes it clear that the former argument that a custom protection system would hinder economic growth is no longer viable, pointing out the strong economic progress that can be seen in both Germany and the US, both countries having protected their industries. But he also says that due to both countries having large domestic markets (creating a large domestic demand), and their growing and educated population, the possibility of creating large-scale industries is good. This does not apply to smaller countries, like Norway, because the domestic market does not create a large enough demand for large-scale domestic production – export markets are needed.

A custom tariff will normally make imports more expensive, the citizens will have to pay for, or buy if possible, the same products from local producers, or reduce their consumption. Customs will also change the domestic pattern of production; labour and capital will be applied less productively in industries that have protection, whereas without the customs, industries that are viable on their own will demand labour and capital and apply them more productively.

Another argument for a protectionist system was that by hindering competition from international industries, domestic entrepreneurs would be likely to stick to their old way of producing goods, whereas competition would force them to be updated on technical advances and apply modern methods of production.

The conclusion that Aschehoug makes after discussing various examples and debates is that, generally, customs on imported goods would make goods more expensive. He also comments on dumping and how this can be damaging to international trade. Aschehoug firmly believes in free trade, especially for smaller countries. He also has a pragmatic attitude when it comes to applying customs, and apart from the importance of transportation, he underlines the importance of entrepreneurial efforts to create viable industries that may successfully compete internationally.

Foreign Trade Policy Development

In terms of the development of foreign trade policy, the main issue is whether it is beneficial for a state to influence trade with customs policies. Aschehoug points out that the theory of free trade gained currency long before it could actually be observed in the trade policies of states. The obvious example is the process of the abolition of the Corn

Laws in England, and just after, the Navigation Act. England's transition from protection to free trade led to important economic progress, which was also noted by other countries and strengthened the belief in the theories of free trade.[19] Aschehoug notes that the last election (in 1906) was won by free trade supporters and, for a country like Norway, a freer trade with England was an advantage.[20] Keilhau later points out that England was becoming more and more alone in their free trade regime after 1878, as protectionist policies were increasingly applied from 1878 to 1914.[21]

In Germany, free trade was implemented with success before the country was united, with customs barriers being abolished between the smaller German states, with economic growth as a result. The free trade policy in Germany was described in Roscher's *Geschichte der National-Oekonomik in Deutschland* and in Schmoller's *Grundriss*. The customs policy of Prussia from 1818 was successfully adapted by the other German states, and a smaller custom was retained in order for local industry to compete with foreign industry.[22] Aschehoug mentions Schmoller and his *Grundriss*, in which he, to some extent, defends mercantilism and under certain conditions prefers the modern protectionist system to free trade.[23] But Germany experienced a serious economic crisis in 1873, leading to a massive claim for a more protectionist customs policy. This was also due to the increasing import of cheaper grain, putting pressure on German agriculture. The only argument for protection that seems suitable to Aschehoug is the protection of domestic agriculture.[24]

An agreement was made between agricultural and industrial sectors to increase protection custom, as both were mainly supplying the domestic market.[25] What Aschehoug attempts to analyse is whether customs work or not. In the case of Germany, he notes that German industry had made huge progress after customs were applied. The customs had, to some extent, hindered the import of industrial goods from England and Belgium, but the main reason for the progress was due to the skilled German industrialists and their ability to develop viable industries and subsequently increase the export of German industrial goods.

In France, free trade policy was defended by most economists, but was opposed by industrialists. In 1860 the trade treaty between France and England was signed. A liberal custom policy was at the same time adapted by Denmark, Sweden, Holland, Belgium, Switzerland and the Kingdom of Sardinia. As Aschehoug points out, the parallel development in transport (railways, steam ships) paved the way to a freer trade – not to use these means of transportation in order to facilitate trade would have been a contradiction.[26]

But free trade met resistance in the US and in Russia; Aschehoug refers to the McKinley Tariff in 1890, followed by Wilson's tariff in 1894 and then again with the more severe Dingley tariff in 1897. He does not agree with the protectionist custom policies of the nineteenth century in Russia. Protectionist policies were also adapted by France and Germany – the French argument was to protect export industries, like the wine producers, and to protect domestic agriculture. According to Aschehoug, the results had not been satisfactory for France, with French foreign trade remaining almost unchanged.

Carey and List had recommended that the US and Germany protect their domestic industries in their development period, in order to establish themselves without too much competition (from England). John Stuart Mill adhered to this to a certain extent, but the danger, says Aschehoug, is that once the industries are used to having protection, they will fight for it. A reduction would be hard to come about, even when the industries are past their founding phase, an argument that is repeated in the Norwegian debates. Aschehoug concludes that free trade defenders want free enterprise and leave the risk of developing industries to the entrepreneur, who is believed to carefully employ resources, whereas protectionist defenders will support them by using customs.[27]

To summarize, Aschehoug here looks through history in order to evaluate theories of trade and compare them to economic development in different countries. His conclusion is still in line with his belief in free trade in smaller countries. The state must to a much larger extent than any individual pay attention to long-term consequences, which may include political actions that will restrict free trade.

Norwegian Trade and Customs Debates from 1842 to 1879

The Norwegian legal development in trade and customs regulations is marked out by the following years: 1818, 1842, 1857, 1866, 1874, 1882, 1897, 1903 and 1906. Not all of them will be commented on, but milestones where Aschehoug participated in the debate will be highlighted. They include both domestic and international trade debates.

From the debates about trade in 1842 and the preparatory works before the passing of the law in 1842, it is stated that changes in domestic trade regulations shall only be done 'if they abolish the prevalent restrictions and no new ones shall be applied'. Harmony between rural and urban trade would come about when trade was as free as possible.[28] If restrictions were to be applied, Schweigaard would concede to them only if they concerned the common good (*almeenvelet*) or if it was necessary regarding Norwegian trade. Norway was largely dependent on trade, and the domestic industries were often small and needed protection in order to be able to compete. It was, then, right that the state interfered with industry 'with the means it had at its disposal'.[29]

In 1842 Aschehoug was still studying, but from 1856 to 1857 he participated in debates about customs and trade. His main views on trade and the right to engage in business can be found in his preparatory work for the Poverty Commission in 1856. His first argument concerned domestic monopolies. Monopolies represented higher prices and consequently more expensive living conditions for workers (as consumers). In the preparatory documents he uses arguments such as, 'village shopkeepers have a monopoly and can set the price they want'. He was also arguing for the possibility of a free occupation, meaning that it should be allowed to be self-employed and run a small business.[30] He wanted competition and saw it as a guarantee of keeping prices lower and thereby bettering the living conditions for the labour class, but it was also an argument in favour of the possibility of becoming self-employed.

When it came to the credit sector, Aschehoug argued for a contribution from the state, suggesting that the state, through the local municipalities, should establish savings banks in the smaller villages. These banks could provide loans for small industrial activities. In this case the state facilitates competition to other credit institutions, and it is not free enterprise that will secure the best solution. This is an example of the rather pragmatic solutions that were chosen in order to modernize and to contribute to 'the best welfare for all'.

He had just started his career and the Poverty Commission was among the first of his larger engagements.

In 1865–66 'den franske traktatsaken' (the French treaty case) was discussed in parliament. In this case Mestad points out that it was of paramount importance to Schweigaard that small countries, like Norway, should not be let out of European trade when it came to the 'power of the seas'.[31] According to Mestad, Schweigaard thought that the fact that other European countries had liberalized their trade was the main reason for the economic growth Norway had experienced for the past 15 years (from 1850 to 1865). As already mentioned, in 1874 Norway signed the free trade treaty with Sweden. Bergh and Hanisch underline that the Norwegian economists argued for a free trade with the usual classical arguments, rejecting raises in customs and other trade-prohibiting means. According to them, all the university professors were 'free trade men'.[32] But again, this is too simple a statement; they were 'free trade men', but they were pragmatic in their practical approach.

During the 1870s, Norway was a more liberal country (in terms of trade policies) than most other European countries.[33] Due to protectionist measures in other countries, Norway eventually surrendered and Aschehoug had to admit in 1879 that 'some years ago the sentiments for the free trade system were strong in many countries, and also in this country, and I believed that I would never have to participate in a debate about this system and have to defend the benefits of free trade'.[34] Economic recessions were, according to Aschehoug, the main reason why protectionist policies were applied internationally, but he added that 'it is unbelievable how it is possible to attribute to free trade any share in this pressure'.[35] Hertzberg defended Aschehoug in a couple of articles in *Morgenbladet* – both agreed that economic depressions usually promoted more protectionist policies, which was the case in the 1870s.

The same year, 1879, Aschehoug was elected chairman for the Customs Commission.[36] The suggestion for a new Customs Commission, during the parliamentary discussions in 1879, showed a concern about the perceived sentiments for a more protectionist regime: '[For] the future of the domestic industry […] it is paramount to remove trade restrictions, and for the time being one has to be content only with theoretical investigations, that could probably not completely satisfy or reassure the doubts that, in these matters, currently seem to have got a certain foothold among those who are more or less directly involved.'[37]

Seip comments, 'In 1873 Aschehoug warned that the boom could continue [being afraid that it would lead to a sharp economic downturn]. He also noted the long term growth due to technical progress, entrepreneurial spirit and insight, a better ability to raise capital and the continuing improvement of transportation.'[38] In the following years a depression came, and questions about protection customs and direct consumption taxes arose. This was the backdrop of the Customs Commission that was established in 1879.[39] Hertzberg and Aschehoug asked the manager of the statistical bureau, Anders N. Kiær, to present statistics showing the value of industrial imports and exports from 1866–79 and later to 1886. This resulted in an article in *Statsøkonomisk Tidsskrift*, 'Om Norges udførsel av industriprodukter' (About the export of Norwegian industrial products). The statistics showed that industrial exports had increased by a factor of 12 and that growth was continuing, whereas imports had grown to a much lesser extent. The recommendation from the Customs Commission was an agreement 'not to principally alter the import tariffs', but the decision was made by eight to seven votes; Aschehoug and Hertzberg were the leading defenders of free trade.[40] Seip tries to draw a line from the 1850s to the 'well-written' proposition from the commission in 1879, and she is right in claiming that this was still a defence for free trade, but not completely, and with nothing to do with laissez-faire.[41] The principles were still specialization when possible, using trade in order to create larger markets for Norwegian industries, and getting reciprocal benefits through free benefits.

The Customs Commission from 1879 argued that all customs meant an increase in prices, and that protectionist tariffs were equal to subsidies for industries. These arguments are also found in Aschehoug's presentation in *Socialøkonomik* written more than twenty years later. What Aschehoug refers to as 'natural industries' must be understood to be industries that had natural conditions for success, either by know-how, entrepreneurial efforts, technology or natural resources, and therefore presumably had no need for protection. What he calls 'artificial industries' were industries that did not have any natural basis, and were, according to Aschehoug, often lacking productivity, so the state should be cautious of supporting them. Such support would often be a hindrance to sound industrial development.[42]

But, the protectionist agitation continued through the 1880s, and in 1887 another Customs Commission resulted in the same votes, eight to seven, but this time with more disagreement than the Aschehoug commission eight years earlier. Two opposing propositions were presented, but still no important protection measures were taken.[43] The conclusion seems to be that Norway gradually had to adapt to the international trade regimes in order not to weaken the country's position.

The 1903 Trade Debate and Lecture at the Statsøkonomisk Forening

In 1904, Aschehoug's colleague Bredo Morgenstierne wrote an article in *Statsøkonomisk Tidsskrift* called 'Vor handelspolitik' (Our trade policy). The article was the basis for a lecture and a discussion at the Statsøkonomisk forening during the autumn of 1903. The chairman of the association was, at the time, Hertzberg (succeeding Aschehoug in 1902), who had been part of the commission for the customs and trade questions of 1879 and who, in 1903, was elected chairman of the new Customs Commission. The intention here is to show how these so-called 'free trade university professors' handled a political issue, and it is worth noting that they were able to discuss the matters without being ardent theoretical free trade believers.

Morgenstierne starts out by saying,

Our industries have recently experienced unfortunate business circles, and in such times the demand for state protection comes up, either as a protection custom or as a rise in an existing one. Our trade system has never really been a free trade system or a fiscal system, like the English, but it was close to it from the 1860s to the 1880s. In 1888 we started a reduction in the fiscal rates and an increase in the protection rates, until we finally in 1897, after the termination of the Swedish–Norwegian free trade treaty, completely adapted a protectionist policy [...] and the agriculture customs have been quite far reaching, although not as considerably as in certain other countries.[44]

These arguments correspond to the presentation of Aschehoug in *Socialøkonomik*.

The result of the more liberal trade policy during most of the nineteenth century was, according to Aschehoug, a huge increase in industrial production and export, especially from 1866 to 1897. He reports that the value of exports grew from 1.5 million Norwegian kroner in 1866 to 44.5 million Norwegian kroner in 1897. No other country had a greater increase in industrial exports in this period.[45] In 1905, a customs tariff of 10 per cent was applied to all imports of machines, with the exception of machines used in shipping, in order to make this important industry more competitive.

The abolition of the free trade treaty with Sweden turned the generally positive opinion towards free trade in Norway to a stricter regime. Norwegian industry had to be protected from Swedish competition.[46] Morgenstierne claimed, in his lecture about trade policies in 1903, that he perceived 'the abolition of the Norwegian–Swedish free trade treaty as the largest folly that has happened between the two nations'. He felt that a lesson should be learned, and from this, 'precautions should be applied in order to pave the way to obtain the goal: the most liberal possible trade relations between the people of the Nordic countries.'[47] Such a trade union would remedy the greatest shortcoming of Norwegian protectionism, namely the size of the home market for the protected industries. Morgenstierne had already defended this free trade treaty with Sweden in his lecture at the Statsøkonomisk forening in 1887, but the treaty was terminated in 1895, and eight years later, in 1903, it was still not showing any signs of a new agreement. A protection policy was approved in 1905.

A typical argument came from Morgenstierne, who claimed that the discussions about customs could be seen in practical terms, which had fortunately almost always been the case. The Norwegian free trade supporters had, for the last generation, at least been as pragmatic as possible. Morgenstierne describes his fellow university professors as free trade supporters who are not doctrinaire and who clearly understand how to evaluate the benefits of stability in customs policies. He says this includes himself and most of his colleagues, and naturally this would include Aschehoug and Hertzberg. An abstract principle of free trade rests on conditions that, under no circumstances, can be applied in the customs policies of a country.[48] He further underlines that at that time (in 1903) there were no disputes between protectionist and free trade policies in Norway, because 'we are all practically protectionists'.[49]

Morgenstierne mentions a brochure called *On Insular Free Trade*, in which the British prime minister Arthur Balfour argued that free trade was the ideal and that protectionist policies always represent a loss to a country. As should be remembered this was Aschehoug's argument both in the 1879 debate and in *Socialøkonomik*, also referring to the British debate and to the brochure by Balfour. The question, according to Balfour, is to what extent this loss is necessary in order to prevent even greater damage.[50] Morgenstierne and Aschehoug have the same understanding of the British debate and arguments.

Furthermore, Morgenstierne wanted to stop the talks about how much an increased customs tariff would better the state finances and how well domestic industries do when they are protected. He acknowledges the argument that growing industries can be better off with protection in their infant period in order to get a grip on the domestic market.[51] He also has to admit that the possibility of a free trade regime seems to have passed: 'The egoistic trade policy that the states are leading have not brought about an idea of solidarity or union, rather it seems that any opportunity to let strangers pay a share of one's country's state expenditures is eagerly grasped.'[52] And he claims, like Aschehoug, that any custom or tariff will eventually directly or indirectly lead to a higher consumer price.[53]

Following Morgenstierne's lecture, the new chairman, Ebbe Hertzberg, conducted the discussions at the Statsøkonomisk forening. Aschehoug did not participate, but both his colleagues Hertzberg and Morgenstierne did.

The first comments came from the secretary of state, Gunnar Knudsen (who later became prime minister in 1908), from the liberal left party, Venstre. He was surprised at the discussions because he was used to generally positive attitudes towards free trade from the university professors: 'In this country we have taken for granted that the learned men at the university are, and will be, free trade defenders, not only in principle, but in the practical application of policies. It is a pleasant surprise for me to find that the old opinions at the university are now broken.'[54]

Knudsen underlined that he saw trade policies not only as something which concerns producers, industries or consumers, but also as a matter of national importance. Considerations should include the whole nation, and the general welfare of all citizens: 'It is a question of how the policies in this country should be organized in order to secure the best possible living conditions for as many people as possible.'[55]

Several debaters raised the issue of the size of the home market and the poor possibilities of specializing when the market is so small.[56] One of them announced, 'I have not yet heard that a protected industry tells the politicians: now I do not need protection any longer.'[57]

Hertzberg agreed with Knudsen, and pointed out that trade policies must be considered in the context of the whole national financial situation.[58] He further agreed with one of the other debaters that it is impossible to conduct free trade if other nations do not apply the same policy. It is a premise that free trade must be reciprocal and applied by all trading nations, otherwise alternatives must be sought, namely an adapted protectionist policy. Hertzberg claimed that the idea of free trade must be universal, and when other nations, even England, protect their industries, the free trade system is broken.[59]

And finally, Morgenstierne was clearly disappointed:

It is true that free trade is the best, and that protection customs generally are an evil that a country must avoid as long as possible. But what should we do? We are forced to accept it. When other countries are becoming protectionist, we have to follow. We must meet them with the same weapons. There is no doubt that this is the most common argument, and in my mind the most important argument for protection, both for becoming protectionist, like England, and for a further strengthening and raising of the customs walls, as in our country.[60]

Conclusion

As has been shown, Aschehoug never abandoned his free trade position, and neither did his fellow scholars. They defended free trade principles both theoretically and in political debates. But, it was never a defence of a laissez-faire principle. The development in international trade towards more protection was the main reason why Aschehoug became more pragmatic in policy discussions, rather than because of a change of opinion. Aschehoug had to review his principles, not because he stopped believing in them, but because the wisest possible policy was to adjust to international developments. As his analysis in *Socialøkonomik* shows, he still defended free trade as the best possible measure for economic growth.

Chapter 12

THE THEORY OF ECONOMIC CRISES

Economic crisis theory is topic of interest that has been extensively discussed among economists in recent times, and many theories have been launched in order to explain economic crises. This chapter will look at what Aschehoug has to say about them and their origins (for example, chapter 94, 'Changing good and bad times; the history of economic crises', and chapter 95, 'The theory of crises'). Aschehoug had, in 1898, published an article in *Statsøkonomisk Tidsskrift* called 'De økonomiske kriser og depressioner i det 19de aarhundrede', containing much of the same theory and history that is later used in *Socialøkonomik*, which was written almost ten years later. The historical parts are updated to include the crises at the beginning of the twentieth century, and his proposed measures and explanations are developed further.

Crises: Necessary to Analyse

The theory of crises was also the focus of another Norwegian economist and jurist, Einarsen, in the article 'Gode og daarlige Tider' (Good and bad times) in *Statsøkonomisk Tidsskrift* in 1904. Together with Aschehoug, this comprises the turn-of-the-century Norwegian literature on the subject. This article included the same theories that Aschehoug later included in *Socialøkonomik*.

The theory of crises is discussed in Part X of *Socialøkonomik*, 'The uneven development of economic activities and results and measures against it'. This part also contains chapters about the distribution of economic wealth, the labour unions and 'social questions'. Looking back at Schweigaard and his thoughts about the 'distribution of economic wealth', Aschehoug has come many steps further in developing his thoughts about the distribution of wealth in society. The 'social question' was, of course, much more pressing after the death of Schweigaard in 1870 than before, and labour unions and labour insurances and laws were not formed in his lifetime. In the opening paragraph, Aschehoug states, 'Even though many things have changed, modern society is still far from reaching its highest purpose: the satisfaction of all rightful and timely needs.'[1] As already pointed out many times, Aschehoug disagrees with the solution of the socialists. He believes in the market economy and the current legal order of the time, but he clearly sees the challenges this system is facing in avoiding serious setbacks and especially in ensuring a stable employment. The main purpose of understanding crises is, of course, understanding how they could be prevented or ameliorated, given a general belief in a market society and not proposing a change in the economic system as such.[2] Economic activity is cyclical, and crises create turning points. Aschehoug's intention is not to operate on a very high level of abstraction, distant from practical relevance. Rather, he argues as someone who is concerned about reality, and therefore his theories become more understandable and he suggests measures to solve or at least cope with the problems of economic crises.

Aschehoug identifies several different economic crises, building on theories found in Conrad's *HWB*, the article 'Krisen' by Herkner and 'Überproduktion' by Lexis. Among his other sources are Schmoller, Roscher and Wirth (*Geschichte der Handelskrisen*), the French writers Juglar (*Des crises commerciales*) and Lescure (*Des crises générales et périodiques de surproduction*), as well as Einarsen's previously mentioned article about crises, *Gode og daarlige tider*, from 1904.[3] Clearly, many new sources were available to Aschehoug ten years after the article he wrote in *Statsøkonomisk Tidsskrift*, and he made an effort to understand the theory behind the crises in more detail than was the case in the earlier article.[4] In this first article only Wirth and Juglar are being used. As mentioned, a colleague of Aschehoug, Einarsen, had written about crises in 1904, pointing out that the impulses that spark the wavelike movements in the economy were difficult to discern. Aschehoug agrees, saying that the explanations for these movements are complex. Aschehoug further states that '[crises] develop and are influenced by many different, more or less important, causes. Finding them and analysing them is a paramount theoretical task.'[5]

Crises and Psychology

To begin with, it seems that Aschehoug bases his analysis on the deeper human psychology. He writes that 'the wavelike movements in the economy have its deepest roots in civilized humanity's urge and ability to ameliorate the human economic condition, and on the strange conditions in which this progress takes place'.[6] He concludes that the theory behind economic crises is a much-debated issue, but he insists that the force behind development is embedded in the civilizing progress of society, due to an everlasting flow of needs and a belief in the human capability and willingness to satisfy these needs. The development is never steady, but always 'rhythmical'. Due to forces like technical progress, curiosity and inventiveness, and improvements in administration and organization, the economy expands and advances. He does not believe in the Marxist theory that the ruin of the economy is inherent in this progress. He states that statistics actually show a long-term growth, even though crises and small setbacks happen in the short run, and he attributes this also to the more developed and prudent interest rate policy of the central banks. This statistical evidence is presented by a historical analysis of economic crises from 1815 onwards, including the continuing crisis in 1907. This analysis demonstrates that none of the crises have diminished the productive forces or the national wealth – on the contrary, wealth increases.[7] Aschehoug believes that economic activity must be seen from a dynamic point of view, meaning that progress will be the natural state of affairs.[8]

The general development of a business cycle is identified through the extensive descriptions of historical economic crises, both in the article in *Statsøkonomisk Tidsskrift* and in *Socialøkonomik*. Aschehoug uses them to outline the different aspects of crises in order to understand why they happen and if anything can be done to prevent them from causing damage in the future. 'Crises seem to be alike in many aspects. When an industry for some time has given a substantial revenue, a general belief spreads that this condition will continue and even become more favourable."[9] The psychology is insightfully described as follows:

> Entrepreneurs and capitalists flow to such an industry. Already established enterprises expand their businesses, new factories are constructed and, since different industries are often related, suppliers also expand. A favourable trend spreads to different parts of society. The businessman cherishes new hopes for the future, new shareholding companies are founded, new factories and buildings pop up, the construction of railways is boosted, and the economy is close to burst. This rise in prices of stocks, property and goods brings forth an even higher demand. Many will want to buy, hoping to sell quickly at an even higher price. This becomes reality for a few that, in a short time, earn a lot of money, something that tempts others to follow. Speculations become wild, and fortunes grow like weed. This movement in the economy is easier if one for some time has had a strong capital accumulation and accordingly a low interest rate. The capitalists do not know where to invest their money safely and acquire decent revenue. Some capital will flow to speculative businesses. The banks will also have huge funds that are difficult to invest. If the bank manager is not modest or careful, the banks will more easily lend money to less sound projects, and generally be less meticulous in their credit evaluation. Turnovers increase, employment rises, salaries rise and personal consumption escalates. The circulation in the money reserve increases. It is what is called fabulous times. But, the change is right outside the door.[10]

All crises follow more or less this kind of pattern.

Identification of Different Crises

All crises are somehow rooted in production or consumption, but they may also be related to money or credit conditions. Aschehoug gives an overview of different kinds of crises, identifying seven types: production or supply crises, money market crises, credit crises, trade crises, stock crises, speculation crises and farming crises.[11] They are typically related, and a crisis in one sector may easily influence another, although this is not always the case. The capital situation is particularly important – the larger the capital accumulation is, the more pressure is on rentable investments and the lower the interest rate will be. This is a typical start for a boom. The greater a boom becomes, the greater the recession will be, and psychology plays an important role – fear and trust are the two important conditions. A downturn in an industry will easily lead to a credit crisis.[12] Aschehoug also identifies that price variations for some important goods in the production process, such as iron and steel, are likely to influence economic business cycles. A rise in prices may indicate that a crisis is on its way.[13] He also identifies the relationship between the general interest rate, the role of the central bank, and the money reserve.

The central postulate in the crisis theory is the variation of the over- or underproduction question and, related to this, the question of a mismatch between production and consumption. Schweigaard had only pointed out partial crises as an economic phenomenon caused by over- or underproduction, basing his analysis on Say, who writes,

> But it may be asked, if this be so, how does it happen that there is at times so great a glut of commodities in the market, and so much difficulty in finding a vent for them? Why cannot one of these superabundant commodities be exchanged for another? I answer that the glut of a particular commodity arises from its having outrun the total demand for it in one of two ways; either because it has been produced in excessive abundance, or because the production of other commodities has fallen short.
>
> It is because the production of some commodities has declined, that other commodities are superabundant. To use a more hackneyed phrase, people have bought less, because they have made less profit; and they have made less profit for one or two causes; either they have found difficulties in the employment of their productive means, or these means have themselves been deficient.[14]

The same arguments can be found in Schweigaard's lectures on political economy.[15] Aschehoug also includes this theory in *Socialøkonomik*. He comments on general economic crises in chapter 95: 'It is often the case that any good is produced in such a large quantity that prices have to be reduced to a level below production cost in order to sell. Supply is then larger than the efficient demand. Such an overproduction, which is still called the changeover between upturn and recession, is connected to economic crises.'[16]

Aschehoug reviews Say's theory of crises and shows that it is based on Say's presumption that all trade is barter trade through money. Say's postulate is that there can be overproduction and underproduction, and that destabilized situations occur because there is overproduction in one area and underproduction in another, which means that general overproduction could not happen. Aschehoug points out that Say slightly changed his mind after debating with Malthus, and later wrote that economic activity that could not cover its costs could not be called production. According to Aschehoug, Say's postulate about the impossibility of general overproduction became invalid, and had no influence on the theory of crises. Several other economists have followed Say, but Aschehoug shows that 'this is an impossible theory'.[17]

It is generally agreed that overproduction may occur in some industries, driven by the psychology and elements found in the description of the business cycle above (technical progress, rise in demand, credit possibilities, etc.), and the marginal value theory underlines this point. All industries compete for capital, resources and labour, and importantly also for demand (or the possibility to sell as much as possible at the highest possible price). The marginal value theory shows price elasticity and the complementary and substitute value of different goods, giving the economists a better tool with which to analyse the business cycle for different goods or industries.[18] An overproduction may occur, but it does not mean that one will simultaneously have an underproduction elsewhere. However, Aschehoug states that even though the production quantity should be at the optimal point (where the marginal cost and marginal income coincide), this does not prevent the fact that production often supersedes this point and overproduction can occur.

The increase in any production needs capital and labour, so the picture that Tugan-Baranovsky presents is too simple. He compares the available free credit to the steam of a steam machine, saying that when the steam pressure is high enough to overcome the resistance of the stamp, it moves to the end of the cylinder and thereby opens for the steam to be let out again, before it returns to its original place.[19] However, if this is the case, crises are bound to happen periodically. Aschehoug adds that if it is the case that free credit is too small, it might be that savings have previously been too small. Crises could have been prevented if credit had been available elsewhere (i.e., internationally). But credit flows internationally and is often hard to get if it is scarce, so the solution could have been to prevent overinvestment in due time before the crisis developed. Another objection is that the available credit is elastic, and that the real problem is not the amount available but the belief that it is so. If there is doubt, the credit will retract.[20]

Overproduction can be understood as a situation where supply exceeds demand in the meaning of felt demand, or as exceeding the real demand. The situation where supply exceeds real demand is most common, and often creates a situation were the price falls below the production cost. This situation will often cause a downturn or a burst in an industry. Eventually there will be easier and cheaper means of production, something that the cleverest entrepreneurs usually will detect and employ first. During the boom, other, less clever entrepreneurs will join, and the 'general glut' is again around the corner. In this process, there is also a lag, depending on the usability and flexibility of the means of production and employment contracts with workers. In many markets, there is a time lag between production and the eventual sale, an early warning often being when new orders stop coming.

Again, Aschehoug comes back to the growing interdependence between the production of goods and credit supply. It turns out that the crisis will be more serious and long lasting if credits are high, meaning that many projects are due to fail and cause a credit crisis along with the original crisis in the industry in question.[21]

Aschehoug also looks at Sismondi's theory described in his *Nouveaux principes d'économie politique*. Sismondi tried to explain crises by pointing out that society's income was wrongly distributed, meaning that the workers had too little and therefore poor purchasing power. Coupled with Malthus's theory that crises were caused by a disparity between production and consumption, the consequence will be underconsumption. Sismondi often pointed to industrialization and its effects on salaries. However, Aschehoug argues that industrialization doesn't necessarily lead to lower salaries, but that, on the contrary, history shows that salaries have in fact increased even though production has been industrialized. Ending his discussion of crises, Aschehoug laconically writes that in an ideal society economic development should be smooth, albeit smaller, with more even growth and no large fluctuations.[22]

What lessons can be drawn here? It is Aschehoug's wish that economic activity be organized in order to smooth out business circles, which would be beneficial for society. This implies that all production factors are easily replaceable and re-employable, which is unrealistic. Change takes time, and the vision of an undisturbed economic development is not attainable as long as economic activity is privately organized. The opposite, a publicly organized economy, would not work either as planning would be insurmountable.[23]

In addition to the general psychology of wanting to become part of a rising market and believing the future to be a continuation of the past (even though it is not the case), Aschehoug believes in the general education of economic leaders, businessmen, and the general public, by using the experience of the past, analysing the effects and the causes in order to prevent them in the future.[24] This might seem naïve, but he adds that the foundation of a sound central bank with a prudent interest rate policy would be a huge step forward. It is important for a country during crises to have a sound central bank. And the interest rate policy of the central bank is of paramount importance, especially during 'dangerous times'.[25]

He points out the difficulties that the US had during their last crisis without such a central bank. Since one of the worst consequences of economic crises is unemployment, Aschehoug finds it mandatory to intervene with a sound interest rate policy, which in many cases might prevent a crisis from becoming devastating. But Aschehoug was cautious, he did not think that the central bank could be used to smoothen economic crises with loans or credits, although assistance to industries in crisis could be given without disturbing the main responsibility of assuring that the currency is kept its nominal value.[26] This interference should only be resorted to if strictly necessary, in order to maintain important industries through serious recessions.

Theories of Crises: What Happened after Aschehoug?

Two Norwegian economists, Einar Lie and Christian Venneslan, point out in their newly published work about the history of the Norwegian Ministry of Finance that 'principles in the Norwegian thought about crises can be found in the teachings of Oscar Jaeger in his *Finanslære* (1930) and in Torkel Aschehoug's *Socialøkonomik*. They both underlined that crises could lead to changes and restructures in industries, because weaker industries were wiped out during crises and the strongest ones were forced to raise productivity.'[27] These teachings were not predominant during the second half of the twentieth century. Political reactions to economic crises were usually a reflex in order to save weak industries, and thereby prevent the natural restructuring process that is a consequence of an economic crisis.

Theories of economic crises are partly forgotten in current economic theory, although the recent financial crises of 2008 have revived these theories.[28] As we have seen, Aschehoug explained many of them over a hundred years ago. Aschehoug is concerned about economic crises because they are damaging, and speculation in various forms will hurt the economy.

The Schumpeterian destruction theory is clearly what Aschehoug has in mind when he points out that economic activity must be seen from a dynamic point of view, meaning that industries that are not viable through crises should not be supported, unless, as I have explained, they are of paramount importance to society. The economist Carlota Perez has pointed out that crises are due to technological change.[29] Her views are that new technology creates financial 'bubbles', and that these bubbles are useful and creative, but that they eventually lead to investments in unsound businesses trying to be a part of the new technology. The consequence is that the investments are gradually financial and not based on the real economy of the production of goods and services. She argues that similar productivity explosions and bursts of financial excitement, leading to economic euphoria and subsequent collapses of confidence, have occurred together before. They are interrelated and interdependent phenomena; they share the same root cause and are in the nature of the system and its workings. She further says that they originate in the way technologies evolve by revolution, and creating potential for the generation of wealth.[30] Her point is that both the entrepreneur creating new business and the financial investor providing capital are important elements in the innovation process, a point that Aschehoug also makes when he points out that financial crises may originate from technological change. Aschehoug says that hard times make people innovative, and thereby encourage technological progress. And if the new businesses create valuable technologies, other entrepreneurs will follow. Aschehoug's analysis couples technological progress and innovation with possibilities and demand of credit, and he explains the underlying mechanisms that may lead to crises. Innovation brings value to capital, and innovation needs capital over time. In this way, the financial sector supports the various economic activities. Aschehoug wanted to make sure that the industrial part of the economy was supported by capital and sound investments and that financial speculation was kept to a minimum.

When Aschehoug talks about the short-term memory and unsound belief in growth and 'easy money', it might be compared to the 'Minsky effect', after the economist Hyman Minsky (1919–1996), who argued that the transformation of the economy, especially its financial system, from 'robust' towards 'fragile' takes place over a very long span of time, with a combination of institutions, regulations, financial practices and memories that together encourage relatively rapid economic growth, high employment, growing incomes and growing confidence in our future. Over time a complex combination of factors means that memories fade, regulations are relaxed or financial institutions come up with innovations, and risky practices emerge. The main contribution of Minsky is his understanding and analysis of what he calls 'destabilizing stability'. Minsky wrote in 1964,

> At present real estate assets seem to be a more important source of financial distress than stock exchange assets. [...] Real estate assets are collateral for an extensive amount of debt, both of households and of business firms, owned by financial institutions. [...] If the price of real estate should fall very sharply, not only will the net worth of households and business firms be affected, but also defaults, repossessions and losses by financial intermediaries would occur.[31]

This destabilizing stability process is explained in the work of Aschehoug (see earlier quote). As pointed out, Aschehoug's emphasis on psychological factors is a key factor. When good times last over a certain period of time, banks will gradually take higher risks when they lend out money. The projects will be more speculative, and entrepreneurs will take higher risks and the banks will be more inclined to agree to loans, in some occasions even to entrepreneurs who cannot even service their mortgages. A crisis can develop because banks get more reckless, and risky projects are approved for loans: 'many banks are easily tempted during booms to exceed all reasonable limits'.[32]

And finally, Aschehoug bases his theories on experience and uses historical examples in order to explain and understand the underlying causes of economic crises, suggesting measures to smoothen them in the future, and at the same time being realistic about their occurrences –they cannot be avoided, but by better understanding them they may be less damaging to the economy.

Aschehoug concludes that the theory behind economic crises is a much-debated issue, and I could add that this has not changed over a hundred years after his death, but Aschehoug insists that the force behind development is embedded in the civilizing progress of society, due to an everlasting flow of needs and a belief in the human capability and willingness to satisfy these needs. According to Aschehoug, the development is never steady, but always 'rhythmical'.

In the current European situation, not even the Nobel Prize winners can agree on what to do. For instance, in 2008 Kenneth Rogoff and Carmen Reinhart published a book with the ironical title *This Time Is Different: Eight Centuries of Financial Folly*, a study of crises in a historical perspective. The title pinpoints the belief that one cannot learn from history, although their research shows among other things that the patterns reappear. The belief that trees grow into heaven will time and again lead to overinvestments through credits and finally speculations. The consequences are great private losses, financial crises and public debt crises. This rings a bell with Aschehoug's analyses. Rogoff and Carmen, as did Aschehoug a hundred years ago, want to find a way to shorten the long and painful downturn. Rogoff argues that the debt should be attacked directly – abolish or reduce through inflation. And so it continues; other economists disagree with him, and the debate will certainly continue.

In the end, Aschehoug's advice still might be valid. The only way to go is to try and avoid coming into the situation in the first place, and to not let the spiral continue too long. By looking and learning from history, the signals should be clear enough, Aschehoug says. That's why his analysis is strikingly modern and relevant. He saw the same causes and mechanisms that are still valid today.

Chapter 13

THE LEGACY OF ASCHEHOUG: CONCLUDING REMARKS

This book has endeavoured to analyse the economic thought of Torkel Aschehoug and to demonstrate that he represented the historical-empirical approach to economics. The reconstruction of his thought has revealed a complexity and sophistication that is rare among his contemporary Norwegian scholars.

Aschehoug's postscript was written in November 1908, only a few months before his death, and provides an overview of his work and thoughts. Aschehoug himself is best described as a reserved optimist. He believed in the power of education to strengthen ideas of equality and democracy, but he did not believe that education would eradicate the self-interested and egoistic tendencies of the human mind. Yet Aschehoug viewed the economic and cultural development on the verge of the twentieth century in an optimistic light, and he was confident that sound use of experience would be the best means of continuous, healthy development. And as the letter below shows, Aschehoug had no intention of quitting his work, despite the fact that his health was quickly deteriorating.

The following letter to Böhm-Bawerk, his last known written words, was composed just a few weeks before he died on 21 January 1909. The letter was never sent. Some words are illegible and their meaning has had to be guessed:

Dear Sir

It has been an exceedingly great pleasure for me to receive your amiable letter from the 26th of December [this letter cannot be found, and there are no traces of a preceding letter to Böhm-Bawerk from Aschehoug, so it might be suggested that Böhm-Bawerk was the one that wrote to Aschehoug in the first place] and the enclosed portrait of you.

As I have [asked], may I later send my student to Vienna [noted by Aschehoug beside the letter text: Böhm-Bawerk has lately been an active professor in Vienna], to benefit from your excellent lectures. You probably know that [unclear] I have heard about your lectures, knowing I may well recommend you [this sentence is unclear]. The acknowledgement and recognition you have shown me and given me in your letter is most dear to me. It is with great expectations that I anticipate the new [edition] of your theory, and I hope to live long enough to be able to use it in my revised edition of Socialøkonomik, although I praise my days in spite of my fears. I am sorry that I haven't been privileged to make your personal acquaintance. My old age of 87 years keeps me at home, and I may not dare to hope seeing you here in my home. If you by any chance would come, you will be received with the utmost gratefulness, not only by me, but also by our whole group of devoted admirers.

Yours T. H. A.

What Böhm-Bawerk wrote to Aschehoug is not known, but he seems to have recognized and known Aschehoug's work, although it is not stated which texts he had read. This points to one of the weaknesses of the legacy of Aschehoug, the fact that he published his works in Norwegian, and they were not translated.

As we have seen, Aschehoug was the chief protagonist of Norwegian economic thought from 1870 until his death, and his works continued to be influential in the first decades of the twentieth century. But the division between economics as a science and practical political life became more visible during the first decades after his death. The science gradually became theoretically stronger, whereas the economist's role as advisor and policymaker became weaker, although it could be argued that later on in the twentieth century the ties between economists and politicians were renewed. The contrast is that different people had different roles, making the 'professor-politician' role redundant. Economics (*statsøkonomi*) became a separate discipline at the university, the first candidates graduating in 1908. Oskar Jaeger was the leading economist after Schweigaard and Aschehoug. Aarum was the other successor, but he died early and did not have the same impact as Jaeger, although his two books about theoretical and practical economics became quite influential after his death.

It is only when Frisch and later Trygve Haavelmo (1911–1999) establish what is later referred to as the Oslo school of economics in the 1930s that *Socialøkonomik* falls into oblivion. The school can be characterized by its introduction of mathematical and quantitative methods into economic teaching and research, and the establishment of econometrics as a new field within economics. Furthermore, the school developed national accounts and budgets and macroeconomic planning models. Aschehoug's views did not fit into this picture, not only due to the Oslo school, but also due to the fact that many of the disciplines that Aschehoug incorporated in his economics gradually became specialized. There is no way back to composing works like *Socialøkonomik*. But this does not mean that it is impossible to find contemporary relevance, and test his contribution in the context of contemporary challenges of theory and policy.

For Aschehoug, history was a tool for any social and economic research that was done in order to address contemporary policy issues and to understand and evaluate economic theories. Aschehoug opens up a wider perspective on economics, reminding us that it is a science of complex human action. For Aschehoug, economics was a policy science concerned with the welfare of the nation and of each individual, economic thinking was profoundly embedded in all social and political thinking, and psychology is in many ways the key to understanding human economic behaviour. His work simultaneously included economic theory, statistics, economic sociology and economic history.

Aschehoug was essentially a child of the European Enlightenment. His background and education was solid, and he was one of the few highly educated Norwegian elite. He stayed updated on international intellectual and political life from his early twenties until his death. His lifespan covered most of what has been presented as the nineteenth century Norwegian economic and political context. Aschehoug was a highly esteemed scientist with a high intellectual capacity, enabling him, quite late in life, to gain a thorough understanding of economics as a second discipline besides law. To Aschehoug, they both concerned society and politics. He continued the work of his teacher, Anton Martin Schweigaard, but as has been pointed out, Aschehoug was first and foremost a professor, not a politician, whereas the opposite was the case for Schweigaard.

The introduction to Schweigaard's lecture on social economics (see Chapter 3) actually points out what Aschehoug is later doing, namely including economics in a comprehensive picture of society and politics, and he followed up the critique that Schweigaard had towards the simplifications of classical economics (as it was in 1847). Aschehoug drew a line between economics as the economic activity and economics as the scientific discipline in his introduction to *Socialøkonomik*, even if the rest of his work did not follow this distinction clearly – something that he was aware of and states in his own conclusion, saying that a sharp division between pure and applied economics is not possible.

Schweigaard never wrote explicitly about method, but as I have tried to argue here, seen together with his political career, it is plausible to assert that his small article on German philosophy was an illustration of his views on scientific methods. There was no *Methodenstreit* in Norway during Aschehoug's lifetime, only a small discussion that took place in the mid-1890s. The empirical tradition dominated, and henceforth also the methods that were applied. Statistics was developed by Aschehoug and his fellow colleagues – first Eilert Sundt, later Anders N. Kiær and others. Aschehoug emphasized the importance of an awareness of history and the national context, which was much closer to a historical, empirical approach than to classical economics. It can be connected both to British empiricism and to the German historical school, and to the general Norwegian opinion that the sciences of society (economics) should stay as close as possible to practical life.

From around 1870 onwards Aschehoug concentrated on scientific economic thought, wrote *Socialøkonomik*, and founded and conducted the Statsøkonomisk forening. There is continuity in Aschehoug's work, as well as an ability to acquire new knowledge, adapt it and process it in the attempt to create a sound foundation for an economic discipline. He preferred the more modern literature and new economic developments in his search for information. The foundation of the Statsøkonomisk forening is of major importance to the development of a professional milieu of economics in Norway. Not only was it an arena for discussions of current economic and social issues, it was also a vehicle for professionalizing economics and presenting new theoretical works. The German Verein für Sozialpolitik was an inspiration, as well as similar associations which were founded in the other Scandinavian countries during the same period.

The French influence throughout *Socialøkonomik* was most valuable in terms of historical, philosophical and partly sociological analysis. The French traditions were used to describe a wider and more detailed analysis of economic history and of economic theory. The most influential French thinker on Norwegian thought was Jean-Baptiste Say. He was of paramount importance to the theory that was developed about the entrepreneur. Aschehoug presented an unique and refreshing perspective on the entrepreneur, emphasizing the unique position the entrepreneur had in economic activity.

The theory of value, originally introduced by Aschehoug, can still be found in curriculums in Norway, but the emphasis on the practical as well as the broad understanding of economics, expressed by both Aschehoug and Marshall, was lost. The influence of Marshall was decisive for Aschehoug in his introduction of marginal theory in Norway.

The central tenet of Aschehoug's views of labour is that he saw the worker as more than just a production factor. The analysis of *Socialøkonomik* and the related debates and papers presented at the Statsøkonomisk forening show that he displays a deep concern and knowledge of 'the social questions'. Inspiration came from Germany and Britain, but mostly these issues were discussed within the Norwegian context and hence were resolved with Norwegian explanations.

Schweigaard adhered to free trade between nations, but he was in many cases willing to adapt his politics to national needs. His modernizing strategy for Norway included many deviations from a free trade theory, because other measures were more adapted to increase national wealth and general welfare. When Aschehoug later wrote about free trade and customs, his continuation of the Schweigaard position is clearly visible. Schweigaard was an adherent of free trade, but not of laissez-faire. This position also accounts for Aschehoug; he and his colleagues did not change radically from Schweigaard's position, but they faced a more difficult international climate, with more widespread protectionist policies. Nevertheless, they were pragmatic in their approach.

The difficult international climate also serves as the backdrop for Aschehoug's extensive analysis of economic crises, in which he aims to understand the different underlying conditions that cause them. Economic crises occurred during Schweigaard's lifetime, but not to the same extent, and the phenomenon was not discussed in detail in his lectures. It is to the Aschehoug's credit that more than a hundred years ago Norwegian economics acquired a comprehensive, and in many aspects modern, understanding of economic crises. A further analysis of the different theories that Aschehoug presented would be a worthwhile topic for a later project.

As stated in the introduction, it has been necessary to choose topics that might be relevant for contemporary economics, because the scope and depth of Aschehoug's work is too extensive to be analysed in full detail within the limits of this thesis. Hopefully the chosen topics will be relevant to scholars who study the history of economic thought and to others who may be interested in exploring the relevance of Aschehoug's thoughts to contemporary economics. Since *Socialøkonomik* in itself is an encyclopaedic work, there are certainly other perspectives to analyse, and hopefully this book will inspire a renewed interest in the work of Torkel Aschehoug and in the way he was able to connect economics to a broader, more nuanced and deeper understanding of society and of human conduct.

Appendix A

OTHER NORWEGIAN TURN-OF-THE-CENTURY ECONOMISTS

The core group of economists consists of Ebbe Hertzberg (1847–1912), Bredo Morgenstierne (1851–1930) and the younger generation, Oskar Jaeger (1863–1933) and Peder Thorvald Aarum (1867–1926). In addition, Anders Nicolai Kiær (1838–1919) and Nicolai Rygg (1872–1957) respectively a statistician and a jurist, were both appointed chairman of Statistisk centralbureau (later Statistisk sentralbyrå or SSB). The latter was, for a short period of time, the successor to Aschehoug as a professor of economics before he became the general manager of Statistisk centralbureau in 1913.

Ebbe Hertzberg, at only 30 years old, was appointed the first professor of economics and statistics in Norway in 1877 after winning a competition. He was a lawyer, an economist and a historian. He was, as commented on in Chapter 3, a strong adherent of Schweigaard, giving him his full approval in his book published in 1883 about Schweigaard and his public affairs. Due to personal reasons, Hertzberg was forced to resign from his post as professor of economics after just a few years in 1886, and he did not take part in the economic debate until the mid-1890s. Aarum later states that Hertzberg had studied with Karl Knies (1821–1898) in Heidelberg and that he was influenced by the historical school.[1] Like Aschehoug, he lectured and published in *Statsøkonomisk Tidsskrift*.[2]

Hertzberg chose 'Statssocialismens theori' (The theory of state socialism) as his topic for the first lecture at the Statsøkonomisk forening in 1884. He described the purpose of his lecture as follows: 'By this theoretical lecture "Statssocialismens theori" I hope to give a short overview of the general and principal situation wherein the contemporary economic discussion takes place.'[3] Bergh and Hanisch argue that Norwegian economists by the turn of the century had begun to use Hertzberg's proposals, making this lecture quite influential.[4] Hertzberg methodically explores the history of economic thought, and quite contrary to his own statements a couple of years earlier when he was lecturing in classical economics, he found that 'such a historical overview today seems the most appropriate way of presenting this topic'.[5] Hertzberg starts out with the idea of individual freedom as opposed to the state, claiming that these two incompatible demands are the origins of different ideas of society. After mercantilism came physiocracy, then the division of labour. The Franco-British free trade treaty accomplished the final 'victory' of free trade in 1860. But, according to Hertzberg, at that moment the general opinion of free trade was overcome by other economic ideas: 'Already within the school of free trade, [alternative ideas grew]; British authors started claiming that historical and social conditions should be taken into account, when questions of reforms according to free trade principles were being discussed.'[6]

Even though Hertzberg here mentions British economists, it is 'reserved for the Germans to systematize the scientific critique towards free trade'.[7] The German historical school had to a large extent 'emphasized the relativity of economic postulates', something that Hertzberg himself seems to acknowledge, but he does not agree with the German claim 'to integrate economic and ethical thought to a higher unit'.[8] Hertzberg further criticized the German historical school, or 'Kathedersozialisten' as he calls them, for not having a theoretical system themselves, only criticizing the old classical economists. He thought it was difficult to perceive how far they wanted to go with their social reforms. On the other hand, he agreed to many of their proposals, for instance the creation of labour unions and social insurances, while also claiming that these ideas could be found in England as well.[9] He picks up on the critical attitude of Schweigaard towards the German ideology, and points out that these social reforms were not a result of some 'ethical, German turn in mentality'; rather it was a practical solution to obvious social problems.

An interesting observation is that Hertzberg credits Albert Schäffle (1831–1903) with the establishment of the German historical school, and notably his development of the term 'collective needs'. Hertzberg says that it was Schäffle who had pointed out that the individual 'could not get his or her needs fully satisfied without the same being the case for all others in the same situation'.[10] Aschehoug also mentions Schäffle when he discusses the limits of the state in his chapter 'The individual and the state'.[11] A comprehensive analysis of different aspects of Schäffle's thought has just been published: *Albert Schäffle (1831–1903): The Legacy of an Underestimated Economist*.[12] Aschehoug did not like his sociological analysis in the *Bau und Leben*, although he does acknowledge his status as a noteworthy economist a little later. Aschehoug sees him as someone who is rather close to socialism, but at the same time takes care to argue for the stronger sides of capitalism, that is, entrepreneurial gain and the possibility of independence. He also praises him for a comprehensive analysis of how socialism could be introduced and to what extent it is possible to accomplish its principles. Both Hertzberg and Aschehoug are influenced by Schäffle when it comes to arguments for an active state, but it remains to analyse how far the two Norwegians would want to go compared to Schäffle.[13] The next economist, Morgenstierne, mentions Schäffle's book *Die Aussichtslosigkeit der Socialdemokratie* and praises him as an outstanding economist. Schäffle is described as a theoretical social democrat, but underlines that a complete social democratic program is unrealistic.[14]

As shown in Chapter 10, Hertzberg was mainly interested in trade policies and was a member of several customs commissions.[15] Together with Aschehoug, he was one of the leading members of the Statsøkonomisk forening from the mid-1890s. He argued, for instance, for a more widespread and thorough economic education in order to make people aware of how important economics was for society as a whole, especially in his article from 1902, 'Om udbredelse af socialøkonomisk kundskab' (About the dispersion of economic knowledge). This was a reaction to the general debate about the national, strained economic situation, and how, in order to get a grip of future state finances, it was necessary to increase the general knowledge about economy. According to Hertzberg, economics was best adapted to increase the general understanding of how bad things could be if the self-interest of individual industries were to grow without a view of the general situation of society. Hertzberg's solution was a kind of economic enlightenment for the growing population.

Hertzberg also had a say in the debate about social issues (Aschehoug's views can be found in Chapter 9 on labour). Economists in general were to have a central role in these debates; they often raised the questions, participated and worked for solutions, and provided theories, statistical facts and practical guidelines, such as law proposals, commission reports and so forth. Hertzberg actively participated, although he published only two articles in *Statsøkonomisk Tidsskrift*. The motto was 'help to self-help', either individually or collectively. The idea was to count on 'associations'. The issues were: how much should the state interfere in these associations, what should be the state responsibility, and how much should be obligatory? Social problems were taken seriously, and it was clear that the state from early on had an important role in securing work and the health of not only the workers, but of all citizens in difficult circumstances. This was a position that Hertzberg shared with the next economist, Bredo Morgenstierne. Further comments on social issues can be found in Chapter 9.

Morgenstierne was appointed professor of the combined chair of law and economics after Aschehoug in 1886. He was a professor until 1919. Morgenstierne was one of the most distinguished conservative voices around the turn of the century. He was the author of several textbooks and an active participant in the economic debate at the Statsøkonomisk forening. He published several articles in *Statsøkonomisk Tidsskrift* between 1887 and 1909.[16]

His *Forelæsninger over statsøkonomien* in four parts was published in handwritten form in 1890. A printed edition was published in 1909. He participated in the debate about making economics a separate discipline, being the only one who claimed that economics should be a part of other disciplines, mainly law. In the end, it was widely accepted that economics should be established as a separate discipline at the university. As shown in Chapter 4, he participated in the 1890s debate about method, publishing his own contribution, *Socialøkonomiens grundtræk*. Morgenstierne also participated in the different customs debates, which are presented in Chapter 11.

Morgenstierne published several articles on social issues, the earliest in 1887 concerning the evil of poverty and socialism. The problems of poverty have always been present, but Morgenstierne states that the consciousness of poverty is a political and economic issue of great importance. He also underlines the importance of the measures that are taken, both by entrepreneurs and by the state through legislation. He contests the socialist view that a complete altering of society is necessary in order to abolish poverty. He believes neither in the socialist order of society, nor that it is possible to abolish poverty. But as he states, even if one disregards the socialist system of distribution or one that is as equal as possible, one should not give up the work to improve the existing distribution of wealth and to some extent even the contrast between those who live in luxury and those who struggle for existence.[17]

The article does not only talk about poverty, it is also a discussion of critical arguments against socialism. It may seem to a modern reader that Morgenstierne perceives social democracy and socialism as radical systems, although he mainly uses the term socialism. He further points out the advances in the more recent German social policies, like the introduction of different workers insurances, and he acclaims these measures, although he adds that 'it is characteristic for the revolutionary character of the social democracy (representatives) to be hostile towards reforms of this kind'.[18] Through British empirical research results, Morgenstierne claims that the last decades have shown a trend towards a more equal distribution of income, not only in England, but in Norway as well. He therefore hopes that it is possible, without a socialist order of society, to achieve a more even distribution of production income.[19] But, he adds, it is an illusion to believe that poverty can be abolished.

Morgenstierne firmly believes in the right of property and individual freedom, and his main issue is that socialism will abolish these two principles, and social democrats will limit them to an extent to which Morgenstierne cannot agree. It is not, then, that he does not want state interference; on the contrary, he believes that on many occasions this is important, especially when it came to social policies. From the last part of the nineteenth century, there was a notable growth in diverse organized welfare measures. The Norwegians were influenced, as is shown, by German measures, but also by the liberal government of Gladstone and the conservative government of Disraeli in Britain. The Norwegian legislation and organization had its distinct Norwegian mark, and it is clear that concerns about a socialist revolution or hidden socialist pacifying policies were unwarranted. These arguments were never relevant, although socialism was refuted both in Morgenstierne's article and in similar arguments by Aschehoug. It is more relevant to say that these economists and the liberal and conservative politicians that alternated in government were genuinely concerned about the welfare of their fellow citizens and a just distribution of income within the limits of a liberal democracy. These issues are further discussed in Chapter 9, and to some extent commented on in parts of Chapter 8.

Morgenstierne's article on 'The evil of poverty and socialism' was a part of the ongoing debates about social issues, something that also engaged the next economist, Oskar Jaeger (1863–1933). Jaeger was appointed as professor of economics in a newly founded chair in 1902. He published many articles in *Statsøkonomisk Tidsskrift* between 1893 and 1908, including his doctoral thesis. Jaeger also published several books between 1915 and 1934.[20]

Oskar Jaeger was 40 years younger than Aschehoug, born in 1863, and outlived him by 25 years, living long enough to experience the 1929 stock market crash, when J. M. Keynes and Ragnar Frisch (1895–1973) were beginning their careers. Jaeger was one of Aschehoug's students. He became acquainted with the thoughts of the Austrians Menger and Böhm-Bawerk during a stay for study purposes in Austria in his youth.[21] He was clearly recognized as the leading economist from 1910 to 1930 (between Aschehoug and the later Oslo school and its protagonist, Frisch), but he was more radical and often in opposition to the earlier economic thought. He became professor of economics in 1902 at the University of Oslo when Aschehoug was busy writing his *Socialøkonomik*. He studied finance, business cycle theory and economics. He was also a politician belonging to the left, liberal side of the political party Venstre (literally, 'Left'), and in 1909 he joined the dissident group of 'Liberal-minded Left' (Frisinnede Venstre), arguing for an antisocialist politics. Svein Carstens comments on his liberal political views in his short biography, as well as on his modern, theoretical economic works.[22] Jaeger was also an ardent defender of finding sustainable solutions to social problems (*fattigondet*/'the evil of poverty'). Around 1900 he published several articles about these solutions, and he was an active member of several commissions dealing with the issue of poverty.

Two of Jaeger's theoretical issues were capital rent and marginal theory, and Aarum states that in this issue Jaeger was in line with Aschehoug.[23] For both issues, he clearly leans on the theory of the Austrian Eugen von Böhm-Bawerk (1851–1914), who, according to Jaeger, gave the ultimate theoretical answer and whose work Jaeger praises and admires. Jaeger lists W. Stanley Jevons (1835–1882), Carl Menger (1840–1921) and Léon Walras (1834–1910), saying that they independently founded the theory. It had been further developed by the Austrian school. He divides clearly between theoretical and practical economics, the latter being economic politics. In theoretical economics, the question is: which laws decide how much or what share of the economic return of production can be given to the different means of production (*produksjonsmidler*). Jaeger lists land, work and capital, and what share each of the 'ones that take over the technical and economic risks of the production' should have.[24] His theory was considered the most progressive in the Nordic countries when it was published in 1922.[25]

Lastly, Peder Thorvald Aarum (1867–1926) was regarded as 'the progressive' among Norwegian economists. He graduated from the University of Oslo in 1893 with a degree in law. From 1899 to 1910 he was a bureaucrat in the Ministry of Justice, and in 1908 he got his doctoral degree in philosophy with a thesis about the labour theory of value. He received a scholarship in economics in 1908 and became a professor of economics at the University of Oslo in 1917. In his short career he managed to publish two textbooks in theoretical and practical economics, *Teoretisk socialøkonomik* (1924) and *Praktisk socialøkonomik* (1928).

Aarum was influenced by Marshall (the eighth and final edition of his *Principles* came in 1920), and he noticed the distinction between the short, intermediate and long term, and adhered to the process that determines price as a result of individual demand and supply functions that merge into a common demand and supply.[26] Sæther and Hanisch further notice that Aarum especially emphasized the different interpretations of the cost of production depending on decreasing, constant and increasing return.

As has already been mentioned, Oskar Jaeger took the Austrian view, which claimed that value was determined by marginal utility alone and that the cost of production had no significance. Aarum, as well as Aschehoug, claimed that the truth lies somewhere in between. Aarum further introduced more graphs and diagrammatic exposition in his lectures and books on economics than Aschehoug ever did.

Ragnar Frisch became Aarum's assistant at the University of Oslo in 1925, one year before Aarum died. In order to summarize these early Norwegian economists, continuation would be a more appropriate term than revolution. The economics of 1920 was certainly more advanced theoretically than that of Schweigaard in 1847. International scientific and political development continued to influence the Norwegian economists, and statistical research was firmly established and developed from the 1850s onwards with Eilert Sundt and Aschehoug. Many economists, and later trained statisticians, did substantial work to ameliorate statistical information, something that is both displayed in the many articles published in *Statsøkonomisk Tidsskrift* and in the lifelong work of the first manager of the Statistical Bureau, Kiær, and his follower Rygg. Finally, I believe that an analysis of the transition from Aschehoug to the Oslo school in the 1930s would be a most interesting perspective for a future project, looking especially into the causes for the development.

Appendix B

DRAFTS FOR *SOCIALØKONOMIK*

These topics are listed in the order they appear in Aschehoug's own archive:

- Several drafts about value and price, a draft about utility, economic value, money and prices, and price theory (it appears he may have been struggling with this as there are the largest amount of drafts for this topic)
- The history of value and price theory (probably used for his article in *Statsøkonomisk Tidsskrift*)
- A critique of socialism
- Several drafts about the law of marginal value, the marginal value
- The relationship between current and future goods (among others, he mentions Nicholson and Jevons)
- Several drafts about production and different aspects of it
- The interest rate
- The organization of economic activity (and whether it should be voluntary or forced)
- Free trade (several drafts, also a discussion of Mill and of the claims of justice and competition)
- International trade
- Exchange value
- The attacks on the economics of Smith: socialism
- The attacks on the classical school (here he mentions Schmollers Jahrbuch 1895)
- Capital (all aspects of capital, here he mentions Böhm-Bawerk)
- The producers, the cost, revenue and organisation of production (Lexis, Marshall, Gide), and a draft about the distribution of production
- Overproduction
- The history of the monetary system (also an article in *Statsøkonomisk Tidsskrift*)
- Money, the change in the value of money
- Exchange rates and trade
- Banks and banking
- The Norwegian Central Bank and its organization (also a draft about the Norwegian Mortgage Bank)
- The history of economics
- The method of economics
- The workings of economic activity
- Economics and the relation to other human activities
- Economic goods (here he mentions Marshall)
- The decision of prices, the objective and subjective value of utility

- The theory of income
- Credit and loans
- Wages and work, several drafts about different aspects of this topic (here he mentions Böhm-Bawerk)
- Supply of work (Marshall)
- The theory of overpopulation (Malthus)
- Workers insurance
- The harmony between demand, supply and work (Schmoller)
- Wages in different economic activities
- Entrepreneurial gain (Schmoller)
- The use of economic goods
- Charity and the public evil of poverty
- The insurance system

Appendix C

DETAILED CONTENTS OF
SOCIALØKONOMIK (FIRST EDITIONS FROM 1903 TO 1908)

The three volumes (four books) contain a total of 2,137 pages. The first edition of Volume I was published in 1903 and consists of 549 pages, 4 parts and 28 chapters. All chapters are also broken down into paragraphs. Volume II was published two years later in 1905. It contains parts 5 and 6, a total of 574 pages, going from chapter 29 to chapter 54. Volume III was published in 1908 and is actually two books, but the pagination is continued throughout the two books, the first part having 514 pages and the second continuing from page 515 to page 1,014. The two books of Volume III consist of parts 7 to 10 and the chapters from 55 to 100. The last book also has a postscript, a list of corrections, an alphabetical author index and a detailed subject index.

The subtitle of *Socialøkonomik* is 'A Scientific Presentation of the Economic Activity of Human Society'.[1] The first volume mainly presents a historical overview of the economic activity of society, but the first part presents the term, method and system of the economic discipline. The second volume has only two large parts: the first goes through all aspects of value, revenue and wealth; the second part discusses production and acquisition (*erhverv*).

The first book of the third volume only contains one part, which presents all aspects of turnover and trade in the economy. The second book of the third volume presents questions of distribution of income, the use of economic goods and finally the instability of economic activity and the solutions and measures that can be taken.

Most of the handwritten manuscripts for *Socialøkonomik* are still in existence; those sections for which none exist are marked with *.

Volume I

Part I: The term *socialøkonomik* (Aschehoug consistently uses *socialøkonomik* when he talks about the economic discipline, and *socialøkonomi* when he describes economic activity).
Chapter 1. The purpose and scope of political economy (*socialøkonomik*) (1–10)
Chapter 2. The method and system of political economy (11–31)

Part II: The history of political economy
Chapter 3. Political economy in the antiquity (32–46)
Chapter 4. The theory and praxis of economic activity in the Middle Ages (47–62)
Chapter 5. Mercantilism (63–75)

Part VI: Production and acquisition

Volume IIIa

Part VII: Turnover and trade

Volume IIIb

Part VIII: Distribution of the returns from economic activity

Part IX: The use of the economic goods

Part X: The instability in economic activity and results, and the solutions and measures that can be taken

NOTES

Chapter 1   Introduction

1 Franklin L. Baumer, *Modern European Thought: Continuity and Change in Ideas, 1680–1900* (New York: St Martin's Press, 1977), 260.

2 Peter R. Senn, 'A Comparison of the Treatment of A. Schäffle in Economic Journals and Economic Thought', in *Albert Schäffle (1831—1903): The Legacy of an Underestimated Economist*, ed. Jürgen Backhaus (Frankfurt: Haag & Herchen, 2010), 223.

3 Trond Berg Eriksen and Øystein Sørensen, *Norsk idéhistorie* (Oslo: Aschehoug, 2001), editors preface, 8. 'På 1800-tallet var nordiske impulser sterke i Norge. Men det var også impulser fra den tyske kulturen, fra Frankrike og fra Storbritannia.'

4 Berg Eriksen and Sørensen, *Norsk idéhistorie*, 9. 'Hovedpoenget i denne sammenheng er at uansett hvor ideer og kulturimpulser er kommet fra, så har de fått sine spesielle uttrykk i Norge. I større eller mindre grad er de blitt bearbeidet. Noen ganger er ideer blitt overtatt uten altfor mye hjemlig bearbeiding, andre ganger kan det norske preget ha blitt så sterkt at vi må snakke om ekte norske tankeformer.'

5 *Socialøkonomik*, 1903–08, 1st edition.

6 The *Methodenstreit* (battle of methods) of economics had – according to Erik S. Reinert, who comments on the German historical school – pointed in a very different direction, arguing that the profession needed to have theories at different levels of abstraction.

7 However, recent revaluations of Mill's economic thought have shown that he was an important forerunner for the modernization of economic thought in the last decades of the nineteenth century. See, for instance, Agnar Sandmo, *Samfunnsøkonomi: En idéhistorie* (Oslo: Universitetsforlaget, 2006), chap. 5.

Chapter 2   Biography

1 In old chronicles the name is spelled Thorkil.

2 As a curiosity, I should mention that Nils Stockfleth Darre Aschehoug is my great-great-grandfather.

3 Joh. K. Bergwitz, 'Til professor Aschehougs karakteristikk, hans ætlegg og stammegaard', special edition of *Statsøkonomisk Tidsskrift* in 1910 (the edition belonged to Sorenskriver Aschehoug, given to his family by the author).

4 A handwritten family tree showing the lineage from Pastor in Rakkestad, Thorkil Aschehoug and wife Anne Cathrine born Olsen, privately owned.

5 Private family notes, privately owned.

6 Elisabeth Christie, '"Aschehoug-epoken" i Rakkestad (1873–1867)', in *Prestegårdsliv*, vol. 2, 2nd ed. (Oslo: Forlaget Land og Kirke, 1976 [1967]), 76.

7 Christie, *Prestegårdsliv*, 82.

8 Christie, *Prestegårdsliv*, 84.

9 Private family notes, privately owned.

10 Bergwitz, 'Til professor Aschehougs karakteristikk', 271 and private family notes, privately owned.

11 Private family notes, privately owned.

12 Private family notes, privately owned.

13 H. Blom Svendsen, 'Julaften på Toten 1797', *Tidens Tegn*, 24 December 1938. The father of Anne Christine later became adjutant for Prince Christian August, company commander, major and chief petty officer at the Generalstaben (general staff) and received on 9 of April 1809, the same year he died, the Danish order Dannebrogordenen from King Fredrik VI, with the personal message, 'It is well deserved'. See also Bergwitz, 271–2.

14 Ulla Meyer, *Norske mødre* (Oslo: Jacob Dybwads forlag, 1945), 42.

15 Meyer, *Norske mødre*, 42.

16 Family tree, privately owned.

17 *Departements-tidende* 58 (35) (1 September 1886), printed in the family tree book by Inger Kloster-Jensen, privately owned.

18 *Departements-tidende* 58 (35), 'Aandslidende og trættende examensarbeide', 'Uforsvarlig misbrug af vore bedste videnskabelige kræfter'.

19 Bergwitz, 'Til professor Aschehougs karakteristikk', 281.

20 Bergwitz, 'Til professor Aschehougs karakteristikk', 281.

21 Originally called Det Kongelige Frederiks Universitetet in Christiania, then Kristiania, and finally changing to Universitetet i Oslo. The current name will be used throughout the text.

22 Francis Hagerup, 'Nekrolog over Torkel Halvorsen Aschehoug', in a special edition of *Tidsskrift for rettsvitenskab* (1909), 1.

23 Harald Westergaard, 'Obituary: T. H. Aschehoug', *Journal of the American Statistical Association* 11 (86): 483. Harald Westergaard was a pioneer in the marginalist thought and had a correspondence with Jevons. Among other things he wrote *Nationalekonomien i Hovedtraek* (1908), which became an important textbook in economics in all the Scandinavian countries. See Johan Lönnroth, 'Nordic Model Political Economic Manuals', preliminary version for a seminar on 11 December 2008.

24 See Anne-Lise Seip, *Vitenskap og virkelighet: Sosiale, økonomiske og politiske teorier hos T. H. Aschehoug* (Oslo: Gyldendal, 2005) and Aschehoug, *Norske universitets og skole-annaler*, part 2, vol. 4 (Christiania: Hartvig Nissen, 1848), 557–71. As a scholarship student, Aschehoug was obliged to write a report to state the purpose and contents of his travel.

25 See Seip.

26 Aschehoug, 'Innberetning fra Cand. jur. T. H. Aschehoug om den av ham med offentlig stipendium foretagende vitenskapelige reise i utlandet', in *Norske universitets og skole-annaler*, 558. 'Enhver der vil danne seg en selvstendig mening om de mangfoldige og kompliserte fenomener i samfunnsutviklingen selv å iaktta Englands institusjoner og økonomiske bedrifter, thi det er på dets jordbunn vitenskapen er oppblomstret, og det er fra den engelske statistikk, statsøkonomene har hentet de fullstendigste, sikreste og verdifulleste kjensgjerninger, hvorfra deres teorier har blitt abstrahert.'

27 Aschehoug, *Norske universitets og skole-annaler*, 558. 'Denne Omstændighed har eller siges av Mange at have givet selve Doctrinen et engelsk Præg, som maa bortages, førend man kan tillægge den almen gyldighed. Hvad man end antager herom, saa er det ialfald vist, at man ei kan overse dette spørgsmaal om Videnskabens character, men for at løse det maa man have ervervet en saa levende opfatelse af Englands sociale forhold, som kun et Ophold i Landet selv kan skjenke.'

28 Aschehoug, *Norske universitets og skole-annaler*, 560–62. 'Under saadanne Forholde, blev det mig naturligviis viktigst, at gjøre mig fortrolig med den brugelige Methode i statistiske Undersøgelser, samt at erhverve mig den fortroligste Kjendskab til den engelske Samfundsutvikling som muligt.'

29 Comments from Aschehoug in *Norske universitets og skole-annaler*.

30 Comments from Aschehoug in *Norske universitets og skole-annaler*.

31 Aschehoug, *Norske universitets og skole-annaler*, 566.

32 George Norman, 'Mine erindringer fra Norge: Meddelt av T. H. Aschehoug', *Historisk tidsskrift* 5 (3) (1899): 181–218.

33 Norman, 'Mine erindringer fra Norge', 217.

34 Lars Roar Langslet, 'Torkel Halvorsen Aschehoug', in *Konservatisme på norsk* (Oslo: Pax, 2011).

35 Aschehoug, 'Norske Universitets og Skole-Annaler', 559. 'Folkets practiske Sands har der medført, at man ikke [...] har givet seg hverken Theorien eller Sædvanen i Vold, men allerede gjennem lange Tider baseret Overlægningen om offentlige Forholdsregler paa en Grundvold av factiske Oplysninger, som kunne erhverves.'

36 Aschehoug, *Norske universitets og skole-annaler*, 560.

37 Aschehoug, *Norske universitets og skole-annaler*, 563.

38 Aschehoug, *Norske universitets og skole-annaler*, 562. 'Studiet av lovgivningen av fast eiendom og dens innflytelse på nasjonalvelstanden, opptok derfor en stor del av den tid jeg tilbrakte i England.'

39 Aschehoug, *Norske universitets og skole-annaler*, 568–9. 'Å bidrage til Landets productive kraft.'

40 Aschehoug, *Norske universitets og skole-annaler*, 557.

41 Lektorat i lovkyndighet.

42 Trond Bergh and Tore J. Hanisch, *Vitenskap og politikk: Linjer i norsk sosialøkonomi gjennom 150 år* (Oslo: Aschehoug, 1984), 51.

43 The debate about the establishment of the chair and Aschehoug's own position is presented in Bergh and Hanisch, *Vitenskap og politikk*, 54–5.

44 Bergh and Hanisch, *Vitenskap og politikk*, 50, 54.

45 Bergh and Hanisch, *Vitenskap og politikk*, 58; Seip, *Vitenskap og virkelighet*, and Hagerup, 'Nekrolog'. Ebbe Hertzberg was in addition a lawyer and was interested in the history of jurisprudence as well as political economy. He participated, like Aschehoug, in several commissions (customs), and was eagerly engaged in different social political subjects, to which he also contributed substantially. He also shared Aschehoug's political views, which could be described as a modified conservative liberalism.

46 Tore J. Hanisch and Arild Sæther, 'Alfred Marshall in Norway', in *The Impact of Alfred Marshall's Ideas: The Global Diffusion of His Work*, edited by T. Raffaelli, G. Becattini, K. Caldari and M. Dardi (Northampton, MA and Cheltenham: Edward Elgar, 2010).

47 Bredo Morgenstierne, 'Professor Aschehoug og hans "Socialøkonomik"', *Statsøkonomisk Tidsskrift* 16 (1902): 198.

48 To be further discussed in Chapter 4.

49 Pål Magnus Lykkja, *Anton M. Schweigaard og Torkel H. Aschehoug sine økonomiske teorier i perioden 1832–82*. Dissertation in economics (*Hovedfagsoppgave*), Department of Economics, University of Oslo, May 2001, 12–13.

50 Seip, *Vitenskap og virkelighet*, 55.

51 Bergh and Hanisch, *Vitenskap og politikk*, 31.

52 Langslet, *Konservatisme på norsk*, 147.

53 Seip, *Vitenskap og virkelighet*, 196.

54 Quoted in Seip, *Vitenskap og virkelighet*, 197.

55 Seip, *Vitenskap og virkelighet*, 205. 'Harmoni og integrasjon, to hovedideer fra 1850-årenes sosiale tenkning, gled i 1870-årene i bakgrunnen både i tanke og i argumentasjon.'

56 Seip, *Vitenskap og virkelighet*, 11.

57 Seip, *Vitenskap og virkelighet*, 125.

58 Seip, *Vitenskap og virkelighet*, 130.

59 Langslet, *Konservatisme på norsk*.

60 Seip, *Vitenskap og virkelighet*, 134.

61 Aschehoug quoted in Seip, *Vitenskap og virkelighet*, 134. 'Og medens Seieren dekker alle Feil, stiller Nederlaget dem ofte i et altfor skarpt Lys.'

62 Seip, *Vitenskap og virkelighet*, 102.

63 Bergh and Hanisch, *Vitenskap og politikk*, 30. The close relationship between Aschehoug and Schweigaard is also mentioned here.

64 Torkel H. Aschehoug, 'Anm. av E. Sundt: Beretning om Fante–eller Landstrygerfolket i Norge', *Norsk tidsskrift for videnskab og literatur* 5 (1851): 74. 'Anstille Sammenligninger og efterspore Forholdet mellem Aarsag og Virkning.'

65 Seip, *Vitenskap og virkelighet*, 31.

66 Hagerup, 'Nekrolog', 5.

67 Bergh and Hanisch, *Vitenskap og politikk*, 53; and Seip, *Vitenskap og virkelighet*, 125–38.

68 Seip, *Vitenskap og virkelighet*, 137.

69 A more thorough analysis of Aschehoug as a politician can be found in Seip, *Vitenskap og virkelighet*; Jens Arup Seip, *Ole Jacob Broch* (Oslo: Gyldendal, 1971); and Rune Slagstad, *De nasjonale strateger* (Oslo: Pax, 2001), parts 1 and 2.

70 Tilsynskommisjonen ved Aas Landbrukshøyskole.

71 Den norske hovedjernbane, later NSB.

72 Statement published by Anna Sewell, privately owned.

73 Norwegens Rechtsenzyklopädie zusammen mit K. J. Berg und A. F. Krieger, vol. 5 (Copenhagen: 1885–99); in vol 1 (1885): 'Den nordiske Statsret' (Das skandinavische staatsrecht).

74 Seip, *Vitenskap og virkelighet*, 185–6.

75 Store Norske Leksikon, 'Bredo von Munthe af Morgenstierne'. Online: http://www.snl.no/.nbl_biografi/Bredo_Von_Munthe_Af_Morgenstierne/utdypning_%E2%80%93_2 (accessed 3 September 2009).

76 Bredo Morgenstierne, 'Professor Dr Iuris T. H. Aschehoug in memoriam', *Norsk retstidende* 13 (1909): 8.

77 Thorstein Veblen, review of T. H. Aschehoug, 'Vaerdi- og Prislaerens Historie', *Journal of Political Economy* (March 1903): 306 (reprinted from *Statsökonomisk tidskrift* 8 (1902): 193).

78 Francis Hagerup, 'Nekrolog over Torkel Halvorsen Aschehoug' in *Norsk Retsvidenskab* (1909): 2.

Chapter 3 Norwegian Economic and Political Context in the Nineteenth Century

1 The summary is by no means aiming to give a complete overview, and many important people are not even mentioned here. The aim is to focus on economic development and to present the main ideas.

2 Gunnar Skirbekk, *Norsk og moderne* (Oslo: Res Publica, 2010), 16. See also Berg Eriksen and Sørensen, eds, *Norsk Idéhistorie*.

3 Kåre Amundsen, *Norsk sosialøkonomisk historie 1814–1890* (Oslo: Universitetsforlaget, 1963), 11.

4 Amundsen, *Norsk sosialøkonomisk historie, 1814–1890*, 12.

5 Amundsen, *Norsk sosialøkonomisk historie, 1814–1890*, 17.

6 Trond Berg Eriksen and Øystein Sørensen, ed., *Norsk Idéhistorie, vol. III: Kampen om Norges sjel 1770–1905* (Oslo: Aschehoug forlag, 2003), 20.

7 Skirbekk, *Norsk og moderne*, 22.

8 The words farmer and peasant will be used. The smallholder was also a farmer, but he did not own his land. He worked on a contract with a farmer, partly helping at the farm and partly being allowed to grow a small plot himself. Øystein Sørensen has helped me with these definitions. The Norwegian *bonde* ('peasant' in a strained English translation) usually denotes a freeholder or a fisherman whose legendary status and property rights were quite unique in pre-nineteenth-century Europe. Øyvind Østerud in Nina Witoszek, *The Origins of the 'Regime of Goodness': Remapping the Cultural History of Norway* (Oslo: Universitetsforlaget, 2011).

9 Berg Eriksen and Sørensen, *Norsk Idéhistorie*, 7.

10 Chapter 10 features an analysis of the reception in Norwegian economics of the entrepreneur, a term that is closely connected to the idea of the independent (but relatively small-scale) farmer.

11 Bo Stråth, 'The Normative Foundations of the Scandinavian Welfare States in Historical Perspective', in *Normative Foundations of the Welfare State: The Nordic Experience*, ed. Nanna Kildal and Stein Kuhnle (London: Routledge, 2005), 38.

12 Stråth, 'Normative Foundations', 42.

13 Nina Witoszek, 'Fugitives from Utopia: The Scandinavian Enlightenment Reconsidered', in *The Cultural Construction of Norden*, ed. Øystein Sørensen and Bo Stråth (Oslo: Scandinavian University Press, 1997).

14 Stråth, 'Normative Foundations', 38–9.

15 Stråth, 'Normative Foundations', 43.

16 Skirbekk, *Norsk og moderne*, 55.

17 *Intelligenskretsen* can be translated as the 'circle of intellectuals'. *Vidar* came out in 1832, *Den constitutionelle* was published from 1836, and these were the journals of the circle. Among others, Anton Martin Schweigaard was actively participating with articles.

18 An interesting analysis of the scientific development of economics in the late eighteenth and early nineteenth centuries can be found in Anton Fredrik Andresen, *Nytte, dannelse og vitenskap?: Universitetet og økonomifaget i det nye Norge 1811–1840* (Oslo: Det historisk-filosofiske fakultet, 2004).

19 Skirbekk, *Norsk og moderne*, 102.

20 Skirbekk, *Norsk og moderne*, 206n4.

21 A detailed analysis of this period can be found in Andresen, *Nytte, dannelse og vitenskap?*

22 Skirbekk, *Norsk og moderne*, 24; Andresen, *Nytte, dannelse og vitenskap?*, 8. 'Debatten pågikk over hele Europa, og hovedtendesen mht. den plass økonomifagene fikk ved universitetene […] var påfallende lik i de fleste land. […] Et nærstudium av det norske tilfelle viser hvilke utslag en allmenn europeisk utvikling på dette område fikk i et land hvor både den politiske, økonomiske og personalmessige situasjonen på mange måter var forskjellig fra de andre landenes.'

23 Witoszek, *'Regime of Goodness'*, 62.

24 Francis Sejersted, *Demokratisk kapitalisme* (Oslo: Pax forlag, 2002), 54.

25 The following description is primarily based on the presentation Sejersted gives in chapter 2 of his *Demokratisk kapitalisme*, 'En teori om den økonomiske og teknologiske utviklingen'. The views of international scholars and other Norwegian perspectives are found in other texts respectively.

26 Fritz Hodne, *Norges økonomiske historie 1815–1970* (Oslo: Cappelen, 1981).

27 David Landes, *The Wealth and Poverty of Nations: Why Some Are So Rich and Some So Poor* (London: Abacus, 1998), 248.

28 Landes, *Wealth and Poverty of Nations*, 249.

29 Frederik Stang was the Prime Minister, he also had other central positions, Schweigaard was never a minister. As David Landes puts it today, 'Getting lucky isn't about culture, but staying lucky often is. When a society, or the controlling parts of a society, is sitting on wealth-making resources, a country can be pretty rich as long as the resources remain. But when the resources are used up and any investments from them exhausted, that country often reverts.' Online: http://www.the-american-interest.com (accessed: January 2011).

30 Fritz Hodne and Ola Honningdal Grytten, *Norsk økonomi i det 19. århundre* (Bergen: Fagbokforlaget, 2000), 16.

31 Schweigaard quoted in Trond Bergh et al., 'Fire transformasjoner i skipsfarten & teknologioverføring og markedserobringer – noen trekk ved industriutviklingen', in *Norge fra u-land til i-land: vekst og utviklingslinjer 1830–1980* (Oslo: Gyldendal, 1983), 140. 'Alt hvad man af Fremtiden kan vente er at Landet ved egne Fabriker vil blive istand til at forsyne sig selv med de fleste grovere og simplere Vevningsprodukter, de finere og kostbarere Manufacturvarer vil Norge vel altid komme til at hente fra Udlandet.'

32 Report from Finansdepartementet in 1842 quoted in Bergh et al., 'Fire transformasjoner i skipsfarten', 140. 'Vanskeligheten ved at concurrere med de udenlandske Fabriker bevirker at denne Næringsvei [the industry] aldrig her i Landet vil kunde drives vidt.'

33 Bergh et al., 'Fire transformasjoner i skipsfarten', 41.

34 Bergh et al., 'Fire transformasjoner i skipsfarten', 184. Fisheries, lumber and shipping was growing with 3 per cent *pro anno* in the period.

35 Bergh et al., 'Fire transformasjoner i skipsfarten', 185.

36 Bergh et al., 'Fire transformasjoner i skipsfarten', 148.

37 Jacob Aall, quoted in Sejersted, *Demokratisk kapitalisme*, 'Alt er i vort Land paa en viss Maade Middelstand', 49.

38 Sejersted, *Demokratisk kapitalisme*, 53.

39 Sejersted, *Demokratisk kapitalisme*, see 53n15.

40 Sejersted, *Demokratisk kapitalisme*, 61.

41 See comments Trond Bergh and Tore J. Hanisch, *Vitenskap og politikk: Linjer i norsk sosialøkonomi gjennom 150 år* (Oslo: Aschehoug, 1984), 13.

42 Bergh and Hanisch, *Vitenskap og politikk*, 13.

43 Wilhelm Keilhau later commented on this article by saying that J. M. Keynes could have signed his arguments without doubt.

44 Andresen, *Nytte, dannelse og vitenskap?*

45 These plans are being described in the works of Oskar Jaeger, *Socialøkonomien* from *Det Kongelige Fredriks Universitet 1811–1911*: Festskrift (Kristiania, Aschehoug, 1911). Quote is found in Bergh and Hanisch, *Vitenskap og politikk*, 16.

46 Slagstad, *De nasjonale strateger*, 15.

47 Olav Bjerkholt, 'Schweigaard og statistikken' in *Anton Martin Schweigaard: Professorpolitikeren*, ed. Ole Mestad (Oslo: Akademisk publisering, 2009), 153. The quote is taken from Nicolai Rygg, 'Statistikken', in *Det Kongelige Fredriks Universitet 1811–1911*. 'Statistikken efter den senere mer rationelle Bearbeidelse har ophørt at være en Samling av Curiositeter og historiske Antiquiteter og er gaaet ind under de juridisk-oeconomiske Statsvidenskabers Classe, idet den deels indeholder Grunlaget for Statens organiske og administrative Lovgivning, deels fremstiller de factiske Data af den anvendte Nationaloeconomie.'

48 Bjerkholt, 'Schweigaard og statistikken', 172.

49 The justification of the chair written by Schweigaard, quoted in Mehlum, 'Samfunnsøkonomen Schweigaard', in *Anton Martin Schweigaard: Professorpolitikeren*, ed. Ole Mestad (Oslo: Akademisk publisering, 2009), 125–6. 'Forholdt dette sig ikke saaledes, saa vilde det være meget let hos os at fremkalde en hel statsøkonomisk Literatur ved Oversættelse af denne Videnskabs Hovedværker i fremmede Sprog. Men hertil utfordres der en ganske anden og selvstændig Virksomhed. En økonomisk Lære, der i den Betydning er norsk, at den kan yde rigtig Veiledning om, hvad der hos os bør rettes og forbedres, og tjene til at lede og befæste Almenanskuelsen angaaende vore egne økonomiske og financielle Anliggender og Foranstaltninger, fremkommer først ved en saadan Gjennemarbeidelse af vort Lands økonomiske Institutioner, at de i deres Grundsætninger, Formaal og Virkninger fremstilles til Beskuelse i Videnskabens Lys.' The quote is originally from Oskar Jaeger, *Socialøkonomien* in *Det Kongelige Fredriks Universitet 1811–1911*.

50 Mehlum, 'Samfunnsøkonomen Schweigaard', 126.

51 Bergh and Hanisch, *Vitenskap og politikk*, 21.

52 Bergh and Hanisch, *Vitenskap og politikk*, 21.

53 Bergh and Hanisch, *Vitenskap og politikk*, 26.

54 Bjerkholt does not agree with Bergh and Hanisch on this point, claiming that they exaggerate the importance of this work in relation to national accounts.

55 This is Bjerkholt's point in his article about Schweigaard, 'Schweigaard og Statistikken', 149–72. In his view, the applied vs the theoretical gets a somewhat negative connotation and a

valuation of the theoretical over the practical or useful. Norges Statistik was originally planned to be two volumes, but only one was written. Bjerkholt, 'Schweigaard og Statistikken', note 4, 150. 'I 1919, da den rettlinjede suksesjon etter Schweigaard når det gjaldt økonomi med Torkel Aschehoug, Ebbe Hertzberg og Bredo Morgenstierne hadde ebbet ut, var det Halvdan Koths opptaninge at "de statsøkonomer vi har havt og har, er alle sammen middelveisfarere, uten originalitet". Med Kohts medvirkning ble rekrutteringen av en "fremragende utlending" forsøkt. Budet gikk til Torstein Veblen [...] Forsøket mislyktes, men problemet løste seg på annen måte da Ragnar Frisch få år senere ga opp en karriere som sølvsmed [and became an economist].'

56 'Om Norges Folkemængde i 1664–1666' was published in *Norsk tidsskrift for videnskab og literatur* in 1848.

57 The office started out as just a small operation in 1851, and in 1867 it was firmly established and directed by Kiær. In 1877 the bureau was founded. A couple of other well-known economists, and also some later ones, becoming the director of the Norwegian Central Bank were for shorter or longer periods closely connected to the Bureau (Einar Einarsen, Nicolay Rygg, Gunnar Jahn and Ingvar Wedervang).

58 Slagstad (in *De nasjonale strateger*) and a couple of other historians have accepted this term as an adequate description of the political period from 1814 to 1884. Norway wrote its constitution in 1814 and parliamentarism was established in 1884.

59 Ole Mestad, 'Schweigaard: mennesket, professoren, politikaren', in *Anton Martin Schweigaard: Professorpolitikeren*, ed. Ole Mestad (Oslo: Akademisk publisering, 2009), 13.

60 This point is also mostly agreed upon among Norwegian historians and commented on earlier in this chapter.

61 Jens Arup Seip, *Utsikt over Norges historie* (Oslo: Gyldendal, 1974), 100–101.

62 Seip, *Utsikt over Norges historie*, 100.

63 Halvor Mehlum, 'Samfunnsøkonomen Schweigaard', in *Anton Martin Schweigaard: Professorpolitikeren*, ed. Ole Mestad (Oslo: Akademisk publisering, 2009), 137.

64 Anton Martin Schweigaard, 'Forelæsninger over den politiske økonomi', in *Ungdomsarbeider*, ed. Oscar Jaeger and Frederik Stang (Kristiania: Aschehoug, 1904), 106. 'Forandringer i de økonomiske Konkjunkturer ere derfor ikke alene en Følge af Natur- eller politiske Aarsager, saasom Aar, Krig, men ogsaa af Uforholdsmæssigheder i Kapitalens anvendelse paa store merkantile og industrielle Foretagende, hvorfor ogsaa Gevinsten her er en meget vaklende Størrelse, i hvilken det Mer til visse Tider kompenseres ved de Mindre til andre.'

65 Bergh and Hanisch, *Vitenskap og politikk*, 22, 23. 'Schweigaards tanke var altså å øke statsøkonomiens praktiske nytte. [...] For til syvende og sist var det ikke vitenskapsmann i mer snever forstand Schweigaard var, men politiker og samfunnstenker.' This is also the point that Lykkja makes in his master thesis.

66 Anton Martin Schweigaard quoted in L. M. B. Aubert, *Historiske Oplysninger om det juridiske Fakultet ved det Norske Frederiks Universitet from 1870*. Statsøkonomien forutsatte: 'en omfattende og indtrængende Indsigt i de Statsinstitusjoner, der betinge de produktive Elementærkræfters Udvikling, og hemmende eller befordrende gribe inn ind i den offentlige og private Økonomien'. Bergh and Hanisch use this quote, see page 22 for their comments.

67 Bergh and Hanisch, *Vitenskap og politikk*, 22. The Schweigaard quote is not indicated, but I presume it comes from Aubert. Schweigaard states, 'En økonomisk Lære, der i den Betydning er norsk, at den kan yde rigtig Veiledning om, hvad der hos os bør rettes og forbedres, og tjene til at lede og befæste Almenanskuelsen angaaende vore egne økonomiske og finansielle Anliggender og Foranstaltninger.'

68 Schweigaard as a modernizer and strategist in the nineteenth century has been a central theme for the Norwegian debate about politics after 1814. Bergh and Hanisch, as two of the few, had an economic starting point in their analysis, whereas for instance Seip, Slagstad and Sørensen have a political approach. Sejersted can be said to have both, and traces of economic debates are also found in Seip, Slagstad and Sørensen.

69 Bergh and Hanisch, *Vitenskap og politikk*, 22. 'Jusen og sosialøkonomiens hovedoppgave var å være hjelpemidler i det politiske reformarbeidet.'

70 Schweigaard, 'Om den tyske filosofi', in *Ungdomsarbeider*, ed. Oscar Jaeger and Frederik Stang (Kristiania: Aschehoug, 1904), 245.

71 Andresen, *Nytte, dannelse, vitenskap?*, 375–6.

72 Andresen, *Nytte, dannelse, vitenskap?*, 376. The debate between Rolf Olsen and Aschehoug is also mentioned by Andresen on the issue of method (see Chapter 4).

73 Nils Rune Langeland, 'Sagens natur', in *Anton Martin Schweigaard: Professorpolitikeren*, ed. Ole Mestad (Oslo: Akademisk publisering, 2009), note 7, 305. 'Mit Rücksicht auf die Natur der Sache, das heisst, mit Rücksicht auf das, was von Bürgern und Bauern als ganz natürlich betrachtet wird, sage ich nur so.' Schweigaard uses the French philosopher of rights Anton Fredrich Justus Thibaut when he explains the expression 'sagens natur' in 1834.

74 Langeland, 'Sagens natur', 303.

75 Ebbe Hertzberg, *Professor Schweigaard i hans offentlige Virksomhed: 1832–1870* (Kristiania: Cammermeyer forlag, 1883), 29. 'Han var jurist, økonom og offentlig personlighed, og disse tre livsopgaver lagde fuldelig beslag paa hans evne og hans tid. Han havde sine grunde for at forkaste den tyske fornuftsfilosofi og at støtte sig til en empirisk verdensanskuelse.' The Norwegian historian Thor Inge Rørvik claims in his article about Schweigaard and philosophy that this critique was more an attack on jurisprudence than a philosophical text about ontology per se. Thor Inge Rørvik, 'Schweigaard og filosofien', in *Anton Martin Schweigaard: Professorpolitikeren*, ed. Ole Mestad (Oslo: Akademisk publisering, 2009), 61–88.

76 Slagstad, *De nasjonale strateger*, 14. 'Mot idealismens "tomme spekulasjon" stilte Schweigaard "erfaringens methode"'.

77 Schweigaard, 'Om den tyske filosofi', 243, 300.

78 Mestad, 'Schweigaard: mennesket, professoren, politikaren', 25. 'Rode i virkeligheten'.

79 Schweigaard, 'Om den tyske filosofi', 248, 255.

80 Schweigaard, 'Om den tyske filosofi', 272. 'Hvad kunne de tyske Filosofer bringe ud af disse tomme Principer? Hvad kunne de fremlægge som det positive Resultat af denne indre Intuition, af denne Fornuft par excellence? […] Er ikke det bedste Middel at løse Stridighederne mellom Partierne […], at bedømme dem efter deres Konsekventser, efter deres Resultater, efter Anvendeligheden af det, som de lære? Ja, det er et Middel, som allerede forlængst har fordrevet denne Maade at filosofere paa fra Frankrige og endu mere fra England, hvor den filosofiske Vilkaarlighed altid er blevet bekjæmpet af rigtig dømmende og kraftige Aander.'

81 Schweigaard, 'Om den tyske filosofi', 282. 'De sociale Videnskaber have, det kan man sige, ganske fjernet sig fra den; det er ikke den lidet vigtige og næsten betydningsløse Gruppering af de tyske Jurister i Historikere og Ikke-Historikere, som jeg sigter til, skjønt de Alle med Enstemmighed modsætte sig denne Filosofis Pretensioner (tyske).'

82 Hertzberg, *Professor Schweigaard i hans offentlige Virksomhed*.

83 Hertzberg, *Professor Schweigaard i hans offentlige Virksomhed*, 22–3. 'Det er de transcendente filosofer, der paa engang paastod at være uafhengige af virkeligheden og at ville beherske denne, som hans forkastelsdom gjælder; en empirisk sammenfatning af en maadeholden og sine egne grænser bevidst abstraction har han saa langt fra udtalt sig mod, at det tværtimod netop er ønskeligheden af en saadan […] han ivrede netop for […] videnskabens og virkelighedens forbindelse.'

84 Hertzberg, *Professor Schweigaard i hans offentlige Virksomhed*, 25.

85 Berg Eriksen and Sørensen, ed., *Norsk Idéhistorie, vol. III: Kampen om Norges sjel 1770–1905*, 117–19. A quote from Schweigaard's rejection of German philosophy is referred: 'En Erkjendelse *par excellence*, høiere end den, som stammer fra Erfaringen, Iagttagelsen og Reflexionen over det Eksisterende i alle de Forhold, som er Gjenstand for Iagttagelse.' Schweigaard believed in the opposite.

86 Langeland, 'Sagens natur', 301–333. The article focuses mainly on juridical issues related to 'sagens natur', but is in general in agreement with the views presented here.

87 Hertzberg, *Professor Schweigaard i hans offentlige Virksomhed*, 26. 'Det umiddelbare, saavel af det historisk given, som af saakaldte almindelige grundsætninger uafhængige hensyn til livets egne, vel forstaaede behov, er saaledes ifølge Schweigaard udviklingens bevægende princip […] med en sikker fod paa det liberale fremskridts standpunkt.'

88 Bergh and Hanisch, *Vitenskap og politikk*, 25.

89 Bergh and Hanisch, *Vitenskap og politikk*, 26.

90 Bergh and Hanisch, *Vitenskap og politikk*, 25.

91 Hertzberg, *Professor Schweigaard i hans offentlige Virksomhed*, 23.

92 Schweigaard, quoted in Hertzberg, *Professor Schweigaard i hans offentlige Virksomhed*, 30. 'Schweigaard indrømmer gjentagende, at den nævte modsætning "for længe siden har ophørt at være skarp, og med hensyn til behandlingsmaaden aldrig har været det. Egentlig gjælder denne forskjel i synsmaaden mer lovgivningsmaadens omfang og pligter, end udviklingen af den bestaaende ret"'.

93 Schweigaard, quoted in Hertzberg, *Professor Schweigaard i hans offentlige Virksomhed*, 30.

94 Bergh and Hanisch, *Vitenskap og politikk*, 24, quote found in Hertzberg, *Professor Schweigaard i hans offentlige Virksomhed*, 12. 'Det rationale gjennemstrømmer ligesaavel tingens som tankens verden. […] Denne karakteristiske udtalelse danner allerede et ligsaa korrekt som kort udtryk for Schweigaards filosofiske standpunkt: Han er empiriker, men i ligesaa høi grad idealist, idet han i den hele tilværelse, "ligesaavel tingenes som tankens verden", ser den rationelle ide bryde sig frem.'

95 Schweigaard, *Ungdomsarbeider*, 'Forelæsninger over den politiske økonomi'. For a detailed analysis see Mehlum, 'Samfunnsøkonomen Schweigaard', 125–46.

96 Editors' note in Schweigaard, *Ungdomsarbeider*, Jæger and Stang, *Vitenskap og politikk*, iv.

97 Mehlum, 'Samfunnsøkonomen Schweigaard', 131.

98 Wilhelm Keilhau and Ragnar Frisch quoted in Mehlum, 'Samfunnsøkonomen Schweigaard', 129. Originally printed in *Sosialøkonomisk utsnitt* (Oslo, 1940).

99 Bergh and Hanisch, *Vitenskap og politikk*, 31.

100 For a detailed analysis see Mehlum, 'Samfunnsøkonomen Schweigaard', 125–46. This article also contains an overview of literature that Schweigaard borrowed at the University Library (UB) from 1844 to 1847. Among the authors we find Bentham, Blanqui, Hermann, McCulloch (3 books), Rau, Senior, Sismondi, Smith and Tocqueville. It is believed that he possessed copies of Smith and Ricardo.

101 Bergh and Hanisch, *Vitenskap og politikk*, 33.

102 Bergh and Hanisch, *Vitenskap og politikk*, 33.

103 Quotes found in Bergh and Hanisch, *Vitenskap og politikk*, 33.

104 Bergh and Hanisch, *Vitenskap og politikk*, 33.

105 Mehlum, 'Samfunnsøkonomen Schweigaard', 131.

106 Jaeger and Stang in their introduction of Schweigaard, *Ungdomsarbeider*, 'Hvori han giver en kortfattet, men fuldstændig Oversigt over, hvad man nutildag kalder den theoretiske Socialøkonomi. […] Det er et slaaende Bevis for Schweigaards mærkværdige Aandsuafhængighed og Skarpblik, at han i 1847 kunde give den theoretiske Økonomi en samlet Fremstilling, hvori det videnskabelige Grundsyn, Bestemmelsen af Videnskabens Omfang og den andvendte Systematik endu er helt ud moderne, og hvori man, efter snart 60 Aars Forløb, skal have vanskeligt for at paavise nogetsomhelst Ensidigt eller Urigtigt i de foredragene Theorier. Der existerer neppe noget samtidigt nationaløkonomisk Værk, som hvilket det samme lader sig sige. Selvfølgelig er der siden Schweigaards Tid foretaget vidtgaaende nye Undersøgelser i den theoretiske Socialøkonomi og fremsat betydningsfulde nye Theorier; men den største Del af dette Nye er endu Gjenstand for videnskabelig Debat. Hvad Schweigaards her trykte Forelæsninger indeholder i elementær og lettilegnelig Fremstilling, er sikkert fastslaaede økonomiske Lærdomme, som burder være den dannede Almeheds aandelige Fælleseie, men som desværre endnu ikke er det.'

107 Amundsen, *Norsk sosialøkonomisk historie 1814–1890*, 94.

108 Schweigaard, 'Forelæsninger over politisk økonomi', in *Ungdomsarbeider*, ed. Oscar Jaeger and Frederik Stang (Kristiania: Aschehoug, 1904), 3. 'Gjenstanden for den politiske Økonomi er at undersøge de almene Aarsager, der virke befordrende eller hemmende paa de borgerlige Samfunds økonomiske Velbefindende eller Velstand, og dens afledede Formaal at medvirke til Forbedring i de udvortes Livsvilkaar, hvis Betryggelse indtager en saa vigtig Plads blandt Betingelserne for Nationernes moralske Fremskridt.'

109 Schweigaard, 'Forelæsninger over politisk økonomi', 3. 'I den form, hvorunder denne Videnskab efter den engelske Skoles Mønster af de Fleste fremstilles, kan det imidlertid ikke siges, at det er den her angivne Retning, der stilles i Spidsen, hvorimod den politiske Økonomi forkynder sig som en Lære, ikke om Almenvelstandens Udbredelse, men om Nationalrigdommens Forøgelse.'

110 Senior, *An Outline of the Science of Political Economy*, first published in 1836, this edition is from 1850, 3rd. print, 1853. Online: http://www.econlib.org/library/Senior/snP1.html (accessed 8 June 2010).

111 Senior, *An Outline of the Science of Political Economy*.

112 Senior, *An Outline of the Science of Political Economy*.

113 Schweigaard, 'Forelæsninger over politisk økonomi', 4. 'For det Første kan det siges, at den politiske Økonomi, naar den ikke indskrænker sig til en Udvikling af de naturlige Love for Nationalrigdommens Dannelse, men fremstiller Betingelserne for Velstandens almene Udbredelse staar Sædelighed samt de politiske og retlige Institutioners Fuldkommenhed i Vigtighed ikke tilbage for Vækkelse af de produktive Kræfter. Men enhver Videnskab maa have sin Begrændsning, og denne vindes her kun ved at betragte de produktive Potenser afsondrede og under et udelukkende Hensyn til den ene Gjenstand, Nationalrigdommens Forøgelse, hvorimod Behandlingen af de moralske Spørgsmål, der blande sig i al menneskelig Virksomhed, maa henvises til den Plads hvor deres Løsning egentlig hører hjemme.'

114 Schweigaard, 'Forelæsninger over politisk økonomi', 5.

115 Aschehoug, *Socialøkonomik*, vol. 1, ch. 1, § 1, 1. 'Økonomi er Betegnelsen for den Virksomhed, ved hvilken Mennesket skaffer sig og bruger de ydre Midler, der ere nødvendige eller tjenlige til at tilfredsstille dets timelige Behov. [...] Virksomheden kaldes Privatøkonomi, naar Hensyn tages udelukkende til det enkelte Individs Interesse. Men for at blive mulig og frugtbar maa Virksomheden drives af flere i Samfund med hverandre staaende Mennesker. Den bliver da Samfunds- eller Socialøkonomi. Det er væsentlig den samme Virksomhed, kun seet fra forskjellige Synspunkter. Denne Virksomhed har fra ældre Tid været kaldt Politisk Økonomi eller Statsøkonomi. Tyskerne, der følte sig som Nation, men som manglede tilstrækkelig Organisation som fælles Stat, begyndte at kalde Virksomheden Nationaløkonomi. I Danmark og Sverige har man uden saadan Foranledning optaget dette Navn fra Tyskland.'

116 Schweigaard, 'Forelæsninger over politisk økonomi', 4.

117 Schweigaard, 'Forelæsninger over politisk økonomi', 9. 'Forkastes altsaa Non-Interventionens Princip som øverste Grundsætning i den politiske Økonomi, saa bliver det Plads for en fra Samfundsvillien udgaaende Paavirkning ogsaa i økonomiske Anliggender.'

118 Schweigaard lectures from 1857 (Ms Forelesn. 878, UB in Oslo, 35), quoted in Øystein Sørensen, *A. M. Schweigaards politiske tenkning* (Oslo: Universitetsforlaget, 1988), 67. 'Det man især maa have for Øie ved Paalæg af Skatterne er at fordele dem saaledes at de komme til at ramme alle i Forhold til deres Bærekraft.'

119 Bergh and Hanisch mention it, and the historian Øystein Sørensen, who wrote his doctoral thesis about Schweigaard, *A. M. Schweigaards politiske tenkning*, gives a broad analysis of Schweigaard's position.

120 Schweigaard, 'Forelæsninger over politisk økonomi', 6–7. 'Hvis man i stedet for den største mulige Produktion sætter den størst mulige Sum af alment Velvære som Videnskabens Gjenstand, saa bliver det uundgaaeligt til Fordel for det sidste Formaal, at opgive den

Grundsætning, der etter den engelske Lære behersker den politiske Økonomi, er, at det størst mulige økonomiske Produkt opnaas ved at lade de menneskelige Bestræbelser og Kræfter følge sin egen Retning uden anden Paavirkning end den, der udkræves til Opretholdelsen af den udvortes retlige Orden.'

121 Sørensen, *A. M. Schweigaards politiske tenkning*, see Chapter 2, 'Schweigaards økonomiske liberalisme: Laissez-faire eller frihandel?', 50–86. A short resume of this position is also found in Berg Eriksen and Sørensen, 'Liberalismen i Norge – laissez-faire?', in *Norsk Idéhistorie, vol. III: Kampen om Norges sjel 1770–1905* (Oslo: Aschehoug forlag, 2003), 106–113. Sørensen also thoroughly investigates the theoretical concepts of free trade and laissez-faire, and the following arguments are found in his presentation.

122 Sørensen mentions the position of two later historians.

123 The opponent to Sørensen's disputation about Schweigaard, Per Maurseth, brings forth the arguments of this more recent article of Seip. Here the main disagreement between Maurseth/Seip and Sørensen is whether, as Sørensen claims, it is continuity in the free trade/ laissez-faire position of Schweigaard or if the 1847 lectures represent a disruption. I do not intend to repeat this disagreement here, because Schweigaard is not my main topic, but in my view, Sørensen presents a plausible and thorough analysis of Schweigaard's position, which I believe also corresponds with the arguments that are found in later debates and writings throughout the century. A further analysis is found in Chapter 11.

124 Sørensen, *A. M. Schweigaards politiske tenkning*, 68. Additionally, Sørensen's analysis does not only take into account what Schweigaard said in his small lecture, but equally looks at what Schweigaard actually said and did in political discussions about trade throughout the 1850s and 1860s. Sørensen states that, 'Strictly speaking, the most interesting analysis to do is not just looking at what Schweigaard said from the lectern. The most interesting issue is how Schweigaard generally – argued theoretically and practiced politically – perceived the laissez-faire doctrine.' Neither Sørensen, nor Hodne or Sejersted (other Norwegian economic historians) or Bergh and Hanisch seem to agree with Seip.

125 For a thorough discussion, see Sørensen, *Schweigaards politiske tenkning*, 56–7. In order to clarify the discussions, Sørensen outlines the views of the classical economists, starting with Adam Smith and continuing with quotes from other liberals like the aforementioned Nassau Senior and J. R. McCulloch, showing that neither of them had an unrestricted view on laissez-faire. Senior claimed in an Oxford lecture from the late 1840s, 'The only rational foundation of government, the only foundation of a right to govern and a correlative duty to obey, is expediency – the general benefit of the community. It is the duty of a government to do whatever is conducive to the welfare of the governed. The only limit to this duty is power.' McCulloch wrote in 1848, 'The principle of laissez-faire may be safely trusted to in some things, but in many more it is wholly inapplicable; and to appeal to it on all occasions, savours more of the policy of a parrot than of a statesman or a philosopher.' Sørensen also gives an account of Schumpeter's view on the classical economists, as well as the views of Lionel Robbins (1898–1984) and Colin Holmes, who both state the opposite view of Schumpeter by underlining the non-laissez-faire position of classical political economy. Colin Holmes claims, 'The scholarship of the last forty years has proved beyond question that the architects of classical political economy cannot be categorised as upholders of the laissez-faire philosophy.' From his 'Laissez-faire in Theory and Practice: Britain 1800–1875', *Journal of European Economic History* 5 (3) (Winter 1976). Sørensen himself seems to side with Robbins and Holmes.

126 William D. Grampp, *The Manchester School of Economics* (Stanford/Oxford: Stanford University Press, 1960). Online: http://oll.libertyfund.org/?option=com_staticxt&staticfile=show.php%3Ftitle=2128&chapter=192980&layout=html&Itemid=27 (accessed 8 June 2010).

127 Sørensen, *A. M. Schweigaards politiske tenkning*, 58.

128 Scott Gordon, 'The Ideology of Laissez-faire', in *The Classical Economists and Economic Policy*, ed. A. W. Coates (London: Methuen, 1965).

129 Schweigaard, 'Om indførselstolden og dens historie', 231.

130 Sørensen, *A. M. Schweigaards politiske tenkning*, 315.

131 Schweigaard lectures from 1857 (Ms Forelesn. 1070a, UB in Oslo, 6), quoted in Sørensen, *A. M. Schweigaards politiske tenkning*, 69. 'Den største Begivenhed i øconomisk Henseende, der er hændt Norge siden 1814, er Navigationsactens Ophævelse i England.'

132 Schweigaard wrote in 'Den Constitutionelle' in 1840, quote found in Bergh and Hanisch, *Vitenskap og Politikk*, 45. 'Gjør den norske skibsfart saa fri som muligt! Dette er en sætning som ikke tidt nok kan gjentages og ikke stærkt nok udtales af enhver, der riktigen har opfattet Norges stilling som søfarende nation. Her er det videste udsigter aabne sig!'

133 Sørensen, *A. M. Schweigaards politiske tenkning*, 88.

134 See Sørensen, Chapter 4, 'Modernisering i praksis: industrialiseringens rolle', in *A. M. Schweigaards politiske tenkning*, 118–39.

135 Sørensen, *A. M. Schweigaards politiske tenkning*, 17. Other historians have analysed the political role of Schweigaard in detail, and this picture is well documented (Keilhau, Bergh and Hanisch, Slagstad).

136 Schweigaard in the 1848 parliamentary debate, quoted in Sørensen, *A. M. Schweigaards politiske tenkning*, 73. 'Man skulde vanskelig kunde paavise noget Værk, som i de sidste 25 Aar havde været drevet med større Omhu og Hensyn til Arbeiderne end dette [...]. Det forekom Taleren at ville være trist, om man ved at afslaa Hjælpen skulde dømme dette Værk til Undergangen.'

137 He wrote 'Om sparebanker og privatbanker, navlig om deres udlånsvirksomhed' (About banking and lending) in 1890, 'Norges hypotekbank' in 1891, 'Om Kapitalrenten og rentefoden' (About capital rent and interest rate) in 1892, 'Den sirkulerende seddelmængde som økonomisk barometer' (Money in circulation as an economic barometer) in 1893, 'Værdi og prislærens historie' (The history of the theory of value and prices) in 1900–1901, 'Kort oversigt over den norske mynt- og pengeværdis historie sammenlignet med Vest-Europas' (A short review of Norwegian monetary history compared to Western European) in 1903, 'About savings banks and private banks, and their lending activities', 'The Norwegian central bank', 'About capital rent and the interest rate', 'The monetary circulation as an economic measure', 'The history of value and prices', 'A short analysis of the Norwegian monetary history compared with Western-Europe', all of which appeared in *Statsøkonomisk Tidsskrift*.

Chapter 4   Norwegian Economic Thought and Method

1 Sources will be *Statsøkonomisk Tidsskrift*, other writings/lectures by Hertzberg, Morgenstierne, Jaeger and Aarum, as well as Norwegian literature on the historical period. Details will follow in an appendix.

2 Eric Grimmer-Solem, *The Rise of Historical Economics and Social Reform in Germany 1864–1894* (Oxford: Clarendon Press, 2003), 3.

3 Trond Bergh and Tore J. Hanisch, *Vitenskap og politikk: Linjer i norsk sosialøkonomi gjennom 150 år* (Oslo: Aschehoug, 1984), 73.

4 Bergh and Hanisch, *Vitenskap og politikk*, 73. See, among others, Bergh and Hanisch, and Lykkja.

5 This is confirmed by Einar Lie and Hege Roll-Hansen in *Faktisk talt: Statistikkens historie i Norge* (Oslo: Universitetsforlaget, 2001).

6 See chapter XVIII in Anton Fredrik Andresen, *Nytte, dannelse og vitenskap?: Universitetet og økonomifaget i det nye Norge 1811–1840* (Oslo: Det historisk-filosofiske fakultet, 2004).

7 Fougner Lundh quoted in Andresen, *Nytte, dannelse og vitenskap?*, 'Statistikken burde "især beskjæftige seg" med å levere de opplysninger som statsøkonomen kunne nyttiggjøre seg.'

8 Andresen, *Nytte, dannelse og vitenskap?*, 373–4.

9 See, for example, the summaries and reviews of all published articles, books, etc. in *Statsøkonomisk Tidsskrift*, starting in 1887.

10 Bredo Morgenstierne, 'Fattigondet og Socialismen', *Statsøkonomisk Tidsskrift* 3 (1889): 1. 'Det er forlængst erkjændt, at staten ikke blot er retstat, men også kulturstat, at den ikke blot har som oppgave at yde den ydre og indre retsbeskyttelse, men ogsaa paa den maade, hvorpaa fra statens side kan ske, at fremme enhver menneskelig interesse og støtte samfundets materielle og aandelige kulturutvikling. De utallige maader, hvorpaa stat og kommune i vor tid faktisk griber regulerende ind i den økonomiske virksomhed, dels gjennem indskrænkninger i den enkeltes frihed, dels gjennem selv at overtage visse bedrifter, vil være kjendt for enhver. Grænserne for statens virksomhed paa dette felt bestemmes just af hensynet til den individuelle frihed. Men hvor disse grænser i det enkelte skal drages, lader sig i sin almindelighed ikke angive. Den ene stat gaar her noget længer i socialistisk, den anden i individualistisk rætning. Den første er f. ex. for tiden tilfældet med Tyskland, det sidste med England, medens vort land kanske kan betegnes som staaende saa nogenlund midt imellem.'

11 Thorvald Aarum, 'Norwegen, Dänemark und Schweden', in *Die Wirtschaftstheorie der Gegenwart*, ed. Hans Mayer (Wien: Julius von Springer, 1927), 122. 'Die Notwendigkeit einer genauen Fühlung mit der Entwicklungen der Wissenschaft im Auslande hat einen gewissen Kosmopolitismus in der Forschung der drei nordischen Länder hervorgerufen, insofern als das Gewicht darauf gelegt wird, die jeweils gemachten Fortschritte für die einheimische Forschung nutzbar zu machen [...] so gibt es auch keine skandinavische Wissenschaft als solche [...]. Demgemäß darf betont werden, daß sich im Gebiete der Ökonomik allerdings gewisse gemeinsame Züge in der Forschung der drei Länder nachweisen lassen, diese aber vielmehr als ein gemeinsames Resultat des intimen Kontaktes mit der ausländischen Forschung, als von irgend welcher internen Gemeinschaft herrührend, anzusehen sind.'

12 Andresen, *Nytte, dannelse og vitenskap?* chapter XVII. 'De sterkeste impulsene mottok han [Fougner Lundh] fra de tyske formidlerne av Adam Smith og hans etterfølgere, både fordi han, liksom de fleste av hans samtidige i Norge, leste mest tysk, og fordi "den tyske lære" i økonomien svarte godt til hans egen tenkemåte.'

13 Andresen, *Nytte, dannelse og vitenskap?*, 342–6.

14 Schweigaard in *Departements-tidende* 36 (1848): 594. 'En økonomisk Lære, der i den Betydning er norsk, at den kan yde rigtig Veiledning om , hvad der bør rettes og forbedres [...], Dette forutsatte en omfattende og indtrængende Indsigt i de Statsinstitutioner, der betinge de produktive Elementærkræfters Udvikling.'

15 Yuichi Shionoya, *The Soul of the German Historical School: Methodological Essays on Schmoller, Weber and Schumpeter* (New York: Springer, 2005), x.

16 Aarum, 'Norwegen, Dänemark und Schweden', 123. 'Der historischen Schule gegenüber, war Aschehoug nicht eben unsympatische gestimmt, konnte sich ihr aber wegen ihrer Vernachlässigung der Theorie nicht anschliessen.'

17 Aarum, 'Norwegen, Dänemark und Schweden', 123. 'Um so mehr empfing er von der österreichischen Wissenschaft beherrscthe tiefe Eindrücke, Ausgehend von der englischen klassischen Lehre, wurde er bald von der Bedeutung der Erneuerung der teoretischen Forschung, die von Menger und seinen Nachfolgern sowie auch von Jevons ihrer Ursprung nahm, gänzlich überzeugt und betrachtete es als seine wichtigste Aufgabe, such seine Schüler in die Gedankengänge dieser Forscher einzuführen.'

18 Pål Magnus Lykkja, *Anton M. Schweigaard og Torkel H. Aschehoug sine økonomiske teoriar i perioden 1832–82* (thesis, Department of Economics, University of Oslo, May 2001).

19 As Lykkja has mainly used the analysis of Schweigaard written by Øystein Sørensens and the doctoral thesis about Aschehoug written by Anne-Lise Seip, there is no need to repeat his findings, unless there are discrepancies or disagreements between us.

20 Lykkja, *Anton M. Schweigaard og Torkel H. Aschehoug*, 7. 'Menneskene, naar de skulle gjennomføre deres Theorier, ere fornuftigere, end naar de blot theoretiserer.'

21 Anathon Aall, *Det historiske og litterære grundlag for filosofien hos A. M. Schweigaard* (Kristiania: Det Norske videnskaps-akademi, 1917), 7.

22 Bergh and Hanisch, *Vitenskap og politikk*, 146, 149.

23 Bergh and Hanisch, *Vitenskap og politikk*, 50.

24 Johan Sverdrup in *Stortingstidende 1869*, quoted in Bergh and Hanisch, 55.

25 Schweigaard, 'Om den tyske filosofi', in *Ungdomsarbeider*, ed. Oscar Jaeger and Frederik Stang (Kristiania: Aschehoug, 1904), 249.

26 Schweigaard, 'Om den tyske filosofi', 249.

27 Schweigaard, 'Om den tyske filosofi', 251.

28 Hertzberg, *Professor Schweigaard i hans offentlige virksomhed: 1832–1870* (Kristiania: Cammermeyer forlag, 1883), 12. 'Denne karakteristiske udtalelse danner allerede et ligesaa korrekt som kort udtryk for Schweigaards filosofiske standpunkt: Han er empiriker, men i ligesaa høi grad idealist, idet han i den hele tilværelse, "ligesaavel tingenes som tankenes verden" ser den rationelle ide bryde sig frem.'

29 John Stuart Mill, *The Collected Works of John Stuart Mill, Volume VIII: A System of Logic Ratiocinative and Inductive Part II* (1843). Online: http://oll.libertyfund.org/index.php?option=com_staticxt&staticfile=show.php%3Ftitle=247&Itemid=28 (accessed 1 November 2010).

30 Lykkja, *Anton M. Schweigaard og Torkel H. Aschehoug*, 20.

31 Aschehoug seems to divide between social economics (*sosialøkonomi*) as the economic activity and social economics (*sosialøkonomik*) or state economics (*statsøkonomik*) as the scientific discipline.

32 Can be translated into the older English 'political economy', the standard use of 'economics' or the German *Staatswirtschaft* or *Volkswirtschaft*.

33 Aschehoug, *Socialøkonomik*, vol. 1, part 1, chap. 1, § 1, 2, note 1. Aschehoug also mentions the arguments that Schmoller brings up in the *HBW* article, where Schmoller apparently defends the use of the term *Nationalökonomie*, but that he seems to be arguing for using *Staatswirtschaft*, since the strongest links between different private economic activities is the state.

34 Andresen, *Nytte, dannelse vitenskap?*, 354.

35 Aschehoug quotes Jevons's *Theory of Political Economy* as well as Roscher's *Grundlagen der Nationalökonomie* and Marshall's *Principles of Economics*.

36 Aschehoug also mentions Pantaleoni and Philippovich.

37 Aschehoug, *Socialøkonomik*, vol. 1, part 1, chap. 1, § 3, 6, note 1 and 2. See Conrad, *Grundriss zum Studium der politischen Ökonomie* (1896); Philippovich, *Grundriss der politischen Ökonomie*; Dietzel, *Theoretische Socialökonomik*, and Schmoller's article in *HBW*, mentioned above. Schmoller makes a distinction between the general *Nationalökonomik* that gives general and universal theories, and the specific *Nationalökonomik* that explains national conditions, history and specific national circumstances.

38 Aschehoug, *Socialøkonomik*, vol. 1, part 1, chap. 1, § 4, 7. 'Nogen skarp Sondering mellem den rene og anvendte Socialøkonomik lader sig ikke gjennemføre. Socialøkonomiken henter baade Grundlaget for sine Theorier og Beviserne for disses Sandhed fra den indre eller ydre Erfarings Kjendsgjerninger. Det var det økonomiske Livs praktiske Opgaver, som kaldte Videnskaben tillive.'

39 Aschehoug, *Socialøkonomik*, vol. 1, part 1, chap. 1, § 4, 7–8. 'Økonomiske Sætninger, som aldrig have havt og aldrig kunne faa nogensomhelst praktisk Anvendelse, ere tome Hjernespind. Videnskabens sidste Opgave bliver til alle tider Praktisk.'

40 Aschehoug, *Socialøkonomik*, vol. 1, part 1, chap. 1, § 4, 8.

41 Aschehoug, *Socialøkonomik*, vol. 1, part 1, chap. 1, § 4, 8. 'Selv om nu Socialøkonomiken ikke formaar at løse alle sine Opgaver, mindst alle praktiske, stifter den Nytte allerede ved at gjøre opmærksom paa dem og fremfor Alt ved at stille dem riktig og paavise, hvad der mangler, for at de skulle kunne løses.' Aschehoug specifically mentions different so-called 'handbooks' or *handbücher* that in his view give an orderly and overall outline of what he refers to as political economy (*politisk økonomi*) and related subjects, written by highly esteemed authors that he describes as having an in-depth knowledge of many subjects. He seems to be using the German *Handwörterbuch der Staatswissenshaften*, 6 volumes, edition from 1898–1901 (1890–1894)

by J. Conrad, L. Elster, W. Lexis and E. Loening, and the *English Dictionary of Political Economy*, three volumes, edition from 1894–1899, by Inglis Palgrave, remarking that this edition has many articles about the English jurisprudence that are of interest for the political economy (*sosialøkonomi*). The two French ones were written by Léon Say and Joseph Chailley in 1891–92, with a supplement from 1897, *Nouveau dictionnaire d'économie politique*, and the older *Dictionnaire d'économie politique* from 1852–53, by Coquelin.

42 Aschehoug, *Socialøkonomik*, vol. 1, part 1, chap. 1, § 5, 9. 'De økonomiske Tilstande afgive i saa Henseende et Sidestykke til de retlige Institutioner. Begge dannes gjennem en under Aarsagernes Lov staaende Udvikling.'

43 Aschehoug, *Socialøkonomik*, vol. 1, part 1, chap. 2, § 1, 12. 'Man maa søge at begribe Mangfoldigheden, følgelig, saavidt muligt, opdage Aarsagsforholdet mellem dens Phænomener.'

44 Aschehoug, *Socialøkonomik*, vol. 1, part 1, chap. 2, § 1, 12. 'Dertil udkræves en Aandsvirksomhed, som paa een Gang er livlig nok til at skabe nye Forestillinger og tilstrækkelig behersket af sund Dømmekraft til at prøve, hvorvidt disse Forestillinger er blotte Indbildninger eller sande Virkelighedsbilleder.'

45 By inductive Aschehoug means the *a posteriori* or analytical method.

46 By deductive Aschehoug means the *a priori* or synthetic, constructive method.

47 Oscar Jæger in *Statsøkonomisk Tidsskrift* from 1895 pages 130–75. 'som har gitt en klar, kritisk Fremstilling af Emnet, i hvilken han væsentlig slutter sig til den østerigske Skole.'

48 Aschehoug, *Socialøkonomik*, vol. 1, part 1, chap. 2, § 1, 14. 'Kjendsgjerningerne ere Videnskabens Fødemidler; men den maa omdanne dem til Kjød og Blod.'

49 Aschehoug, *Socialøkonomik*, vol. 1, part 1, chap. 2, § 5, 17.

50 Myntvesenet, *Bankvesenet og handelskrisenes historie*.

51 Aschehoug, *Socialøkonomik*, vol. 1, part 1, chap. 2, § 7, 19, note 1.

52 Aschehoug refers to the introduction to Marshall's *Principles*, pages xii–xiii and appendix xiv.

53 Aschehoug, *Socialøkonomik*, vol. 1, part 1, chap. 2, § 8, 20.

54 Aschehoug gives an extensive list of different views in this debate, see note 1, § 8.

55 Aschehoug, *Socialøkonomik*, vol. 1, part 1, chap. 2, § 8, 22. 'Det er derfor unøiagtigt og vildledende at kalde disse Sætninger (eller de Kræfter, hvis Virksomhed de beskrive) naturlige Love.'

56 See discussion in § 9, Aschehoug, *Socialøkonomik*, vol. 1, part 1, chap. 2, § 9, 23.

57 Aschehoug, *Socialøkonomik*, vol. 1, part 1, chap. 2, § 9, see discussions. 'Videnskabens Sætninger ere kun Abstraktioner, Almensætninger, byggede paa Erfaringer om, hvad der finder Sted i Økonomiens fleste, sædvanligste eller eiendommeligste Livsytringer.' Aschehoug points out the danger in believing that these are postulates that can be applied directly, the discussion of conditions and circumstances is more important. Postulates can only be used for guidance and to show straightforward relations.

58 Aschehoug, *Socialøkonomik*, vol. 1, part 1, chap. 2, § 9, 25. 'teknisk Kyndighed og sundt praktisk Blik.'

59 See end of § 9, 26.

60 Aschehoug, *Socialøkonomik*, vol. 1, part 1, chap. 2, § 10, 26, note 1. Aschehoug here refers to Malthus, Cairnes, Sidgwick, J. N. Keynes, Marshall, Cossa, Neumann and Schmoller (article 'Volkswirtschaft' in Conrad's *HWB*, paragraph 10).

61 Aschehoug, *Socialøkonomik*, vol. 1, part 1, chap. 2, § 10, 29.

62 Hagerup, 'Nekrolog over Torkel Halvorsen Aschehoug', 6–7. 'Dette træder i hans historiske Arbeider frem i en omhyggelig, kritisk Sigtning af Kildematerialet i Forbindelse med en stor Nøiaktighed i Detaljpaavisningen af de enkelte Institutioners Udvikling og indbyrdes Sammenhæng. Derimod laa ham fjernt de nødvendigvis usikrere og til dels paa mer hypotetisk Grundlag hvilende Bestræbelser for at paavise de drivende Kræfter i Udviklingen. [...] Som Retsdogmatiker følger Aschehoug i metodisk Henseende nærmest Schweigaard. [...] Ligesom England var det eneste Land undenfor Norden, som han haved besøkt i Studieøiemed, saaledes fulgte han i sin statsretslige Fremstilling mer engelske end tyske Forbilleder. Hans Metode var

den, som Schweigaard har kaldt den 'analytisk-deskriptive' rettet paa en positiv Udredning af det givne Retsstof og dets Forhold til de mødende individuelle Retsforhold samt en Intrængen i disse Retsforholds konkrete Natur.'

63 Joseph Schumpeter, *Das Wesen und der Hauptinhalt der theoretischen Nationalökonomie* (1908), 6–7, quoted in Yuichi Shionoya, *The Soul of the German Historical School*, 97.

64 As far as I am concerned, the small dispute between Rolf Olsen and Schweigaard and Aschehoug in Morgenbladet during the 1850s is the only dispute about method before the dissertation of Oskar Jaeger published in 1895. See discussion details in Lykkja and in Seip. I should add that a general discussion of the position of economics (including how it should be) was an issue since the foundation of the University of Oslo in 1811 and is, for instance, discussed thoroughly in the doctoral thesis of Anton Fredrik Andresen, *Nytte, dannelse, vitenskap?*.

65 Aarum, 'Norwegen, Dänemark und Schweden', 125. 'daß man bisher diese Lehren Smiths zu sehr durch die Augengläser Ricardos gesehen hat und daß sie, von ihren eigenen Ausgangspunkten heraus beurteilt, volle innere Einheit und Zusammenhang besitzen.'

66 Aarum, 'Norwegen, Dänemark und Schweden', 125. 'In seiner Methodenlehre schließt er sich Menger an, der bekanntlich eine scharfe Scheidenlinie zieht zwischen der Statistik und der Geschichte der Volkswirtschaft auf der einen und der theoretischen und praktischen Volkwirtschaftlehre auf der anderen Seite und somit die Sozialökonomik als einetheoretisch-praktische Wissenschaft auffaßt, von welcher wieder die praktische Prinzipienlehre und die volkswirtschaftliche Praxis zu trennen ist.'

67 Bergh and Hanisch, *Vitenskap og politikk*, 85.

68 Bergh and Hanisch, *Vitenskap og politikk*, 83.

69 Oskar Jaeger, 'Den theoretiske Statsøkonomis opgave og videnskabelige methode', *Statsøkonomisk Tidsskrift* 9 (1895): 132–3. 'Det, som man I vort land med en maaske ikke ubetinget heldig betegnelse officielt kalder statsøkonomi, men som andensteds i verden pleier at gaa under navn af politisk økonomi, nationaløkonomi eller socialøkonomi, er da ikke nogen historisk videnskab. Den indeholder derimod sammenfatningen af al theoretisk og praktisk videnskab paa det økonomiske livs omraade og falder følgelig I en theoretisk og en praktisk del, hvorav den første, den theoretiske statsøkonomi, har til opgave at undersøge de økonomiske fænomeners generelle væsen og lovmæssighed, medens man i den praktiske del derimod stræber at fastslaa de grundsætninger eller maximer, hvorefter menneskene, under de forskjellige samfundsforhold, paa den bedste made kan realisere sine økonomiske hensigter.'

70 Jaeger, 'Den theoretiske Statsøkonomis opgave og videnskabelige methode', 134. 'Man vil da let forstaa, hvor overordentlig vigtigt det er, at disse praktiske videnskaber paa det økonomiske omraade holdes skarpt ude fra den theoretiske statsøkonomi, hvis opgave og hvis videnskabelige methode er en fra deres fundamentalt forskjellig. […] Den videnskabelige systematic kræver derfor af de moderne forskere, at de behandler den theoretiske statsøkonomi for sig afsondret fra den økonomiske politik og finansvidenskaben.'

71 Jaeger, 'Den theoretiske Statsøkonomis opgave og videnskabelige methode', 136–7.

72 Jaeger, 'Den theoretiske Statsøkonomis opgave og videnskabelige methode', 138. 'Med at fremstille alle disse økonomiske fænomener i deres individuelle beskaffenhed beskjæftiger den theoretiske statsøkonomi sig, som allerede anført, slet ikke; det overlader den til den økonomiske historie og den økonomiske statistik. Hvad den sætter sig til opgave er tvertimod udelukkende at udforske deres generelle væsen og generelle sammenhæng i rent økonomisk retning.'

73 Jaeger, 'Den theoretiske Statsøkonomis opgave og videnskabelige methode', 140.

74 Jaeger, 'Den theoretiske Statsøkonomis opgave og videnskabelige methode', 151, 153. '[…] i alle tilfælde handlede fuldstændig i overensstemmelse med den psykologiske lov, at menneskene under sin økonomiske virksomhed med den mindst mulige opofrelse søger at oppnaa den største mulige fordel (151). […] siges de, som allerede antydet, at handle økonomisk, idet de jo aabenbart derved realiserer sine økonomiske formal paa den i rent økonomisk henseende fuldkomneste maade (153).'

75 Jaeger, 'Den theoretiske Statsøkonomis opgave og videnskabelige methode', 142.
76 Jaeger, 'Den theoretiske Statsøkonomis opgave og videnskabelige methode', 146.
77 Aarum, 'Norwegen, Dänemark und Schweden', 126. 'Die exakte Induktion und Deduktion ist etwas ganz anderes. Durch die exakte Induktion macht man eine spekulative Folgerung aus den zutage liegenden Wirkungen auf die verborgenen Ursachen und durch die exakte Deduktion sucht man von den gefundenen Ursachen die Wirkungen abzuleiten, von denen man ausging.'
78 Jaeger, 'Den theoretiske Statsøkonomis opgave og videnskabelige methode', 157.
79 Jaeger, 'Den theoretiske Statsøkonomis opgave og videnskabelige methode', 163. 'Kun under betingelsen: Cæteris paribus, eller som engelskmændene ogsaa udtaler det samme forbehold: in the absence of disturbing causes, holder, med andre ord, de exakte typer og love stik i virkeligheden. [...] I den theoretiske statsøkonomi kan man derfor aldrig virkelig isolere de enkelte aarsager, men maa lade sig nøie med blot at tænke dem isolerede og rent fornuftmæssig slutte sig til deres særskilte virkninge.'
80 Jaeger, 'Den theoretiske Statsøkonomis opgave og videnskabelige methode', 166–9.
81 Jaeger, 'Den theoretiske Statsøkonomis opgave og videnskabelige methode', 168. 'Man er nødt til at specialisere videnskaben, om man skal kunne naa frem til en virkelig theoretisk forstaalese af det sociale livs fænomener.'
82 Jaeger, 'Den theoretiske Statsøkonomis opgave og videnskabelige methode', 169. 'Den reform af den theoretiske statsøkonomi, hvis nødvendighed man følte, kom saaledes ikke og kunde selvfølgelig heller ikke komme fra statsøkonomer af den historiske skole. Derimod er det i løbet af de par sidste aartier lykkedes en række fremragende forskere af forskjellig nationalitet – vi nævner blandt dem her kun engelskmanden Jevons, schweizeren Walras, østerrigerne Carl Menger og maaske den største af dem alle, Eugen von Böhm-Bawerk – at gjenoptage de gamle mesteres arbeide og uden nogen principiel forandring i den videnskabelige forskningsmethode at vinde nye resultater af en saadan betydning, at de i virkeligheden betegner et gjennembrud i den statsøkonomiske videnskabs historie. Alle disse forfattere lægger hovedvægten paa den exakte forskning baade som den betydningsfuldeste, vanskeligste og derfor ogsaa hidtil ufuldkomneste del af den theoretiske statsøkonomi.'
83 Jaeger, 'Den theoretiske Statsøkonomis opgave og videnskabelige methode', 172–4.
84 Jaeger, 'Den theoretiske Statsøkonomis opgave og videnskabelige methode', 174. 'Den beundringsverdigste af alle disse nyere forfattere herhenhørende arbeider er i vore øine Böhm-Bawerks: *Positive Theorie des Kapitales*, hvori han for første gang giver den I alt væsentligt fyldestgjørende forklaring af det helt fra oldtiden af saa uafladelig omstridt kapitalrenteproblem [...] er den af ham ved spekulativ induktion [...] kjendte psykologiske lov: at menneskene gjennemgaaende pleier at værdsætte nutidsgoder høiere end fremtidsgoder [...] har han med overordentlig skarpsindighed og logisk kraft deduceret sin nye, epokegjørende kapitalrentetheori.'
85 Aarum, 'Norwegen, Dänemark und Schweden', 126. 'Sowohl auf dem Gebiete der empirischen, als auch auf dem Gebiete der exakten Forschung unterscheidet Jaeger zwischen dem induktiven und deduktiven Verfahren. Die empirische Induktion heißt vom Besonderen auf das Allgemeine, die empirische Deduktion umgekehrt vom Allgemeinen auf das Besondere schließen. So kommt auch Schmoller mit seiner bekannten Aussage: Wie der rechte und linke Fuß zum Gehen, so gehören Induktion und Deduktion gleichmäßig zum wissenschaflichen Denken. Ich habe stets betont, daß, wenn wir schon alle Wahrheit besäßen, wir nur deduktiv verführen, daß aller Fortschritt der Induktion uns deduktiv verwertbare Sätze bringe, daß die vollendetsten Wissenschaften am meisten deduktiv seien, nicht aus der empirischen Forschung hinaus, er bleibt innerhalb seiner induktiven Methode.'
86 Aarum, 'Norwegen, Dänemark und Schweden', 126. 'Durch Erfahrung kann ein jeder zur Kenntnis der Wahrheit der anderen Wissenschaften angehörigen empirischen Gesetze kommen, welche die im volkswirtschaftlichen Leben auftretenden ersten Ursachen bilden;

dazu bedarf es sicherlich keiner spekulativen Induktion. Das Kausalitätsverhältnis selbs oder, mit anderen Worten, die Erkenntnis, welche von den empirischen Gesetzen der verschiedenen Wissenschaften eben ökonomische erste Ursachen sind, ist dagegen vollkommen unempirische und muß durch exakte Induktion aufgedeckt werden [...]. Erst als auf neue originelle Theoretiker unter den Nationalökonomen erschienen, die unter den Gesetzen der Psychologie neue ökonomische erste Ursachen durch spekulative Induktion entdeckten, gelang es neue exakte Theorien zu deduzieren, welche fast die ganze theoretische Nationalökonomie erneuert haben.'

87 Schweigaard, *Ungdomsarbeider*, 233, 243.
88 Witoszek, *The Origins of the 'Regime of Goodness'*, 47–9.

Chapter 5   Development of the Economic Thought of Aschehoug: Statsøkonomisk Forening and the *Socialøkonomik* Project

1 Francis Sejersted, interview by the author, 17 November 2010.

2 Rune Slagstad, *Rett og politikk: Et liberalt tema med variasjoner* (Oslo: Universitetsforlaget, 1987), 83. 'Det bemerkelsesverdige ved Aschehougs teoretiske posisjon er nettopp kombinasjonen av antidemokratisk konservatisme og konstitusjonell liberalisme.'

3 Anne-Lise Seip, *Vitenskap og virkelighet: Sosiale, økonomiske og politiske teorier hos T. H. Aschehoug 1845–1882* (Oslo: Gyldendal, 1975), 24.

4 Aschehoug, 'Norske universitets og skole-annaler' (catalogue, National Library of Norway), 557–8 (my emphasis). 'Den, der vil studere Statistik og Statsoekonomie i Storbritanien, kan – forsaavidt han iforveien er tilstrækkelig bekjendt med Videnskabens Theorie – have et dobbelt Maal for Øie. Han kan nemlig ønske, deels at vinde en levende og klar Oversigt over det engelske Samfunds Tilstand og Virksomhed, deels at blive fortrolig med den Methode, hvorefter Englænderne samle og behandle de Kjendsgjerninger, som tjene den sociale Videnskab til Grundlag.'

5 *Statsøkonomisk Tidsskrift* 1 (1887): 62, account from the founding meeting. 'Etter forudgaaende indydelse utstedt af d'hrr. professor Aschehoug, konsul Heftye, professor Hertzberg, direktør Kiær, borgermester Rygh og statsraad Schweigaard samledes den 4de december 1883 paa universitetets juridiske auditorium et antall af omtrent 60 herrer for at drøfte dannelsen af en statsøkonomisk forening. Efterat professor Aschehoug havde angivet mødets hensigt, besluttedes enstemmig at stifte en saadan forening, hvorpaa man efter endel diskussion vedtog foreningens statuter. Af de deltagende eller indikere regnede sig dels paa stedet, dels ved senere henvendelse til bestyrelsen ialt 74 herrer. Til medlemmer af bestyrelsen valgtes paa det samme forberedende møde: professor Aschehoug, konsul Heftye, professor Hertzberg, direktør Kiær og borgermester Rygh. Foreningens første møde holdtes fredag den 25. januar 1884 i Kristiania handelsstands foreningslokale.'

6 Interview with Francis Sejersted, 17 November 2010.

7 Trond Bergh and Tore J. Hanisch, *Vitenskap og politikk: Linjer i norsk sosialøkonomi gjennom 150 år* (Oslo: Aschehoug, 1984), 52–3.

8 Bergh and Hanisch, *Vitenskap og politikk*, 58.

9 Interview with Francis Sejersted, 17 November 2010.

10 Tore Jørgen Hanisch and Arild Sæther, 'Alfred Marshall in Norway', in *The Impact of Alfred Marshall's Ideas: The Global Diffusion of his Work*, ed. T. Raffaelli, G. Becattini, K. Caldari and M. Dardi (Northampton, MA and Cheltenham, UK: Edward Elgar, 2010).

11 *Statsøkonomisk Tidsskrift* 1 (1887): 64, account from the founding meeting. statutes. 'Statutter, paragraf 1, Foreningens formaal er ved foredrag, diskussion og utdgivelse af skrifter at virke for oplysning om statsøkonomiske og sociale spørgsmaal; Paragraf 2, Foreningen avholder mindst et møde i hver af maanederne oktober–april; Paragraf 3, Foreningens anliggender ledes af en

bestyrelse, bestaaende af 5 medlemmer, der sig imellem opnævne formand, viceformand og sekretær.'

12 Bergh and Hanisch, *Vitenskap og politikk*, 59–60.

13 Aschehoug quoted in Bergh and Hanisch, *Vitenskap og politikk*, 63.

14 'Folk lå under for den almindelige og skjæbnesvangre tilbøielighed til at overvurdere øieblikkets og undervurdere fremtidens krav og at tro mer, hva de haaber paa, end hva de burde frygte.'

15 Bredo Morgenstierne, 'Professor Aschehoug og hans "Socialøkonomik"', *Statsøkonomisk Tidsskrift* 16 (1902): 198.

16 Aschehoug in *Stortingstidende* (1869), quoted in Bergh and Hanisch, *Vitenskap og politikk*, 54. 'fremstille Statsøkonomien [...] i Løbet af et eneste Halvaar med 6 Timers Forelæsninger om Ugen; større Omfang har den ikke.'

17 See article Arild Sæther, Niels Kjærgård and Bo Sandelin, 'Economics in Scandinavia', in *New Palgrave Dictionary of Economics*, edited by Steven N. Durlauf and Lawrence E. Blume (Palgrave Macmillan, 2006).

18 Hanisch and Sæther, 'Alfred Marshall in Norway', 2.

19 Aschehoug archive, Nationalbiblioteket, Håndskriftssamlingen, visited October 2010.

20 Bredo Morgenstierne, 'Professor Aschehoug og hans socialøkonomik', *Statsøkonomisk Tidsskrift* 16 (1902): 202. 'Professor Aschehoug har udført dette verv paa en udmerket made, har været kjendt i alle interesserede kredse. Allerede den ovenfor nævnte række af afhandlinger har dannet et af vidnesbyrdene derom. Men med hvilken energi han har vendt sig mod dette andet hovedemne for sit livs arbeide, hvilken arbeidskraft han har lagt for dagen i tilegnelsen af den uhyre stofmasse, som den nyere nationaløkonomiske litteratur frembyder, og med hvilken videnskabelig overlegenhed han har behersket dette stof, det har hidtil været dem forbeholdt fuldt ud at vurdere, som enten har hørt eller paa anden made havt de øvrige sider af samfundslivet. Hans 'Socialøkonomikens historie' som Endnu ikke er afsluttet i det foreliggende hefte, nærmer sig derved til at blive en skisse af samfundsudviklingen overhovedet. Fremstillingen er overalt klar og letlæst; de korte sætninger gjengiver ofte tanken med en epigrammatisk knaphed, der fæster sig i erindringen.'

21 Morgenstierne, 'Professor Aschehoug og hans Socialøkonomik', 202. 'I en universel videnskab som socialøkonomiken eller nationaløkonomien bliver det lille lands videnskabsmænds første opgave at danne vinduet ud mod verdenslitteraturen. Og ingen kan i sandhed gjøre det bedre og fyldigere end Aschehoug i det nu paabegyndte værk. Dette er naturligvis ogsaa i første række skrevet for hans landsmænd og for de øvrige folk af den skandinaviske sprogstamme. Men lykkeligvis er de smaa folk ikke blot modtagende, men ogsaa ydende i sit forhold til verdenslitteraturen. Professor Aschehougs Socialøkonomik tilhører selv denne. Holder dette værk – som jeg er forvisset om – hvad det lover, vil det i alsidighed, universelt overblik og paa samme tid videnskabelig stringent og almenfattelig fremstilling neppe have sit sidestykke i noget lands litteratur. Det tør da forudsættes, at oversættelser paa fremmede sprog neppe vil lade vente længe paa sig [...] betydningsfulde arbeide paa den teoretiske og praktiske nationaløkonomis omraade, og da atter i ganske særlig grad til hans "Socialøkonomik", hans lange og grundige studiers og rige erfaringers modne frugt.'

22 William Scharling, 'Professor Dr. Iuris T. H. Aschehoug in memoriam', *Norsk retstidende* 13 (1909): 1. 'det kom hefte etter hefte, og det tok lengre og lengre tid, etter som Aschehoug gjerne ville ha med seg den aller siste litteratur innen forskjellige felt, slik at hans fremstilling ville være så aktuell som mulig.'

23 Westergaard, 'Obituary T. H. Aschehoug'.

24 Fredrik Stang, 'Aschehoug', in *Norsk biografisk leksikon*, vol. 1 (Aabel–Bjørnson), ed. Edvard Bull, Anders Krogvig, Gerhard Gran (Kristiania: Forlaget av Aschehoug (W. Nygaard), 1923), (275–89) 282. 'Da A. trak sig tilbake fra det offentlige liv, la han hele sin kraft i sit vitenskabelige arbeide. Efterhaanden samlet han det helt om statsøkonomien. Uagtet han i sin ungdom med forkjærlighet hadde studert statsøkonomi, var det i virkeligheten en ny videnskap, han stod

overfor, da han nu paany vendte sig til den, og det var en verdensomspænende litteratur han begav sig ind i. A. kastet sig med lidenskab ind i arbeidet, og det var fortrinsvis i den nyere litteratur og i nyere økonomiske foreteelser han søkte sit stof. Med en mottagelighet og en utviklingsevne, som selv hos en meget yngre mand vilde været forbauset, levet han sig ind i den nye tankeverden og optok den i sig. Faa dager før han fyldte 80 aar kunde han begynde trykningen av en omfattende fremstilling av socialøkonomiken. Da han var 87 aar, var værket færdigtrykt. Han gik straks ivei med at revidere det med en ny utgave for øie. En maaneds tid efter avbrøt imidlertid døden hans rastløse arbeide.'

25 Lönnroth, 'Nordic Modell Political Economic Manuals': 'He must have read practically everything important of contemporary writings on the subject. He used *Nouveau Dictionnaire d'économie politique* from France, *Cyclopaedia of Political Science and Political Economy* from the US, *Handwörterbuch der Staatswissenschaften* from Germany and Palgrave's *Dictionary of Political Economy.*'

26 Sæther et al., 'Economics in Scandinavia'.

27 Bergh og Hanisch, *Vitenskap og politikk*, 51. 'En begivenhet både i norsk og nordisk sosialøkonomi var Aschehougs store 4-binds *Socialøkonomik* som forelå kort før hans død. Det var den første grundige norske læreboken i faget og en så omfattende og lærd fremstilling at det internasjonalt neppe fantes mange paralleller til den.'

28 Scharling, 'Professor Dr. Iuris T. H. Aschehoug in memoriam', 1. 'en berøring med livet og dets aktuelle forhold.'

29 Besides Schmoller's own Grundriss, for instance, Wagner's *Allgemeine oder theoretische Volkswirtschaftslehre*; Schönberg's *Handbuch der politischen Ökonomie*; Mangoldt, Grundriss and Roscher, *Grundlagen der Nationalökonomik.*

30 See pages 29–30. He mentions Say, MacCulloch and Rau not treating trade separately, Mill and Cherbuliez not treating consumption, and Marshall treating consumption as part of his whole system.

31 Aschehoug, *Socialøkonomik*, vol. 1, part 1, chap. 2, § 11, 31. 'Deres Exempel skal her blive fulgt.'

32 Aschehoug, *Socialøkonomik*, vol. 1, part 1, chap. 2, § 11, 31, note 1. Aschehoug emphasizes the works of Hermann, *Staatswirthschaftliche Untersuchung* (1870, 2nd edition). Of more resent works, Aschehoug calls attention to the works of Wagner, *Grundlegung der Politischen Oekonomie* (1892–1894, 3rd edition); Neumann, *Grundlagen der Volkswirtschaftslehre* (1889); and Roscher, *Grundlagen der Nationalökonomie* (1897, 22nd edition). Of others that have the same structure, Aschehoug mentions Sidgwick's *Principles of Economics*; Marshall's *Principles*; Leroy-Beaulieu's *Traité*; Gide's *Principles*; Cauwés's *Cours d'économie politique*; and Leffler's *Det ekonomiska samhällslivet.*

33 Aschehoug, *Socialøkonomik*, vol. IV, 'Postscript', 977.

34 Thorvald Aarum, 'Norwegen, Dänemark und Schweden', in *Die Wirtschaftstheorie der Gegenwart*, ed. Hans Mayer (Vienna: Julius von Springer, 1927), 124. 'Aschehoug hat überhaupt seine Stärke mehr in der plastischen Darstellung des Stoffes, der sorgfältigen Wiedergabe der Ideen und Tatsachen und unparteischen Würdigung der verschiedenen Meinungen, als in origenellem Denken und scharfem Durchdringen der Probleme.'

35 Francis Hagerup, obituary of Torkel Aschehoug, *Tidsskrift for retsvitenskab* (1909), 5, 6.

36 Aarum, 'Norwegen, Dänemark und Schweden', 124. 'Sein hauptverdienst bleibt, daß er in einer Zeit rascher Entwicklung der theoretischen Forschung die Fühlung mit dieser Entwicklung vermittelt und ihre Ergebnisse für die einheimische Forschung verwertet hat. Sein Bemühen, den Meinungen anderer gerecht zu sein, hat ihn häufig veranlaßt, eine vermittelnde Stellung in Streitfragen einzunehmen, weshalb er auch als Eklektiker bezeichnet worden ist.'

37 Aarum, 'Norwegen, Dänemark und Schweden', 124–5. 'Diese Bezeichnung darf jedoch nicht als Charakteristik seiner wissenschaftlichen Stellung im allgemeinen gebraucht werden, da er in den Hauptfragen sehr wohl eine selbständige Meinung zu behaupten weiß.'

38 Thorvald Aarum, foreword to *Socialøkonomik*, revised edition (Oslo: Aschehoug forlag, 1910).

39 Thorvald Aarum, professor of Oslo from 1917, revised, updated and enlarged Aschehoug's *Socialøkonomik*. Aarum also published his own textbook, *Læren om Samfundets Økonomi*, in two volumes in 1924.

40 Aarum, 'Norwegen, Dänemark und Schweden', 125. 'Dieses Werk hat bis auf den heutigen Tag eine große erzieherische Bedeutung für die studierende Jungend und wird als Hand- und Lesebuch seine Stellung noch lange behaupten.'

41 Scharling, 'Professor Dr. Iuris T. H. Aschehoug in memoriam', 3. 'Naar jeg dog med fuld Bevidsthed om dens Ufuldkommenhed fremsender denne rent skizzemessige Udtalelse om et saa betydelig Værk, sker det med det Haab, at den vil blive suppleret med en mere indgaaende Vurdering fra en eller anden yngre norsk Nationaløkonom, en af Aschehougs egne Disciple.'

42 Bergh and Hanisch, *Vitenskap og politikk*, 103.

43 Aarum, 'Norwegen, Dänemark und Schweden', 125.

44 Aarum, 'Norwegen, Dänemark und Schweden', 127. 'Ein zeitgemäßes Lehrbuch passenden Umfanges fehlte den Studenten bisher, denn Aschehougs Socialøkonomik ist als solches zu weitläufig und auch nicht in allen Teilen den letzten Ergebnissen der Forschung ganz angepaßt.'

45 Aarum, 'Norwegen, Dänemark und Schweden', 127. 'Jeder, der akademische Lehrtätigkeit ausgeübt hat, wird die erfahrung gemacht haben, daß es trotz der großen Anzahl Lehrbücher in allen Sprachen doch an solchen fehlt, welche die letzten Resultate der Forschung eingeschaltet haben und hinreichende Auskünfte über den heutigen Stand er Wissenschaft geben. In der Regel lenken sie ihre Darstellung in die alten Bahnen nach der herkömmlichen Systematik mit einer heterogenen Mischung von altem und neuem Stoffe, ohne ein einheitliches Lehrgebäude zu bilden. Diesen Mängeln abzuhelfen und den Studierenden eine hinreichende Orientierung mit rücksicht auf den heutigen Stand der theoretischen Forschung zu geben, war die Aufgabe, die sich der Verfasser stellte.'

46 Aarum, 'Norwegen, Dänemark und Schweden', 127. 'Mit Rücksicht auf den Stand der theoretischen Forschung im allgemeinen ist der Verfasser der Meinung, daß die Differenzen der verschiedenen Richtungen in der Theorie, welche bisher eine so großten Teile ausgeglichen worden sind, weshalb die ökonomische Theorie zurzeit weit mehr zu einem einheitlichen System ausgebaut worden ist als je vorher. Was unsere Zeit fordert, ist nicht ein fortgesetzter Streit um akademische Lehrmeinungen und haarsplitternde Auseinandersetzungen begriffsmäßiger Art, sondern eine folgerichtige Anwendung der Theorie zur Beantwortung der vielen Fragen, die dem Volkswirtschaftslehre überall in großer Fülle von der Wirklichkeit gestellt werden.'

47 Aarum, 'Norwegen, Dänemark und Schweden', 130. 'Als Gesamtcharakteristik der neueren norwegischen Ökonomik ist zu bezeichnen, daß sie sich noch in ihrer Jugendperiode befindet, in dem Sinne, als sie sich noch vorwiegend mit den theoretischen Prinzipienfragen und Grundproblemen beschäftigt und noch nicht an die Behandlung der konkreten Fragen und die Anwendung der Theorie auf die aktuellen Probleme herangerückt ist. Die Aufgabe der nächsten Zukunft scheint vielmehr die Verwertung der theoretischen Erkenntnisse für die Lösung praktischer Fragen zu sein, und Zeichen, daß diese Aufgabe angegangen wird, sind vorhanden.'

Chapter 6   The German Historical School: Similarities, Influences and Discrepancies

1 For instance the *Handwörterbuch der Staatswissenschaften* of Johannes Conrad, the *Jahrbücher für Nationalökonomie und Statistik* of Fischer, Schmoller's *Jahrbuch für Gesetzgebung, Verwaltung und Volkswirtschaft im deutschen Reich*, and *Zeitschrift für die gesamte Staatswissenschaft* of Schäffle.

2 In addition to these mentioned publications, he extensively used the *Handwörterbuch der Staatswissenschaften* edited by Johannes Conrad.

3 Kåre Amundsen, *Norsk sosialøkonomisk historie 1814–1890* (Oslo: Universitetsforlaget, 1963), 103. 'I Norge var den politiske situasjonen mer lik den engelske enn den som var rådende i de tyske stater, f. eks., så noen større tilslutning til den historiske skolen får vi ikke blant norske økonomer i det nittende århundre.'

4 Underlined by several authors such as Grimmer-Solem and Benny Carlson (in *De institutionalistiska idéernas spridning*), who has looked at the close connection between Swedish economists and the German and the American institutionalism.

5 Eric Grimmer-Solem, *The Rise of Historical Economics and Social Reform in Germany 1864–1894* (Oxford: Clarendon Press, 2003), 8.

6 Charles Gide and Charles Rist, *A History of Economic Doctrines from the Time of the Physiocrats to the Present Day* (Boston: D. C. Heath, 1915), 384. Online: http://www.archive.org/stream/historyo feconomi00gideiala#page/384/mode/2up (accessed November 2010).

7 Grimmer-Solem, *The Rise of Historical Economics*, 3.

8 Yuichi Shionoya, *The Soul of the German Historical School: Methodological Essays on Schmoller, Weber and Schumpeter* (New York: Springer, 2005), 33.

9 Alfred Marshall, 'The Present Position of Economics' (1885), quoted in Grimmer-Solem, *The Rise of Historical Economics*, 19.

10 Gide and Rist, *A History of Economic Doctrines*, 386.

11 Shionoya, *The Soul of the German Historical School*, 18.

12 Nicholas W. Balabkins, *Not by Theory Alone…: The Economics of Gustav von Schmoller and Its Legacy to America* (Berlin: Duncker & Humblot, 1988), 14.

13 Balabkins, *Not by Theory Alone*, 22.

14 Shionoya, *The Soul of the German Historical School*, 33.

15 Yuichi Shionoya, ed., *The German Historical School: The Historical and Ethical Approach to Economics* (London and New York: Routledge, 2001), 1.

16 Quoted in Grimmer-Solem.

17 See comment from Schmoller's student Arthur Spiethoff in *Festgaben für Adolph Wagner zur siebenzigsten Wiederkehr seines Geburtstages* (1905), 'Preface', quoted in Benny Carlson, *De institutionalistiska idéernas spridning* (Stockholm: SNS Forlag, 1995), 20.

18 Grimmer-Solem, *The Rise of Historical Economics*, 15–16.

19 Joseph Schumpeter, *History of Economic Analysis* (New York: Oxford University Press, 1954), 810.

20 Grimmer-Solem, *The Rise of Historical Economics*, 22.

21 According to Balabkins, his methodology was as follows: 'Roscher's specific methodology consisted of four basic principles: 1) he combined economics with the history of law, government, and cultural evolution; 2) he cultivated economic history; 3) he used comparative methods of economic doctrines in different nations and different time periods; and 4) he used relativism to explain different economic policies over time.' Quote from G. Eisermann, *Die Grundlagen des Historismus in der deutschen Nationalökonomie* (Stuttgart: F. Enke Verlag, 1956), in Balabkins, *Not by Theory Alone*, 26.

22 Quote from Eisermann, *Die Grundlagen*, in Balabkins, *Not by Theory Alone*, 27. Balabkins further notes that Hildebrand sought to keep economics from being a strictly academic discipline and to bridge the gap between the owners and nonowners of property via social legislation. In addition, he prepared adequately for legislative reforms by a careful and detailed analysis of social and economic matters.

23 Gide and Rist, *A History of Economic Doctrines*, 384. 'Hildebrand's absolutism had no more influence than Roscher's eclecticism, unless we make an exception of his generalisation concerning the three phases of economic development [...] beyond that he merely contented himself with publishing a number of fragmentary studies [...] without [...] making any attempt to modify the Classical theory of production and distribution.'

24 Balabkins, *Not by Theory Alone*, 28.

25 Gide and Rist, *A History of Economic Doctrines*, 384.

26 Balabkins, *Not by Theory Alone*, 29.

27 Shionoya, *The Soul of the German Historical School*, ix. See also Shionoya, *The German Historical School*, chap. 1.

28 Shionoya, *The Soul of the German Historical School*, 7. He adds, 'The ethical method thus has two functions in historical economics: first, ethics is understood empirically as a determinant of human behaviour and social systems; second, it is assumed methodologically as a teleological principle of social inquiry. [...] The status of ethics in the Historical School should be interpreted as a value premise, not as a value judgement.'

29 This summary is made by Benny Carlson, *De institutionalistiska idéernas spridning*, 22–3.

30 Shionoya, *The Soul of the German Historical School*, x. Economics was originally called political economy in English, not as an ideological dogma but to distinguish it from household economy. It meant the economics of society or polity. During the late nineteenth century, there was a strong move to discard the unwieldy name political economy in favour of something more up to date and scientifically precise.

31 Grimmer-Solem, *The Rise of Historical Economics*, 39–40.

32 Harald Hagemann, 'The Verein für Sozialpolitik from its foundation (1872) until World War I', in *Societies of Political Economy and Associations of Economists*, ed. Massimo Augello and Marco E. L. Guidi (London: Taylor & Francis, 2001), (1–23) 4. I have chosen to use Hagemann as my main source of the Verein since Franz Boese's authoritative overview from 1936 only exists in German. Hagemann uses Boese extensively as his source in his article.

33 *Samfunnsvitenskapelig* (social sciences faculty): economics did not become a part of this faculty at the University of Oslo until much later; it was for a long time part of the faculty of law.

34 Shionoya, *The Soul of the German Historical School*, 5.

35 Grimmer-Solem, *The Rise of Historical Economics*, 255.

36 Jürgen Backhaus, preface to Balabkins, *Not by Theory Alone*, 8.

37 Carl Menger quoted in Grimmer-Solem, *The Rise of Historical Economics*, 263–4.

38 Shionoya, *The Soul of the German Historical School*, 6.

39 Schmoller originally quoted in Boese. Hagemann comments in a note that Boese is the authoritative source, although he is clearly siding with Schmoller, being his former assistant and having a strongly 'conservative-centrist' perspective. Hagemann, 'The Verein für Sozialpolitik', 12, note 9.

40 Hagemann, 'The Verein für Sozialpolitik', 12.

41 See for instance Shionoya.

42 Bruce Caldwell, *Hayek's Challenge* (Chicago/London: University of Chicago Press, 2004), 77–8.

43 See Caldwell, *Hayek's Challenge*, 39–45, and his chapter about the *Methodenstreit*.

44 See Hagemann, 'The Verein für Sozialpolitik', part 5, 'Some famous controversies: The *Methodenstreit* and the *Werturteilsstreit*'.

45 Aschehoug, *Socialøkonomik*, vol. 1, part 2, chap. 8.

46 Aschehoug, *Socialøkonomik*, vol. 1, part 2, chap. 7, 82, note 1.

47 Aschehoug, *Socialøkonomik*, vol. 1, part 2, chap. 8, 99.

48 Aschehoug, *Socialøkonomik*, vol. 1, part 2, chap. 8, 101. Quoted from the 'Vorwort' in *Grundriss zu Vorlesungen über die Staatswirtschaft nach geschichtlicher Methode* from 1843 by Roscher.

49 Aschehoug, *Socialøkonomik*, vol. 1, part 2, chap. 8, 101, note 1. 'Saavel hans overordentlige Lærdom som hans modne Omdømme, Upartiskhed og ædle Livsanskuelse gjør dem til Prydelser for det 19de Aarhundredes Litteratur.'

50 Aschehoug, *Socialøkonomik*, vol. 1, part 2, chap. 8, § 4, 103. 'Fuldstendig sande Theorier kan Videnskaben ikke opstille, førend den har gjennemgransket alle de historisk given Forudsætninger, paa hvilke Theorierne maa bygges. Da nu disse Forudsætninger idelligen forandres, maatte det følgeriktigen nægtes, at der overhovedet kan opstilles nogen theoretisk

Socialøkonomik. Videnskaben kan ikke komme længre end til, saavidt muligt, at beskrive det økonomiske Livs historisk beviselige Kjendsgjerninger og Sammenhængen mellem dem, saavidt denne lader seg udfinde. Dette er kun at slaa Vrag paa al Videnskab, som ikke svarer helt ud til sitt Ideal.'

51 See Backhaus, Balabkins, Shionoya and Grimmer-Solem.

52 Aschehoug, *Socialøkonomik*, vol. 1, part 2, chap. 8, § 4, 104. 'Med at indsamle alle de historiske og statistiske Oplysninger, som udkræves til en uangribelig Lærebygning, bliver man aldrig færdig. Ligesaalidt som Arbeidet med at indsamle nyt Materiale maa standses, ligesaalidt tør man udsætte den videnskabelige Tilgodegjørelsen af det Materiale, man til enhver Tid allerede besidder.'

53 Yuval P. Yonay, *The Struggle over the Soul of Economics: Institutionalist and Neoclassical Economics in America between the Wars* (Princeton, New Jersey: Princeton University Press, 1998), 42.

54 Stang, 'Aschehoug', in *Norsk biografisk leksikon*, vol. 1 (Aabel—Bjørnson), ed. Edvard Bull, Anders Krogvig, Gerhard Gran (Kristiania: Aschehoug, 1923), 282.

55 Backhaus, preface to Balabkins, *Not by Theory Alone*, 5.

56 Schmoller, *Grundriss II*, quoted in Balabkins, *Not by Theory Alone*, 81.

57 Aschehoug, postscript to *Socialøkonomik*, vol. IV, 977. 'Jeg lige fra Begyndelsen af har sat mig som Maal i Værket at indarbeide det Allervigtigste af den nye økonomiske Lovgivning og Litteratur, som under Undgivelsen maatte komme frem.'

58 Following the English translation and presentation of Balabkins in Balabkins, *Not by Theory Alone*, 56–62.

59 Carlson, *De institutionalistiska idéernas spridning*, chap. 2.

60 Schmoller, *Grundriss*, quoted in Balabkins, *Not by Theory Alone*, 104.

61 Aschehoug, *Socialøkonomik*, vol. 1, part 1, chap. 1, § 6, 11. 'De Kræfter, hvis Virksomhed udvikles i Mekaniken, tilhører blot den ydre Natur, de Kræfter, med hvilke Socialøkonomiken beskjæftiger sig, tilhører ogsaa den psychiske Verden.'

62 Shionoya, 'Reconstruction of the German Historical School', in *The German Historical School*, 15.

63 Farnam in the *Yale Review* 9 (2) (August 1900): 164–74.

64 Balabkins, *Not by Theory Alone*, 67.

65 Reginald Hansen, 'Gustav Schmoller as a Scientist of Political Economy', in *Handbook of the History of Economic Thought: Insights on the Founders of Modern Economics*, ed. Jürgen Backhaus (New York: Springer, 2011), introduction: 'Controversial Opinions about Schmoller: Was He a Historian or an Economist?'.

66 Hansen, 'Gustav Schmoller as a Scientist of Political Economy', part 4: 'The Scientific Background of Gustav Schmoller and His Efforts for a Modernised Methodology of Social Sciences: Schmoller's Method of Historical Research'.

67 Yuval P. Yonay, *The Struggle over the Soul of Economics: Institutionalist and Neoclassical Economists in America between the Wars* (Princeton, New Jersey: Princeton University Press, 1998), 47.

68 Hansen, 'Gustav Schmoller as a Scientist of Political Economy'.

69 Hansen, 'Gustav Schmoller as a Scientist of Political Economy', part 4.

70 Aschehoug, 'Anmeldelse av B. M. Tvethe: Norges Statistik', *Norsk tidsskrift for videnskab og literatur* 2 (1848): 203. 'Data maa sættes i Forbindelse med hinanden, først herigjennem faar man klar Indsigt i, hvad de betyde.'

71 Aschehoug, 'Om Norges Folkemængde i 1664–1666', *Norsk tidsskrift for videnskab og literatur* 2 (1848): 305. 'Begivenhedernes Historie [...] Hjælpemiddel til at bedømme Nationens forhenværende indre Forholde [...] fremfor Alt nødvændigt for en videnskabelig Sammenligning mellem Nutidens og Fortidens Økonomi.'

72 Neurath, quoted in Grimmer-Solem, *The Rise of Historical Economics*, 278–9.

73 Balabkins, *Not by Theory Alone*, 45.

74 Hagemann, 'The Verein für Sozialpolitik', 14–15.

75 Balabkins, *Not by Theory Alone*, 'Preface' Backhaus, 7.

76 Balabkins, *Not by Theory Alone*, 'Preface' Backhaus, 8.

77 Joseph Schumpeter, 'Gustav von Schmoller und die Probleme von heute', *Schmollers Jahrbuch für Gesetzgebung, Verwaltung und Volkswirtschaft* 50 (1926): 373–88 (1–52), quoted and translated by Jürgen Backhaus in Balabkins, *Not by Theory Alone*, 5–6.

78 Backhaus, preface to Balabkins, *Not by Theory Alone*, 6.

79 Balabkins, *Not by Theory Alone*, 57.

80 Gustav von Schmoller, *Grundriss der allgemeinen Volkswirtschaftslehre*, 111, quoted in Balabkins, *Not by Theory Alone*, 57.

81 Schmoller is quoted from *Preußische Jahrbücher* (1867) in Grimmer-Solem.

82 Hansen, 'Gustav Schmoller as a Scientist of Political Economy', part 4.

83 Bredo Morgenstierne, review of *Socialøkonomik*, *Statsøkonomisk Tidsskrift* 16 (1902): 199–202.

84 Aschehoug, *Socialøkonomik*, vol. 1, part 4, chap. 23, § 20, 400.

85 Quoted in Balabkins, *Not by Theory Alone*, chap. 5.

86 Hildebrand quoted in Grimmer-Solem, *The Rise of Historical Economics*, 128–9.

87 Grimmer-Solem, *The Rise of Historical Economics*, 153.

88 Hagemann, 'The Verein für Sozialpolitik', 1.

89 Hagemann, 'The Verein für Sozialpolitik', 9.

90 Balabkins, *Not by Theory Alone*, 47.

91 Invitation to meeting in Eisenach in 1872 by Schmoller, quoted in Grimmer-Solem, *The Rise of Historical Economics*, 176.

92 Hagemann, 'The Verein für Sozialpolitik', 15.

93 Jürgen Backhaus, 'The German Economic Tradition: From Cameralism to the Verein für Sozialpolitik', in *Political Economy and National Realities*, ed. M. Albertone and A. Masoero (Torino: Fondatione Luigi Einaudi, 1994), 352.

94 Ernst Engel was also the patron of Engel's law and Engel curves, and he had been investigating historically and statistically the living conditions of the labour class.

95 See comment in Hagemann.

96 Grimmer-Solem, *The Rise of Historical Economics*, 12; and Balabkins, *Not by Theory Alone*, 31.

97 It was not until 1972 that it officially became the periodical for the Verein under the name of *Zeitschrift für Wirtschafts- und Sozialwissenschaften*. Hagemann adds that this 'renaming' implicitly tells a lot about the development of economics as a discipline. See Hagemann, 'The Verein für Sozialpolitik', 16, for a detailed overview.

98 The speech of Schmoller from the *Verhandlungen der Eisenacher Versammlung*, quoted and facilitated by Grimmer-Solem.

99 Hagemann, 'The Verein für Sozialpolitik', 6.

100 Hagemann, 'The Verein für Sozialpolitik', 7.

101 Aschehoug, *Socialøkonomik*, vol. 1, part 2, chap. 11, § 1, 133.

102 Hansen, 'Gustav Schmoller as a Scientist of Political Economy', part 5: 'Schmoller's Activities as a Chair Holder for Statistics at Halle University: The Practical Significance of His Theoretical Approach to Political Economy', 17, 26.

103 Hansen, 'Gustav Schmoller as a Scientist of Political Economy', part 1, 2–3.

104 See Hansen, part 5.

105 Hansen, 'Gustav Schmoller as a Scientist of Political Economy', 22.

106 Grimmer-Solem, *The Rise of Historical Economics*, 281.

107 I may add here that a more thorough and recent revaluation of Adam Smith shows that the German perception at the time (the last part of nineteenth century) was too simplified, and that the laissez-faire label of Smith is not correct in its simple form.

108 Grimmer-Solem, *The Rise of Historical Economics*, 263.

109 Grimmer-Solem, *The Rise of Historical Economics*, 274.

110 Bertram Schefold's article on Schmoller in *The New Palgrave Dictionary of Economics*, my translation from Carlson, *De institutionalistiska idéernas spridning*.

111 Grimmer-Solem, *The Rise of Historical Economics*, 284.
112 Quoted in Caldwell, *Hayek's Challenge*, 52.

Chapter 7   Alfred Marshall: Aschehoug and the Adoption of Marginal Theory

1 Mark Skousen, *The Making of Modern Economics: The Lives and Ideas of the Great Thinkers*, 2nd edition (Armonk, NY: M. E. Sharpe, 2009). 'Marshall made a singular change that reflected this transformation [marginal revolution].'
2 Skousen, *The Making of Modern Economics*, 198.
3 Alfred Marshall, *Principles of Economics*, abridgement of the 8th edition (1920) (New York: Prometheus Books, 1997), 14.
4 Mark Blaug quoted in Skousen, *The Making of Modern Economics*, 197.
5 Earl Beach, 'Alfred Marshall', in *Handbook of the History of Economic Thought: Insights on the Founders of Modern Economics*, ed. Jürgen Backhaus (New York: Springer, 2011), Introduction, n.p.
6 Beach, 'Alfred Marshall', Assessments, n.p.
7 Also mentioned by Bergh and Hanisch, *Vitenskap og politikk*, 78. Aschehoug started using marginal theory immediately in his manuscripts and drafts for *Socialøkonomik*.
8 Chapter 30, 'Den klassiske Skoles Værdilære'; chapter 31, 'Grænseverdilæren. Grænseværdibegrebet i en isoleret Husholdning'; chapter 32, 'Fortsættelse; Grænseværdibegrebet i Bytteøkonomien'; chapter 35, 'Forholdet mellem Produktionsomkostningerne og Produktets Værdi'; chapter 56, 'Prislærens Grundbegreber. Efterspørgsel og Tilbud' and chapter 57, 'Prisbestemmelsen'. Translation can be found in Chapter 4, where a complete layout of *Socialøkonomik* is given.
9 Hanisch and Sæther, 'Alfred Marshall in Norway', in *The Impact of Alfred Marshall's Ideas: The Global Diffusion of his Work*, ed. T. Raffaelli, G. Becattini, K. Caldari and M. Dardi (Northampton, MA / Cheltenham UK: Edward Elgar, 2010).
10 Hanisch and Sæther, 'Alfred Marshall in Norway'.
11 Hanisch and Sæther, 'Alfred Marshall in Norway', 2.
12 Hanisch and Sæther. 'Alfred Marshall in Norway', 4.
13 Marshall himself tells that he 'borrowed' the term marginal from von Thünen's *Der isolierte Staat*, which is commonly used by German economists. He further says that he considered and adopted Jevons's term 'final', but that he was gradually convinced that 'marginal' is better. See Marshall, *Principles*, xvi.
14 Agnar Sandmo, *Economics Evolving: A History of Economic Thought* (Princeton, NJ: Princeton University Press, 2011).
15 Sandmo, *Samfunnsøkonomi: En idéhistorie* (Oslo: Universitetsforlaget, 2006), 185.
16 Aschehoug, *Socialøkonomik*, vol. 1, part 1, chap. 2, § 6, 17. 'Det træffer heller ikke sjelden, at man er ude av Stand til at bringe paa det Rene, hvilke økonomiske Virkninger en tilstrækkelig fastlaaet historisk Kjendsgjerning har havt.' The quote is from Marshall, *Principles*, book 1, chap. 6, § 4.
17 Aschehoug, *Socialøkonomik*, vol. 1, part 1, chap. 2, § 11, 29–30. 'Som allerede før sagt, har det været sædvanligt at inddele den økonomiske Virksomhed i Produktion, Omsætning, Fordeling og Forbrug af de økonomiske Goder. [...] Mod denne Systematikk har der dog været gjort adskillige Indvendiger. [...] Andre tillægge vel Forbrugen Betydning for Samfundets Velstand, men sige, at den maa medtages under Udviklingen af alle Virksomheders Grene. Denne Anskuelse ligger til Grund for Marshalls Systematik.'
18 Aschehoug, *Socialøkonomik*, vol. 1, part 1, chap. 1, § 6, 10. 'Fuldkommen er denne Likevægt, naar de modsatte økonomiske Kræfter gjensidigen opveie hverandre, saaledes at ingen Forandring indtræder i deres Virkninger og Forholdet mellem dem. En saadan Stabilitet er dog

ikke stort mere end tænkelig. Den vil i alle Fald aldrig vare længe. [...] Vaklende eller instabilt siges Ligevægtspunktet at være, naar Ligevægten efter en Gang at have været forstyrret, men først fremkommer paa et nyt, derfra væsentlig forskjelligt. Det økonomiske Ligevægtspunkts bevægelighed har sin Betydning ikke blot i Læren om Markedsprisen, Grundrenten, Kapitalrenten, Arbeidslønnen, men ogsaa overhovedet i alle økonomiske Kræfters Samspil, saaledes ogsaa i Befolkningslæren og Finansvidenskaben.'

19 It seems though that Aschehoug must have had at least an edition from around the turn of the century, because he quotes a motto in the preface that is not found in the first edition, and henceforth must be from a later edition.

20 Marshall, *Principles of Economics*, preface to the first edition, xi–xii.

21 Yuval P. Yonay, *The Struggle over the Soul of Economics: Institutionalist and Neoclassical Economists in America between the Wars* (Princeton, NJ: Princeton University Press, 1998), 32.

22 Hanisch and Sæther, 'Alfred Marshall in Norway'.

23 Aschehoug, *Socialøkonomik*, vol. 1, part 1, chap. 2, § 7, 19. 'Men Mathematiken kan misbruges, dels til Forklaring af, hvad der allerede uden dens Bistand er klart nok, dels til Forsøg paa at forklare, hvad den ikke magter, fordi Antallet af de søgte ubekjendte Størrelser bliver enten større eller mindre end Antallet af de Ligninger, man kan opstille for at finde dem. Mathematiken bliver derfor mindre og mindre anvendelig, jo mer forviklede de undersøgte Forhold blive.'

24 Marshall, *Principles*, xvi, preface to the first edition.

25 Marshall, review of Jevons's *Political Economy* in 1872, quoted in John Maynard Keynes, *Essays on Biography* (New York: Norton & Company, 1951 [1933]), 159.

26 Earl Beach, 'Alfred Marshall', Contributions.

27 Marshall, *Principles*, 8th ed., book 5 (1920), 461.

28 Yonay, *The Struggle over the Soul of Economics*, 32.

29 Earl Beach, 'Alfred Marshall', Contributions, see note 9.

30 Marshall, *Principles*, book 1, chap. 3, 36. 'The term "law" means then nothing more than a general proposition or statement of tendencies, more or less certain, more or less definite.'

31 Marshall, *Principles*, book 1, chap. 3, 32–3.

32 See, for instance, comments in Beach about various twentieth century economists and Marshall.

33 Yonay, *The Struggle over the Soul of Economics*, 32.

34 Marshall, *Principles*, xii.

35 Marshall also says that Ricardo and his chief followers misapplied economic dogmas, instead of building on universal truths, they were applying a certain class of truth. Marshall from *Principles* quoted in Keynes, *Essays on Biography*, 171.

36 Marshall, *Principles*, xii.

37 Aschehoug, *Socialøkonomik*, vol. 1, part 4, chap. 18, § 8, 271. 'Der det er Tale om Sammenhængen mellem de menneskelige Bevæggrunde, som gjøre sig gjældende i og udenfor Samfundsøkonomien, er det selvfølgelig dennes Forhold til Ethiken, som er af Interesse. Spørgsmaalet erkjendes at have faaet en saa alvorlig Betydning, at det nu bliver omhandlet, tildels meget indgaaende, saavel af Philosopherne som af Socialøkonomerne.'

38 Aschehoug, *Socialøkonomik*, vol. 1, part 4, chap. 18, § 9, 271. 'Om een Ting er man væsentlig enig. Mellem den sande Moral og den sunde Samfundsøkonomi hersker der god Forstaaelese.'

39 Keynes, *Essays on Biography*, 136.

40 Marshall, *Principles*, 4.

41 Keynes, *Essays on Biography*, 137.

42 Quoted in Keynes, *Essays on Biography*, 138.

43 Aschehoug, *Socialøkonomik*, vol. 4, 'Efterskrift', 977. 'Grunden er, at jeg lige fra Begyndelsen af har sat mig som Maal i Værket at indarbeide det Allervigtigste af den nye økonomiske Lovgivning og Litteratur [...] og at dette nye Stof har strømmet ind i en Mængde, der for mig har været næsten overvældende.'

44 Keynes, *Essays on Biography*, 140.

45 Keynes, *Essays on Biography*, 141.

46 Yonay, *The Struggle over the Soul of Economics*, 46.

47 Quoted in J. M. Keynes, 'Alfred Marshall, 1842–1924', *Economic Journal* 34 (135) (September 1924): 350.

48 Keynes, *Essays on Biography*, 183.

49 Marshall, *Principles*, xvi, preface to the first edition.

50 Aschehoug, *Socialøkonomik*, vol. 2, part 5, chap. 30, § 3, 24. 'Men baade Efterspørgselen og Tilbudet paavirkes af Markedsprisen. Falder denne, saa utvides Kredsen af dem, som have Lyst og Raad til at kjøbe, og det siges da, at Efterspørgselen stiger. Omvendt pleier Prisfald meføre, at Tilbudet indskrænkes. Stiger Markedsprisen, pleier dette have den modsatte Virkning baade paa Efterspørgselen og Tilbudet. Mellem disse og Markedsprisen er det saaledes et stærkt fremtrædende Vexelvirkningsforhold.'

51 Aschehoug, *Socialøkonomik*, vol. 2, part 5, chap. 30, § 8, 29–30.

52 Aschehoug, 'Værdi- og prislærens historie', part 1 (185–230) in *Statsøkonomisk Tidsskrift* 14 (1900): 195.

53 Agnar Sandmo, *Samfunnsøkonomi: En idéhistorie*, chap. 9.

54 Aschehoug, *Socialøkonomik*, vol. 1, part 1, chap. 2, § 7, 18.

55 Aschehoug, *Socialøkonomik*, vol. 1, part 1, chap. 2, § 7, 18.

56 Aschehoug, *Socialøkonomik*, vol. 2, part 5, chap. 31, § 1, 31, note 1, 'Læren har vundet stor Udberedelse, navnlig gjennem Marshalls *Principles*.'

57 Aschehoug, *Socialøkonomik*, vol. 2, part 5, chap. 31, § 1, 31. '[…] først og fremst ved at vise, at det er den subjective Brugsværdi (Nytten), der er bestemmende for Menneskenes økonomiske Handlemaade og derigjennem tillige for Bytteværdien.' Aschehoug. *Socialøkonomik*, vol. 2, part 5, chap. 29, § 10, 14. 'Liden Brugsværdi for ham, men høi Bytteværdi, det vil sige, hvis han som Vederlag for den kan faa meget af et vist andet Slags Gjenstande, han tiltrænger eller ønsker. Omvendt bliver han utilbøieligere til at skille sig ved den, hvis den har stor Brugsværdi for ham, medens dens Bytteværdi er liden. Dette er den nyere Værdilærens Udgangspunkt.'

58 Aschehoug, *Socialøkonomik*, vol. 2, part 5, chap. 31, § 2, 32–3. 'Den moderne Værdilære søger sit Grundlag i følgende sætninger, som allerede før ere fremhævede, nemlig i Kapitel 16, §§1–7, jfr. Kapitel 18, §§1–5, og Kapitel 29, § 5: a) At intet Behov har økonomisk Betydning medmindre det fremkalder økonomiske Handlinger, positive eller negative. b) At en Gjenstand, for at have økonomisk Værdi, maa være eller antages at være skikket som Middel til at tilfredsstille et saadant Behov. c) At et Behov, for at faa økonomisk Betydning, maa være subjektivt og konkret, gjøre sig gjældende hos en eller flere bestemte Personer og ved en bestemt Leilighed. Det bliver da ham eller dem, som værdsætte Tilfredsstillelsesmidlet. d) At ethvert Behov ialfald midlertidigt kan mættes, saaledes at det indtil videre taber enten hele sin Styrke eller en Del deraf. e) At et Behov ophører at være økonomisk virksomt, ikke blot naar det er mættet, men ogsaa naar dets Tilfredsstillelse er fuldstændig sikret, nemlig ved Besiddelsen af de for Tilfredsstillelsen nødvendige Midler, og Behovet altsaa er dækket.'

59 Aschehoug, *Socialøkonomik*, vol. 2, part 5, chap. 31, § 6, 35. 'Maalestokken for den Nytte eller Værdi, han tillægger enhver Brøkdel af Forraadet, ligger i det svageste Behov, for hvilket han kan anvende denne Brøkdel uden derved at efterlade noget stærkere Behov udækket. Denne Nytte er det, den moderne Værdilære kalder Foraadets Grænsenytte.'

60 Aschehoug, *Socialøkonomik*, vol. 2, part 5, chap. 31, § 8, 38–9. 'For den abstrakteste, rent mathematiske Anskuelse ligger denne Løsning af Spørgesmaalet nærmest [the general postulate]. Hvilken [løsning] der i Virkeligheden bliver valgt, maa bero paa de i hvert enkelt Tilfælde foreliggende Omstendigheder, navlig paa Eierens Individualitet og paa, hvorvidt Forraadet lader sig dele i store eller mindre Brøkdele. Læren maa forstaaes med det selvsagte Forbehold, at Enhver indretter sin Økonomi efter en fornuftig Plan.'

61 Thorvald Aarum, 'Norwegen, Dänemark und Schweden', in *Die Wirtschaftstheorie der Gegenwart*, ed. Hans Mayer. (Vienna: Julius von Springer, 1927), 124. Bei Erweiterungen oder Verkleinerungen der produktiven Aufopferungen wird die Produktmenge größer oder kleiner und dadurch wird sich ein Gleichgewicht auf dem Punkte einstellen, wo der Grenznutzen des eine weitere

Ausdehnung der Produktion sich nicht als vorteilhaft erweist, weil sie einen verkleinerten Grenznutzen einem vergrößerten Grenzopfer gegenüber bedeutet und deshalb nicht mehr als ökonomisch zulässig anzusehen ist.

62 Aschehoug, *Socialøkonomik*, vol. 2, part 5, chap. 32, § 4, 56. 'Der maa altsaa være en Forskjel mellem den Bortbytnings- og Tilbytningsværdi, enhver af Parterne tillægger Ombytningsgjenstandene.'

63 Aschehoug, *Socialøkonomik*, vol. 2, part 5, chap. 32, § 5, 57–8. 'Sætningens sande Mening er kun, at man skal ordne sit Forbrug paa en saadan Maade, at man faar den bedst mulige Tilfredsstillelse af sine Behov.'

64 Aarum, 'Norwegen, Dänemark und Schweden', 124. 'Auch für die Bildung des Tauschwerts im geldlichen Markverkehr führt Aschehoug den Nachweis, daß sowohl Kosten als Nutzen den Wert bestimmen, und daß beide Momente, in Verbindung miteinander wirkend, prinzipiell als Elemente der Wertbildung anzusehen sind.'

65 Aschehoug, *Socialøkonomik*, vol. 2, part 5, chap. 34, § 2, 78. 'Ordet Produktionsomkostninger bruges i to Betydninger. Snart tænker man paa de Opofrelser, som de i Frembringelsen av en vis Gjenstand delagtige Personer i saadant Øiemed have gjort, navnlig gjennem den dermed forbundne Arbeidsanstrengelse og Savnet af de deri forbrugte materielle Hjælpemidler. Snart mener man de Pengeudgifter, den producerende Driftsherre virkelig har havt, samt den Pengegodtgjørelse, han har beregnet sig for sine egne, ved Produktionen forvoldte Opofrelser. [...] Videnskaben tiltrænger imidlertid begge Begreber, Marshall, *Principles*, Bog V, Kap. III, § 2.'

66 Aschehoug, *Socialøkonomik*, vol. 2, part 5, chap. 35, § 7. 'Tvisten om den øverste Maalestok for de økonomiske Goders Værdi'.

67 Aschehoug, *Socialøkonomik*, vol. 2, part 5, chap. 35, § 9, 112. 'Marshall har erklæret sig uenig med Böhm-Bawerk i det her omhandlede Punkt. Efter Marshall's Opfatning lider saavel den klassiske som den østerrigske Skole av en vis Eensidighed. Hin fæstede sin Opmerksomhed for stærkt ved Produktets Omkostninger, denne ved dets Nytte. Begge, baade den positive og den negative Nytte, indgaa som Led i Bestemmelsen af Produktets Normalværdi. Og heri synes Marshall os at have fuldkommen Ret.'

68 Aschehoug, *Socialøkonomik*, vol. 2, part 5, chap. 35, § 9, 112–13. The conclusion of Marshall is as follows in the words of Aschehoug: 'Man maa gaa tilbake til Grundprincipet i al Økonomi. Forat et vist Slags Produkter skal faa Bytteværdi og kunne sælges, er det ikke nok, at de tilfredsstille Menneskers Behov. Det kræves ogsaa, at dette Slags Gjenstande ikke staa dem til Raadighed i saa stor Mængde, at de med denne kunne dække sine Behov fuldt ud, uden al Antstrængelse.' Aschehoug says: 'Produktets Værdi har derfor et dobbelt Grunlag, nemlig at dets Brug bringer Tilfredsstillelse, og at dets Frembringelse koster Anstrængelse eller anden Opofrelse.'

69 Marshall, *Principles*, 8th edition (London: Macmillan, 1920). Online: http://www.econlib. org/library/Marshall/marP43.html#Bk.VI,Ch.I (accessed 29 May 2013). In Aschehoug's copy of Marshall's *Principles* this is found in § 10. Aschehoug, *Socialøkonomik*, vol. 2, part 5, chap. 35, § 5, 103, note 1. 'Grænsen for Anvendelsen af ethvert Produktionsmiddel, Grundeiendommene indbefattede herunder, afhænger af Efterspørgselen i Forhold til Tilbudet, det vil sige paa den Side af Intensiteten af alle de Behov, der kunne tilfredsstilles ved Hjælp af dette Produktionsmiddel, samt alle de Kjøbelystnes Kjøbeevne, og paa den anden Side det disponible Forraad af dette Produktionsmiddel, hvad enten Forraadet er en uforanderlig Størrelse, saasom Grundeiendommene, eller dets Mængde kan forøges, saaledes som Tilfældet er med Arbeidet. Grænseandvendelserne af ethvert Produktionsmiddel, det vil sige dettes Grænseproduktivitet i hver Andvendelse og hermed dets Bytteværdi i denne, bero følgelig alle samtidigt paa det almindelige Forhold mellem Efterspørgsel og Tilbud. Endelig bemærkes, at Ligheden mellem dets Værdi i forskjellige Andvendelser oppretholdes ved den frie Konkurrences stadige Tendents til at overføre Produktionsmidlet fra mindre til mere lønnende Andvendelser.'

70 Aschehoug, *Socialøkonomik*, vol. 2, part 5, chap. 35, § 2, 97. 'Denne kommer tilsyne som det Ligevægtspunkt, hvorom Markedspriserne paa et Produktionsmiddel svinge. [...] Utjevningen

kan da kun foregaa eferhaanden og tage lang Tid. Det Ligevægtspunkt, hvorom Priserne paa Produktionsmidlerne svinge, er langtfra uforanderligt. Det kan endog forandre sig temmelig hurtigt, navlig hvis det beror paa en Lovforskrift eller en Skat eller en Mangel paa Kommunikationsmilder. Men et Ligevægtspunkt i denne Prisbevægelse er der altid, naar Konkurrencen paa enhver af Siderne er fri.'

71 See also the theory of composite demand in Marshall.

72 See Chapter 36 in *Socialøkonomik*. He summarizes in § 9: 'Det er det praktiske Livs Kjendsgjerninger, Domme og Efaringer, Værdilæren benytter som sit Grundlag. Herunder maa den ikke fortabe sig i usikre eller uoverskuelige Enkeltheder, men søge at give en saavidt muligt klar og sammenhængende Oversigt over de Kræfter, der med størst Almindelighed, Styrke og Tydelighed gjøre sig gjældende i den økonomiske Virksomheds Vurderinger.'

73 Aschehoug, *Socialøkonomik*, vol. 3, part 7, chap. 57, § 10, 36. 'De Forudsætninger, paa hvilke dette Schema er bygget, ere i det virkelige Liv neppe nogensinde tilstede. Det indeholder blot en Veiledning for Tanken. Lidt nærmere Virkeligheden kommer man, hvis man tænker sig, at hvert enkelt Trin i Efterspørgselen og Tilbudets Række repræsentereres ikke af en enkelt, men af flere og helst mange Personer med nogenlunde lige Kjøbelyst og Kjøbeevne, altsaa en hel Gruppe. [...] Men Schemaet yder i denne Skikkelse bedre Hjælp til at forstaa den vigtige Sandhed. [...] Prisdannelsen kan, som sagt, ogsaa fremstilles graphisk; men for Andre end Mathematikere bliver Læren derved i det Hele taget neppe mere letfattelig eller klarere.' Aschehoug here refers to the method of price setting found in Westergaard, 'Innledning til Studiet af Nationaløkonomien', his own paper in *Statsøkonomisk Tidsskrift*, 'Værdi- og prislærens historie'.

74 Aschehoug, *Socialøkonomik*, vol. 2, part 6, chap. 45, § 5, 243.

75 Beach, 'Alfred Marshall', Context, n.p.

76 Aschehoug, *Socialøkonomik*, vol. 1, part 4, chap. 28, § 19, 549. Marshall, *Principles*, book 4, chap. 12, § 10. 'Nok er her blevet sagt til at vise, at Verden just er begyndt at blive færdig for den kooperative Bevægelses høiere Arbeide, og at dettes mange forskjellige Former med Rimelighed kunne ventes at lykkes bedre i Fremtiden end i Fortiden.'

77 Aschehoug, *Socialøkonomik*, vol. 4, part 8, chap. 89, 'Samfundsindtægtens endelige Fordeling'.

78 § 7, 'Interessefællesskabet mellem de produktive Samfundsklasser', § 8, 'Den dobbelte Kappestrid mellem dem om Indtægtens Fordeling', and § 9, 'Grænseværdilærens Tillempning paa Indtægtsfordelingen'.

79 Aschehoug, *Socialøkonomik*, vol. 4, part 8, chap. 89, § 7, 702. 'Den ældre Theori sagde derfor, at den almindelige Efterspørgsel (*the general demand*) falder sammen med det almindelige Tilbud (*the general supply*). Nu udtrykker man Tanken noget forsigtigere, nemlig ved at sige, at ligesom Samfundsintægten er Samfundsvirksomhedens Produkt, saaledes er den ogsaa den eneste Kilde til Efterspørgselen efter Produktionsmidlerne.' The quote from Marshall is from *Principles*, book 6, chap. 1, § 11, and chap. 11, § 4.

80 Aschehoug, *Socialøkonomik*, vol. 3, part 8, chap. 89, § 9, 703. 'Ligesom al anden økonomisk Kappestrid beherskes Kappestriden om Samfundsintægtens Fordeling af Grænseværdiens Lov. Forstaaelsen heraf har mere end noget andet bidraget til at bringe større Klarhed over Fordelingen og at fjerne de gamle Tvistespørgsmål.'

81 Marshall, *Principles*, book 6, chap. 1, § 10, quoted in Aschehoug, *Socialøkonomik*, vol. 3, part 8, chap. 89, § 11, 708.

82 Marshall, *Principles*, 6th edition (1910).

83 Ragnar Frisch, *Notater til økonomisk teori*, 2nd, 3rd and 4th editions (Oslo: Sosialøkonomisk institutt, 1947), n.p.

84 Ragnar Frisch, 'Alfred Marshall's Theory of Value', *Quarterly Journal of Economics* 64 (4) (November 1950): 495–524 (my emphasis).

85 Thorstein Veblen, review of 'Vaerdi- og prislaerens historie' by T. H. Aschehoug, *Statsökonomisk tidskrift* 8 (1902).

Chapter 8   The French Influence: Adopting Say and Refuting Socialism

1 Aschehoug borrowed McCulloch's definition of economics that McCulloch had attributed to Adam Smith's works. Economics as a discipline was defined as: 'The theory of the laws that regulate production, distribution and consumption of the goods or products that have an exchange value and at the same time are necessary, useful or valuable for humans', *Socialøkonomik* vol. 1, part 2, chap. 2, 20.

2 *Stortingsmelding* (1868–69), 'Debatt om Lov om det høyere skolevesen', 431.

3 Aschehoug quoted in Anne-Lise Seip, *Vitenskap og virkelighet: Sosiale, økonomiske og politiske teorier hos T. H. Aschehoug 1845–1882* (Oslo: Gyldendal, 1975), 187.

4 Ottar Dahl, *Norsk historieforskning i det 19. og 20. århundre*, 4th edition (Oslo: Universitetsforlaget, 1990), chapter 5.

5 Quoted in Seip, *Vitenskap og virkelighet*, 258.

6 'Begrebet Socialøkonomik'.

7 Aschehoug, *Socialøkonomik*, vol. 1, part 1, chap. 1, 2.

8 Aschehoug, *Socialøkonomik*, vol. 1, part 1, chap. 1, § 2, 3.

9 Aschehoug, *Socialøkonomik*, vol. 1, part 1, chap. 1, § 2, 3. 'Adam Smith sagde at den var Læren om Nationalvelstandens Natur og Aarsager. Under Paavirkning av Jean Baptiste Say have de fleste senere Forfattere defineret den som Læren om de økonomiske Goders Frembringelse (Produktion), Omsætning (Cirkulation), Fordeling (Distribusjon eller Repartition) og Forbrug (Konsumtion).'

10 Aschehoug, *Socialøkonomik*, vol. 1, part 1, chap. 1, § 3, 7. 'Ogsaa i Frankrige have enkelte Forfattere sondret mellem Socialøkonomiken som theoretisk og som praktisk Videnskab. (Corcelle-Seneuil, Cherbuilez, Maurice Block slutter sig til dem.) Men de fleste franske Forfattere se Videnskaben fra begge Sider. Herved vinde deres Fremstillinger unægtelig mer Liv og Interesse. (Leroy-Beaulieu og Gide, begge disse utmærkede Værker vise, hvor sandt dette er.)'

11 Aschehoug, *Socialøkonomik*, vol. 1, part 1, chap. 1, § 4, 7. 'Økonomiske Sætninger, som aldrig have havt og aldrig kunne faa nogensomhelst praktisk Andvendelse, ere tomme Hjernespind. Videnskabens sidste Opgave bliver til alle Tider praktisk.'

12 Aschehoug, *Socialøkonomik*, vol. 1, part 1, chap. 1, § 6, 10. 'kun Selvinteressens og Nyttens Mekanikk eller at den er Mekanikk anvendt på de sosiale rikdommenes likevektspunkt og bevegelse.'

13 Aschehoug, *Socialøkonomik*, vol. 1, part 2, chap. 5, § 1, 63. 'mere et praktisk, handelspolitisk System end en fuldt udviklet vitenskabelig Theori.'

14 Aschehoug, *Socialøkonomik*, vol. 1, part 2, chap. 5, § 5, 67–8. Aschehoug uses, among others, Levasseur, Clement, Noël, Cohn 'at hæve den store Industri, Fabrikvirksomhed, selv om det skede på den lille Industris, Haandværkets Bekostning.'

15 Aschehoug, *Socialøkonomik*, vol. 1, part 2, chap. 5, § 5, 68.

16 Aschehoug, *Socialøkonomik*, vol. 1, part 4, chap. 23, § 4, 374. 'Statens Berettigelse ligger i dens Evne til at virke for det menneskelige Samfunds Øiemed. [...] Statens Formaal kan nemlig ikke gaa videre, end dens Virkemidler tillade. [...] Men Spørgsmaalet om, hvor langt Kredsen strækker sig af de Formaal, for hvilke Staten kan virke, har været og er fremdeles Gjenstand for en Tvist, som er af den allerstørste praktiske Betydning ogsaa for Samfundsøkonomien.'

17 Aschehoug, *Socialøkonomik*, vol. 1, part 4, chap. 23, § 7, 379. Aschehoug adds in footnote 3 that this was also the case for Turgot, see Michel, *L'idée de l'état*. 'vare Tilhængere af Enevældet og haabede ved "sine kloge Raad" at bevæge Kongerne til at indføre økonomisk Frihed.'

18 Aschehoug, *Socialøkonomik*, vol. 1, part 4, chap. 23, § 7, 385. 'Begge disse udmærkede Forfattere saa med Ugunst på Statens Indgreb i den individuelle Frihed. Toqueville udviklede for det Første hvorledes og hvorfor det moderne Demokrati gjør sig gjældende med uimodstaalig Magt, dernæst hvilke Farer de medfører, og endelig med hvilke Midler disse efter hans Mening kunne hemmes.'

19 Aschehoug, *Socialøkonomik*, vol. 1, part 2, chap. 6, § 1, 76. 'vældig aandelig Bevægelse, først i økonomisk, siden i politisk Retning.'

20 Aschehoug, *Socialøkonomik*, vol. 1, part 2, chap. 6, § 1, 76. 'Den begyndte i 1706 med Vaubans Kritikk over Skattevæsenet (*Dime Royale*) og optoges av Boisguillebert, som i sin *Détail de la France* (1707) forlangte Handels- og Næringsfrihed. Men varig intryk paa den almindelige Mening gjorde først Physiokraternes Skole. Den grundlagdes av Lægen Quesnay, hvis skrifter udkom i Aarene 1756–1768.'

21 Ronald L. Meek, *The Economics of Physiocracy* (London: Routledge, 2003 [1962]), 17.

22 Aschehoug, *Socialøkonomik*, vol. 1, part 2, chap. 6, § 2, 77. 'Ethvert Menneske er altsaa Retssubjekt. Dette er Systemets inderste Tanke.'

23 Aschehoug calls it 'politistaten'.

24 Aschehoug, *Socialøkonomik*, vol. 1, part 2, chap. 6, § 2, 78. 'Menneske ere, siger han, underkastede en dobbelt Rettsorden, den naturlige og den positive. Den naturlig Retsordens Love udledes gjennem den menneskelige Fornuft af den almindelige Menneskenatur og dens Plan. Disse love ere de for det menneskelige Samliv tjenligste. Den positive Retsorden har kun den Opgave gjennem sine Love at bringe de naturlige Love til ret.'

25 Aschehoug, *Socialøkonomik*, vol. 1, part 2, chap. 6, § 2, 79. 'et naturlig Tilbageslag, at Physiokraterne overvurderte det.'

26 Aschehoug, *Socialøkonomik*, vol. 4, part 8, chap. 88, 666. 'Arbeidslønnen; dens "Bestemmelsesgrunde"', gir en oversikt over arbeidslønn og arbeidsforhold i vid forstand, men som vanlig, 'før vi tage fat paa de vanskeligere Spørgsmaal vedkommende Arbeidslønnens Bestemmelsesgrunde, skulle vi kaste et Blikk paa Lærens Historie.'

27 See Agnar Sandmo, *Samfunnsøkonomi: En idéhistorie* (Oslo: Universitetsforlaget, 2006), 31–3 about the physiocrats and Turgot.

28 Aschehoug, *Socialøkonomik*, vol. 4, part 8, chap. 88, 666. 'Turgot, som synes at have været den første, der søgte at danne sig et Begreb om Fordelingen af Samfundsvirksomhedens Afkastning, og som delte Physiokraternes Produktionslære maatte jo ved denne ganske naturligen ledes ind paa den Tanke, at hverken Arbeidslønnen eller Kapitalrenten kunde hæve sig over et vist naturlig Lavmaal, og i denne Tanke fandt han sig styrket ved det praktiske Livs Erfaringer. Det var en velkjendt Sag, at Kapitalrenten var sunken, og Turgot troede, at den ikke kunde holde sig høiere, end at den afgav tilstrækkelig Opfordring til at spare.'

29 Aschehoug, *Socialøkonomik*, vol. 1, part 2, chap. 6, § 2, 81. 'De bragte desuden Socialøkonomiken i en Forbindelse med Retsphilosophien, som øvede stor og varig Inflydelse paa begge Videnskaber.' 'Turgot har forfattet en Række udmærkede Skrifter, blant hvilke maa fremhæves *Réflexions sur la formation et la distribution des richesses*, trykket i 1770.'

30 Aschehoug, *Socialøkonomik*, vol. 1, part 2, chap. 6, § 2, 82. As a small curiosity, Aschehoug mentions in a footnote that some had claimed that Smith got his most important economic terms from Turgot, but his is now rejected because examples of Smiths lectures, held years before, have now been discovered. In these lectures Smith introduces many of these theorems and terms (Lectures on justice, police and revenue, 1763).

31 Aschehoug, *Socialøkonomik*, vol. 1, part 2, chap. 6, § 2, 84.

32 Aschehoug, *Socialøkonomik*, vol. 1, part 2, chap. 10, § 3, 118. 'Den historiske Skole staar, som allerede antydet, i et vist Slægtskapsforhold til en anden Aandsretning, der har gjort mindst ligesaa megen Opsigt, nemlig Positivismen. Dens Hjem er Frankrige, dens grundlægger Auguste Comte.'

33 Frans Gregesen and Simo Køppe, ed., *Idéhistorie: Ideer og strømninger i det 20. århundrede*, vol. 1 (Århus: Amanda forlag, 1994), 100.

34 Gregesen and Køppe ed. *Idéhistorie: Ideer og strømninger*, 101.

35 Aschehoug, *Socialøkonomik*, vol. 1, part 2, chap. 10, § 3, 119.

36 Aschehoug, *Socialøkonomik*, vol. 1, part 2, chap. 10, § 3, 119. 'Samfundet er et høiere organisk System, en kollektiv eller social Organisme.'

37 Alfred Fouillée, *Le mouvement idéaliste et la réaction contre la science positive* (Paris: Germer Baillière, 1896), xiii.

38 Aschehoug, *Socialøkonomik*, vol. 4, part 10, chap. 101, § 11, 975. 'Tvivlen om Menneskeslægtens økonomiske Fremtid ligger paa Raavareproduktionens Side. Der er jo en nærliggende Mulighed for, at denne bliver utilstrækkelig for Behovet, og Trykket heraf gjør sig altid følt i gamle Kulturstater, der have udnyttet sine naturlige Produktionskilder, saalangt det for Tiden lønner sig, og hvor Trykket da giver sig tilkjende ved en Formindskelse av Fødselshyppigheden eller stærk Utvandring. Det kan lettes ved nye tekniske Opdagelser, som forøge den svigtende Raastofproduktion; men om saadanne end kunne haabes, kunne de ikke forudsees med nogen Vished.'

39 Franklin L. Baumer, *Modern European Thought: Continuity and Change in Ideas, 1680–1900* (New York: St Martin's Press, 1977), 371.

40 Aschehoug, *Socialøkonomik*, vol. 1, part 2, chap. 10, § 3, 120. Aschehoug quotes Comte: 'reorganisation des opinions pour passer ensuite aux moeurs et finalement aux institutions.'

41 Aschehoug, *Socialøkonomik*, vol. 1, part 2, chap. 10, § 4, 122.

42 Aschehoug, *Socialøkonomik*, vol. 1, part 2, chap. 7, § 7, 127. 'Det maa regnes Comte til Forjeneste, at han vakte større Opmærksomhed for den indre Sammenhæng melem de særskilte Videnskaber, der omhandle Samfundslivets forskjellige Sider. Dette har bidraget til, at enhver af dem nu studeres med stadigere Hensyn til de øvrige og derved paa en frugtbarere Maade. Navnligen gjælder dette om Socialøkonomiken, Retsvidenskaben og Historien.'

43 Aschehoug, *Socialøkonomik*, vol. 1, part 2, chap. 10, § 9, 137.

44 Seip, *Vitenskap og virkelighet*, chapter 10.

45 Aschehoug, *Socialøkonomik*, vol. 1, part 2, chap. 11, § 2, 134, note 1.

46 Aschehoug, *Socialøkonomik*, vol. 1, part 2, chap. 11, § 2, 134.

47 Aschehoug, *Socialøkonomik*, vol. 1, part 2, chap. 11, § 2, 136; http://en.wikipedia.org/wiki/Simonde_de_Sismondi (accessed 1 June 2013).

48 Aschehoug, *Socialøkonomik*, vol. 1, part 2, chap. 11, § 3, 136. 'Sismondi havde skjærpet Opmerksomheden for, at der var noget Galt paafærde med Forholdet mellem Ethikken og Socialøkonomiken og følgelig mellem hin og en Socialøkonomik, som lukkede øinene for denne Disharmoni.'

49 Aschehoug, *Socialøkonomik*, vol. 1, part 2, chap. 7, § 3, 84. 'nemlig at Gjennemførelsen af fuldkommen Retfærdighet, fuldkommen Frihet og fuldkommen Lighed er det meget simple Middel, ved hvilket man virksomst sikrer alle Samfundsklasser den største Velstand.'

50 Aschehoug, *Socialøkonomik*, vol. 1, part 4, chap. 17, § 1, 250, note 1. 'Det franske Sprog har Ordene *Richesses* og *Biens*, hvilket sidste nærmest svarer til vort Sprogs "økonomiske goder". Men ved *Biens* forudsættes, at de hermed betegnede Gjenstande ere Eiendele, og ihvorvel enkelte Forfattere ere tilbøielige til at foretrække det, er Ordet *Richesses* fremdeles det almindeligste anvendte.'

51 Aschehoug, *Socialøkonomik*, vol. 1, part 4, chap. 23, § 10, 386–7.

52 Aschehoug, *Socialøkonomik*, vol. 1, part 4, chap. 23, § 15, 393. In footnote 3, Aschehoug states that Rambaud, Bechaux and also the French edition of Pareto's work defend individualism.

53 Aschehoug, *Socialøkonomik*, vol. 1, part 4, chap. 28, § 1, 394.

54 Aschehoug, *Socialøkonomik*, vol. 1, part 2, chap. 7, § 4, 88 (footnote).

55 Ib E. Eriksen and Arild Sæther, 'Hvor ble det av entreprenøren i norsk samfunnsøkonomi?' *Norsk økonomisk tidsskrift* 124 (2010): 1–32; Arild Sæther, 'Jean-Baptiste Say's Influence in Norway', in *Jean-Baptiste Say: Influence, critiques et postérité*, ed. André Tiran (Paris: Éditions Classique Gariner, 2010).

56 Aschehoug, *Socialøkonomik*, vol. 1, part 2, chap. 7, § 4, 87.

57 Aschehoug, *Socialøkonomik*, vol. 1, part 2, chap. 8, § 3, 100. 'Say led paatageligen af Mangel paa historiske Sands. Han satte liden Pris paa Smiths historiske Undersøgelser, og han forkastede det Forsvar for ældre Ideer, at de dog maatte have havt nogen Berettigelse, naar de havde været almindelige hos alle Folk.'

58 Aschehoug, *Socialøkonomik*, vol. I, part II, chapter 8, § 6, 106. 'Den historiske Skole har imidlertid i Frankrige faaet et Sidestykke i Positivismen, men et Sidestykke med et særeget philosophisk Tilsnit.'

59 Aschehoug, *Socialøkonomik*, vol. 2, part 5, chap. 43, § 2, 202.

60 Aschehoug, *Socialøkonomik*, vol. 2, part 6, chap. 44, § 8, 227.

61 Aschehoug, *Socialøkonomik*, vol. 2, part 6, chap. 50, § 1, 409–410.

62 Aschehoug, *Socialøkonomik*, vol. 2, part 6. Aschehoug refers to works and authors such as: Michel Chevalier, *La monnaie*; Leroy-Beaulieu, *Traité*; Walras, *Théorie de la monnaie*; Auguste Arnauné, *La monnaie, le credit et le change*; A. Beaure, *Théorie et pratique de la monnaie*.

63 Aschehoug, *Socialøkonomik*, vol. 3, part 7, chap. 75, § 14, 364. 'J.-B. Say har i et berømt kapitel gjort opmærksom paa at al Omsætning egentlig er Tuskhandel, selv om den er formidlet ved Penge (Say, *Traité*, 1, Kap. 15).'

64 Aschehoug, *Socialøkonomik*, vol. 3, part 7, chap. 80, § 8, 452, note 1.

65 Aschehoug, *Socialøkonomik*, vol. 3, part 7, chap. 80, § 2, 457. 'Det lod altsaa til, at Frihandelstanken tilsidst skulde seire i den civiliserede Verdens Handelspolitik. Heraf lovede man sig den største Fordel baade for Verdens Fred og for dens Velstand.'

66 Aschehoug, *Socialøkonomik*, vol. 3, part 7, chap. 80, § 4, 459–60.

67 Aschehoug, *Socialøkonomik*, vol. 4, part 8, chap. 83, § 4, 521, 546–7.

68 Aschehoug, *Socialøkonomik*, vol. 4, part 8, chap. 84, § 4, 559, note 2.

69 Aschehoug, *Socialøkonomik*, vol. 1, part 2, chap. 7, § 5, 92.

70 Seip, *Vitenskap og virkelighet*, 68. 'Når Aschehoug omkring 1850 sluttet seg til den optimistiske skole, sluttet han seg til en retning som hadde gjort nye framstøt og fått nytt teoretisk tilsig i slutten av 1840-årene. I Frankrike gav Frédéric Bastiat det best populariserte uttrykk for denne retningen, som i sin mest konsekvente utforming fikk navnet harmoni-økonomien, etter tittelen på Bastiats hovedverk "Harmonies Économiques".'

71 Aschehoug, *Socialøkonomik*, vol. 4, part 8, chap. 84, § 4, 566. 'Bastiat sluttede sig væsentlig til Senior og fandt ligesom han, at Opsamling af Kapital er en Opofrelse (privation) eller ialfald en Opsættelse (delai) med at tage den Behovtilfredsstillelse, Kapitalgjenstandenes Forbrug kan give. Men Bastiat fremhævede stærkere og mer iøinefaldende end Senior, at Kapitalgjenstandenes Eier ved at anvende dem i Produktionen forøgede dennes Afkastning. Han gav sin Tanke til det Udtryk, at Kapitalisterne ved å stille sin Kapital til produktivt Forbrug gjorde saavel Driftsherrerne som Forbrugerne en Tjeneste. Modtagelsen af denne Tjeneste forpligter til Gjenteneste. Derfor har Kapitalisten berettiget Krav paa Renter.'

72 Aschehoug, *Socialøkonomik*, vol. 4, part 8, chap. 85, § 19, 611. 'Tankengang indeholder sikkerlig nogen Sandhed, men er ikke fri for Indvendinger og kræver paalidelig Undersøgelse.'

73 Aschehoug, *Socialøkonomik*, vol. 4, part 8, chap. 87, § 6, 642–3.

74 Aschehoug, *Socialøkonomik*, vol. 4, part 9, chap. 90, § 1, note 1, 723.

75 Aschehoug, *Socialøkonomik*, vol. 4, part 9, chap. 91, § 1, 735, 737. 'Videre kunne vi ei oppholde os ved Luxusnydelsernes Historie, men henvise derom til Leroy-Beaulieus og Roschers fortræffelige Skildringer deraf.'

76 Aschehoug, *Socialøkonomik*, vol. 4, part 9, chap. 91, § 5, 737. 'tilladelige Luxus baner Veien for bedre fremtidige Konsumtionsforhold. Heri ligger dens fornemste økonomiske og kulturelle betydning.'

77 Aschehoug, *Socialøkonomik*, vol. 1, part 2, chap. 12, § 2, 142.

78 Aschehoug, *Socialøkonomik*, vol. 1, part 2, chap. 12, § 2, 143.

79 Gerschenkron, *Economic Backwardness in Historical Perspective* (Cambridge, MA: Belknap Press of Harvard University Press, 1962), 23.

80 Gerschenkron, *Economic Backwardness in Historical Perspective*, 24.

81 Aschehoug, *Socialøkonomik*, vol. 1, part 2, chap. 12, § 2, 143, footnote 2.

82 Erik S. Reinert, 'The Terrible Simplifiers: Common Origins of Financial Crises and Persistent Poverty in Economic Theory and the new "1848 Moment"', DESA Working Paper no. 88, ST/ESA/2009/DWP/88, December 2009.

83 Aschehoug, *Socialøkonomik*, vol. 1, part 4, chap. 28, § 1, 515.

84 Aschehoug, *Socialøkonomik*, vol. 1, part 4, chap. 21, § 1, 330. 'Undersøgelsen om det nuværende Samfunds retlige Grundlag er Spørgesmaalet om Eiendommens Berettigelse det mest omtvistede.'

85 Aschehoug, *Socialøkonomik*, vol. 1, part 4, chap. 23, § 4, 374.
86 Aschehoug, *Socialøkonomik*, vol. 1, part 2, chap. 12, § 4, 144. 'Overhovedet kan det ikke nægtes Proudhon, at han var rig paa nye Tanker eller ialdefald forstod at iklæde gamle Tanker nye og overraskende Former. Men naar han gav sig ifærd med at forklare, hvorledes den økonomiske Virksomhed skulde ordnes ad frivillig Vei, altsaa uden Støtte i Statens straffende og tvingende Myndighed og dog saaledes, at den tilveiebragte Midler nok til at tilfredsstille Menneskenes Behov, glippede for ham.'
87 Aschehoug, *Socialøkonomik*, vol. 1, part 2, chap. 12, § 4, 144. 'Tilsidst kom dog Proudhon til den Overbevisningen, at Anarkismen er et uopnaaligt Ideal, og at man, praktisk taget, ikke kan komme længere end til "Føderalismen", nemlig en Forening mellem autonome Kommuner.'
88 Aschehoug, *Socialøkonomik*, vol. 2, part 5, chap. 39, § 4, 160–61.
89 Aschehoug, *Socialøkonomik*, vol. 2, part 5, chap. 39, § 4, 161. 'Paa grund af alt dette har det været sagt, at Værdibegrebet lider af en indre Modsigelse. Det er Proudhon, der er fremkommen med denne Sætning, som derfor kaldes Proudhons Værdiantonomi. Han sagde: "Eftersom vi blot leve ved Arbeide og Ombytning, og vi ere rigere, jo mere vi producere og omsætte, maa Enhver producere saa store Brugsværdier som muligt for saameget mer at forøge sine Omsætninger. Godt og vel. Men den første og denne er at forringe deres Værdi. Jo mere Varens Mængde stiger, desto mere synker dens Bytteværd."' Aschehoug has a thorough note to this paragraph in which he mentions Proudhon's *Système des contradictions économiques*, chapter 2, and the critique of this postulate in Marx's *Misère de la philosophie*, chapter 1, § 1.
90 Aschehoug, *Socialøkonomik*, vol. 2, part 5, chap. 39, § 4, 163. 'Af sine to Funktioner udfører Bytteværdien den sidste meget bedre end den første.'
91 Aschehoug, *Socialøkonomik*, vol. 4, part 10, chap. 101.

Chapter 9   Views of Labour in the Work of Aschehoug

1 Work is of course treated in the texts of all major classical economists. Aschehoug chooses to mention at the beginning of chapter 47, 'The human labour', John Stuart Mill and his *Principles*, Jevons's *Theory*, Marshall's *Principles*, Nicholson's *Principles*, Clark's *Philosophy of Wealth*, Gide's *Principes*, Leroy-Beaulieu's *Traité*, Hermann's *Untersuchungen*, Roscher's *Grundlagen*, Schönberg's article 'Arbeit' in Conrad's *HWB*, Lehr's *Production und Konsumtion* and articles by Buch, Liesse, Walker, Lexis and Lothmar.
2 Nicholas Balabkins, 'What Did Schäffle Teach Schumpeter?', in *Albert Schäffle (1831–1903): The Legacy of an Underestimated Economist*, ed. Jürgen Backhaus (Frankfurt: Haag & Herchen, 2010), 50 and 38.
3 Balabkins, 'What Did Schäffle Teach Schumpeter?', 40.
4 The following paragraphs about labour are based on a joint paper between myself and Sylvi Endresen entitled 'Torkel Aschehoug: Seeing workers as more than just a production factor', paper presented at the 23rd Heilbronn seminar: 'Liberation of the serfs', June 2010. Published as 'More than Just a Production Factor: The View of Labour in the Works of the Norwegian Economist Torkel Aschehoug (1822–1909)', in *The Liberation of the Serfs: The Economics of Unfree Labor*, ed. Jürgen Backhaus (New York: Springer, 2011).
5 His background and appointments are outlined earlier in Chapter 2.
6 Letter from Aschehoug to his friend Helgesen in 1840. Aschehoug was only 18 years old.
7 Hagerup, 'Nekrolog over Torkel Halvorsen Aschehoug', *Tidsskrift for rettsvitenskab* (1909): 6. 'Aschehougs videnskabelige Forfatterpersonlighed har derfor et udpræget realistisk Tilsnit. Han savnede tilvisse ikke Sans for de ideelle Værdier. Han havde i sin Ungdom sammen med sin Studenterkamerat og senere Kollega Filosofen M. J. Monrad modtaget Impulser fra den Hegelske Filosofi, og han var hele sit Liv igjennem en dybt religiøs Natur. Men denne Idealisme havde vistnok mere Betydning for hans Følelsesliv end for hans Intelligens, hvis mest udprægede Karaktertræk var den skarpe Sans for det empirisk givne, de positive Realiteter.'

8 Letter from Aschehoug to his friend Henrik Helliesen in 1843, Håndskriftssamlingen, Nationalbiblioteket, Oslo.

9 Anne-Lise Seip, *Vitenskap og virkelighet: Sosiale, økonomiske og politiske teorier hos T. H. Aschehoug 1845–1882* (Oslo: Gyldendal, 1975), 33.

10 See quote in Seip, *Vitenskap og virkelighet*, 212, note 42.

11 Balabkins, 'What Did Schäffle Teach Schumpeter', 50.

12 Seip, *Vitenskap og virkelighet*, 35.

13 Seip, *Vitenskap og virkelighet*, 37.

14 Report of the Poverty Commission (*Fattigkommisjonen betenkning*) 58 (1856): 62. '[Arbeiderklassen er] hvad Forholdene have gjort den til.'

15 Proposition of the Smallholder Commission (*Husmannskommisjonen innstilling*) (1851), 20. 'Vi ved ikke engang om Fattigdommen vokser eller avtar.'

16 *Stortingstidende* (1868–69), L 665.

17 *Stortingstidende* (1868–69), L 665, 666. 'væsentlig [...] et moralsk Onde og ikke et økonomisk [...] Arbeiderbefolkningen steg [...] i Forhold til Formuen og Kapitalen, altsaa i Forhold til de eiendomsbesiddende Klasser [...] de, der levede fra Haanden til Munden og havde liden Indtægt og ingen Formue, giftede sig for tidlig. Men paa samme Tid steg deres Fordringer [...] [arbeidernes lettsind var] Hovedaarsagen til Fattigdommen.'

18 Anders N. Kiær, 'Nogle bidrag til bedømmelsen af den økonomiske udvikling med særligt hensyn til Norge (fortsat)', *Statsøkonomisk Tidsskrift* 1 (1887).

19 Discussions of papers in *Statsøkonomisk Tidsskrift* were stenographed in the meetings and printed in the journal. This discussion is printed in the journal of 1887, 76–9.

20 Aschehoug says in the discussions, 'Trykkende tider for alle? – ja, for alle driftsherrer. Der er ogsaa trykkede tider for kapitalisterne [...]. Men der er ikke trykkede tider for arbeidsklassen.'

21 Quote from the discussion: 'at der egentlig foregaar en stor omvæltning i indtægts- og formuesfordelingen i de civiliserede samfund, idet driftsherrer og kapitalister faar en mindre andel av udbyttet, mendens arbeiderklassen faar en større.'

22 Aschehoug, *Socialøkonomik*, vol. 2, chap. 45, § 1, 239.

23 See later paragraph about entrepreneurs.

24 Aschehoug, *Socialøkonomik*, vol. 4, chap. 87, § 5, 641–2. Aschehoug also mentions that it could be decided publicly through tariff negotiations.

25 Aschehoug. *Socialøkonomik*, vol. 2, chap. 47, § 4, 310–11. 'Man tænkte sig, at lav Arbeidsløn var en Betingelse for billig Produktion og navnlig for stor Exportvirksomhed, en Forestilling, som endnu tildels gjør sig gjældende i Forretningsverdenen.'

26 Aschehoug, *Socialøkonomik*, vol. 2, chap. 47, § 28, 346. 'Godt lønnende Arbeidere ere ved bedre Mod og ivrigere i sin Gjerning. De ere ikke blot Producenter, men udgjøre ogsaa den talrigeste Klasse af Konsumenterne. Jo høiere deres Lønninger ere, desto større Kjøbeevne have de, og desto sikrere Afsætning finde alle de Slags Varer, de forbruge. Dette kommer de Driftsherrer tilgode, som producerer disse Varer.' Aschehoug mentions in a footnote to this statement that economists like Brassey, Brentano and Walker also take his point of view.

27 Aschehoug, *Socialøkonomik*, vol. 2, chap. 47, § 28, 346. 'Arbeidet gjerne er mest effektivt i de Lande, hvor Arbeidslønnen er høi i Forhold til Arbeidstiden, og at Driftsherrerne i saadanne Lande for samme Pengebeløb faa udrettet mere Arbeide end i Lande hvor Arbeidslønnen er lav.'

28 The point is extensively discussed in chapter 98 of *Socialøkonomik*.

29 Aschehoug, *Socialøkonomik*, vol. 4, chap. 88, § 11. 'Naar arbeidslønnen stiger og stadigen holder sig høiere end før, uden at Priserne paa Arbeidernes Forbrugsgjenstande stige i samme grad, kunne Arbeiderne benytte denne Bedringen af deres økonomiske Vilkaar paa forskjellige Maader.'

30 Discussions at the Statsøkonomisk forening about the paper 'Vort landbrugs økonomiske stilling' (About the economic situation of Norwegian farming) by J. Smith, printed in *Statsøkonomisk Tidsskrift*

10 (1896): 217. 'En beskyttelsestold paa landmandsprodukter vilde ramme arbeiderklassen, selv om kornet forblev toldfrit. Naar en arbeiders kaar forbedres, søgte han i almindelighed først at faa sig en bedre bolig, og dernæst forøgede han sin konsumtion af animalsk næring, hvorved hans arbeidskraft og hans energi forøgedes. Det vilde derfor være meget uheldig, om man ved toldpaalæg formindskede arbeidernes konsumtion af animalske fødemidler.'

31 Aschehoug, *Socialøkonomik*, vol. 4, chap. 87, § 6, 643.

32 See also Aschehoug, *Socialøkonomik*, vol. 4, chap. 52, § 12, 455.

33 Quoted in Seip, *Vitenskap og virkelighet*, 212, note 42.
    Balabkins, 'What Did Schäffle Teach Schumpeter', 44. This view is discussed by Schäffle in his *Bau und Leben des sozialen Körpers*, published in 1896.

34 Adam Smith, *The Wealth of Nations* (New York: Bantam Classics, 2003 [1776]), book 5, chap. 1, 987.

35 Aschehoug, *Socialøkonomik*, vol. 2, chap. 51, § 6, 434.

36 Aschehoug, *Socialøkonomik*, vol. 2, chap. 47, § 19, 333. 'ligget under for Trykket av et Forlangende fra Arbeiderne, navlig hvor Forlangendet er udgaaet fra en vel organiseret og talrig Fagforening.'

37 Aschehoug, *Socialøkonomik*, vol. 2, chap. 47, § 19, 353. 'en længere Arbeidstid endog i fri luft siges at være omtrent uudholdelig under Australiens Klimat.'

38 Thorvald Aarum, 'Norwegen, Dänemark und Schweden', in *Die Wirtschaftstheorie der Gegenwart*, ed. Hans Mayer (Vienna: Julius von Springer, 1927), 124. 'Übrigens wird auch, meint er, durch die Tätigkeit der Gewerkvereine auf dasselbe Ziel direkt hingesteuert, und zwar mit Erfolg, da es gelungen ist, eine Verkürzung der täglichen Arbeitszeit Hand in Hand mit Lohnerhöhungen durchzuführen.'

39 Aschehoug, *Socialøkonomik*, vol. 4, chap. 97, § 1, 871. 'de Kræfter, som ere i Bevægelse for at bedre de Ubemidledes økonomiske Kaar'.

40 Aschehoug refers to, among others, *hilfskassen, krankenversicherung, unfallversicherung, invaliditätsversicherung.*

41 Aschehoug uses Palgrave's dictionary and the equivalent, Conrad's *HWB*, and the article 'Arbeiterschutzgesetzgebung', to explain the development.

42 Aschehoug uses many German and British sources in these paragraphs, such as Schmoller, Conrad's *HWB*, Schäffle, Brentano, Palgrave and Trap.

43 Aschehoug, *Socialøkonomik*, vol. 4, chap. 97, § 21, 900–901. 'Derimod er der hos os endu ikke istandbragt nogen Lov hverken om Syge- eller om Invaliditets- og Alderdomsforsikring. Forberedelserne dertil ere dog aldrig stansede.'

44 Aschehoug, *Socialøkonomik*, vol. 4, chap. 90, § 7, 730. 'Mennesker producere ikke for at samle Formue, men for at leve paa menneskeværdig Maade. Endog fra et rent økonomisk Synspunkt kan man gjerne sige, at den personlige Konsumption, naar den ordnes forstandig, er den nyttigste Anvendelse af de økonomiske Goder; thi den tjener da til at vedligeholde, styrke og udvikle det fornemste af alle Produktionsmidler, den menneskelige Arbeidskraft.'

45 Discussions at the Statsøkonomisk forening about the paper 'Om menneskets økonomiske værd' (About the economic value of humans) by A. N. Kiær, printed in *Statsøkonomisk Tidsskrift* 6 (1892): 44–5. 'Vi er her komne ind paa en side av menneskelivet, som vistnok har en vis økonomisk interesse, men hvis væsentlige betydning gaar langt dybere. Hvad man her først og fremst maa vogte sig for, er at begtragte denne gjenstand fra et blot og bart økonomisk standpunkt. Derved vilde man komme ind i store vanskeligheder, idet man da opererede med begreber, som er dannede for menneskelig virksomhed, som gaar ud paa at efhverve og bevare formue, og som ikke passer eller kan komme til at passe paa sider ved det menneskelige liv, hvor disse formaal træder i baggrunden eller endog helt forsvinder. […] Jeg har derfor aldrig kunnet lægge stor vægt paa spørgsmaalet om, hvorvidt et menneskes opdragelse kan siges at have lønnet sig i økonomisk henseende, og som følge heraf heller ikke paa spørgsmaalet om, hvilken rentefod man maatte lægge til grund for beregningen.'

46 Aschehoug, *Socialøkonomik*, vol. 4, chap. 92, § 10, 762. 'Det er nu almindelig anerkjendt, at Staten maa sætte sig som Opgave at drage Omsorg for visse Klasser af Trængende, som ikke

blive hjulpne paa anden Maade. [...] Omtvistet er det derimod, hvorvidt det Offentlige bør sætte sig som Opgave at understøtte Trængende, som vel have kunnet sørge for sig selv, men som senere ere blevne ude af Stand dertil, enten fordi de have mistet sin Arbeidsdygtighed, eller fordi de ikke kunde finde Arbeide.'

47 *Renteutligningssystemet.*

48 Hjælp mod Arbeidsløshed (Help against unemployment); law no. 3, 12 June 1906, om Stats- og Kommunebidrag til norske Arbeidsledighedskasser (about the government and municipal contribution to Norwegian unemployment funds); and law no. 2, 12 June 1906, i hver kommune en opprettelse av et offentlig kontor til formidling av arbeid (in each municipality establish a public office for employment distribution).

49 Aschehoug, *Socialøkonomik*, vol. 4, chap. 101, § 10, 973. 'Almendannelsen formindsker gjennem sin Udvikling og Udbredelse Klasseforskjellen, vækker og styrker Bevidstheden om Ligheden mellom Mennesker.'

50 Aschehoug, *Socialøkonomik*, vol. 2, chap. 47, § 4, 312. 'og selv den stærkeste mand er svag, hvis han kun betragtes og vurderes som en Maskine.'

51 Aschehoug, *Socialøkonomik*, vol. 2, chap. 47, § 18, 330. 'Arbeidstiden har endog for voxne Mænd i gamle Dage saagodtsom overalt i Europa været sat altfor lang (see Brentano, Liesse and Sidney and Beatrice Webb). Baade Farbrikanterne, Godseierne og Bøndene mente, at Arbeiderne udrettede mer, jo længere Arbeidstiden udstraktes. Nu forstaar man, at denne Forestiling er urigtig.'

52 Aschehoug, *Socialøkonomik*, vol. 2, chap. 47, § 4, 310. 'I ældre Tider, da der var forholdsvis Arbeidere nok at faa til at udrette det simpleste Slags Arbeide, og da Lønnen for dem, som ikke kunde paatage sig andet, følgelig var lav, var man tilbøielig til at undervurdere det. Endog Videnskaben var paa Veie til at betragte Legemsarbeiderne som blotte Produktionsredskaber og glemme, at de vare Mennesker og udgjorde Samfundets store Flertal.'

53 Aschehoug, *Socialøkonomik*, vol. 2, chap. 47, § 9, 320. 'Kun den Legemsenergi, som ikke behøves til at vedligeholde Livet, kan anvendes til frivillig ydre Arbeide.'

54 Aschehoug, *Socialøkonomik*, vol. 2, chap. 47, § 2, 308. 'Ethvert Menneskes Arbeidskraft er en begrænset Størrelse. Intet Mennneske kan yde et Arbeide, som overstiger dets Kræfter.'

55 Aschehoug, *Socialøkonomik*, vol. 2, chap. 47, 314–317. Aschehoug uses an article in Palgrave's *Dictionary*, 'Efficiency of Labour', that gives an overview of recent articles, statistics and authors that have investigated this subject in order to make his point.

56 Aschehoug, *Socialøkonomik*, vol. 2, chap. 47, § 8, 318. 'Og tilsidst kommer der et Tidspunkt, da Anstrengelsen bliver uudholdelig eller endog ganske umulig og Trangen til Hvile uimodstaaelig.'

57 The first ideas for this section were brought forth in a symposium at Sørmarka, Oslo, November 2009 to commemorate the 100th anniversary of the death of Aschehoug in 1909. I owe part of this paragraph to my cooperation with Sylvi Endresen.

58 As treated in chap. 47, 'The human labour'.

59 Positivism refers to a set of epistemological perspectives and philosophies of science which hold that the scientific method is the best approach to uncovering the processes by which both physical and human events occur.

60 Aschehoug, *Socialøkonomik*, vol. 2, chap. 47, § 11, 323. Arbeidsmøie, Tid og Intensitet. 'bliver Arbeidsmøien, mathematisk seet, en Funktion af [...] Arbeidstiden og Arbeidsintensiteten.'

61 Aschehoug, *Socialøkonomik*, vol. 2, chap. 47, § 24, 341. 'I nogen Grad vilde dette rettes, hvis det lykkedes at bibringe den store Almenhed og hermed ogsaa Arbeidstanden bedre Indsigt i Sundhedspleien, større Kjendskab til de forskjellige Fødemidlers Næringsværdi og større Forstand paa disse Tillavning. Men selv i Vore Tider er der mange, som savne tilstrækkelig Evne til at kjøbe de Fødemidler, de helst burde have. Ere disse Personer arbeidsdygtige, ligger Hjælpen kun I en høiere Arbeidsløn.'

62 Aschehoug, *Socialøkonomik*, vol. 2, chap. 47, § 15, 328. 'Forlænges Arbeid ud over den rette Grænse, slider man sig for tidlig ud. Livet bliver for eensformigt og glædesløst. Man lever ikke

blot for at udrette økonomisk Arbeide, men for at opfylde sine Pligter mod sin Familie og mod sit Land samt at fremme sit eget Aandsliv. Ogsaa disse Livsøiemed tage nødvendigen Tid i Beslag. Men paa den anden Side staa dog Hensyn, som ogsaa ere af stor Vægt. Saafremt Arbeidstiden forkortes for meget, producers der for lidet, og hverken Individets eller Samfundets Behov blive i saa Fald tilfredsstillede i ønskelig Grad.'

63 See discussion in Aschehoug, *Socialøkonomik*, vol. 2, chap. 47, § 21. 'De Fleste vilde vel anse det som en stor Anbefaling for 8 Timers Normalarbeidsdag, om den kunde fjerne eller i væsentlig Grad formindsket denne Ujevnhed i Efterspørgselen efter Arbeid. Vexlingen mellem gode og slette Tider ønskes ligesaa lidet af Driftsherrernes som af Arbeidernes store Flertal.'

64 Aschehoug, *Socialøkonomik*, vol. 2, chap. 47, § 22, 339. 'Erfaring har vist, at 8 Timers Arbeidsdagen efterhaanden i alle Bedrifter, hvor den medfører overveiende Gavn for de deri Interesserede, vinder stigende Utberedelse ad de frivillige Overenskomsters Vei.'

65 Aarum, 'Norwegen, Dänemark und Schweden', 124. 'Auf die Arbeit als Primäre Form der Kosten angewendet, wird dieser Zusammenhang auch nicht bestritten, und selbst Böhm-Bawerk gibt zu, daß die Arbeitsmühe Einfluß auf den Wert überall da ausübt, wo der Arbeiter frei ist und seine Arbeitszeit nach Belieben wählen kann. Dies ist jedoch seiner Meinung nach nicht der Fall unter der arbeitsteiligen Anordnung der Produktion, wo der Arbeiter sich nach der festgesetzten Arbeitszeit und den sonstigen Bedingungen der Arbeit einrichten muß. Demgegenüber wendet Aschehoug ein, daß selbst wenn der Arbeiter nicht auf die Länge des Arbeitstages einwirken könne, er doch im großen Ganzen über die Intensität der Arbeit Herr sei und durch Änderung dieser im Stande sei, eine Anpassung der Arbeitsmühe an die Entlohnung herbeizuführen.'

66 Aschehoug, *Socialøkonomik*, vol. 2, chap. 47, § 28, 347. 'Arbeid maa for saa vidt betragtes som en Vare. Enhver kyndig Mand forstaar, at det ofte lønner sig bedre at kjøbe kostbarere, men bedre Tøi fremfor billigt og daarligt.'

67 Aschehoug, *Socialøkonomik*, vol. 2, chap. 47, § 4, 312. 'De med saakaldt legemligt Arbeide sysselsatte Mennesker gjøre sig derfor Uret, hvis de betragte sig selv som Maskiner og sætte sin økonomiske Betydning i sin Muskelkraft.'

Chapter 10   The Entrepreneur: The Fourth Production Factor

1 Aschehoug, *Socialøkonomik*, vol. 1, part 4, chap. 27, § 13, 510–512. 'Hvilke slags Erhvervsvirksomheder en Kommune bør kaste sig ind i eller forbeholde sig, er et spørgsmaal, som maa afgjøres efter de forhaandenværende Omstændigheder. […] Hvis en Erhvervsvirksomhed allerede drives af Private til rimelige Priser og paa en for Kunden iøvrigt tilfredsstillende Maade, er der sjelden tilstrækkelig Føie for en Kommune til at kaste sig ind i Konkurrance med de private Driftsherrer. […] Det er da ogsaa sjelden, der for Alvor bliver Tale om, at en Kommune for Gevinstens Skyld skal indlade sig paa frie Erhvervsvirksomheder til Fortrængsel for private Driftsherrer eller i Konkurrence med dem. Af og til fremkastes der i fremmede Lande Ønsker f. ex. om, at en Kommune skal oprette Bageri for at forskyne Befolkningen med godt Brød til billigst mulige Priser. Men den almindelige Mening stiller sig gjerne afgjort ugunstig mod deslige Idéer.'

2 Arild Sæther and Ib E. Eriksen, 'Aschehoug and the Role of Entrepreneurship: A Key Factor Lost in Neo-Classical Economics', presentation at the Sørmarka seminar (University of Agder, November 2009). The paper and the Sørmarka presentation have inspired me to investigate how the entrepreneur was adopted and seen by the Norwegian economists of the nineteenth century.

3 Aschehoug, *Socialøkonomik*, vol. 2, part 6, chap. 50, § 1.

4 Kåre Amundsen, *Norsk sosialøkonomisk historie, 1814–1890* (Oslo: Universitetsforlaget, 1963), 132–3.

5 Say is also treated separately in Chapter 8 on the French influence.

6 Arild Sæther, 'Jean-Baptiste Say's Influence in Norway', 186–90.

7 Ib E. Eriksen and Arild Sæther, 'Hvor ble de av entreprenøren i norsk samfunnsøkonomi?', *Norsk økonomisk tidsskrift* 124 (2010): 6

8 Jean-Baptiste Say, *Traité d'economie politique*, book 1, chap. 14. Online: http://www.librairal. org/wiki/Jean-Baptiste_Say:Trait%C3%A9_d'%C3%A9conomie_politique_-_Livre_I_-_ Chapitre_XIV (accessed 3 June 2013).

9 Eriksen and Sæther, 'Hvor ble det av entreprenøren i norsk samfunnsøkonomi?', 2. Eriksen and Sæther quote the British translation by C. R. Prinsep of Say's term entrepreneur: 'The term entrepreneur is difficult to render in English; the corresponding word, undertaker, being already appropriated to a limited sense. It signifies [...] the person who takes upon himself the immediate responsibility, risk, and conduct of concern of industry, whatever upon his own or borrowed capital. For want of a better word, it will be rendered into English by the term adventurer.'

10 Aschehoug, *Socialøkonomik*, vol. 2, part 6, chap. 50, § 1, 409–10.

11 Schumpeter, *History of Economic Analysis*, 555.

12 Jean-Baptiste Say, *Traité d'economie politique*, book 2, chap. 7, part 3. Online: http://www.librairal. org/wiki/Jean-Baptiste_Say:Trait%C3%A9_d'%C3%A9conomie_politique_-_Livre_II_-_ Chapitre_VII (accessed 10 February 2011).

13 Jean-Baptiste Say, *Traité d'economie politique*, book 2, chap. 7, part 3. Online: http://www.librairal. org/wiki/Jean-Baptiste_Say:Trait%C3%A9_d'%C3%A9conomie_politique_-_Livre_II_-_ Chapitre_VII (accessed 10 February 2011).

14 An analysis of Schweigaard's adoption of this distinction is found in Amundsen, *Norsk sosialøkonomisk historie, 1814–1890*, 96. For Aschehoug, see *Socialøkonomik*, vol. 4, part 8, chap. 83, § 2, 524. 'Naarman i Forretningsverdenen taler om Driftsherrer, tænker man paa dem, der drive Erhvervsvirksomhed i nogelunde stor Maalestok, saaledes at den faar merkbar Betydning for Andre end dem selv. Dette er naturligt, hvor det gjælder at paavise Viktigheden af den Rolle, Driftsherrerne spille i Samfundets Økonomi. Men Fordelingslæren skal forklare, hvilken Andel af dettes Indtægt der tilfalder alle selvstændige Næringsdrivende, hvad enten de virke i stor eller liden Maalestok, kun til eget Forbrug eller til Salg, kun ved egne Midler eller tillige med leiede Arbeidere.'

15 For a further analysis of the Say tradition in Norway before Schweigaard see Sæther, 'Jean-Baptiste Say's Influence in Norway' and also Eriksen and Sæther, 'Hvor ble det av entreprenøren i norsk samfunnsøkonomi?'.

16 Schweigaard, *Ungdomsarbeider*, 'Om Produktionen', 15–16. 'Utbyttet av menneskelig Arbeide er ikke alene afhængigt af dets Styrke og udholdenhed, men i en vesentlig Grad ogsaa af den Indsigt, hvoraf det ledes, og af den Frihed for forstyrrende Indvirkninger, under hvilken den foregaar. Dette viser sig især tydelig deri, at naar en Virksomhed antager en mer sammensat Skikkelse, saa maa dens Ledelse ovedrages til en særskilt Styrer, der selv ikke deltager i det legemlige Arbeide, men hvis Virksomhed dog i strængeste Forstand er produktiv, da Foretagendets heldige Gang væsentligen beror paa ham.'

17 Anton Martin Schweigaard, 'Om Produktionen', in *Ungdomsarbeider*, ed. Oscar Jaeger and Frederik Stang (Kristiania: Aschehoug, 1904), 25. 'Kapitalens Akkumulation fremkalder en Mangfoldighed af Virksomheder, der i sin mere fuldendte og kunstmæssige Skikkelse ikke lykkes uden med Bidstand af Personer, der ere udrustede med store Indsigt og Færdighed og derfor kunne gjøre Fordringer paa en store Andel i Udbyttet, og forsaavidt virker Kapitalens Anvendelse til at skabe et større Antal af bedre Samfundsstillinger selv for den Ubemidlede.'

18 Eriksen and Sæther, 'Hvor ble det av entreprenøren i norsk samfunnsøkonomi?', 9.

19 Anton Martin Schweigaard, 'Driftsherreindtægt', in *Ungdomsarbeider*, ed. Oscar Jaeger and Frederik Stang (Kristiania: Aschehoug, 1904), 105. 'De, der stille sig i Spidsen for økonomiske Foretagender, hvortil en mærkelig Del Kapital fordres, saasom Skibsrederi, Fabrikdrift, Handel, Jordbrug, vinde i Gjennemsnit deraf et Udbytte udover Renten af de anvendte Virkemidler, hvilket Udbytte udover Renten af de anvendte Virkemidler, hvilket Udbytte vi

ovenfor have kaldt Driftsherreindtægt. Uagtet denne Næringsindtægt kan ansees som Vederlag for Driftsherrens Arbeide og Møie, hvilken Begtragtningsmaades Rigtighed fornemmeligen viser sig deri, at Driftens heldige gang især beror paa hans Duelighed og Virksomhed, saa vilde man dog ikke danne sig et fuldverdig Begreb om Tingen ved ganske at sætte denne Indtægt i Klasse med Arbeidslønnen, da den Størrelse saa væsentligt er afhengig af den anvendte Kapital.'

20 Amundsen, *Norsk sosialøkonomisk historie, 1814–1890*, 132–3.

21 Schweigaard, 'Driftsherreindtægt', 106.

22 The point is taken from Sæther's presentation at the Sørmarka conference.

23 Sæther and Eriksen, 'Aschehoug and the Role of Entrepreneurship', in Eriksen and Sæther, 'Hvor ble det av entreprenøren i norsk samfunnsøkonomi?'. Morgenstierne's views are also quoted (from 1891), showing that he had the same opinion on the theory and importance of the entrepreneur (10–11).

24 Aschehoug, *Socialøkonomik*, vol. 2, part 6, chap. 50, § 1, 410. 'Man har kaldt dem Produktionens Høvdinger'.

25 Aschehoug, *Socialøkonomik*, vol. 2, part 6, chap. 50, § 2, 411. 'I Driftsherrernes inbyrdes Konkurrence er det altid Dygtigheden, ikke Kapitalrigdommen som i Længden gjør Udslaget, ihvorvel denne Dyktighedens Haand ofte betrygger Seieren.'

26 Aschehoug, *Socialøkonomik*, vol. 2, part 6, chap. 45, § 5, 243–4.

27 Aschehoug, *Socialøkonomik*, vol. 2, part 6, chap. 45, § 5, 243, 245. 'Alt vel overveiet, tør der alligevel være mest Grund til at omhandle Forretningstalentet som særegen Produktionsfaktor. Af alt aandeligt Arbeide er Bedriftsorganisasjonen og Bedriftsledelsen af den mest umiddelbare Betydning for Produktions- og Erhvervsvirksomheten.'

28 Sæther and Eriksen, 'Aschehoug and the Role of Entrepreneurship', 3.

29 Aschehoug, *Socialøkonomik*, vol. 2, part 6, chap. 50, § 2, 410. 'For at den skal blive kraftig, maa den de være tilstede i passende Forhold, af fornøden Brugbarhed og bringes i hensiktsmæssig Forbindelse med hverandre. Dette er Driftsherrenes Sag. Og heri ligger det stærkeste Forsvar for en Systematik, der nævner Forretningstalentet som Produktionsmiddel ved Siden av Naturen, Arbeidet og Kapitalen.'

30 Aschehoug, *Socialøkonomik*, vol. 2, part 6, chap. 50, § 2, 412–13.

31 Aschehoug, *Socialøkonomik*, vol. 2, part 6, chap. 50, § 2, 413.

32 Aschehoug, *Socialøkonomik*, vol. 1, part 1, chap. 1.

33 Aschehoug, *Socialøkonomik*, vol. 4, part 8, chap. 83, § 3, 526.

34 Aschehoug, *Socialøkonomik*, vol. 4, part 8, chap. 83, § 3, 526.

35 Aschehoug, *Socialøkonomik*, vol. 2, part 6, chap. 49, § 13, 409.

36 Aschehoug, *Socialøkonomik*, vol. 4, part 8, chap. 83, § 7, 531. 'Under begrebet Arbeidsløn vil denne Theori henregne hele den Godtgjørelse, Driftsherren kan beregne sig ikke blot for Udførelsen af almindeligt Arbeide, men ogsaa for Planlæggelse, Iværksettelse og Ledelse af Bedriften. Thi ogsaa dette Arbeidet kan udføres af Andre end den egentlige Driftsherre. Dette kommer klart tilsyne ved Aktieselskaberne. I ethvert saadant er det selve Selskabet, altsaa alle Aktieeiere tilsammentagne, som er Driftsherre. Det bærer Risikoen for Forretningens Gang. Gaar den uheldigt, taber Aktieselskabet sin Kapital; gaar det heldigt, faar Aktieeierne Dividende, det vil sige Driftsherregevinst. Men Aktieeierne styre ikke Forretningen. Dette Hverv er overdraget en Direktion med eller uden Bistand af en enkelt Mand, en Direktør. Den særskilte Godtgjørelse, Bestyrerne erholde for Ledelsen af Virksomheden, er Arbeidsløn.'

37 Aschehoug, *Socialøkonomik*, vol. 2, part 6, chap. 50, § 6, 417.

38 Aschehoug, *Socialøkonomik*, vol. 2, part 6, chap. 50, § 7, 419. 'Bestyrelsen af et Aktieselskab har ikke samme økonomiske Interesse af, at Forretningen gaar godt, som en Enkeltmand vilde have, om han eiede den, og endnu mindre samme Tab, om den gaar uheldigt. De større Aktieselskaber søge i nogen Grad at bøde herpaa ved at give sine Bestyrere ikke alene høi Løn, men ogsaa en Brøkdel (Tantieme) af Selskabets Nettofortjeneste i sidste Regnskabsaar. Men det er langtfra,

at dette System sikrer Selskaberne Styrere, der ere ligesaa dygtige og kraftfulde som de bedste private Driftsherrer. [...] De smaa Selskaber, hvis Aktier ere fordelte paa mange Hænder og saaledes, at intet Medlem har nogen stor Interesse af Driften, blive ofte meget slet styrede.'

39 Aschehoug, *Socialøkonomik*, vol. 4, part 8, chap. 82, § 2, 517. 'I Almindelighed eier en Driftsherre nogen del af den Kapital han har sysselsat i sin Bedrift. I ældre Tider under mindre udviklede Kreditforhold var det almindeligvis Tilfælde, at han eiede den væsentlige Del af Kapitalen, og paa Grund heraf var det, Adam Smith [...] betragtede Driftsherrerne væsentlig som Kapitalister og slog deres Andele i Virksomhedens Afkastning sammen under den fælles Benævnelse Profit [...] senere Tid, efterat det er blevet Flere, som blot udlaane sine Kapitaler og leve af Renterne, og paa den anden Side almindeligere, at Driftsherrer laane den største Del af sine Driftskapitaler. Det er blevet tydeligere, at de to forskjellige Funktioner, den ene at opspare Kapitalen, den anden at bringe den til produktiv Anvendelse, at det er to forskjellige Samfundsklasser, som gjøre det, og at deres Andele i Virksomhedens Afkastning bero paa meget forskjellige Omstændigheder. Sammenblandingen av Kapitalrente og Driftsherreindtægt har givet Anledning til den Forestilling, at det er med Kapitalisterne, Arbeiderne have sin fornemste Interessekamp. Det er dog ikke med Kapitalisterne, men med Driftsherrerne, Arbeiderne kjæmpe om sin Løn.'

40 Aschehoug, *Socialøkonomik*, vol. 4, part 8, chap. 82, § 4, 518.

41 Jürgen Backhaus, 'Unternehmer in Wirtschaft und Politik', Serie A, no. 152, July 1980, 11. 'Insbesondere im Hinblick auf die Theorie des Unternehmergewinns ist die Feststellung wesentlich, daß Unternehmer und Kapitalgeber durchaus nicht identisch sein müssen.'

42 Backhaus, 'Unternehmer in Wirtschaft und Politik', 11–12.

43 Backhaus, 'Unternehmer in Wirtschaft und Politik', 10.

44 Backhaus, 'Unternehmer in Wirtschaft und Politik', 10.

45 Aschehoug, *Socialøkonomik*, vol. 4, part 8, chap. 82, § 6, 520–21. '[alle fire produksjonsfaktorer] staa altsaa i et særeget Forhold til hverandre, idet de danne komplementære Goder, medens ethvert af dem ialfald i nogen Grad kan substitueres for et eller flere af de øvrige. Deres Værdi og Priser afhænge af de ved deres Hjælp frembragte Produkters Værdi. Hvorledes denne skal fordeles mellem Yderne af de dertil anvendte Produktionsmidler, er et Spørgsmaal af saa stor Betydning for Socialøkonomiken, at det fortjener at behandles som et af dens Hovedproblemer.'

46 Aschehoug, *Socialøkonomik*, vol. 4, par 8, chap. 83, § 1, 522.

47 Anne-Lise Seip, *Vitenskap og virkelighet: Sosiale, økonomiske og politiske teorier hos T. H. Aschehoug 1845–1882* (Oslo: Gyldendal, 1975), 70. Quotes taken from a variety of articles and reports during the 1850s.

48 Statistics quoted in Aschehoug, *Socialøkonomik*, vol. 2, part 6, chap. 52, § 17, 465.

49 Aschehoug, *Socialøkonomik*, vol. 2, part 6, chap. 52, § 21, 476. 'Mange nære den Tro, at den lille Industri vil lettes derved, at den navnligen gjennem Elektriciteten kan skaffe sig billig Drivkraft for de smaa Maskiner, den kan behøve. Andre betviler dette, fordi Driften alltid bliver forholdsvis dyrere, naar Maskinerne ere smaa, end naar de ere store. Nogen Lettelse maa dog den nævnte Omstendighed medføre. Hvor stor Betyning den i saa Henseende vil faa, kan kun Tiden vise.'

50 Aschehoug, *Socialøkonomik*, vol. 2, part 6, chap. 52, § 235, 497–8. 'Slutligen bemærkes, at Trustorganisationen kun er anvendelig i Bedrifter, som egne sig til at drives i meget stor Maalestok. Efter hvad der overfor er forklaret, er dette ikke Tilfældet engang med alle Stofforædlingsvirksomheder. Den lille Industri vil efter all sandsynlighed hævde sin Plads i Fremtidens Økonomi. Udenfor den egentlige Industri gives der vistnok Næringsveie, som drives bedst i stor Maalestok og kunne overtages af Stat eller Kommune. [...] Men om den vigtigste af alle Næringsveie, det egentlige Agerbrug, gjælder dette ikke. Og saalenge dette er Tilfældet, kommer de individuelle Driftsherrer til i det Store taget at raade i Samfundsøkonomien.'

51 I owe the analysis here to the insights of Eriksen and Sæther in their recent article 'Hvor ble det av entreprenøren i norsk samfunnsøkonomi?' and to discussions with Professor Sæther.

52 Morgenstierne quoted in Sæther and Eriksen, 10.

53 Morgenstierne quoted in Sæther and Eriksen, 15.

54 Jaeger quoted in Sæther and Eriksen, 18.

55 Aarum quoted in Sæther and Eriksen, 27.

56 Quote from Sæther and Eriksen, 28.

57 Textbooks mostly from published in the US appearing in curriculums of economics.

Chapter 11   Trade and Customs Debates from 1840 to 1906

1 Rune Slagstad, *De nasjonale strateger* (Oslo: Pax, 2001), 66.

2 Slagstad, *De nasjonale strateger*, 66. 'Etter sitt møte med engelsk liberalisme doserte Aschehoug for sine studenter høsten 1848 en ideologi som var mer i slekt med Hegels statslære enn med Adam Smiths laissez-faire. Aschehoug viste til det nye syn på staten som var brutt frem i "den aller seneste tid", i kontrast til den foreldede oppfatningen av staten som en "nyttig" sammenslutning, Staten var ifølge Aschehoug "en nødvendig Form for Menneskeaandens ydre Aabenbarelse, en Organisme, et virkelig Individ, ikke sammenfaldende med det fysiske Individ, men analogt med dette".'

3 Anton Michael Schweigaard, 'Forelæsninger over den politiske økonomi', in *Ungdomsarbeider*, ed. Oscar Jaeger and Frederik Stang (Kristiania: Aschehoug, 1904), 10.

4 Schweigaard, 'Forelæsninger over den politiske økonomi', 4.

5 Wilhelm Keilhau, *Den økonomiske og den politiske liberalisme* (Oslo: Universitets studentkontor, 1948), 27.

6 Fritz Hodne and Ola Honningdal Grytten, *Norsk økonomi i det nittende århundre* (Bergen: Fagbokforlaget, 2000), 141.

7 Aschehoug, *Socialøkonomik*, vol. 3, part 9, chap. 80, § 8, 464. 'Statsstyrelsen brød med Merkantilismen ved Forordningen af 1ste Februar 1797. Denne gik vel i afgjort frihandlersk Retning, men bibeholdt dog en vis moderat Beskyttelse for den indenlandske Industri.'

8 Keilhau, *Den økonomiske og den politiske liberalisme*.

9 Aschehoug, *Socialøkonomik*, vol. 3, part 9, chap. 80, § 9, 466. 'Da Norge herved havde tabt Toldbeskyttelsen i Sverige og saa sin Indførsel derhen i høi Grad indskrænket, erkjendtes det af Alle, endog av af de varmeste Frihandelsvenner, at Norge maatte beskytte sine produktive Virksomheder mod Konkurrencen fra Sverige.'

10 Keilhau, *Den økonomiske og den politiske liberalisme*, 25.

11 Ole Mestad, 'Schweigaard og den franske traktatsak 1865', in *Anton Martin Schweigaard: Professorpolitikeren*, ed. Ole Mestad (Oslo: Akademisk publisering, 2009), 229.

12 Aschehoug, *Socialøkonomik*, vol. 2, part 5, chap. 37, § 1, 133. 'lærte den klassiske skole [...] at deres Værdi beror paa de komparative Produktionsomkostninger [...] International Handel var opprinnelig Tuskhandel [...] Og Forholdet mellem begge Varers Produktionsomkostninger paavirker igjen Produktionsvirksomheden i begge Lande. [...] Landet maa derfor anvende dem paa den fordelagtigst mulig Maade, altsaa i de Næringsveie som give den værdifuldeste Afkastning i Forhold til de anvendte Produktionsopofrelser.'

13 He quotes Sidgwick, Nicholson, Bastable, Edgeworth, Palgrave's *Dictionary*, Cournot, Cherbuliez, Jourdan, Cauwès, Block, Rau, Mangoldt, Roscher, Held, Marshall and Pantaleoni.

14 Keilhau, *Den økonomiske og den politiske liberalisme*, 4. 'På dette området kan en si at den liberalistiske ideologi hadde hele sitt grunnlag i eller endog falt sammen med den frihandelsteori som ble utviklet av den klassiske skole i britisk økonomi.'

15 Aschehoug, *Socialøkonomik*, vol. 2, part 5, chap. 37, § 4, 139. 'Den nuværende Verdenshandel ser imidlertid ganske annerledes ud. Saagodtsom alle Lande ere dragne ind i Samhandelen. Den omfatter en stor Mængde Varer, nemlig alle dem der taale Transport. Og den omfatter ikke blot materielle Gjenstande, men ogsaa Tjeneste.'

16 Mentioned by Aschehoug in chapter 54, also mentioned by recent economic historians as an important factor of industrialization.

17 Aschehoug, *Socialøkonomik*, vol. 2, part 6, chap. 54, § 20, 574. 'Allervigtigst er dog maaske, at det er Samfærdselen, som bærer tanken om Verdensfreden. For hundrede Aar siden næredes Tanken kun af de største Aander samt af de vildeste Drømmere. Nu er den bleven en anerkjendt praktisk Opgave for Statsmændene. Den vil neppe nogensinde opgives, og det er aabenbart Samfærdselen, som holder Liv i den.' Keilhau, *Den økonomiske og den politiske liberalisme*, 25. 'Alt i bevegelsens [liberalismens] første tid tok de derfor opp et kraftig arbeid for å fremme freden mellom folkene. Frihandel og fredssak hører sammen.'

18 Aschehoug, *Socialøkonomik*, vol. 3, part 9, chap. 78, § 4, 436.

19 Aschehoug, *Socialøkonomik*, vol. 3, part 9, chap. 80, § 2, 455.

20 Aschehoug, *Socialøkonomik*, vol. 3, part 9, chap. 80, § 7, 464. 'Den almindelige Mening i Storbritannien holder endnu fast ved Frihandelen. Dens Tilhængere vandt nemlig ved Valgene til Underhuset i Januar 1906 en overraskende stor Seir. [...] Baade Norge og de øvrige skandinaviske Stater have selvfølgelig al Grund at ønske, at Storbritannien opretholder sin nuværende Handelspolitik.'

21 Keilhau, *Den økonomiske og den politiske liberalisme*, 45.

22 Aschehoug, *Socialøkonomik*, vol. 3, part 9, chap. 80, § 2, 455–6.

23 Aschehoug, *Socialøkonomik*, vol. 3, part 9, chap. 80, § 1, 452, note 1. 'Schmoller, *Grundriss*, Bog IV, Afsnitt 3, hvor han søger at paavise, at den ældre Merkantilisme vel var hensynsløs, men at den for sin Tid har havt sin Berettigelse, samt at det moderne Beskyttelsessystem under visse Betingelser endnu er at foretrække for Frihandel. [...] Det bedste Hjælpemiddel til Studiet af den ydre Handelspolitik have vi i W. Scharling, *Handels- og Toldpolitik*.' The German customs debates are also commented on by Harald Hagemann in his essay on the Verein für Sozialpolitik.

24 Aschehoug, *Socialøkonomik*, vol. 3, part 9, chap. 80, § 17, 476–7.

25 Aschehoug, *Socialøkonomik*, vol. 3, part 9, chap. 80, § 5, 460.

26 Aschehoug, *Socialøkonomik*, vol. 3, part 9, chap. 80, § 2, 457. 'Denne Bevægelse indeholdt en Nærmelse til Frihandelssystemet og sluttede sig naturligen til de store Fremskridt, Samfærdselsmidlerne gjorde. Det fremstillede sig lettelig som en Selvmodsigelse at bygge Jernbanelinier og Dampskibe i mængdevis, men samtidigt holde fast ved en Handelspolitik, som hemmede deres Benyttelse til international Vareførsel.'

27 Aschehoug, *Socialøkonomik*, vol. 3, part 9, chap. 80, § 15, 474. 'Frihandlerne mene, at man bør overlade private Driftsherrer paa egen Haand, uden Beskyttelse at anstille saadanne Forsøg. Det kan da ventes, at de blive anstillede med størst Omhu og Kraft. Beskyttelsesmændene mene, at Staten maa lette dem Forsøgene.'

28 From the preparatory works, 'Betænkning og udkast til en lov om handelen' from 1841. 'udelukkende bestaae i at ophæve gjældende Indskrænkninger og ikke i at indføre nye.'

29 Schweigaard, 'Forelæsninger over den politiske Økonomi', 17–18. 'Den virkelige Statspraxis er dog herfra forskjellig, idet den ved Anvendelse af de Midler til at paavirke Produktionen, hvilke den har til sin Raadighed. [...] For Overgangstiden vil den praktiske Regel være at styrke, hvad der er svagt, og at fremhjælpe, hvad er har Begyndelsens Vanskeligheder at overvinde.'

30 Aschehoug, report of the Poverty Commission (*Fattigkommisjonens betenkning*) (1856). 'simpel Retfærdighed kræver at der gjøres saa liden Indskrænkning som muligt i Adgangen til at ernære sig ved egne hender.'

31 Mestad, 'Schweigaard og den franske traktatsak 1865', 270. 'det almindelige europæiske Samfund med Hensyn til Magten paa Havet.'

32 Trond Bergh and Tore J. Hanisch, *Vitenskap og politikk: Linjer i norsk sosialøkonomi gjennom 150 år* (Oslo: Aschehoug, 1984), 86.

33 Sejersted, *Demokratisk kapitalisme*, 238–9. Generally, Sejersted draws a picture of the trade and customs development during the nineteenth century that corresponds to the main ideas in this chapter. His focus is more on economic facts, and he analyses different industries and their development.

34 Aschehoug in *Stortingstidende* from 1879: 'For nogle Aar siden var Stemningen for Frihandelssystemet i mange andre Lande og navnlig her hos os saa stærk, at jeg virkelig ikke troede, at jeg nogensinde skulde behøve at tage Del i en Debat om dette System og forsvare dets Fortrin.'

35 Aschehoug in *Stortingstidende* (annual governmental report) from 1879: 'det er mig utfatteligt, hvorledes man kan ville tilskrive Frihandelen nogen Andel i dette Tryk.'

36 *Stortingsproposition* 5 (1879).

37 *Stortingsproposition* 5 (1879). And the purpose is stated: 'Den indenlanske Industris fremtidige stilling ligeoverfor Toldbefatningen, som det naa er magtpaaliggende at søge fjernet [...] paa Sagens nuværende Trin være nødfanget til at indskrænke sig til theorietiske Undersøgelser, der neppe kunde være fuldt ud tilfredsstillende for Øiemedet eller ventes at indeholde tilstrækkelig Beroligelse liegoverfor de Tvivl, som paa dette Feldt synes for Tiden at have vundet en ikke ringe Udbredelse blandt de i denne Sag nærmest og mest direkte Interesserede.'

38 Anne-Lise Seip, *Vitenskap og virkelighet: Sosiale, økonomiske og politiske teorier hos T. H. Aschehoug 1845–1882* (Oslo: Gyldendal, 1975), 196. Seip is quoting Aschehoug's opinions in *Stortingstidende* from 1873.

39 The eight elected pro–free trade members in this commission were the chairman, Aschehoug, customs inspector Andersen, consul Christian Christiansen, professor Ebbe Hertzberg, apothecary Hvoslef, secretary Isachsen, farmer Lindstøl and stadshauptman Onsum. The drafts were written by Hertzberg, but they were finished by Aschehoug and other commission members, and the result must be seen as a joint declaration.

40 Wilhelm Keilhau, *Det norske folks liv og historie gjennem tidene: tidsrummet fra omkring 1875 til omkring 1920*, vol. 10 (Oslo: Aschehoug, 1935), 348. 'Det viste seg at den hadde et frihandelsvennlig flertall på 8 medlemmer med Aschehoug og Ebbe Hertzberg i spissen, mens 7 medlemmer holdt på beskyttelse. Likevel blev innstillingen samlet, idet – som premissene sier – begge fraksjoner var 'enige om utilrådeligheten av å gjøre noen prinsipiell forandring i vår innførselstolltariff.'

41 Seip, *Vitenskap og virkelighet*, 196.

42 These arguments are found in the different propositions, the commission report and the debates in the parliament between 1879 and 1881. My summary here builds on quotes found in Seip.

43 Keilhau, *Det norske folks liv og historie gjennem tidene*, 348.

44 Bredo Morgenstierne, 'Vor handelspolitik', *Statsøkonomisk Tidsskrift* 17 (1903), 97. 'Vore næringsveie eller ialfald flere af dem har i de sidste aar lidt under uheldige konjunkturer, og i saadanne tider melder sig efter al erfaring kravene paa statshjælp, særlig i form af beskyttelsestold eller forøget saaden. Vort toldsystem har jo aldrig været et egentligt frihandelssystem eller fiskalsystem som det engelske. Men det nærmede sig dertil i 1860- til 80-aarene. Saa begyndte fra 1888 saa smaat en vending til nedsættelse af fiskalsatserne og forhøielse af beskyttelsessatserne, indtil vi endelig i 1897, efter mellemrigslovens ophævelse, helt gik over til en protektionistisk tariff. [...] For agrartoldens vedkommende var den indførte beskyttelse noksaa vidtgaaende, om end paa langt nær i samme grad som enkelte andre landes.'

45 Aschehoug, *Socialøkonomik*, vol. 3, part 9, chap. 80, § 9, 465.

46 Aschehoug, *Socialøkonomik*, vol. 3, part 9, chap. 80, § 9, 466. 'Frihandelens Grundsætninger haved ikke tabt sit Hold paa den almindelige Mening. En Forandring heri fandt først Sted ved Mellemrigslovens Ophævelse. Da Norge herved havde tapt Toldbeskyttelsen i Sverige og saa sin Indførsel derhen i høi Grad indskrænket, erkjendtes det af Alle, endog af de varmeste Frihandelsvenner, at Norge maatte beskytte sine produktive Virksomheder mod Konkurrencen fra Sverige.'

47 Morgenstierne, 'Vor handelspolitik', 118–19. 'anser den norsk-svenske mellemrigslovs ophævelse som den største daarskab, der er begaaet i forholdet mellem de to riger [...] der tages lærdom, og at saadanne forholdsregler jo overhovedet alene kunde sigte til at bane veien for overenskomster, der kunde nærme os maalet: det friest mulige handelssamkvem mellem

Nordens folk. [...] Vilde en saadan sammenslutning afhjælpe den anden store hovedmangel ved en norsk protektionisme: hjemmemarkedets snæverhed for selve de beskyttede produktionsgrene.'

48 Morgenstierne, 'Vor handelspolitik', 99.

49 Morgenstierne, 'Vor handelspolitik', 98. 'Dertil er lykkeligvis vore frihandelsmænd altfor lidet doktrinære og forstaar for godt at vurdere fordelene ved stabilitet i toldpolitiken. Der staar med andre ord for tiden ingen aktuel strid mellem principiel toldbeskyttelse og principiel frihandel i vort land. Vi er forsaavidt alle praktisk talt protektionister.'

50 Morgenstierne, 'Vor handelspolitik', 99. 'Jeg gaar da i det følgende ud fra, at alle, som er berettigede til at have nogen mening om disse ting, erkjender, saaledes som f. eks. den engelske premierminister Balfour i sin bekjendte brochure [On Insular Free Trade], at frihandel, det friest mulige handelssamkvem mellem landene, er idealet, og at beskyttelsessystemet altid for et land betyder et tab, et offer af national kraft. Spørgesmaalet er da kun, om eller i hvilken udstrækning dette offer er nødvendigt til forebyggelse af videre større skade.'

51 Morgenstierne, 'Vor handelspolitik', 101.

52 Morgenstierne, 'Vor handelspolitik', 102.

53 Morgenstierne, 'Vor handelspolitik', 106.

54 Statsraad Gunnar Knudsen in the discussions at the Statsøkonomisk forening, printed in *Statsøkonomisk Tidsskrift* 17 (1903), 97ff.: 'Man har jo været vant til her i landet at ga ud fra som et aksiom, at de lærde herrer ved universitetet er og vil vedblive at være frihandelsmænd, ikke alene i principet, men i det hele taget ogsaa i den praktiske utførelse. Det var mig imidlertid en behagelig overraskelse at finde at den gamle opfatning nu er brudt ved universitetet.'

55 Statsraad Gunnar Knudsen, *Statsøkonomisk Tidsskrift* 17 (1903), 97ff.: 'Da bliver det jo spørgsmaal om, hvorledes man kan indrette dette land saaledes, at de flest mulige mennesker kan leve bedst muligt.'

56 General manager of Nydalens kompani, Niels Christian Nielsen, General Manager Sunde and Redaktør (publisher) Sundt.

57 Participant in the discussion in 1903 in Statsøkonomisk forening, printed in *Statsøkonomisk Tidsskrift* 17 (1903).

58 Ebbe Hertzberg in the discussions at the Statsøkonomisk forening, printed in *Statsøkonomisk Tidsskrift* 17 (1903): 'For at slutte med, hvad jeg begyndte, vil jeg gjentage, at man maa se beskyttelsessystemet i lys af den hele statsøkonomiske stilling i landet og udenfor det.'

59 Professor Hertzberg: 'Hvad jeg begyndte med at fremhæve, var imidlertid, at beskyttelsessystemet maatte sees i forbindelse med de nationale og politiske bestræbelser overhovedet. Det staar paa det nøieste i forbindelse med statens financer, og disse staar jo naturligvis atter i intim rapport med statens hele skattevæsen [...] nei, jeg siger: lad os være saa meget frihandelsmænd i principet, som vi vil, lad os indrømme, at de argumenter, hr. Sundt anførte, er saa logisk riktige, de være vil, saa er det dog saaledes at den hele frihandel kommer til at halte, saalenge vi ikke kan bringe de øvrige nationer til ligeledes at være frihandlere lige overfor os. [...] Den selvfølgelige forudsætning for dette system er, at det gjælder for og gjennemføres af alle nationer. Er det ikke tilfælde, maa der skaffes et slags lighed, et slags balance paa anden basis, og det maa da blive en efter omstændighederne afpasset beskyttelse. Jeg kan ikke komme til anden opfatning, end at firhandelen kræver universal frihandel for at svar til sin idé. Men naar de aller fleste nationer ikke har den, og endog den af de større nationer, som hidtil holdt paa den, nemlig England, nu viser sterke tegn til at opgive den, saa er systemet ramlet sammen.'

60 Morgenstierne, 'Vor Handelspolitik', 109. 'Det er sandt, at frihandel er det beste, og at beskyttelsestold i det store og hele er et onde, som et land længst muligt og i størst mulig udstrækning maa holde sig fra livet. Men hvad skal vi gjøre? Vi tvinges jo ligefrem dertil. Naar alle andre stater bliver protektionistiske, maa ogsaa vi følge efter. Vi maa møde udlandet med lige vaaben. [...] Det er ingen tvil om, at vi her staar lige overfor det baade mest anvendte og efter mit skjøn i visse henseender ogsaa det vægtigste argument, det være sig for overgang til

beskyttelse i et land med frihandel, som England, eller for en yderligere befæstelse og forhøielse af toldskrankerne som hos os.'

Chapter 12   The Theory of Economic Crises

1 Aschehoug, *Socialøkonomik*, vol. 4, part 10, chap. 93, § 1, 769.

2 Aschehoug, *Socialøkonomik*, vol. 4, part 10, chap. 94, § 8, 781. 'Betydning for den rette Forstaaelse af Krisernes Aarsager og Virkninger, saavel som for Løsningen af det vigtigste praktiske Spørgsmaal, nemlig hvorvidt denne Ujevnhed i den økonomiske Virksomhed kan forebygges eller dens uheldige Følger mildnes.' See also: chap. 93, § 1, 769.

3 Preben Munthe comments on Einarsen's *Gode og daarlige tider* (1904,) saying that it had a greater originality and provided a fresh, unconventional insight on crises. It had been written quickly for a competition for a post at Copenhagen University; Einarsen's paper won. His analysis consists of two parts: an empirical, showing the last fifty years' history of crises in Denmark and Norway, and a theoretical, discussing different causes of business cycles. Munthe gives credit to both parts. An interesting feature in his theoretical analysis is his division between what he calls impulses and transmission (*impulser* and *forplantninger*). The first one is difficult to explain, but the next one intends to explain how a boom or a burst might transfer from one industry to another, or from one country to another. Munthe claims that the impulse phenomenon was difficult to explain in the beginning of the century: 'Paa en rutschbane kan der dog ikke rutsches op og ned i det uendelige, og dette gjælder ogsaa den økonomiske udviklings rutschbane. Der maa være selvstændige kræfter, der stadig virker og holder de op- og nedadgaaende bevægelser vedlige', the same way the moon attracts the earth and makes the tides. The Swedish economist Knut Wicksell argued that the economy was constantly exposed to arbitrary shocks from the outside, when he continued this thought, and that these shocks were transformed to regular movements. Preben Munthe, biography of Einar Einarsen, Norsk Biografisk Leksikon. Online: http://www.snl.no/.nbl_biografi/Einar_Einarsen/utdypning (accessed 29 July 2010).

4 Among them we find Bergmann, *Die Wirthschaftskrisen* (1895); E. D. Jones, *Economic Crises* (1900); Tugan-Baranowsky, *Studien zur Geschichte und Theorie der Handelskrisen* (1901); Wicksell, 'Krisernas gåta', printed in *Statsøkonomisk Tidsskrift* from 1907; Herkner's article in Conrad's *HWB*, 'Krisen'; Marshall's *Economics of Industry* from 1892, and Pareto's *Cours d'économie politique*.

5 Aschehoug, *Socialøkonomik*, vol. 4, part 10, chap. 94, § 8, 780. 'at den stedfindende Afvexling af Opgangs- og Nedgangstider i Samfundets økonomiske Virksomhed er et overmaade complex Phænomen. Den fremkaldes og paavirkes af en Mængde forskjellige, mere eller mindre væsentlige Aarsager. At udfinde og udrede disse er Forholdets fornemste theoretiske Opgave.'

6 Aschehoug, *Socialøkonomik*, vol. 4, part 10, chap. 95, § 7, 822. 'Bølgebevægelsen har sit dybeste Udspring i den civiliserede Menneskeheds Trang og Evne til at forbedre sin økonomiske Tilstand samt i de eiendommelige Vilkaar, under hvilke denne Fremgang finder sted.'

7 Aschehoug, *Socialøkonomik*, vol. 4, part 10, chap. 94, § 26, 814–15.

8 Aschehoug, *Socialøkonomik*, vol. 4, part 10, chap. 95, § 10, 825. 'Samfundets økonomiske Liv maa betragtes fra et dynamisk Standpunkt, og Fremskridtet viser sig da at være et normalt Phænomen.'

9 Aschehoug, 'De økonomiske kriser og depressioner i det 19de aarhundrede', in *Statsøkonomisk Tidsskrift* 13 (1898): 6. 'Disse kriser ligner hverandre i sine hovedtræk. Naar en næringsvei i nogen tid har givet rigelig afkastning, udbreder gjerne den forestilling sig, at denne tilstand skal vare og kanske endog blive endnu gunstigere.'

10 Aschehoug, 'De økonomiske kriser og depressioner i det 19de aarhundrede', 6–7. See also paragraphs 4 to 7 in chapter 94 of *Socialøkonomik*.

11 See explanations in *Socialøkonomik*, vol. 4, part 10, chap. 94, § 1, 2, 772–4. 'Produktions- eller Afsætningskriser, Pengekriser, Kreditkriser, Varhandelskriser, Børskriser, Spekulationskriser and Agrarkriser.'

248 TORKEL ASCHEHOUG

12 Aschehoug, *Socialøkonomik*, vol. 4, part 10, chap. 94, § 5, 779. 'Naar det saaledes viser sig, at den økonomiske Tilstand er usund, svækkes den almindelige Tillid Mand og Mand imellem. [...] Tilstanden kan forværre sig til en ren Panik, hvorunder alle Kreditomsætninger i Groshandelen standse, og det bliver umuligt selv for solide Næringsdrivende at faa Kredit. Den almindelige Afsætningskrise ledsages da af en Kreditkrise.'

13 Aschehoug, *Socialøkonomik*, vol. 4, part 10, chap. 94, § 5, 783.

14 Jean-Baptiste Say, *Traité d'économie politique*, book 1, chap. 15. Online: http://www.librairal. org/wiki/Jean-Baptiste_Say:Trait%C3%A9_d'%C3%A9conomie_politique_-_Livre_I_-_ Chapitre_XV (accessed 13 February 2011).

15 Schweigaard, *Ungdomsarbeider*, 18–19.

16 Aschehoug, *Socialøkonomik*, vol. 4, part 10, chap. 95, § 15, 833. 'Derimod er det et hyppigt Tilfælde, at hvilketsomhelst Slags Gjenstande produceres i saa stor Mængde, at de, for at blive solgte, maa sælges til saa lave Priser, at disse ikke dække Produktionsomkostningerne. Der er da produceret for meget i Forhold til den effektive Etterspørgsel. Det er en saadan Overproduction, som fremkalder Omvexlingen fra Opgang til Nedgang og den dermed muligens forbunden Krise.' See also: chap. 71, § 18; chap. 72, § 12, 295; and § 15, 299. 'En Seddelbanks første Opgave er at sørge for sin Vederhæftighed og sine Sedlers Indløselighed. Dernæst maa den i gode Tider sanke Kræfter til daarlige Tider at yde de Næringsdrivende den Hjælp, disse ikke kunne faa hos Andre.'

17 Aschehoug, *Socialøkonomik*, vol. 4, part 10, chap. 95, § 2, 816–17.

18 Aschehoug, *Socialøkonomik*, vol. 4, part 10, chap. 95, § 12, 829.

19 Aschehoug, *Socialøkonomik*, vol. 4, part 10, chap. 95, § 13, 831. 'Tugan-Baranowsky har oplyst denne Sætning ved en fra Mekaniken hentet Lignelse, Den frie Laanekapital kan, siger han, sammenlignes med Dampen i en Dampmaskine. Naar Dampens Tryk paa stemplet opnaar den bestemt Styrke, overvinder den Stemplets Modstand, Stemplet bevæger sig til Cylinderens Ende, hvor der aabner sig en fri Udgang for Dampen, og Stemplet vender da tilbage til sin gamle Plads.'

20 Aschehoug, *Socialøkonomik*, vol. 4, part 10, chap. 95, § 14, 832. 'Det er først naar der opstaar Tvivl, om den paatænkte eller fortsatte Bedrift er og forbliver lønnede, Krediten svigter.'

21 This seems to be the view of Aschehoug that he also attributes to Juglar.

22 Aschehoug, *Socialøkonomik*, vol. 4, part 10, chap. 95, 837.

23 Aschehoug, *Socialøkonomik*, vol. 4, part 10, chap. 95, § 18, 838–9. 'Disse forandringer tage Tid. [...] Samfundets økonomiske Virksomhed er overhovedet næsten i alle Stykker behæftet med en Uvished, der gjør Tanken om en proportional Afpasning efter Konsumtionen ugjennemførlig. Herom kan der ikke være mindste Tvil, saalenge Virksomheden foregaar i private Bedrifter. [...] De ville ikke blive vissere, om al økonomisk Virksomhed dreves for offentlig Regning; men Planlæggelsen vilde da blive ulige vanskeligere, fordi den blev saa meget mere omfattende.'

24 Aschehoug, *Socialøkonomik*, vol. 4, part 10, chap. 95, § 19, 839. 'Jo bedre oplyst Almenheden og dens økonomiske Ledere blive om den stedfindende Virksomheds Gang og Resultater, og jo klarere Forstaaelse de faa af Fortidens Erfaringer, desto mere ville de blive istand til at undgaa de Feil, som have fremkaldt eller skjærpet ældre Kriser.'

25 Aschehoug, *Socialøkonomik*, vol. 4, part 10, chap. 95, § 19, 839.

26 Aschehoug, *Socialøkonomik*, vol. 3, part 7, chap. 69, § 8, 231. 'Seddelutstedelsen, bliver godt styret, opretholder den sin Kredit baade indenrigs og udenrigs, ogsaa i kritiske Tider da all andre Banker maa sørge for sig selv og længere vove paa at give nye Lån. Under saadanne Omstændigheder er det af uvurderlig Nytte for Samfundet at have en Bank, der kan hjælpe Forretningsverdenen med Laan, medens ingen anden kan gjøre det.'

27 Einar Lie and Christian Venneslan, *Over evne: Finansdepartementet 1965–1992* (Oslo: Pax forlag, 2010), 214.

28 A short overview of different theories using a historical approach can be found in Erik S. Reinert, 'The Terrible Simplifiers: Common Origins of Financial Crises and Persistent Poverty in Economic Theory and the New "1848 Moment"'; and in Erik S. Reinert, 'Finanskrisenes teori', appendix to *NOU* (Official Norwegian Reports) (2011: 1), *Bedre rustet mot*

finanskriser: Finanskriseutvalgets utredning, 25 January 2011. Reinert has also pointed out different theories that can be found in the work of Aschehoug.

29 Carlota Perez, *Technological Revolutions and Financial Capital: The Dynamics of Bubbles and Golden Ages* (Cheltenham, UK: Edward Elgar, 2002).

30 Perez, introduction to *Technological Revolutions and Financial Capital*. Online: http://www.carlotaperez.org/TRFCbook/TRFCintrod.pdf (accessed 10 January 2011).

31 Quoted from Reinert, 'Finanskrisenes teori', appendix to *NOU* (2011: 1).

32 Aschehoug, *Socialøkonomik*, vol. 4, part 10, chap. 95, § 17, 836. 'At Omslaget i de moderne Samfund saa ofte antager Formen af en Krise, hidrører klarligen derfra, at Bevægelsen i begge Retninger er i høi Grad forstærket ved den almindelige og ofte vovelige Brug av Krediten. Viser det sig under en begynende Opgangsperiode, da der er megen disponibel Kapital, at mange nye Foretagender lønne sig, saa voxer saavel Driftsherrernes Foretagelseslyst som de private Kapitalisters og Bankernes Evne og Trang til at undersøtte dem ved Laan. Under en Opgangsperiode kommer derfor Krediten gjerne til en mere utbredt Anvendelse, som ikke altid er uberettiget, selv om den medfører mærkbar Risiko for Laangiveren. [...] Men mange Banker fristes under saadanne Omstændigheder let til at gaa ud over alle rimelige Grænser.'

Appendix A Other Norwegian Turn-of-the-Century Economists

1 Thorvald Aarum, 'Norwegen, Dänemark und Schweden', in *Die Wirtschaftstheorie der Gegenwart*, ed. Hans Mayer. (Vienna: Julius von Springer, 1927), 127. 'Nebst Aschehoug war 1877 bis 1886 Ebbe Hertzberg als Professor an der Universität zu Oslo tätig. Er hatte bei Professor Knies in Heidelberg studiert und war von der historischen Schule beeinflußt. Seine Arbeiten beschäftigen sich mit dem Zettelbank- und Kreditwesen.'

2 The following are articles and economic works by Hertzberg between 1880 and 1909:
Lecture: 'Behovenes økonomi' (The economy of needs);
Lecture: 'Den statsøkonomiske videnskap' (The science of state economics);
Lecture: 'Vor handelspolitik' (Our trade policy);
Lecture: 'Om norsk næringsliv og økonomi' (About Norwegian industrial and economic life);
Lecture: 'Om sparebankens virksomhed og kassekreditenes anvendelse' (About the activity of saving banks and the use of overdraft facilities);
Lecture: 'Norges statistikk' (Norwegian statistics);
Lecture: 'Konsumtion og befolkning' (Consumption and population);
'Om kredittens begreb og væsen' (About the term credit and how it works), *Statsøkonomisk Tidsskrift* (1877);
'En kritisk fremstilling af grundsætningerne for seddelbankers indretning og virksomhed med særligt hensyn til de skandinaviske seddelbanker i deres nuværende skikkelse' (An analysis of the central banks, their foundation and activity, with special emphasis on Scandinavian banks), *Statsøkonomisk Tidsskrift* (1877);
'Professor Schweigaard i hans offentlige virksomhed: 1832–1870' (Schweigaard and his public affairs 1832–1870), *Statsøkonomisk Tidsskrift* (1883);
'Om udbredelse af socialøkonomisk kundskab' (About the currency of economic knowledge), *Statsøkonomisk Tidsskrift* (1902);
'Beskyttelsesspørgsmaalet, (The protection question), *Statsøkonomisk Tidsskrift* (1904).

3 The analysis of this handwritten lecture is based on the presentation in Trond Bergh and Tore J. Hanisch, *Vitenskap og Politikk: Linjer i norsk sosialøkonomi gjennom 150 år* (Oslo: Aschehoug, 1984), the quote from Hertzberg, 70. 'et theoretisk foredrag, der kunde give en korfattet oversigt over den almindelige principmæssige stilling hvori den økonomiske diskution overhodet for tiden befinder sig.'

4 Bergh and Hanisch, *Vitenskap og politikk*, 98.

5 Ebbe Hertzberg, 'Statssocialismens theori', handwritten opening lecture held at the Statsøkonomisk forening, 1884, quoted in Bergh and Hanisch, *Vitenskap og politikk*, 70. 'En saadan oversigt meddeles i det nærværende øiblik uden tvivl mest hensigtssvarende i form af en historisk anlagt redegjørelse for den nye økonomiske retning, der under betegnelsen "statssocialisme" har ladet saa meget tale om sig.'

6 Hertzberg, 'Statssocialismens theori'. 'Allerede inden den store frihandelskole selv. [...] Engelske forfattere av utvilsom autoritet gjorde oppmerksom på historiske og sosiale forhold som nødvendigvis måtte tas med i betraktninge naar det spurgtes om at indføre bestemte reformer i overenstemmelse med det i theoretisk henseende almengyldige frihandelprincip.'

7 Hertzberg, 'Statssocialismens Theori'. 'forbeholdt Tyskland at sætte den videnskabelige kritik lige overfor frihandelstheorien saa at sige i system.'

8 Hertzberg, 'Statssocialismens theori'.

9 Hertzberg, 'Statssocialismens theori'.

10 Hertzberg, 'Statssocialismens theori'. 'ikke kan faa dem fuldt ud tilfredsstillede uden derigjennem at de øvrige individer i og med det samme se sine tilsvarende behov tilfredsstillet.'

11 Aschehoug does seem to know Schäffle quite well, although not quoting him as much as other Germans like Schmoller, he had read many of his books and articles, I list them here: *Bau und Leben des socialen Körpers*; *Quintessenz des Socialismus*; 'Die Aussichtslosigkeit der Socialdemokratie'; *Nationalökonomische Theorie der ausschliessende Absatzverhältniesse*; 'Gesselschafftliches System'; 'Die Steuern: Besonderer Teil, Kapitalismus und Socialismus mit besonderer Rücksicht auf Gescäfts- und Vermögensformen'; 'Zeitschrift für die gesammte Staatswissenschaft, Die Steuern Allgemeiner Teil'; 'Kern-und Zeitfragen'; 'Neue Folge: Die Inkorporation des Hypothekarkredits'.

12 Jürgen Backhaus, ed., *Albert Schäffle: The Legacy of an Underestimated Economist* (Hanau: Haag & Herchen, 2010). The article 'What Did Schäffle Teach Schumpeter?' by Nicholas W. Balabkins gives a comprehensive analysis of different aspects of Schäffle; some aspects are in line with Aschehoug's own.

13 Bergh and Hanisch, *Vitenskap og politikk*, 72. The two authors mention that Schäffle was probably more socialistic than both Hertzberg and Aschehoug.

14 Bredo Morgenstierne. 'Fattigondet og Socialismen', *Statsøkonomisk Tidsskrift* 3 (1889): 143.

15 See Chapter 11 about trade policies.

16 'Om bestræbelserne for en nordisk toldforening' (1888) (About a Nordic customs union);
    'Fattigondet og Socialismen' (1889) (The evil of poverty and socialism);
    'En tysk Henry George' (1892) (A German, Henry George);
    'Mellemrigelovens opsigelse' (1896) (The termination of the free-trade law between Sweden and Norway);
    'Om tidsmomentet ved de menneskelige vurderinger' (1899) (About the time dimension in human considerations);
    'Om principerne ved en retfærdig skattefordeling' (1901) (About the principles of a just tax distribution);
    'Arveskat' (1901) (Inheritance tax);
    'Professor Aschehoug og hans *Socialøkonomik*' (1902) (Aschehoug and his *Socialøkonomik*);
    'Vor handelspolitikk' (1903) (Our trade policy);
    'Om folkesparebanker og folkeforsikring' (1907) (About saving banks and public insurance);
    'Forelæsninger over Statsøkonomien' (1909) (Lectures on Political Economy);
    and a book: *Norsk Socialstatistik* (1912) (Norwegian social statistics).

17 Morgenstierne, 'Fattigondet og Socialismen', 138. 'Men om man end saaledes ikke kan betragte det socialistiske fordelingssystem eller overhovedet den ligeligst mulig fordeling som maalet for en god fordelingspolitik, bør man dog derfor ingenlunde opgive arbeidet for at forbedre den nuværende fordeling og i nogen grad udjevne kontrasten mellem de ophobede millioner og det uhyre luxusforbrug paa den ene og massernes kamp for tilværelsen paa den anden side.'

18 Morgenstierne, 'Fattigondet og Socialismen', 139. 'I denne henseende frembyder den nyere tyske socialpolitik (ulykkesforsikringer, sygekasser, alderdomsforsikring, etc.) sin store interesse, og det er karakteristisk for socialdemokratiets revolutionære karakter, at det optræder fiendtligt mod reformer av denne art.'

19 Morgenstierne, 'Fattigondet og Socialismen', 139. 'Det er navnlig af engelske forfattere gjennem de omhyggeligste undersøgelser godtgjort, at udviklingen i de sidste haøvhundrede aar er gaaet i retning af at formindske de store indtægter og forøge de mindre [...] ogsaa hos os. [...] Det er da grund til at haabe, at man uden en socialistisk samfundsgrund, skulde kunne naa til en noget større udjevning af produktionsudbyttets fordeling.'

20 'Den moderne statsøkonomis grundlæggelse ved Adam Smith' (1893) (The foundation of modern political economy by Adam Smith, doctorate dissertation at the University of Oslo);

'Udsigt over de forandringer, som Norges Banks virksomhed har undergaaet ved den nye Banklov' (1894) (About the Norwegian Central Bank);

'Den theoretiske statsøkonomis opgave og videnskabelige methode' (1895) (The task and method of theoretical economics);

'Eugen von Böhm-Bawerk og hans videnskabelige betydning' (1901) (Eugen von Böhm-Bawerk and his scientific influence);

'Tobaksmonopol' (1904) (The monopoly of tobacco);

'Den departementale komités forslag til lov om stats- og kommunebidrag til de norske arbeidsledighetskasser' (1906) (About the law of government support of unemployment funds);

'Bør forslaget om indførelse af folkeforsikring gjenoptages?' (1906) (About public insurance);

Socialøkonomi 1: Socialøkonomiens historie ([1915] 1934) (The history of economics);

Teoretisk socialøkonomik (1922), a positive review by Professor Birck (Theoretical economics);

Praktisk socialøkonomik (Næringspolitik og socialpolitik) (sm.m. I. Wedervang, 1928) (Practical economics);

Finanslære (1930) (The theory of finance).

21 Aarum, 'Norwegen, Dänemark und Schweden', 125. 'Jaeger ist Schüler von Aschehoug und hat, wie dieser, seine ersten Eindrücke aus der englischen klassischen Schule empfangen. Schon in seiner Jugendzeit ist er jedoch, besonders während eines Studienaufenthaltes in Wien, wo er u. a. Menger und Böhm-Bawerk kennen gelernt hat, von der österreichischen Schule beeinflußt worden.'

22 Svein Carstens, biography of Oscar Jaeger, Store Norske Leksikon, 26 April 2010. Online: http://www.snl.no/.nbl_biografi/Oskar_J%C3%A6ger/utdypning (accessed 6 June 2013).

23 Aarum, 'Norwegen, Dänemark und Schweden', 125. 'Der reine Grenznutzenlehre gegenüber nimmt er jedoch dieselbe Stellung ein wie Aschehoug.'

24 These two paragraphs about Jaeger have been composed by reading his lecture notes at Håndskriftssamlingen at the National Library in Oslo in 2010.

25 Svein Carstens, 'Oscar Jaeger', *Norsk Biografisk Leksikon* (Oslo: Kunnskapsforlaget, 2002), 175–6.

26 Tore Jørgen Hanisch and Arild Sæther, 'Alfred Marshall in Norway', in *The Impact of Alfred Marshall's Ideas: The Global Diffusion of his Work*, ed. T. Raffaelli, G. Becattini, K. Caldari and M. Dardi (Northampton, MA and Cheltenham: Edward Elgar, 2010).

Appendix C Detailed Contents of *Socialøkonomik* (First Editions from 1903 to 1908)

1 *Socialøkonomik: En vitenskapelig fremstilling af det menneskelige samfunds økonomiske virksomhed.*

LITERATURE

Works and Documents by Aschehoug Used in This Book

Works for which Aschehoug was not the sole author (acting as a contributor or being quoted extensively, as in governmental documents) are marked with *.

Letter from Aschehoug to his friend Henrik Helliesen. Oslo: Håndskriftssamlingen, National Library, 1843.

'Anmeldelse av B. M. Tvethe: Norges statistik'. *Norsk tidsskrift for videnskab og literatur* 2 (1848).

'Om Norges folkemængde i 1664–1666'. *Norsk tidsskrift for videnskab og literatur* 2 (1848).

Norske universitets og skole-annaler, no. 2, vol. IV. Christiania: Hartvig Nissen, 1848.

'Anm. av E. Sundt: Beretning om fante- eller landstrygerfolket i Norge'. *Norsk tidsskrift for videnskab og literatur* 5 (1851).*

Husmannskommisjonen innstilling (proposition of the Smallholder Commission) (1851).*

Fattigkommisjonens betenkning (report of the Poverty Commission) (1856).*

Stortingsmelding (white paper) (1868–69).*

Stortingstidende (annual governmental report) (1868–69).*

Stortingsproposition (governmental proposition) 5 (1879).*

Stortingstidende (annual governmental report) (1879).*

Departements-tidende (ministry report) 58, no. 35 (1 September 1886), printed in the family tree book by Inger Kloster-Jensen, privately owned.*

'De økonomiske kriser og depressioner i det 19de aarhundrede'. *Statsøkonomisk tidsskrift* 13 (1898).

Socialøkonomik, vol. I–IV. Oslo: Aschehoug, 1903–1908.

'Værdi- og prislærens historie', part 1. *Statsøkonomisk tidsskrift* 14 (1900): 185–230.

Handwritten family tree showing the lineage from Thorkil Aschehoug, pastor of Rakkestad, and wife Anne Cathrine née Olsen, privately owned.

Private family notes, privately owned.

Published Works by Aschehoug

All published in Kristiania (now Oslo). Economic and statistical works are marked in bold.

'Indledning til den norske retsvidenskab' (booklet, 1845).

Om Norges folkemængde i aarene 1664 til 1666 (book, 1848).

Retsfilosofi (book, 1856).

'Det europæiske pengemarked' (article, 1856).

Utkast til ny föreningsakt mellom Norge og Sverige, with Nils Vogt (1817–1894), (draft, 1860).

'Beretning, afgiven til departementet for det indre, fra tilsynscommissionen ved Aas høiere landbrugsskole', with Frederik Stang (1808–1884), (report, 1861).

17 May 1864, Slotspladsen i Kristiania (Referat af Taler), with Bjørnstjerne Bjørnson (1832–1910) and Bernhard Dunker (1809–1870), (speeches, 1864).

Norges offentlige ret (book, 1866).

Statsforfatningen i Norge og Danmark indtil 1814 (book, 1866).
'Appel: Efter Professor Aschehougs forelæsninger: Høstsemester 1867' (lecture, 1867).
'Om unionskomiteens udkast til en ny foreningsakt' (report, 1870).
Nordisk retsencyklopædi / samlet og udgivet af T. H. Aschehoug, K. J. Berg og A. F. Krieger (book, 1872).
'Om formuesforholdet mellem ægtefæller' (article, 1872).
Norges nuværende statsforfatning (book, 1875).
'Om retsforholdet mellem naboeiendomme' (article, 1877).
'Om den konstitutionelle regnskabskontrol' (article, 1884).
Den nordiske statsret (book, 1885).
Retskilderne og statsretten, with Ebbe Hertzberg (book, 1885).
'De nugjældende regler om stemmerets erhvervelse' (article, 1885).
Das staatsrecht der vereinigten køningreiche Schweden und Norwegen (book, 1886).
'Festskrift til Hans Majestæt Kong Oscar II ved Regjerings-Jubilæet den 18de September 1897 / fra det Kongelige Frederiks Universitet', with Sophus Bugge (1833–1907), Moltke Moe (1859–1913) et al., (article, 1897).
'De norske communers retsforfatning før 1837: Universitetsprogram for 1ste semester 1896' (lecture, 1897).
Socialøkonomik: En videnskabelig fremstilling af det menneskelige samfunds økonomiske virksomhed, vol. I (book, 1903).
Yhteiskunnallisen taloustieteen historia (Finnish edition of *Socialøkonomik*, vol. I; book, 1904).
Socialøkonomik: En videnskabelig Fremstilling af det menneskelige samfunds økonomiske virksomhed, 4 vols, revised by Thorvald Aarum (book, 1910).

Articles published in Statsøkonomisk Tidsskrift (Journal of political economy)

'Studier over kornprisenes historie i Norge siden Amerikasoppdagelse' (Studies of the history of grain prices in Norway since the discovery of America), vol. 2 (1887).
'Om Norges udførsel av industriprodukter' (About the export of Norwegian industrial products), vol. 3 (1888).
'Om Sparebanker og privatbanker, navlig om deres udlaansvirksomhed' (About saving banks and private banks and their lending activity), vol. 5 (1890).
'Statistiske studier over folkemængde og jordbrug i Norges landdistrikter i det 17. og 18. aarhundre' (Statistical studies of the population and of agriculture in the Norwegian countryside in the seventeenth and eighteenth century), appendix to *Statsøkonomisk Tidsskrift* vol. 5 (1890).
'Norges Hypotekbank', vol. 6 (1891).
'Om kapitalrenten og rentefodens historie' (About the capital rent and the history of the interest rate), vol. 7 (1892).
'Den circulerende seddelmængden som økonomisk barometer' (The circulation of money as an economical barometer), vol. 8 (1893).
'Kornprisernes fremtidsudsigter' (The future of grain prices), vol. 9 (1894).
'Om pantegjældens størrelse i Norge' (About the size of the mortgage debt), vol. 9 (1894).
'Om de forskjellige slags mekanisk drivkraft, som bruges i økonomisk tjenste' (About different mechanical forces to produce energy being used in economic activity), vol. 9 (1894).
'Til orientering i spørgsmaalet om bygning af arbeiderboliger' (An outline of the question of the building of workers housing), vol. 10 (1895).
'De økonomiske kriser og depressioner i det 19. aarhundre' (The economic crises and depressions in the nineteenth century), vol. 13 (1898).
'Afkastning og indtækt' (Revenue and income), vol. 13 (1898).
'Værdi- og prislærens historie' (The history of value and prices), vols 15–17 (1900–1902).

'Kort oversigt over den norske mynt- og pengeværdis historie, sammenlignet med Vesteuropas' (A short history of Norwegian money compared to Western Europe), vol. 18 (1903).
Review of K. A. Wieth-Knudsen, *Formerelse og Fremskridt* (Multiplicity and progress), vol. 23 (1908).

Comments on articles between 1887 and 1989

The first of Aschehoug's articles to appear in *Statsøkonomisk Tidsskrift* was 'Studier over kornprisenes historie i Norge siden Amerikasoppdagelse', a study of the history of grain prices in Norway since the exploration of America, from 1887. The following year he published 'Om Norges udførsel av industriprodukter', which was about the export of industrial products. In 1890 he produced an article about the banking system in Norway focusing on lending and loans, 'Om sparebanker og privatbanker, navlig om deres udlaansvirksomhed'. Aschehoug also published a historical and statistical account of the population and agriculture in the seventeenth and eighteenth century in 1890, 'Statistiske studier over folkemængde og jordbrug i Norges landdistrikter i det 17. og 18. aarhundre', as an appendix to *Statsøkonomisk Tidsskrift*. The next year he continued his work on the mortgage bank system with an article called 'Norges Hypotekbank'. He continued with the theme of banking and credit in his 1892 article about the history of capital rent and interest rates, 'Om kapitalrenten og rentefodens historie'. In 1893, he wrote about the money in circulation as a barometer for the economy in 'Den circulerende seddelmængden som økonomisk barometer'. The year 1894 was a productive one, with three articles in *Statsøkonomisk Tidsskrift*: the first about prospects for corn prices, 'Kornprisernes fremtidsudsigter'; the second about the size of mortgage loans in Norway, 'Om Pantegjældens størrelse i Norge'; and the third about sources of mechanical energy which were being used in economic activity, 'Om de forskjellige slags mekanisk drivkraft, som bruges i økonomisk tjenste'. The year after he commented on the construction of adequate housing for workers in 'Til orientering i spørgsmaalet om bygning af arbeiderboliger'.

Letters from Aschehoug (1822–1909)

Ordered by correspondent and date.

Aarum, Petter Thorvald 1898.12.31
Aftenbladet, 1871.10.21
Aschehoug, Anna Christine, f. Darre 1833.01.09
Aschehoug, Nils Stockfleth Darre 1870.08.25
Aubert, Ludvig Mariboe Benjamin 1878.01.03
Aubert, Ludvig Mariboe Benjamin 1878.04.09
Aubert, Ludvig Mariboe Benjamin 1880.12.30
Aubert, Ludvig Mariboe Benjamin 1883.08.09
Aubert, Ludvig Mariboe Benjamin 1885.12.21
Aubert, Ludvig Mariboe Benjamin 1892.03.31
Aubert, Ludvig Mariboe Benjamin 1893.03.29
Bergens Aftonblad 1890.11.20
Bjerknes, Carl Anton 1879.02.08
Bjerknes, Carl Anton 1899.05.13
Bricka, Carl Fredrik 1893.09.20 (copy; original is in Det KongeligeBibliotek, Copenhagen)
Böhm-Bawerk, Eugen von 1909 (not sent)
Carlson, Fredrik Ferdinand 1853.10.30 (copies; originals are in Riksarkivet, Stockholm)
Carlson, Fredrik Ferdinand 1854.06.11
Carlson, Fredrik Ferdinand 1859.07.26
Carlson, Fredrik Ferdinand 1863.06.22
Carlson, Fredrik Ferdinand 1867.01.03

Carlson, Fredrik Ferdinand 1867.04.07
Carlson, Fredrik Ferdinand 1867.05.29
Carlson, Fredrik Ferdinand 1869.04.22
Carlson, Fredrik Ferdinand 1869.11.06
Carlson, Fredrik Ferdinand 1872.03.18
Carlson, Fredrik Ferdinand 1872.04.22
Carlson, Fredrik Ferdinand 1873.09.17
Carlson, Fredrik Ferdinand 1874.01.09
Carlson, Fredrik Ferdinand 1874.12.06
Carlson, Fredrik Ferdinand 1876.01.06
Carlson, Fredrik Ferdinand 1877.06.30
Carlson, Fredrik Ferdinand 1877.07.09
Carlson, Fredrik Ferdinand 1879.09.04
Carlson, Fredrik Ferdinand 1881.07.09
Carlson, Fredrik Ferdinand 1881.07.22
Carlson, Fredrik Ferdinand 1881.09.29
Christiania Magistrat 1886.05.31
Daae, Ludvig Ludvigsen 1874.08.26
Daae, Ludvig Ludvigsen 1876.01.29
Daae, Ludvig Ludvigsen 1886.03.28
Daae, Ludvig Ludvigsen 1886.09.26
Daae, Ludvig Ludvigsen 1896.12.24
Daae, Ludvig Ludvigsen 1901.02.18
Daae, Ludvig Ludvigsen 1904.12.07
Dareste, Rodolphe 1878.11.20 (draft; enclosed letters from Rodolphe Dareste to Torkel Halvorsen
    Aschehoug, dated 1878.11.20)
Dareste, Rodolphe 1885.11.04
Dietrichson, Lorentz 1879.06.03
Drage, Geoffrey 1889.11.20 (draft written on letter from Geoffrey drage to Torkel Halvorsen
    Aschehoug, dated 1889.11.20)
Drolsum, Axel Charlot 1905.03.03 (appendix: copy of letter fromAxel Drolsum to Torkel Halvorsen
    Aschehoug, dated 1905)
Forssell, Hans 1873.03.26 (copies; originals are in Kungliga Biblioteket, Stockholm)
Forssell, Hans 1873.04.06
Forssell, Hans 1873.04.24
Forssell, Hans 1882.03.05
Forssell, Hans 1887.10.29
Forssell, Hans 1889.12.15
Forssell, Hans 1891.11.29
Forssell, Hans 1894.02.04
Forssell, Hans 1898.01.02
Forssell, Hans 1900.01.06
Frølich, Theodor Christian Brun 1893.07.26
Hage, Hother 1848.05.03 (copies; originals are in Det Kongelige Bibliotek, Copenhagen)
Helliesen, Henrik Laurentius (original letters and copies)
Helliesen, Henrik Laurentius 1839
Helliesen, Henrik Laurentius 1839.10.11
Helliesen, Henrik Laurentius 1839.10.14
Helliesen, Henrik Laurentius 1840.02.08
Helliesen, Henrik Laurentius 1840.02.17
Helliesen, Henrik Laurentius 1840.03.12
Helliesen, Henrik Laurentius 1840.04.05

Helliesen, Henrik Laurentius 1840.05.13
Helliesen, Henrik Laurentius 1840.07.02
Helliesen, Henrik Laurentius 1840.09.08
Helliesen, Henrik Laurentius 1840.09.23
Helliesen, Henrik Laurentius 1840.10.04
Helliesen, Henrik Laurentius 1840.10.24
Helliesen, Henrik Laurentius 1841.01.21
Helliesen, Henrik Laurentius 1841.03.24
Helliesen, Henrik Laurentius 1841.09.27
Helliesen, Henrik Laurentius 1841.11.22
Helliesen, Henrik Laurentius 1843.05.30
Helliesen, Henrik Laurentius 1870.08.18
Helliesen, Henrik Laurentius 1872.12.26
Helliesen, Henrik Laurentius 1872.12.30
Helliesen, Henrik Laurentius 1872.12.31
Helliesen, Henrik Laurentius 1873.01.05
Helliesen, Henrik Laurentius 1873.01.23
Helliesen, Henrik Laurentius 1873.05.11
Helliesen, Henrik Laurentius 1878.05.18
Helliesen, Henrik Laurentius 1879.10.19
Helliesen, Henrik Laurentius 1879.12.28
Helliesen, Henrik Laurentius 1883.12.14
Helliesen, Henrik Laurentius 1884.01.18
Holm, Edvard 1892.04.21 (copies; originals are in Det Kongelige Bibliotek, Copenhagen)
Ihlen, Jacob 1895.07.20 (draft enclosed letters from Jacob Ihken to Torkel Halvorsen Aschehoug, dated 1895.07.19)
Kielland, Alexander 1895 (draft on letter from Alexander Kielland to Torkel Halvorsen Aschehoug, dated 1895.04.05)
Koht, Halvdan 1901.09.27
Krieger, Andreas Frederik 1848 (approx. 100 letters; copies, catalogue on paper)
Lehmann, Halfdan 1890.03.26
Lindstedt, Anders 1898.12.27 (copy; original is in Kungliga Biblioteket, Stockholm)
Maurer, Konrad von 1875 (draft on letter from Konrad von Maurer to Torkel Halvorsen Aschehoug, dated 1875.04.10)
Monrad, Marcus Jacob (n.d.)
Morgenstierne, Bredo von Munthe af 1881.01.28
Morgenstierne, Bredo von Munthe af 1886.12.12
Morgenstierne, Bredo von Munthe af 1891.01.26
Morgenstierne, Bredo von Munthe af 1891.06.16
Morgenstierne, Bredo von Munthe af 1892.10.15
Morgenstierne, Bredo von Munthe af 1895.02.25
Morgenstierne, Bredo von Munthe af 1895.12.14
Morgenstierne, Bredo von Munthe af 1896.02.18 (endorsement on letter from Bredo Morgenstierne to Torkel Halvorsen Aschehoug, dated 1896.02.18)
Morgenstierne, Bredo von Munthe af 1899.04.17
Morgenstierne, Bredo von Munthe af 1901.02.13
Nansen, Fridtjof
Naumann, Christian 1859.04.28 (copies; originals are in Riksarkivet, Stockholm)
Naumann, Christian 1864.09.21
Naumann, Christian 1866.12.03
Naumann, Christian 1883.10.11
Naumann, Christian 1885.06.29

Naumann, Christian 1885.10.10
Naumann, Christian 1885.11.22
Naumann, Christian 1886.04.03
Nielsen, Yngvar 1894.12.07
Olsen, Olaj 1886.09.02
Orland, Christian August 1908.04.21
Ploug, Carl 1846.02.15 (copies; originals are in Det Kongelige Bibliotek, Copenhagen)
Ploug, Carl 1872.09.27
Richter, Ole Jørgensen 1880 (draft on letter from Ole Richter to Torkel Halvorsen Aschehoug, dated 1880.10.05)
Schjelderup, Hjalmar 1888.01.04
Schwartz, Johan Jørgen 1874.01.19
Sibbern, Georg Christian (draft enclosed letter from Georg Sibbern to Torkel Halvorsen Aschehoug, dated 1867.5.28)
Sibbern, Georg Christian 1866.12.23
Sibbern, Georg Christian 1867.06.01 (copy)
Sibbern, Georg Christian 1867.08.02
Sibbern, Georg Christian 1867.08.25
Sibbern, Georg Christian 1867.08.28
Sibbern, Georg Christian 1867.09.24
Sibbern, Georg Christian 1867.11.03
Sibbern, Georg Christian 1868.09.05
Stang, Emil (n.d.)
Stang, Emil 1881.09.23
Stang, Emil 1883.06.07
Stang, Emil 1885.03.01
Stang, Emil 1888.02.03
Stang, Emil 1889.06.25
Stang, Emil 1890.03.24
Stang, Emil 1890.04.17
Stang, Emil 1892.02.27
Stang, Emil 1892.07.02
Stang, Emil 1892.07.27
Stang, Emil 1892.07.27
Stang, Emil 1892.07.28
Stang, Emil 1892.07.28
Stang, Emil 1892.07.28
Stang, Frederik 1865.05.11 (about union committee)
Stang, Frederik 1865.05.18
Stang, Frederik 1865.05.23
Stang, Frederik 1865.06.06
Stang, Frederik 1867.08.04
Stang, Frederik 1867.08.09
Stendahl, Fridleiv 1898 (draft on letter from Fridleiv Stendahl to Torkel Halvorsen Aschehoug, dated 1898.02.27)
Strandberg, Carl Gustaf 1867.03.12 (copy, original is in Kungliga Biblioteket, Stockholm)
Trap, Cordt 1892.03.31 (copy, original is in Det Kongelige Bibliotek, Copenhagen)
Ueland, Ole Gabriel 1867.05.04 (draft enclosed letter from Ole Gabriel Ueland to Torkel Halvorsen Aschehoug, dated 1867.05.04)
Veterinærklassen in Selskabet for Norges Vel 1889.01.25 (on the same document, a comment from Professor F. Lochmann)
Vibe, Nils Andreas 1890.11.18

Vogt, Hans Holmboe 1887.11.15
Vogt, Hans Holmboe 1898.12.31
Vogt, Nils 1903.09.23
Vult von Steyern, Nils 1882.05.14 (draft on letter from Nils Vult von Steyern to Torkel Halvorsen
    Aschehoug, dated 1882.05.14)
Waage, Lars 1884.02.09 (draft enclosed letter from Lars Waage to Torkel Halvorsen Aschehoug,
    dated 1884.01.21)
Wergeland, Harald Titus Alexis 1872.02.03 (no. 2)
Wille, Nordal (n.d.)
Wille, Nordal 1891.06.12
Wille, Nordal 1904.04.10
Wille, Nordal 1904.10.22
Wille, Nordal 1907.02.25

Reviews of Aschehoug (1822–1909)

From private documents and documents in the National Library of Norway. Dates are given where available.

Torkel Halvorsen Aschehoug: Different papers concerning his life
References, testimonials and academic records
Diplomas from honorary doctorates, Lund and Königsberg
Diplomas for membership in nine academic societies
Order diplomas, hereby included one for Hanna Aschehoug
Celebrations for Aschehoug, notification about his death, etc.
1872 Political sympathy announcements to Torkel Halvorsen Aschehoug from Horten 1872 and
    1880, Sigdal 1881, Stord 1881, Sandeherred and Sandefjord 1881.
Invitation to formal dinner on the occasion of the 40th anniversary of Torkel Halvorsen
    Aschehoug's career as university scholar in 1892 (76 signatures)

Lectures by Torkel Halvorsen Aschehoug (1822–1909)

Including lectures refereed by Aschehoug. Derived from hand-written notes, dates for lectures are given where available.

T. Aschehoug. 'Administrationsret' (Administration law; 2 small notebooks).
_____. 'Administrativ ret' (Administration law; 1 pamphlet).
_____. 'Administrativ ret' (Administrative law; 115 pages).
_____. 'Appel' (Appeals). Referee: J. N. Brøgger (1 booklet).
_____. 'Appel' (Appeals). Referee: O. Platou (82 pages, 2 pages loose).
_____. 'Appell' (Appeals). Referee unknown; owned by Peter Brinch-Reichenwald.
_____. 'Commentar over Kongeriget Norges Grundlov' (Comments on the constitution of the
    Norwegian monarchy). Referee: G. Rubach (parts 1–2, pages 1–148 and 1–44).
_____. 'Forelæsninger over administrativretten af Lektor Aschehoug' (Lectures about the
    administrative law by Assistant Professor Aschehoug). Referee: Carl A. Folvig (?).
_____. 'Forelæsninger over administrativretten' Lectures about the administrative law).
    Booklets 1–5.
_____. 'Forelæsninger over Appel' (Lectures about Appeals) 2nd semester 1867.
_____. 'Forelæsninger over appel'. Autumn 1867 (booklets 1–2).
_____. 'Forelæsninger over den norske personret' (Lectures about Norwegian private law). 2nd
    semester 1863 until 1st semester 1864. Referee: Evald Rygh.

_____. 'Forelæsninger over Norges offentlige ret I–III' (Lectures about Norwegian public law I–III).

_____. 'Forelæsninger over Norges offentlige ret' (Lectures about Norwegian public law). Referee: Evald Rygh.

_____. 'Forelæsninger over retsfilosofien' (Lectures about the philosophy of law). 2nd semester 1862. Referee: Evald Rygh.

_____. 'Forelæsninger over Statsøkonomi I–IV' (Lectures about state economics I–IV). Referee: F. Stang.

_____. 'Forelæsninger over Statsøkonomi' (Lectures about state economics I–IV). Referee: Waldemar Eckell.

_____. 'Forelæsninger over statsret' (Lectures about Government law). Referee: F. Stang.

_____. 'Forelesninger over appel' (Lectures about appeals).

_____. 'Grundlov (I–III)' (The constitution I–III). Referee: O. Platou. 2 booklets.

_____. 'Om uthinglyste forpagtningscontracter som stemmerettsfundament' (About nonregistered lease contracts as a foundation for the right to vote). No date (after 1896). Ms. to article, sent to Morgenbladet (2 pages).

_____. 'Personrett' (Private law). Referee: P. Birch-Reichenwald ('Med et vedheng fra 1870' [with an appendix from 1870]).

_____. 'Personrett' (Private law). Referee: Peter Birch-Reichenwald.

A. M. Schweigaard: 'Forelæsninger over den norske administration' (Lectures about the Norwegian administration). Referee: T. H. Aschehoug. (On the front page it is written: 'Forelæsninger over personretten' [Lectures about private law].)

_____. 'Forelæsninger over processen' (Lectures about the process). Referees: W. and T. H. Aschehoug (booklets 1–5).

G. F. Hallager: 'Lovhistorie' (History of law). Referee: T. Aschehoug.

Primary Sources other than Aschehoug and Secondary Sources

Aall, Anathon. *Det historiske og litterære grundlag for filosofien hos A. M. Schweigaard*. Kristiania: Det Norske videnskaps-akademi, 1917.

Aarum, Thorvald. 'Norwegen, Dänemark und Schweden'. In *Die Wirtschaftstheorie der Gegenwart*. Edited by Hans Mayer, 122–35. Vienna: Julius von Springer, 1927.

Amundsen, Kåre. *Norsk sosialøkonomisk historie 1814–1890*. Oslo: Universitetsforlaget, 1963.

Andresen, Anton Fredrik. *Nytte, dannelse og vitenskap?: Universitetet og økonomifaget i det nye Norge 1811–1840*. Oslo: Det historisk-filosofiske fakultet, 2004.

Backhaus, Jürgen. 'Unternehmer in Wirtschaft und Politik', serie A, no. 152, July 1980.

_____. 'The German Economic Tradition: From Cameralism to the Verein für Sozialpolitik'. In *Political Economy and National Realities*. Edited by M. Albertone and A. Masoero, 329–56. Torino: Fondatione Luigi Einaudi, 1994.

Balabkins, Nicholas W. *Not by Theory Alone…: The Economics of Gustav von Schmoller and Its Legacy to America*. Berlin: Duncker & Humblot, 1988.

_____. 'What Did Schäffle Teach Schumpeter'. In *Albert Schäffle (1831–1903): The Legacy of an Underestimated Economist*. Edited by Jürgen Backhaus 35–52. Frankfurt: Haag & Herchen, 2010.

Baumer, Franklin L. *Modern European Thought: Continuity and Change in Ideas, 1680–1900*. New York: St Martin's Press, 1977.

Beach, Earl. 'Alfred Marshall'. In *Handbook of the History of Economic Thought: Insights on the Founders of Modern Economics*. Edited by Jürgen Backhaus, 495–512. New York: Springer, 2011.

Berg Eriksen, Trond and Øystein Sørensen. Preface to *Norsk idéhistorie*. Oslo: Aschehoug, 2001.

_____, eds. *Norsk idéhistorie, vol. III: Kampen om Norges sjel 1770–1905*. Oslo: Aschehoug, 2003.

Bergh, Trond, Tore Hanisch, Even Lange and Helge Pharo. 'Fire transformasjoner i skipsfarten and Teknologioverføring og markedserobringer: Noen trekk ved industriutviklingen'. In *Norge fra u-land til i-land: vekst og utviklingslinjer 1830–1980*, 86–186. Oslo: Gyldendal, 1983.

Bergh, Trond and Tore J. Hanisch. *Vitenskap og Politikk: Linjer i norsk sosialøkonomi gjennom 150 år*. Oslo: Aschehoug, 1984.

Bergwitz, Joh. K. 'Til Professor Aschehougs karakteristikk, hans ætlegg og stammegaard'. Special edition of *Statsøkonomisk tidsskrift* (1910).

Bjerkholt, Olav. 'Schweigaard og Statistikken'. In *Anton Martin Schweigaard: Professorpolitikeren*. Edited by Ole Mestad, 149–74. Oslo: Akademisk publisering, 2009.

Blom Svendsen, H. 'Julaften på toten 1797'. *Tidens tegn*, 24 December 1938.

Caldwell, Bruce. *Hayek's Challenge*. Chicago/London: University of Chicago Press, 2004.

Carlson, Benny. *De institutionalistiska idéernas spridning*. Stockholm: SNS Forlag, 1995.

Carstens, Svein. 'Oskar Jæger'. In *Norsk biografisk leksikon*. Oslo: Kunnskapsforlaget, 2002.

_____. 'Oskar Jæger'. *Store norske leksikon*. Online: http://www.snl.no/.nbl_biografi/Oskar_J% C3%A6ger/utdypning (accessed 26 April 2010).

Christie, Elisabeth. *Prestegårdsliv*, vol. 2, 2nd edition. Oslo: Forlaget Land og Kirke, 1967, 1976. 'Aschehoug-epoken', i Rakkestad (1873–1867).

Dahl, Ottar. *Norsk historieforskning i det 19. og 20. århundre*, 4th edition. Oslo: Universitetsforlaget, 1990.

Drechsler, Wolfgang. 'Christian Wolff and Law & Economics: The Heilbronn Symposia in Economics and the Social Sciences: An Introduction'. In *Christian Wolff and Law & Economics: The Heilbronn Symposium*. Edited by Jürgen G. Backhaus, v–x. Hildesheim, Zürich, New York: Gerog Olms Verlag, 1998.

Eriksen, Ib E. and Arild Sæther. 'Hvor ble det av entreprenøren i norsk samfunnsøkonomi?'. *Norsk økonomisk tidsskrift* 124 (2010): 1–32.

Farnam, H. W. *The Yale Review* 9 (2) (August 1900): 164–74.

Fasting, Mathilde and Sylvi Endresen. 'Torkel Aschehoug: Seeing Workers as More than Just a Production Factor'. Paper presented at the 23rd Heilbronn Seminar, 'Liberation of the Serfs', June 2010. Published as 'More than Just a Production Factor: The View of Labour in the Works of the Norwegian Economist Torkel Aschehoug (1822–1909)'. In *The Liberation of the Serfs: The Economics of Unfree Labor*. Edited by Jürgen Backhaus, 44–60. New York: Springer, 2012.

Fouillée, Alfred. *Le mouvement idéaliste et la réaction contre la science positive*. Paris: Germer Baillière, 1896.

Frisch, Ragnar. 'Alfred Marshall's Theory of Value'. *Quarterly Journal of Economics* 64 (4): November, 1950.

Gerschenkron, Alexander. *Economic Backwardness in Historical Perspective*. Cambridge, MA: Belknap Press, 1962.

Gide, Charles and Charles Rist. *A History of Economic Doctrines from the Time of the Physiocrats to the Present Day* (Boston: D. C. Heath, 1915), 384. Online: http://www.archive.org/stream/historyo feconomi00gideiala#page/384/mode/2up (accessed November 2010).

Gordon, Scott. 'The Ideology of Laissez-Faire'. In *The Classical Economists and Economic Policy*. Edited by A. W. Coates. London: Methuen, 1965.

Grampp, William D. *The Manchester School of Economics*. Stanford/Oxford: Stanford University Press, 1960. Online: http://oll.libertyfund.org/?option=com_staticxt&staticfile=show.php%3 Ftitle=2128&chapter=192980&layout=html&Itemid=27 (accessed 8 June 2010).

Gregesen, Frans and Simo Køppe, eds. *Idéhistorie: Ideer og strømninger i det 20. århundrede*, vol. 1. Århus: Amanda forlag, 1994.

Grimmer-Solem, Eric. *The Rise of Historical Economics and Social Reform in Germany 1864–1894*. Oxford: Clarendon Press, 2003.

Hagemann, Harald. 'The Verein für Sozialpolitik from its Foundation (1872) until World War I'. In *Societies of Political Economy and Associations of Economists*. Edited by Massimo Augello and Marco E. L. Guidi. London: Taylor & Francis, 2001.

Hagerup, Francis. 'Nekrolog over Torkel Halvorsen Aschehoug'. Special edition of *Tidsskrift for rettsvitenskab* (1909).

Hanisch, Tore Jørgen and Arild Sæther. 'Alfred Marshall in Norway'. In *The Impact of Alfred Marshall's Ideas: The Global Diffusion of his Work*. Edited by T. Raffaelli, G. Becattini, K. Caldari and M. Dardi. Northampton, MA and Cheltenham: Edward Elgar, 2010.

Hansen, Reginald. 'Gustav Schmoller as a Scientist of Political Economy'. In *Handbook of the History of Economic Thought: Insights on the Founders of Modern Economics*. Edited by Jürgen Backhaus, 389–414. New York: Springer, 2011.

Hertzberg, Ebbe. *Professor Schweigaard i hans offentlige virksomhed: 1832–1870*. Kristiania: Cammermeyer forlag, 1883.

_____. 'Statssocialismens theori'. Handwritten opening lecture held at the Statsøkonomisk forening, 1884. Reprinted in Trond Bergh and Tore J. Hanisch. *Vitenskap og Politikk: Linjer i norsk sosialøkonomi gjennom 150 år*. Oslo: Aschehoug, 1984.

Hodne, Fritz. *Norges økonomiske historie 1815–1970*. Oslo: Cappelen, 1981.

Hodne, Fritz and Ola Honningdal Grytten. *Norsk økonomi i det nittende århundre*. Bergen: Fagbokforlaget, 2000.

Holmes, Colin. 'Laissez-faire in Theory and Practice: Britain 1800–1875'. *Journal of European Economic History* 5 (3) (winter 1976).

Jaeger, Oskar. 'Den theoretiske statsøkonomis opgave og videnskabelige methode'. *Statsøkonomisk tidsskrift* 9 (1895).

_____. *Socialøkonomien* from *Det Kongelige Fredriks Universitet 1811–1911. Festskrift*. Christiania: Aschehoug, 1911.

_____. *Teoretisk socialøkonomik* (Christiania 1922). *Nationaløkonomisk tidsskrift* 3 (31) (1923). Online: http://www.tidsskrift.dk/visning.jsp?markup=&print=no&id=91467 (accessed 23 April 2010).

Keilhau, Wilhelm. *Det norske folks liv og historie gjennem tidene: Tidsrummet fra omkring 1875 til omkring 1920*, vol. 10. Oslo: Aschehoug, 1935.

Keilhau, Wilhelm. *Den økonomiske og den politiske liberalisme*. Oslo: Universitets studentkontor, 1948.

Keynes, John Maynard. *Essays on Biography*. New York: Norton & Company, 1951 (1933).

Kiær, Anders N. 'Nogle bidrag til bedømmelsen af den økonomiske udvikling med særligt hensyn til Norge (fortsat)'. *Statsøkonomisk tidsskrift* 1 (1887).

_____. 'Om menneskets økonomiske værd'. *Statsøkonomisk tidsskrift* 6 (1892).

Landes, David. *The Wealth and Poverty of Nations: Why Some Are So Rich and Some So Poor*. London: Abacus, 1998.

Langeland, Nils Rune. 'Sagens natur'. In *Anton Martin Schweigaard: Professorpolitikeren*. Edited by Ole Mestad, 301–34. Oslo: Akademisk publisering, 2009.

Langslet, Lars Roar. 'Torkel Halvorsen Aschehoug'. In *Konservatisme på norsk*, 138–50. Oslo: Pax, 2011.

Lie, Einar and Hege Roll-Hansen. *Faktisk talt: Statistikkens historie i Norge*. Oslo: Universitetsforlaget, 2001.

Lie, Einar and Christian Venneslan. *Over evne: Finansdepartementet 1965–1992*. Oslo: Pax forlag, 2010.

Lovejoy, Arthur O. *Essays in the History of Ideas*. Baltimore: Johns Hopkins Press, 1948.

_____. 'Reflections of the History of Ideas'. *Journal of the History of Ideas* 1 (1) (January 1940).

_____. *The Great Chain of Being*. Cambridge, MA/London: Harvard University Press, 1964.

Lykkja, Pål Magnus. *Anton M. Schweigaard og Torkel H. Aschehoug sine økonomiske teoriar i perioden 1832–82*. Dissertation in economics, Økonomisk Institutt, Universitetet i Oslo, May 2001.

Lönnroth, Johan. 'Nordic Model Political Economic Manuals'. Preliminary version for a seminar, 11 December 2008.

Marshall, Alfred. *Principles of Economics*, abridgement of the 8th edition (1920). New York: Prometheus Books, 1997.

_____. *Principles of Economics*, 8th edition, book VI, chapter 1. London: Macmillan, 1920. Online: http://www.econlib.org/library/Marshall/marP43.html (accessed September 2010).

Maurseth, Per. 'Anton Martin Schweigaards politiske tenkning'. *Historisk tidskrift* 1 (1990).

Meek, Ronald L. *The Economics of Physiocracy*. London: Routledge, 2003 (1962).

Mehlum, Halvor. 'Samfunnsøkonomen Schweigaard'. In *Anton Martin Schweigaard: Professorpolitikeren*. Edited by Ole Mestad, 125–48. Oslo: Akademisk publisering, 2009.

Mestad, Ole. 'Schweigaard: Mennesket, professoren, politikaren'. In *Anton Martin Schweigaard: Professorpolitikeren*. Edited by Ole Mestad, 1–36. Oslo: Akademisk publisering, 2009.

_____. 'Schweigaard og den franske traktatsak 1865'. In *Anton Martin Schweigaard: Professorpolitikeren*. Edited by Ole Mestad, 229–76. Oslo: Akademisk publisering, 2009.

Meyer, Ulla. *Norske mødre*. Oslo: Jacob Dybwads forlag, 1945.

Michalsen, Dag. Biography of Bredo Von Munthe Af Morgenstierne. Store Norsk Leksikon, Online: http://www.snl.no/.nbl_biografi/Bredo_Von_Munthe_Af_Morgenstierne/utdypning_%E2%80%93_2 (accessed 3 September 2009).

Mill, John Stuart. *The Collected Works of John Stuart Mill, vol. VIII: A System of Logic Ratiocinative and Inductive, part II* (1843). Online: http://oll.libertyfund.org/index.php?option=com_staticxt&staticfile=show.php%3Ftitle=247&Itemid=28 (accessed 1 November 2010).

Morgenstierne, Bredo. 'Book review, *Socialøkonomik*'. *Statsøkonomisk tidsskrift* 16 (1902).

———. 'Fattigondet og Socialismen'. *Statsøkonomisk tidsskrift* 3 (1889).

———. 'Professor Aschehoug og hans "Socialøkonomik"'. *Statsøkonomisk tidsskrift* 16 (1902).

———. 'Professor Dr. Iuris T. H. Aschehoug in memoriam'. Norsk retstidende 13 (1909).

———. 'Vor Handelspolitik'. *Statsøkonomisk tidsskrift* 17 (1903).

Munthe, Preben. Biography of Einar Einarsen. Norsk Biografisk Leksikon. Online: http://www.snl.no/.nbl_biografi/Einar_Einarsen/utdypning (accessed 29 July 2010).

Nordenstam, Tore. *Fra kunst til Vitenskap*, 2nd edition. Oslo: Fagbokforlaget, 2000.

Norman, George. *Mine erindringer fra Norge: Meddelt av T. H. Aschehoug: Historisk tidsskrift*, part 3, vol. 5. Kristiania: 1899.

Perez, Carlota. Introduction to *Technological Revolutions and Financial Capital: The Dynamics of Bubbles and Golden Ages*. Online: http://www.carlotaperez.org/TRFCbook/TRFCintrod.pdf (accessed February 2011).

———. *Technological Revolutions and Financial Capital: The Dynamics of Bubbles and Golden Ages*. Cheltenham: Edward Elgar, 2002.

Reinert, Erik S. 'Compensation Mechanisms and Targeted Economic Growth: Lessons from the History of Economic Policy'. In *The Employment Impact of Innovation*. London: Routledge, 2000.

———. 'Finanskrisenes teori'. Appendix to NOU 2011: 1. 'Bedre rustet mot finanskriser'. *Finanskriseutvalgets utredning*, 25 January 2011.

———. 'The Terrible Simplifiers: Common Origins of Financial Crises and Persistent Poverty in Economic Theory and the New "1848 Moment"'. DESA Working Paper no. 88, ST/ESA/2009/DWP/88. December 2009.

Rygg, Nicolai, 'Statistikken'. In *Det Kongelige Fredriks Universitet 1811–1911: Festskrift*. Christiania: Aschehoug, 1911.

Rørvik, Thor Inge. 'Schweigaard og filosofien'. In *Anton Martin Schweigaard: Professorpolitikeren*. Edited by Ole Mestad, 61–90. Oslo: Akademisk publisering, 2009.

Sandmo, Agnar. *Samfunnsøkonomi: En idéhistorie*. Oslo: Universitetsforlaget, 2006.

Say, Jean-Baptiste. *Traité d'economie politique*. Online: http://www.librairal.org/wiki/Jean-Baptiste_Say:Trait%C3%A9_d'%C3%A9conomie_politique (accessed 6 June 2013).

Scharling, William. 'Professor Dr. Iuris T. H. Aschehoug in memoriam'. *Norsk retstidende* 13 (1909).

Schmidt, Karl-Heinz. 'Friedrich List Striving for Economic Integration and Development'. In *Handbook of the History of Economic Thought: Insights on the Founders of Modern Economic*. Edited by Jürgen Backhaus. New York: Springer, 2011.

Schumpeter, Joseph. 'Gustav von Schmoller und die Probleme von heute'. In *Schmollers Jahrbuch für Gesetzgebung, Verwaltung und Volkswirtschaft* 50 (1926).

———. *History of Economic Analysis*. New York: Oxford University Press, 1954.

Schweigaard, Anton Martin. *Ungdomsarbeider*. Edited by Oscar Jaeger and Frederik Stang. Kristiania: Aschehoug, 1904.

Seip, Anne-Lise. *Demringstid: Johan Sebastian Welhaven og nasjonen*. Oslo: Aschehoug, 2007.

———. *Vitenskap og virkelighet: Sosiale, økonomiske og politiske teorier hos T. H. Aschehoug 1845–1882*. Oslo: Gyldendal, 1975.

Seip, Jens Arup. *Ole Jacob Broch*. Oslo: Gyldendal, 1971.

———. *Utsikt over Norges historie*. Oslo: Gyldendal, 1974.

Sejersted, Francis. *Demokratisk kapitalisme*. Oslo: Pax forlag, 2002.

Senior, William Nassau. *An Outline of the Science of Political Economy*, first published in 1836, this edition is from 1850, 3rd print, 1853. Online: http://www.econlib.org/library/Senior/snP1.html (accessed 8 June 2010).

Senn, Peter R. 'A Comparison of the Treatment of A. Schäffle in Economic Journals and Economic Thought'. In *Albert Schäffle (1831–1903): The Legacy of an Underestimated Economist*. Edited by Jürgen Backhaus, 13–34. Frankfurt: Haag & Herchen, 2010.

Shionoya, Yuichi. *The German Historical School: The Historical and Ethical Approach to Economics*. London and New York: Routledge, 2001.

_____. *The Soul of the German Historical School: Methodological Essays on Schmoller, Weber and Schumpeter*. New York: Springer, 2005.

Sismondi, Jean-Charles-Léonard. *A History of the Fall of the Roman Empire, Comprising a View of the Invasion and Settlement of the Barbarians*, vol. 2. Online: http://www.ebooksread.com/authors-eng/j-c-l-simonde-de-jean-charles-lonard-simonde-sismondi/a-history-of-the-fall-of-the-roman-empire-comprising-a-view-of-the-invasion--s-msi/page-2-a-history-of-the-fall-of-the-roman-empire-comprising-a-view-of-the-invasion--s-msi.shtml (accessed August 2010).

Skousen, Mark. *The Making of Modern Economics: The Lives and Ideas of the Great Thinkers*, 2nd edition. Armonk, NY: M. E. Sharpe, 2009.

Skirbekk, Gunnar. *Norsk og moderne*. Oslo: Res Publica, 2010.

Slagstad, Rune. *De nasjonale strateger*. Oslo: Pax, 2001.

_____. *Rett og politikk: et liberalt tema med variasjoner*. Oslo: Universitetsforlaget, 1987.

Smith, Adam. *The Wealth of Nations*. New York: Bantam Classics, 2003 (1776).

Smith, J. 'Vort landbrugs økonomiske stilling'. *Statsøkonomisk tidsskrift* 10 (1896).

Stang, Fredrik. 'Aschehoug'. In *Norsk biografisk leksikon*, vol. 1 (Aabel–Bjørnson). Edited by Edvard Bull, Anders Krogvig and Gerhard Gran. Kristiania: Aschehoug, 1923.

Stråth, Bo. 'The Normative Foundations of the Scandinavian Welfare States in Historical Perspective'. In *Normative Foundations of the Welfare State: The Nordic Experience*. Edited by Nanna Kildal and Stein Kuhnle. London: Routledge, 2005.

Sæther, Arild. 'Jean-Baptiste Say's Influence in Norway'. In *Jean-Baptiste Say: Influence, critiques et postérité*. Edited by André Tiran, 177–217. Paris: Éditions Classique Gariner, 2010.

Sæther, Arild and Ib E. Eriksen. 'Aschehoug and the Role of Entrepreneurship: A Key Factor Lost in Neo-Classical Economics'. Presentation at Sørmarka Seminar, University of Agder, November 2009.

Sæther, Arild, Niels Kjærgård and Bo Sandelin. 'Economics in Scandinavia'. In *New Palgrave Dictionary of Economics*, 2nd edition. Palgrave Macmillan, 2008.

Sørensen, Øystein. *A. M. Schweigaards politiske tenkning*. Oslo: Universitetsforlaget, 1988.

Veblen, Thorstein. Review of *Vaerdi- og Prislaerens Historie* by T. H. Aschehoug (Reprinted from *Statsökonomisk tidskrift* 8 (1902), 193. *Journal of Political Economy* 11 (March 1903).

Westergaard, Harald. 'Obituary T. H. Aschehoug' from 1909.

Wilson, Daniel J. *Arthur O. Lovejoy and the Quest for Intelligibility*. Chapel Hill: University of North Carolina Press, 1980.

Wikipedia, 'Jean Charles Léonard de Sismondi'. Online: http://en.wikipedia.org/wiki/Simonde_de_Sismondi (accessed August 2009).

Witoszek, Nina. 'Fugitives from Utopia: The Scandinavian Enlightenment Reconsidered'. In *The Cultural Construction of Norden*. Edited by Ø. Sørensen and Bo Stråth. Oslo: Scandinavian University Press, 1997.

_____. *The Origins of the 'Regime of Goodness': Remapping the Cultural History of Norway*. Oslo: Universitetsforlaget, 2011.

Yonay, Yuval P. *The Struggle over the Soul of Economics: Institutionalist and Neoclassical Economists in America between the Wars*. Princeton, NJ: Princeton University Press, 1998.

INDEX

Lightning Source UK Ltd.
Milton Keynes UK
UKOW04n0901290913

218118UK00001B/4/P